Norfolk Blues

"With kindest regards, (signed) John Walters."

Courtesy of the Norfolk Masonic Temple

Norfolk Blues

The Civil War Diary
of the
Norfolk Light Artillery Blues

WITHDRAWN

BY
John Walters

EDITED AND INTRODUCED BY
Kenneth Wiley

 Burd Street Press

All maps and photographs not otherwise credited are from the author's collection.

This Burd Street Press publication
was printed by

Beidel Printing House, Inc.
63 West Burd Street
Shippensburg, PA 17257 USA

In respect for the scholarship contained herein, the acid-free paper used in this book meets the guidelines for permanence and durability of the Committee on Production Guidelines for Book Longevity of the Council on Library Resources.

For a complete list of available publications
please write

Burd Street Press
Division of White Mane Publishing Company, Inc.
P.O. Box 152
Shippensburg, PA 17257 USA

Library of Congress Cataloging-in-Publication Data

Walters, John, 1835–1918.
    Norfolk Blues : the Civil War diary of the Norfolk Light Artillery
Blues / by John Walters ; edited and introduced by Kenneth Wiley.
        p.   cm.
    Includes bibliographical references.
    ISBN 1-57249-019-5 (acid-free paper)
    1. Confederate States of America.   Army.   Virginia Artillery.
Grandy's Battery.   2. Walters, John, 1835–1918--Diaries.   3. United
States--History--Civil War, 1861–1865--Personal narratives,
Confederate.   4. United States--History--Civil War, 1861–1865-
-Regimental histories.   5. Virginia--History--Civil War, 1861–1865-
-Personal narratives.   6. Virginia--History--Civil War, 1861–1865-
-Regimental histories.   7. Soldiers--Virginia--Norfolk--Diaries.
8. Norfolk (Va.)--Biography.   I. Wiley, Kenneth, 1952–
II. Title.
E581.8.G73W35   1997
973.7'455--dc21
[B]   96-51428
                                                                 CIP

PRINTED IN THE UNITED STATES OF AMERICA

Table of Contents

Foreword .... **ix**

Chapter 1. John Walters Joins the Blues **1**
Walters' early life, the origins of the Norfolk Light
Artillery Blues, The War Between North and South, Op-
erations Around Norfolk in 1861 and early 1862

Chapter 2. John's Diary Begins **18**
Petersburg Camp, Marches and Skirmishes, With The
Army of Northern Virginia, Fredericksburg, Winter Camp,
Chancellorsville, and the Road to Gettysburg

Chapter 3. On the Defensive **79**
The Road Back to Virginia, Holding the Fords, Winter
Camp, the Wilderness, Spotsylvania Court House, Cold
Harbor, and Richmond

Chapter 4. The Siege of Petersburg **127**
Battle of the Crater, Life in the Trenches, and the Coming
of Winter

Chapter 5. The Last Battles **184**
A Visit to Richmond, A New Position in the Lines, The
Thin Line Breaks, Appomattox, and the Long Road Home

Chapter 6. Reconstruction and Resumption **230**
A Return to Peace, Walters' Later Years, and the Rebirth
of the Norfolk Light Artillery Blues

Roster of the Men of the Norfolk Light Artillery Blues **239**
A Roster of the Company from 1861 to 1865 with brief
biographical sketches of some of its members

Bibliography **314**

Index **316**

List of Maps

Norfolk and Vicinity in 1861 7
Northern Virginia and the route to Gettysburg 75
Richmond and Petersburg Area 146

List of Illustrations

John Walters in Masonic Regalia .... frontispiece

Advertisement for Clark & Walters Bookbinders 3

U.S.S. *Monticello* 10

State Flag of the Blues 12

Command Flag of the Blues 12

Poplar Lawn 21

6-Pounder Field Piece 25

Drewry's Bluff 26

Exchange Hotel, Gordonsville, Virginia 39

Orange Court House 41

12-Pounder Field Howitzer 48

Bank's Ford 55

White Post, Virginia 70

Charles Town Court House 72

3-Inch Rifle 78

Potomac River 81

Mill at Edinburg, Virginia 87

Madison Court House 89

Rapidan River 92

Clark Mountain 95

Manor House and Fields 95

10-Pounder Parrott Rifle 112

Napoleon Gun 123

Commemorative Marker at Jerusalem Plank Road 126

Houses on Harding Street 202

Battery 45 205

vii

Boisseau House 212

Blues' Cemetery Plot 232

Sewell's Point 235

Armory of the 111th Field Artillery 238

John C. Ashton 244

Smith N. Brickhouse 250

Walter H. Doyle 259

Dr. Frank Fletcher 264

Alexander Goodrich 268

Captain Charles R. Grandy 270

Advertisement for C. W. Grandy & Sons 271

Point Lookout, Maryland in 1865 279

Melville C. Keeling 281

John Walters 303

Walters with Men of McKendree Church 305

Foreword

How many a glorious name for us,
How many a story of fame for us,
They left, – Would it not be a blame for us,
If their memories part
From our land and our heart,
And a wrong to them, and a shame for us?

an excerpt from *C.S.A.*
by Father Abram Ryan,
poet-priest of the Confederacy

As with most diaries, this is not intended to be an all-encompassing history of the American Civil War, but merely the personal account of one eyewitness who was caught up in this great national tragedy. It originated with the typewritten copy in the possession of the city of Norfolk's Kirn Library, Sargeant Memorial Room. It is my belief that this document was typed by Walters' daughter, Mary, from his handwritten originals. It is an interesting narrative of the war which required very little clarification or correction. Except for punctuation and the correction of the spelling of the names of a few towns and leaders, John Walters' diary is presented substantially as I found it. The introductory and postscript chapters and the brief biographies of soldiers I have added should help to provide a more complete history of the Norfolk Light Artillery Blues. The notes which I have included within the diary are primarily intended for the reader who is not intimately familiar with the local geography or with the American Civil War, and who I hope will be encouraged to read further into this fascinating and never exhausted subject. In some small way, I hope this work by John Walters and me will add to the written history of Norfolk, and engender an even greater pride in this fine old Southern city and in the Norfolk Light Artillery Blues.

My thanks to the many people who have graciously given their time, assistance, and encouragement to see this book through, especially my patient family, the late Carroll Walker, Sr., Peggy Haile of the Sargeant Memorial Room, Rick Cox and the many re-enactors who introduced the life of a Confederate cannoneer to me, Vincent Newby and the helpful staff at Norfolk's Elmwood Cemetery, Tom Crew of Richmond, the Old Dominion University Archives, the Hampton Roads Naval Museum, and to JoAnne Clay for her frequent assistance and encouragement in uncovering material for the individual biographies.

Ken Wiley
October 1993

CHAPTER ONE

John Walters Joins the Blues

John H. Walters was a typical citizen of Virginia in the middle of the 1800s. Like many others, he served as a private during war, raised a family, and was active in his community. His life story forms a single common thread which, with the threads of hundreds of similar lives, forms an important part of the colorful strand known as the Norfolk Light Artillery Blues, one of the most unique and impressive of such strands to be found in the historic fabric of its home city.

Similarly, the Norfolk Light Artillery Blues was a company in many ways typical of the militia units called to serve in the monumental struggle known as the American Civil War. The marches, the drills, the camp life, and the sudden terrors of battle were experiences shared by hundreds of similar companies on both sides of the conflict. What makes the Norfolk Blues particularly significant among these is the spirit of its men. These were men with a conviction to duty and honor burned deeply into their hearts. The Blues served from the start of the fighting to the very end in some of the heaviest battles, they resolved never to surrender, they increased their ranks while other companies diminished or dissolved, and they never lost a single man through desertion.

Walters was born near Amsterdam, Holland on January 12, 1835. He came to America as a young man and lived in Albany, New York where he worked for a time in an office of the New York State legislature. He then moved to the seaport of Norfolk, Virginia where he met and befriended people who were in his words "kinder to me

1

than any other I have ever met." It was here in Norfolk that he entered a partnership with Fredrick W. Clark and became a bookbinder, a trade that would sustain him for much of his life. It comes then as no surprise that when Virginia voted to leave the Union of States, Walters chose to join the Norfolk Light Artillery Blues. Not only was it a well established, prestigious militia company, but its captain, Jacob Vickery, Jr., owned one of Norfolk's most prosperous book stores.

The Blues had come into being even before Walters was born. From its earliest days, Virginia had required that all its voting citizens serve in the state militia, either as members-at-large, who were subject to be called to service in times of emergency and assigned wherever needed, or as volunteers who met in companies and drilled at regular monthly meetings. These volunteer militia companies were generally considered to be exclusive clubs as well as military units, and it was common for men to apply to whichever company appealed to their social as well as their martial interests. Possibly because the borough of Norfolk at that time had no active artillery unit, and perhaps inspired by the exploits of the neighboring Portsmouth Artillery who had immortalized themselves at the Battle of Craney Island during the War of 1812, a group of Norfolk gentlemen decided to form a volunteer company of cannoneers in 1829.

The earliest known authentic record of this group is a notice published in the newspapers of Norfolk on September 22, 1829: "Those gentlemen of the Borough who have consented to enroll themselves in a volunteer company of artillery should meet this evening at Town Hall at half past seven o'clock." The minutes of that meeting, glued into the front of the company Secretary's Book, tell us that those in attendance signed their names to a written pledge of support for the proposed company and appointed temporary officers. These officers, in turn, assigned committees to draft appropriate by-laws, design a company uniform, and to collect the names of others who were "disposed to join the company." This work was rapidly completed, and the by-laws committee presented its draft at the next meeting on September 26, 1829.

Another newspaper story in the *Norfolk Beacon* in October 1829 reported the company "has selected the name Norfolk Light Artillery Blues," and "is rapidly becoming an asset to the Borough." The term "light artillery" refers to the mobility of the unit; light artillery consists of cannons (field pieces) and equipment which are easily transported, whereas heavy or siege artillery uses more cumbersome cannon which may have to be transported in separate parts and reassembled before service. The "Blues" designation referred to the color chosen for the company's uniform. Blue, gray, and even green were popular colors for American militia units. In antebellum

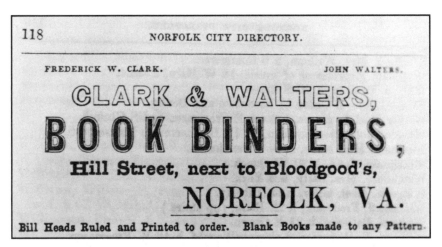

118   NORFOLK CITY DIRECTORY.

FREDERICK W. CLARK.   JOHN WALTERS.

CLARK & WALTERS,
BOOK BINDERS,
Hill Street, next to Bloodgood's,
NORFOLK, VA.

Bill Heads Ruled and Printed to order.   Blank Books made to any Pattern.

This advertisement for the bookbinding shop of Clark and Walters appeared in the 1860 Norfolk City Directory.
Courtesy of the Norfolk Public Library

Virginia alone, there were some 14 companies dressed in blue, and 79 in gray. By February of 1830, the company had elected Miles King, mayor of Norfolk Borough, as their captain, and were fully uniformed in dark blue jackets and trousers and tall leather hats. Their first public appearance was in the Washington's Birthday parade on February 22, 1830. That evening, the Blues hosted the first of many grand balls, and from 1830, Washington's Birthday has also been celebrated as the birthday of the Norfolk Light Artillery Blues.

The Blues continued their peacetime pursuits of parties and parades for the next thirty years without interruption. Their ranks continued to be filled by some of Norfolk's finest young men, and many of the officers were civic leaders as well. Other than being occasionally called out to restore the peace at a fire or some other disturbance, militia service in the Blues meant the sound of boots tramping in unison on the cobblestone streets of the seaport in time to some lively military music, while trying not to obviously acknowledge the admiring glances of the ladies from behind their fluttering fans. It also meant waking the populace with a ceremonial blast from the company cannon on the three national holidays: Washington's Birthday, Independence Day, and Yorktown Victory Day. Occasionally, it included a day-long excursion to a nearby city where the company would be hosted and toasted by brother militia brigades, or a return of the favor at the Blues' own gun room which stood near City Hall.

In these early days of the company, the rolls usually listed about sixty members, with only about half of those being truly active. The Blues usually received a single application for membership and also about the same number of resignations at most of their monthly meetings. This situation changed drastically after John Brown's Raid on Harpers Ferry, Virginia on October 16, 1859. The entire South became alarmed by the possibility that other abolitionists would incite slaves to take up arms, and men rushed to join the militia. Throughout the election year of 1860, several applications for membership were approved at nearly every gathering of the Blues. By January 14, 1861, the company had reached full strength and was divided into four complete gun squads or platoons.

A typical battery of light artillery in the regular army at this time consisted of one captain, two first lieutenants for a six-gun battery or one for a four-gun battery, two second lieutenants, one first sergeant, one quartermaster sergeant, one sergeant and two corporals for each gun in the battery, two buglers, one guidon bearer, two artificers (mechanics), and from 65 to 125 privates. One gun with its limber and a caisson with its limber formed a platoon headed by a sergeant. Two of these gun platoons headed by a lieutenant formed a section. Thus a fully equipped, six-gun battery would consist of three sections.

The Blues were a four-gun battery, equipped with brass howitzers in addition to the percussion cap muskets carried by each private. Most official records show these four cannon were 6-pounder smoothbores, but a few sources refer to them as 12-pounders, with "pounder" referring to the weight of the solid cannonball which would fit the barrel of the gun. It is most likely that the Blues had the smaller 6-pounder guns, as these were popular pieces when the company received their first cannon barrel from the state in 1833. The Blues fired it publicly on the Fourth of July that year, then had it mounted on a carriage at the Gosport Navy Yard in 1836.

The uniform of the Blues at this time differed only in slight details from that which had been adopted by the company when it was formed in 1829. It consisted of a dark blue wool jacket and trousers, generously trimmed with gold cord and lace, and adorned with three rows of 20 brass buttons. White-crossed belts, black cartridge and cap boxes, and a tall, bell-shaped hat were reminiscent of the Napoleonic or "tin soldier" style of army uniforms in use during the War with Mexico in 1846. On January 12, 1860, the Blues voted to update their uniform slightly by adopting a fatigue cap of the type then becoming popular. This was the French hat or "kepi" which would soon be in widespread use. The Blues adorned their version with crossed cannon barrels and a number "4" on the front, denoting the 4th Virginia Regiment of Militia to which the company was assigned. Each man in the company was responsible for buying his own uniform, and since many of the men had only recently enlisted, most of the uniforms at this time would have been practically new. As late as March of 1861, the Blues placed an order with a clothing supplier in New York for matching blue overcoats or "greatcoats."

The ranks of the company continued to swell as "war talk" increased and events propelled the nation toward war. Abraham Lincoln won the presidential election in November of 1860 after stating at the start of his campaign that "a house divided against itself cannot stand" and that the nation "could not exist as half slave and half free." Many Southerners saw Lincoln's election as an end to the compromises between the agricultural South and the industrialized North and as a direct threat to their rights, particularly their right to own slaves, and vowed the time had finally come to leave the Union of States. On December 21, 1860, South Carolina voted to secede and declared itself to be independent. Mississippi, Alabama, Florida, Georgia, Louisiana, and finally Texas followed suit. In February 1861 they banded together in a loose alliance known as the "Confederate States of America."

Opinions in Norfolk over secession varied widely. Most citizens seemed to favor keeping Virginia in the Union, but at the same time, they were content to let the states to the South leave peacefully if that was their wish. On two occasions, an ordinance of secession was introduced in the Virginia legislature, and it was twice voted down.

There were some however who disagreed with this position of the Commonwealth and campaigned for its secession. On April 2, 1861, a Confederate States flag, consisting of one white and two red stripes with seven stars in a field of blue encircling the letters "Va", was flown from a house on Wolfe Street in Norfolk. Julius Augustus Elliott, one of the many recent enlistees in the Blues, took credit for hoisting this flag.

With each day, the escalation toward conflict gathered momentum. Finally, on April 12, 1861, Confederate forces fired on the Federal garrison which had refused to leave Fort Sumter, South Carolina. The fort surrendered the following day and President Lincoln quickly responded by calling on all loyal states to provide 75,000 militiamen to put down the armed rebellion. On April 16, 1861, Governor John Letcher refused to commit Virginia troops "for any such use or purpose as envisioned" and the next day the Commonwealth of Virginia voted to present a referendum on secession to its citizens, to allow it to leave the Union rather than fight against her sister states to the South. War had come.

On April 18, Letcher called up all state militia units, and the Norfolk Light Artillery Blues were one of the first companies to respond, drawing to a close their first thirty-one years of peaceful service. Walters and many others rushed to enlist in the company as quickly as they could.

With Virginia moving toward secession from the Union, the citizens of Norfolk fully expected an immediate occupation by Northern troops from Fort Monroe. The militia companies assembled to protect Norfolk and Portsmouth, but in the first few days, things seemed to be in a confused state. One member of the Norfolk Light Artillery Blues, Private Richard Banks, set out with a small group to destroy the lights and buoys in the channel of the Elizabeth River to prevent Union ships from approaching Norfolk. On the evening of April 19, the Blues and other local militia groups went to Fort Norfolk just down the river from the city, overpowered its caretaker, a Mr. Oliver, and took possession of the navy magazine and its store of 60,000 pounds of gunpowder. Thirteen hundred barrels of this powder were loaded on a boat for Richmond as two of the Blues' guns stood guard on the dock. The following day, the entire company was ordered to intercept the steamer arriving from Baltimore. A rumor had been spread that a group of U.S. Marines were aboard and were on their way to reinforce the small Union force stationed at the Gosport Navy Yard. The Blues searched the steamer but no marines were found. Later that night, the U.S.S. *Pawnee* crept up the Elizabeth River with a force of about 500 men who burned and then abandoned the navy yard to the Virginia State troops.

Following this, the situation became somewhat more organized as the Virginia troops took control and began to fortify the area around Norfolk and Portsmouth. On April 22, the Blues were posted at the old fort at Craney Island, where the approach to both cities by the Elizabeth River had been successfully defended in 1813. The Blues spent about three weeks helping to repair and improve this fort. About the middle of May they were moved to Crossroads, a community at the intersection of several main roads in Norfolk County, and a large detachment of the battery was sent to the shore of the Elizabeth River near the mouth of Tanner's Creek known as "Boush's Bluff." The Blues, the Norfolk "Juniors" and the Norfolk "Harbor Guards" began setting up a battery here to complement the Craney Island fort across the Elizabeth River.

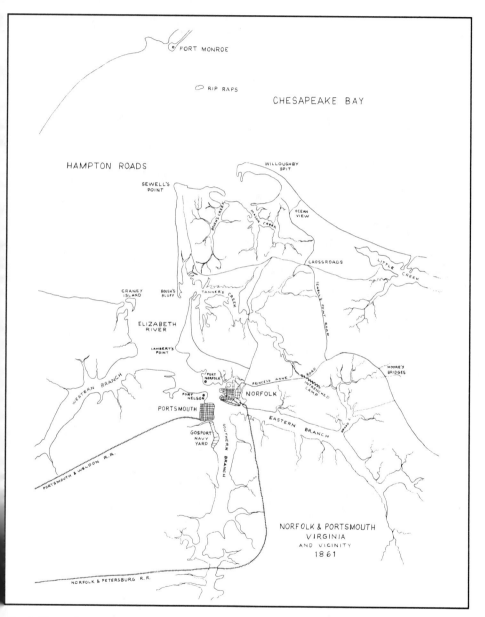

Norfolk and Portsmouth, Virginia and vicinity in 1861.

On Saturday, May 18, the tugboat *Kahukee* steamed past Boush's Bluff with laborers and supplies to begin building another earthen fort to further defend the approach to Norfolk. The tug was en route from Norfolk to Sewell's Point, a low lying area of farmland which jutted out into Hampton Roads across from Union-held Fort Monroe at the tip of Old Point Comfort. The lookouts at Fort Monroe evidently saw the tug as it unloaded its cargo, and a short time later the screw-steamer U.S.S. *Monticello* weighed anchor. This gunboat had just been purchased for the United States Atlantic Blockading Squadron and in its first action its crew was determined to sink the tug and drive the Rebels away from Sewell's Point before any stronghold could be built.

The *Monticello* opened fire with its two 32-pounders and its rifled 10-pounder as it approached the *Kahukee,* and the tug quickly cast off and headed back up the Elizabeth River for the safety of Norfolk with the *Monticello* in pursuit. As the two vessels came in range of the Virginia militia at Boush's Bluff, Captain John J. Young of the "Harbor Guard" fired a shot at the Yankee boat with his 32-pounder naval gun, and the *Monticello* abandoned the chase and returned to anchorage in Hampton Roads for the night.

The following day, the U.S.S. *Monticello*, supported by the makeshift gunboat U.S.S. *Thomas Freeborn*, returned to finish off the new position. A letter written by an unidentified member of the Blues contained this short account of the action:

> At eleven o'clock am, Sunday, the 19th of May, the detachment of the Norfolk Blues stationed at this post (Boush's Bluff) under Lt. Thomas Nash, Jr. and a detachment of the Norfolk Juniors under Lt. Holmes, received orders to march immediately to Sewell's Point and report there for duty. Upon our arrival we found the Columbus (Georgia) Light Guard under Capt. Colquit, and the Woodis Rifles, just up from Ocean View, under Capt. William Lamb. General Gwynn, with his aide Major William E. Taylor was on the ground giving orders. At four o'clock pm, one gun was mounted on its carriage but not fastened. Two others were at that hour buried in the sand. By five o'clock they also were mounted and one of them fastened. While the work of arranging the guns for action was hastily but steadily progressing, a shot came whizzing from a U.S. Government steamer and struck the battery, throwing the turf some distance in the air.
>
> All the battery was now in confusion, but immediate preparation was made to return the fire with the two 32-pounders, and the two rifled cannon brought and manned

by the Woodis Rifles. Captain Colquit being in command of the forces at this time, called for a Virginian to hoist the Georgia flag (that being the only flag available), and Major William E. Taylor of Norfolk mounted the ramparts and unfurled it to the breeze in defiance of the enemy, who had initiated the battle. Orders were then given to open fire, and the first gun was discharged by the detachment of the Juniors, Thad Gray having command of the gun. The Georgians, who had worked manfully in mounting the guns (in conjunction with the Juniors, Blues, and Rifles) took charge of the other two and fought bravely during the whole engagement. Every man acted the true soldier, and though our forces only numbered 250 men, every one stood at his post, whether in the battery or out of it, ready to answer the call of his commanding officer. Those present on this occasion will scarcely ever forget the sound of a bomb or the whistle of a ball, and though they cracked the trees and plowed the ground around us, nobody was hurt and everyone lived to tell the tale.

The *Monticello* had turned broadside about three-quarters of a mile from the shore and began shelling their position. During the height of the battle, three of the Georgia troops openly defied the guns of the *Monticello* by climbing over the embankments to shovel sand out of the way of their cannons. Both the gunboat and the shore battery fired as furiously as they could. Thad Gray, stripped to the waist, worked the Juniors' gun crew and urged on the other cannoneers. Even though none of their cannons had their sights mounted, several of their shots found their mark, wounding two of the gunboat's crew. Captain Henry Eagle (or Engle) ordered the *Monticello* to retire only after the vessel had fired fifteen stands of grape, twelve 10-inch shot, thirty-two 10-inch shell, ten 32-pounder shell, and forty-five 32-pounder shot, which exhausted his ammunition, but his report also admitted there were five holes in the hull as well as two men wounded as the gunboat sailed back toward Fort Monroe. The *Monticello* had failed to drive the Rebels off.

This minor exchange became known locally as the "Battle of Sewell's Point." Although typical of the earliest fights between the North and South, it can hardly be called a battle when compared with the massive actions and tremendous losses which would soon follow. The initial expectations of both sides for a quick and relatively bloodless war would soon be proven to be terribly naive.

The following day, the Sewell's Point Battery was reinforced by even more troops. When the U.S.S. *Monticello* returned on April 21,

The Federal gunboat U.S.S. Monticello which fired against the Sewell's Point Battery on May 19, 1861.

Courtesy of the Hampton Roads Naval Museum

it found the battery fully prepared and eager to fight, and only exchanged a few shots before retreating to the safety of Fort Monroe. This gunboat, which would continue in service with the blockading fleet, would no longer attempt to control all of Hampton Roads. Sewell's Point was now securely in Southern hands.

Work continued steadily at Sewell's Point as men and materials continued to arrive. The sandy soil was piled up to form thicker ramparts, a large flagstaff was raised, a barracks built, and several more 32-pounder naval guns were mounted. On May 27, the battery took the offensive and fired on an expedition under the command of General Benjamin Butler which was sailing to Newport News from Fort Monroe.

At the same time, the Federals were strengthening both Fort Monroe some five miles across the water and also the man-made island known as the "Rip-Raps" or Fort Nelson which lay only two and a half miles from Sewell's Point. On May 30, 1861, an experimental rifled gun designed by Sylvanus Sawyer of Fitchburg, Massachusetts was erected at the Rip-Raps by the newly arrived 99th New York Volunteers. In the middle of June, the garrison at Sewell's Point was startled as the Sawyer Gun fired eleven shells, seven of which struck their battery. A farm house adjacent to the Confederate fort ran up a white flag, probably hoping to show it was not a military target. For the remainder of the summer the Sewell's Point garrison was periodically annoyed by the fire of this long range gun, but never had the range to return the fire. Major General

Benjamin Huger (pronounced "Yoo-gee"), the Confederate commander of the Norfolk area, sent several loads of railroad iron to Sewell's Point to be used as reinforcement against the Sawyer Gun and the Union navy.

The Norfolk Blues were quite aware of the Sawyer Gun as the entire company had been moved to Sewell's Point following their first reorganization on May 21. After a month of recruiting, the ranks of the Blues had swelled to about 150 eager men; however, the unit was informed that state regulations limited the size of a battery to 105 men, and so before the members of the battery could be officially accepted into the state army, the unit was divided. The new company formed by this division chose the name "Norfolk Light Artillery." They elected Lieutenant Frank Huger, a West Point graduate and the son of Major General Benjamin Huger, as their captain. Huger's Battery was assigned duty at the "Intrenched Camp" guarding the approach to Norfolk across Princess Anne Road, and they took the four light smoothbore guns which had belonged to the Blues for nearly thirty years. The similarity between the names of these two batteries, and the fact that most of Huger's men had originally begun their service with the Blues, caused a bit of confusion later for those trying to decide which unit was which.

The old Norfolk Light Artillery Blues, still under the command of Captain Jacob Vickery, Jr., were officially mustered into the 6th Virginia Army on June 4 and were posted at Sewell's Point. On June 8, the troops were inducted into the Confederate States Army. On July 1, they were designated Company H of the 16th Virginia Regiment. In September, the Blues were presented with a beautiful new command flag by the ladies of Norfolk, represented by Miss Kate Lee. This flag was patterned after the Virginia State colors, and used the center emblem from the company's original 1830 flag. A second flag carried by the company featured a blue field with a portrait of George Washington and the motto "Our Cause is Just, Our Rights We Will Maintain." While part of the Confederate army was fighting its first major engagement against the Federal troops at Manassas, Virginia on July 21, the Blues were spending the summer of 1861 in relative comfort at Sewell's Point, expanding the railroad iron casemates and other defenses, firing an occasional shot at a Union vessel in the harbor, and doing battle daily with the ever present mosquitoes.

The Battle of Manassas (or Bull Run) did have one immediate effect on the Blues and other militia troops. Up to that time, a great many militia companies from both North and South had continued to wear their traditional uniforms of nonstandard colors and designs. In fact, many Southerners were paid an allowance

Virginia State Flag of the Norfolk Light Artillery Blues, presented to them by the Ladies of Norfolk in September of 1861.

Courtesy of the Chrysler Museum, Norfolk, Virginia.
A gift of the city of Norfolk

The Command Flag carried by the Norfolk Light Artillery Blues during the war.

Courtesy of the Chrysler Museum, Norfolk, Virginia.
A gift of the city of Norfolk

for furnishing their own uniform, since the states were unable to meet the sudden demand for clothing. This caused a great deal of confusion when the armies clashed at Manassas as multi-colored units with similar looking flags fired on both friend and foe alike. Almost immediately afterward, the Confederates adopted the red battleflag with a blue Saint Andrew's Cross, and issued official descriptions with color illustrations of standardized gray uniforms. It is easy to imagine that every available scrap of gray cloth in Norfolk and Portsmouth was then quickly put to use in clothing the local troops. The Blues turned in their cherished namesake blue jackets and trousers (possibly to be re-styled and re-dyed in gray or "butternut" brown) as the women of Norfolk cut and stitched them new clothes of gray trimmed in artillery red. Although many soldiers like Walters would occasionally have to depend on "battlefield plunder" to keep themselves clothed, for the rest of the Civil War the Blues adopted Confederate gray as their official color.

In July, the Blues' position at Sewell's Point came under a unique form of observation. The aeronaut John LaMountain was personally hired by Butler, commander of Fort Monroe, to observe their battery by balloon. LaMountain made several ascents with his hydrogen-filled balloons, sketching the Sewell's Point works and estimating its strength. On August 3, 1861, LaMountain got a closer look at the Blues and other Confederates when his balloon ascended from the deck of the gunboat *Fanny* anchored halfway across Hampton Roads. As he drew the battery, LaMountain probably gave little thought to expanding the novel idea of using the *Fanny* as a support vessel for his balloon, and of course had no way of knowing that the area he was sketching would someday be a home port to a fleet of aircraft carriers.

LaMountain did report that the Confederate positions were being continuously strengthened. During the summer months the earthen fort was gradually enlarged as a large rampart facing Hampton Roads was completed. Bastions were built on the left and right of this work around a central parade ground and barracks. By October 16, 1861, the commander reported 29 guns mounted at the fort, including twenty 32-pounders, three 42-pounder carronades, and six 9-inch rifles. As the annoying fire from the Rip-Raps (later renamed Fort Wool for the general in command) continued, additional batteries were begun about a half mile east of the main fort, and these were trained at the rock pile in the center of the harbor.

In November, the battery fired without apparent effect on the steamer *Express*. The following month, this same ship was not so lucky. As it attempted to tow the schooner *Sherwood* through Hampton Roads, it was fired on by both the Sewell's Point Battery and the gunboat *Northampton*. The *Express* cut loose its load and escaped, but the *Sherwood* was captured by the Confederates.

The Blues lost two of their officers that same autumn. On September 25, First Lieutenant William Nimmo died of illness, and his remains were returned to the city for burial. On December 4, Captain Jacob Vickery resigned as commander of the company at the age of 48, citing his failing health. Vickery had first served as captain of the Blues in the 1840s and was no doubt proud of his company's reputation as artillerists. It is quite possible that in addition to being sickly and somewhat old for field command, he also resented losing his company's four howitzers to the Norfolk Light Artillery, then being stuck doing garrison duty at a relatively quiet outpost. He returned to his book store in Norfolk and, ironically, lived until well after the war. Vickery was replaced by the youthful attorney Charles R. Grandy of Company B of the 6th Virginia Regiment. Grandy, the eldest son of the prominent Norfolk cotton commission merchant C. W. Grandy, was elected captain of the Blues on December 21, 1861, and was destined to remain in command until after the War Between the States was over. The Norfolk Light Artillery Blues would henceforth be referred to in official Confederate dispatches and reports as "Grandy's Battery."

The Confederates began the year 1862 with the belief that their position in Norfolk was secure, and that their new ironclad ship being finished at the Gosport Navy Yard would soon drive the Yankee fleet from Hampton Roads. It was then only a matter of time before Fort Monroe itself would fall. The Blues enjoyed the relatively mild winter, and drilled with the rest of the Sewell's Point garrison under Commander W. L. Maury for the decisive action sure to come.

Unfortunately all was not as peaceful and secure as it seemed, particularly just to the south. In January, Brigadier General Henry Wise, the commander of the Confederate fort on Roanoke Island in North Carolina, asked that the Norfolk Light Artillery Blues be transferred to him since he feared an attack was imminent and he had no experienced cannoneers to defend the island. Major General Huger refused his request, saying that all available troops were needed for the defense of Norfolk. Roanoke Island was attacked the next month by a Union amphibious force which had sailed from Fort Monroe. The island fell on February 8, 1862, and Elizabeth City, North Carolina was captured two days later, opening the "back door" to the cities of Portsmouth and Norfolk to possible attack from the south by way of the Dismal Swamp Canal.

On March 8, 1862, the quiet of Hampton Roads was broken by the chugging of steam engines as a small fleet of Confederate ships made their way down the Elizabeth River to the open harbor. This was the shakedown cruise of the C.S.S. *Virginia*, the old U.S.S. *Merrimack* which had been burned when the Gosport Navy Yard was abandoned and then rebuilt as an ironclad, and her commander, Flag Officer Franklin Buchanan, and crew were anxious to put the new warship to the test. From the shore of Sewell's Point, the Blues and other troops cheered as the *Merrimac* (as the re-commissioned ship was commonly called) began firing at the helpless wooden Union ships. The U.S.S. *Cumberland* was rammed and quickly sank, and soon after the U.S.S. *Congress* was ablaze and sinking from the *Merrimac*'s hot shot. The Sewell's Point fort added to the battle by firing at a number of scurrying ships which passed within range. The U.S.S. *Roanoke* and *Mystic* were fired on as they abandoned Hampton Roads to the *Merrimac*, and the U.S.S. *Minnesota* was hit by at least one shot from the battery before running aground. With the tide going out, the *Merrimac* broke off the battle, and anchored off Craney Island to resupply for the next day, when she would surely finish off the remaining wooden ships of the Federal navy.

The next morning as the *Merrimac* began its attack on the grounded U.S.S. *Minnesota*, the Blues and the rest of the Confederates were surprised by the sight of a small, peculiar looking ironclad vessel which audaciously approached the *Merrimac* and opened fire. It was the U.S.S. *Monitor* which had arrived during the night, and for the next four hours it dueled the *Merrimac* to a draw. Success had apparently eluded the Confederacy by just one day, as without the timely intervention of the *Monitor*, the *Merrimac* would have made short work of the remaining ships. After that initial battle of the two ironclads, an uneasy truce seemed to fall over Hampton Roads as neither one of the naval commanders was permitted to risk reopening the fight.

This stalemate lasted just less than a month. On May 8, a Union fleet of five ships led by the U.S.S. *Monitor* approached the Sewell's Point battery. The *Monitor* opened fire with Birney incendiary shells and the other ships, the U.S.S. *Seminole, San Jacinto, Dacotah,* and *Susquehanna* quickly joined in. The Blues and the rest of the garrison bravely returned the fire, and the fighting continued for nearly an hour. A Columbiad gun manned by several of the Blues including Privates James Watters and Joseph Allyn was hit and dismounted. One building within the fort was set ablaze, and the defiant Confederate flag was knocked from its staff twice by the heavy Union hail of fire. Suddenly, the *Merrimac* appeared coming up the Elizabeth River from the south, and the Federal ships, under orders not to engage the enemy ironclad, retreated to the shelter of the guns of Fort Monroe. The *Merrimac* anchored off Sewell's Point that evening.

Sewell's Point had been attacked to test its strength after a small tugboat had brought word to Fort Monroe that the Confederates were abandoning Norfolk. President Abraham Lincoln happened to be visiting the fort and when this news was received, he urged his officers to immediately invade the city, deprive the *Merrimac* of her secure port, and force the ship into a fight.

Regardless of the firm stand taken by the Sewell's Point battery, the reports of troop withdrawals were ironically true. The commander of the Virginia State forces, General Robert E. Lee, had worried for some time that Federal troops slowly massing on the Peninsula around impregnable Fort Monroe would eventually make an attack to connect with their forces in North Carolina, and reasoned that if Suffolk were taken, his army in Norfolk and Portsmouth would be cut off and useless for the defense of Richmond. In spite of a plea for the continued defense of Norfolk from Mayor W. W. Lamb directly to President Jefferson Davis on May 1, Lee had given orders to begin evacuating all forces in the area to Petersburg.

On May 9, after another brief shelling from the *Monitor* and their old friend the Sawyer Gun, the Norfolk Light Artillery Blues left Sewell's Point and marched to Norfolk. One of the Blues, Private Joseph Allyn, remembered this day as the most exhausting of his service. After serving a night on picket duty, followed by an afternoon of rowing a scouting party around Sewell's Point, he marched with his company the seven miles back to Norfolk where he was then detailed to unload sand-covered tents. He spent one last night with his family, then with the others they said their goodbys, assembled at their armory in the morning, marched down Main Street, and boarded a train for Petersburg.

Many of the citizens took this opportunity to enlist in the Blues and other units as they were separated from their homes and families, but John Walter's business partner, Fred Clark, was not among them. Perhaps Clark, who had been born in Burlington County, New Jersey, was one of the many Unionists of the area, or perhaps he could not bear to leave his new wife (Clark had married a local girl, one of the sisters of Private John Gamage of the Blues, just the previous November), or it even could have been that he agreed to stay and take care of their business. In any event, the two partners were an example of the divided opinions and differing paths of the people in the old port city. For the rest of this war, the Union would hold sway in Norfolk.

On the same day, May 10, a Federal expedition of 6,000 men under General Wool landed on the sandy beach at Ocean View, a few miles to the east of Sewell's Point. Wool's troops marched cautiously toward Norfolk, expecting at any time to meet a sizable resistance. A few shots were fired as they approached Indian Pole Bridge across Tanner's Creek and they found the bridge in flames, but by the time his forces circled back and approached the city from Princess Anne Road, all the enemy troops, including the Norfolk Light Artillery Blues, had completed their withdrawal and were already on their way to Petersburg. The city had fallen without a fight, and Lincoln's objective was met. The *Merrimac* was deprived of her safe port and, unable to escape up the James River due to her deep draft, she was destroyed by her crew while at anchor off Craney Island before dawn on May 11.

The following day, a Lieutenant John Watters of the U.S.S. *Minnesota* landed at Sewell's Point and took inventory of the recently abandoned battery. He found 45 cannons, including three rifled guns, six 42-pounder carronades, seven 9-inch smoothbores, twenty-two 32- pounders, and another seven dismounted guns. None of the guns were spiked or disabled. His report stated that the guns were mounted in well prepared positions including an earthen wall fort complete with a moat, palisades, bombproof shelters, and a full barracks, and in remote batteries provided with ironclad casemates. The garrison had been well prepared to defend Norfolk, Portsmouth, and the Gosport Navy Yard against an invasion, but they never got the chance. The Norfolk Light Artillery Blues were now on their way to join the force which would go down in history as the Army of Northern Virginia, and Private John H. Walters had begun the diary which would record much of this history.

CHAPTER TWO

John's Diary Begins

Nothing is farther [*sic*] from my mind than the keeping of a journal, yet as the times are as stirring as any which I expect to see no matter how long my life may be spared, I have thought that by dotting down an event here, or an incident there, I might in the future be reminded of the past. I shall by no means mark down the events of each day as they occur, but shall only select the most interesting, taking Friday, the 8th of May, 1862 as a starting point for these notes. I have selected this day for the reason that upon it I bade farewell to many acquaintances and a few friends, the latter of whom I have found as true and faithful as any that man ever was blessed with, friends tested in the crucible of adversity when being weighed in the scales were never found wanting. "May God bless them!" will always be the prayer of one who left them with a smile upon his lips, but with a heart aching as it never, never ached before. Without further preamble, I shall now at once begin, deeming it necessary to say that everything will be condensed to the smallest space possible.

May 8, 1862 Left Norfolk at 10 am (having been sent there the day previous on a corporal's guard after Blockaders) and arrived at Tanner's Creek Wharf about 12 meridian. Shortly afterward we heard firing in the direction of one battery on Sewell's Point whereupon the party with whom I was put for the scene of action, on arriving there, found one steam frigate, three steam sloops-of-war, three gun boats, and the *Monitor* shelling our battery. During the bombardment, which lasted about four hours, the enemy fired some eight hundred or one thousand shot to which we replied by sixty or eighty shot and shell. We do not know what damage we did, but all that we received was three wounded, two slightly and one severely, besides which our quarters were spirred [*sic*] in a number of places. At about 4 pm the long looked for *Merrimac* hove in sight whereupon the Yankee fleet turned tail and fled for protection to the guns of Old Point; comment upon this is unnecessary.

May 9, 1862 During the morning an old acquaintance, the old Sawyer Gun, threw a number of shells on the point without damage. The *Monitor* also appeared off our battery and threw a couple of shells at us without effect. In the afternoon, we were ordered to Norfolk where we arrived about 10 pm. Shortly after, I retired to the luxury of an elegant feather bed with the rather uncomfortable conviction that it was to be perhaps the last time for months that I should be able to enjoy that luxury.

May 10, 1862 At 8 am we assembled at our gun room with knapsack and everything else ready for a march at about 11 am. We proceeded to the N & P RR Depot and in an hour thereafter, the whistle blew, the cars moved, hands were shaken, handkerchiefs waved, we gave a parting cheer, and bade farewell to glorious old Norfolk to return! When? After a most tiresome ride of some seven hours (in freight cars, where I took care to obtain a seat near the door), we arrived in Petersburg, and were marched to Dunn's Hill where we encamped.

> -The Norfolk & Petersburg Railroad had been making scheduled runs since September of 1859. Its president was William Mahone, who was now also serving as a brigadier general in the Confederate army. After the last trainload of Norfolk troops passed the Blackwater River north of Zuni, the trestles were burned, and the N & P RR remained severed for the rest of the war. Mahone was now free to devote more of his time to soldiering.-

May 11, 1862 Woke up early this morning, cold and stiff, from laying on the damp ground. This wore off after a brisk walk down to the spring where I performed my ablutions. I then ate for breakfast what I had left in my haversack, and after dressing and brushing up, went to town. At 9 am I went to the Market Street M.E. Church where, after being requested by the Sunday school Superintendent, I took charge of a class. That over, I went upstairs in company with a number of the Blues and listened to a very fine sermon by the Reverend Mr. Slade, the pastor of that church. After service, I went to Jarrett's Hotel and was charged one dollar for my dinner, paid it of course, but nearly bursted myself in an heroic endeavor to get the worth of my money. I walked around town all afternoon, took supper (75 cents) at Jarrett's (how long will this last on $11.00 per month?), and then went to camp to sleep on the bosom of Mother Nature. I think I would prefer a bosom not quite so damp and a little softer.

May 12, 1862 I make a note of this day for the following purpose: this morning I went down to the mill dam at the foot of the hill on which our camp is pitched, with two handkerchiefs and one pair of socks which needed washing, and while sitting there, I was forced to laugh at the idea of a man paying two dollars and seventy-five cents a day for his board, and between meals washing his stockings, thereby making a clear savings of ten cents. Such is a soldier's life. On second thought, I will have my washing done, and eat one less meal at the hotel.

May 17, 1862 We moved our camp this morning to Poplar Lawn, I think I shall like it better than Dunn's Hill. I do not know what our camp is named, but the most appropriate name for it would be "Camp of Half Rations", as those who live at camp (and I shall soon be of that number) generally get about half enough to eat. We get one half a loaf of bread each man per day, one half an ounce of sugar, no coffee, one half pound of bacon (generally all fat), middling, and some peas. This is bad enough when half of the men eat in town. What will it be when we have no such resources to run to?

-Poplar Lawn is a large open area that lies on Sycamore Street in the middle of Petersburg. It was purchased by the city in 1844 as a park. Volunteer companies assembled and recruited here when Virginia declared secession, and in 1863, a large wooden hospital was erected here. It later became known as Central Park.-

May 18, 1862 Went to church this morning, and toward the close of the service, I was taken with a chill which lasted about two hours, and the fever which followed lasted more than as long again. I feel very sick.

May 20, 1862 Another very severe chill and fever. I feel nearly used up. Dr. Baylor attends me.

May 24, 1862 It seems that Saturday is the only day upon which we can do anything. On this day we move our camp from the Lawn to Oak Grove, near to the Model Farm, in the midst of a pelting rain storm. I heard that the ladies were the cause of our removal, as they objected to having the lawn trampled by our horses. If this is so, it may be all right, and yet I think I can remember that when troops first began to arrive in Norfolk no place was too good for them, and where they first pitched they might have remained til the

Poplar Lawn or Central Park, Petersburg, Virginia. The stone in the foreground marks the site of a Confederate hospital built in 1863.

"crack of doom" before our ladies would have requested their removal. However, my informant may have been mistaken, and if so I do not wish to be guilty of injustice.

May 25, 1862 During the past week I have been slowly improving in health, and today I feel as though Richard would soon be himself again. During my recent illness, while lying one night in my tent, unable to go to sleep, the very peculiar and startling question presented itself to my mind; am I, with all my other faults, a hypocrite? I was led to ask this by having one of my mess mates attempting to ridicule me for bowing my head during prayer in church, saying that by this I led people to believe that I was praying, while out of church I was the greatest scamp unhung. Now I will freely acknowledge that my present walk and conversation is highly reprehensible, but yet those only who are perfect have cast the first stone, and however great a sinner I may be, I can yet find no word or passage in the Bible which prohibits my making use of the publican's prayer, and God only can know in what agony of spirit I sometimes cry out "God, be merciful to me, a sinner". And for this, I am ridiculed. Well, let them talk as they will, they know me not as I am, and it will be folly to let their judgment influence me. Today, I attended the High Street Episcopal Church and by invitation dined at the house of Mr. John B. Ege, a brother book-binder whose acquaintance I made since my arrival here. I also took supper there, or rather here, for I am writing this in his house at half past eleven at night, so the inference is easily drawn that I am to sleep here, and I must say that on looking around, that the bed looks rather more inviting than my allotted space in our tent. I am impatient to learn whether it is softer than my earthly couch; who can doubt that it will not!

> -Mr. Ege was a job printer, book publisher, and editor of the short lived *Petersburg Sun* newspaper. He had moved to Petersburg in 1841 from Richmond where he had been born on August 5, 1819, and had served as an apprentice printer. He was a member of the Odd Fellows, and the Petersburg Benevolent Mechanic Association. The High Street Episcopal Church was generally known as Grace Church. It was begun in 1859 and was located in the most fashionable residential section of Petersburg. Mr. Ege, his wife, and daughter lived near Grace Church on Old Street, a few blocks from Mr. Ege's bookbinding shop at $64^1/_2$ Sycamore Street. Walters would visit all of these places many times.-

June 1, 1862 I again attended the Episcopal Church and dined and took supper at the house of Mr. Ege. The excitement in the city has been intense today in consequence of the reports constantly being received in regard to the battle being fought near Richmond. The reports are so very contradictory that I expect that after the battle is over, though we will have gained a great victory and driven the enemy back any number of miles, each party will yet return to occupy their original position. This may be all very fine, but like the French officer when viewing the charge of the Light Brigade at Balaklava, I doubt whether it is war. The news of the death of the gallant Lamax of the 3rd Alabama has just been received; we could not have lost a better man. I have just heard of an incident which leads me to think that the people of this place will greatly regret his death, it appears his regiment passed through this place en route for Norfolk, but were not permitted to proceed until they had partaken of a splendid collation prepared by the ladies. Upon taking their departure, Colonel Lamax thanked the ladies in a neat and feeling speech in the course of which he remarked that if ever the enemy desecrated this beautiful city, it could only be done after his arm should have lost the power to wield a sword in its defense. His stalwart arm has lost that power, his manly voice is hushed in death, but the remembrance of his worth will nerve his men to deeds of daring which will lead them, not only to defend this place for which he expressed so great a regard, but also to terribly avenge his death.

June 12, 1862 I had another chill this morning, followed of course by a fever, but neither of them were very severe. This afternoon I was pleasantly reminded that I have friends in the city by the receipt of a most delicious rice pudding, and large enough for my whole mess. It is almost needless to say that the boys did it ample justice. It was sent to us by Mrs. J. B. Ege.

June 14, 1862 I had another chill and a very severe fever accompanied by excessive vomiting, not withstanding I took 18 grams of quinine before it came on. Oh! for a lodge in some vast wilderness where these things are unknown. I wonder if I am never to be rid of this incubus. I think I shall try arsenic. I have heard that mentioned as being very effective.

-Walters was not the only member of his company to fall ill. Private J. S. Sterrett, a twenty-year-old enlistee from Maryland, died on this date of illness in a Petersburg hospital.-

June 15, 1862 Feeling a little better this morning, I went to Mr. Ege's house to stay a few days until I get better; he having frequently invited me to do so.

June 20, 1862 Not having had any chill since last writing, I reported to camp early this morning, though pressed to stay til next Monday by all at Mr. Ege's. In my twenty-seven years of life, it has been my good fortune to meet with many kind and hospitable people, but never, til I came to Virginia have I found such free hearted, open handed hospitality as I found in Norfolk and this place. It seems to be as natural a thing here for people to show kindness to a stranger as to breathe, and it is all done in such a way that the moment a stranger sets foot in a house he feels as much at home as if he had lived there some years.

June 26, 1862 This morning I took a walk to town and in the course of my ramble went to Mr. Ege's place of business. While there, I saw a large number of troops passing on their way to Richmond, and great was my surprise to see our company in the line. One minute saw me a spectator of, the next a figure in this warlike panorama as it took me about that length of time to say good-bye and run to and get up on the piece to which I am attached. We went as far as Swift Creek, about three miles from Petersburg on the road to Richmond, where we halted as though for the night. At about 9 o'clock pm heavy cannonading was heard to the right ahead of us and about an hour after, just as I was looking for a soft place, the bugles sounded to harness up, and the drums from several regiments encamped in our neighborhood beat the long roll, and in twenty minutes we were on the march to what we thought would be a battle, as it was reported that the enemy were landing in force. After marching about four miles on a road that seemed to be all hills going up and none to go down, we came to a halt and bivouacked for the night, as we learned that the reported landing was a fabrication of some frightened man who saw four or five men coming ashore in a boat and imagined thousands following them.

-By this time, Captain Grandy had been largely successful in equipping his company as a light artillery unit. This was no small task, as the Blues had served for nearly a year as infantry, but fortunately Petersburg was the rail center for all supplies coming into the Richmond area. The Blues were at first given two three-inch ordnance rifles, two bronze 12-pounder howitzers, and two Napoleons. All of these were popular and effective guns. The howitzers, when loaded with canister, were especially suited to close range fire against massed battle lines of infantry. The rifled guns were accurate, dependable weapons for long-range work, particularly counter-battery fire. The Napoleons, smooth-bores with heavier, longer barrels than the howitzers, were effective in either role. Thus supplied, the Blues were well equipped for any type of fight. Unfortunately, before the Blues could see action, the Napoleons were taken and they received two less effective, antiquated 6-pounder pieces in their place. Walters was assigned as the number three man on one of these guns.

The primary need of the Blues or any other artillery company, even greater than cannons or uniforms, was for horses. Cannons were distributed to the artillery alone, but every branch of the army competed for good horses. Considering that a regulation team of six healthy horses was supposed to pull each gun and each caisson, it literally took as many horses as men to keep each field piece in service. Added to this were the teams needed to pull the forage and supply wagons and the traveling forge, and the mounts for the officers and guidon bearer. A field artillery battery was certainly never idle, even while encamped, with all those horses to care for and feed. Unfortunately, the whole Confederate Army would be plagued by a chronic shortage of horses throughout the war. Grandy's battery received only four horses for each of its teams, and this would be the most horses the Blues would ever have available.-

June 27, 1862 This morning, as the wagon was going to Petersburg for forage, I received permission to go with it to get my coat and blanket, as my hasty departure of yesterday prevented my getting them from camp. I, of course, intended to return with the wagon, but by some accident or other missed it, and so found that I would be obliged to walk. Thinking that a six mile walk would not be much, I waited until half past five pm when I left town, but fancy my feelings when after walking about five miles, I learned that all the artillery had gone on, as I was told, to Richmond. This was awful, five miles already walked and sixteen more to go over was nearly enough to turn me back, but as the evening was beautiful and the night promised to be cool, I pushed on hoping that the company would bivouac somewhere on the road. This hope was realized, for on reaching the house of a Mr. Drewry in the neighborhood of a formidable bluff of that name, I found our boys. On inquiring the distance from there to Petersburg I was told it was fifteen or sixteen miles, but if anyone should ask me I should say that it was about one hundred and fifty. I slept so soundly that night that all the bugles in the Confederate Army would have failed to wake me.

July 1, 1862 For the last three days a great battle has been fighting near Richmond of which we have received the most glowing accounts. God grant that it all is as we hear for we sadly stand in need of a great victory to save us from subjugation, while MacClellan requires one to save his reputation for which he will fight harder now, and where the difference is so great, as between a man and a nation's welfare, surely the God of Battles will smile on our arms.

This morning our battery, supported by three companies of North Carolina troops, was ordered down to Bermuda Hundred to look after some Yankee transports which were in the river at that place.

This 6-pounder gun is an example of the type used early in the war by the Norfolk Light Artillery Blues. Most units traded their 6-pounders for larger Napoleons or for rifles at the first opportunity.

This heavy gun mounted en barbette in Fort Darling at Drewry's Bluff guards the approach to Richmond by way of the James River.

After going some twelve miles over very bad roads for the artillery, having but four horses to a piece, we came to a halt, being about two miles from the Hundreds. The officers went forward to reconnoiter, and after being absent some two hours or more the Colonel who had charge of us (a North Carolinian, by the way) said that it was not advisable to fire on a large transport which lay in the river in full sight and which we could have approached within a few hundred yards. This did not please our boys at all but of course we did not dare say a word to him, though the fact that we were to do nothing pleased me well enough, as I was laying under a tree shaking with all the energy of which I was capable, having been taken with a chill a short time before, caused most probably by the sun, which had been oppressive all morning. After remaining about an hour longer, to give me as the Colonel said, an opportunity to finish my exercises, we were on the point of returning when the Colonel ordered two of our pieces down for the purpose of giving the Yankees just the last taste in the world of our metal. By this time my chill had passed off, and I was indulging in the questionable luxury of a perspiration bath, the fever having set in, and as my gun was one of those going, I mounted the limber chest, determined to go where duty called me though I had rather gone to bed if one had been convenient. While going down to take up a position, a scout reported the *Monitor* and a gun boat coming down the river. As these would be a little too much for our small guns we returned and going back a couple of miles, encamped for the night with orders to be ready at day break to return to our old camp at Drewry's house.

-Grandy's Battery was now assigned to the Department of North Carolina under Major General Theophilus Holmes. The "Colonel who had charge of us" was Colonel James Deshler, the department chief of artillery. Deshler's fitness report of July 15 notes the Blues were equipped with the guns mentioned previously, namely two 6-pounders, two 12-pounders, and two 3 inch rifles, that they still need harness for one of their guns, and that the company was among those needing drill. He did finish his report by saying the Blues "have only been under my command for a few days, so that the remarks regarding efficiency, and etc. are necessarily more or less imperfect".-

July 2, 1862 According to orders, at day break we got ready and were soon on our way back. With day light came rain, in no very gentle shower but one continuous pour which made the roads, bad at best, almost impossible for our pieces. So much so, that we were two or three times compelled to take all the horses off one piece and hitch them to another and drawing it a mile or so return and get another, til all were once more together, while twice the order was given for the cannoneers to go to the front with the axes, to cut a road through the woods, the main road being perfectly impassable. In this way we worked on til about four o'clock pm when we arrived at an old camp, wet to the skin, hungry, and tired. Someone has said that "angels weep when sinners die". If today's rain had not been so heavy, and with an occasional smile from the sun between, I could very readily have imagined that angels were weeping over the large number of souls that were cancelled suddenly before their God within the last few days.

July 3, 1862 Another dark day for me in the chill and fever line, thought the weather had cleared up. While lying in our wagon line, our Captain came and told me that he was going to send the wagon to Petersburg tomorrow, and that I had better go in it to get medicine, and stay til I got better. I tried hard to keep my teeth shut long enough to tell him there was nothing wrong with me, but it was no go, they would rattle in spite of me, and as I was of no service there, I thought it better to do as he said.

July 4, 1862 This morning, after passing a most wretched night, I got in our wagon and in the course of three or four hours jolting over a very rocky road, arrived and went to the house of Mr. Ege, though I did so with the feeling as if I were imposing on good nature, but my reception was so kind that it would have been churlish to have doubted my welcome.

July 5, 1862 Today I had another chill, but not by any means so severe as those which I have lately had, owing no doubt to the kind attention which I received from Mrs. Ege. Really this lady must have been born to elevate the already high standard of herself, and to shed sunshine around the path of every unfortunate who may come in contact with her. Far be it from me to sit in judgment upon her, but if she and such like her do not go to heaven, who does?

July 13, 1862 This morning, I went to our camp at Oak Grove to get some clean clothes, and while there was made very happy by the weight of a letter from my home in Norfolk, which informed me that all were well but very anxious to hear from me. This was very hard, to learn that none of my letters or messages had reached them, notwithstanding that I paid three dollars some weeks ago to have one carried. However I also learned that a lady was going to Norfolk next Tuesday, so writing a letter I called on her with the request to carry it there, with which she kindly complied. During the past week I have escaped chills owing I think, to a solution of arsenic which a doctor gave me, and as this is I believe, the last medicine given, I trust that I have had my last chill.

-Other "medicines" commonly in use included quinine, strychnine, turpentine, castor oil, and a mercury-based camomile. "Black Draught" was a common laxative. Quinine was the only one of these popular treatments to prove medically effective.-

July 17, 1862 This afternoon, while at dinner, we were startled by the loud report of what seemed to be a field piece in our vicinity, and a short time after we learned, a few doors above us on the other side of the street, a man was engaged in unloading a shell while his father-in-law was looking on, when suddenly it exploded, shockingly wounding both men in such a manner that I feel satisfied they cannot live.

August 3, 1862 Since writing the above both the unfortunate men spoken of have died, a terrible warning to those who know but little of the danger of handling such uncouth Yankee pets. I feel very sad tonight, as I intend to report for duty tomorrow morning, and as our company is at present some few miles from the city, it may be some time before I shall have another opportunity of being with this family who, notwithstanding the short acquaintance that I have with them, have grown inexpressibly dear to me, by reason of their overwhelming kindness. And what is so strange is that though there is so little in or about me for anyone to like or admire, they really seem, and I cannot but think, are sorry that I am going. I can only account for the latter on ground that as there is more pleasure in giving than receiving they regret losing the opportunity of adding to their already many kindnesses.

Since my last writing I have sent two letters to Norfolk. Will they be received? Or will those dear friends still labor under the sad mistake of believing that, forgetting all their many acts of friendship, I do not even send them word that I am yet where I can look back with fond regret upon the many happy hours spent in their society.

What a singular influence a dream, even though there be nothing prophetic in it, sometimes has over us. Last week I had a very blue day caused by what might almost be called a cosmopolitan dream, a dream of three homes, or rather two homes and a face, one home far away with which my earliest recollections of life are associated, a home where I was surrounded with the love of such a mother as few are ever blessed with, who if living, recreant though I am, still prays for her wild, wandering boy, and if dead and permitted, watches over him with the solicitude which only a mother can feel. The other, a home where during a residence of three years I met with nothing but kindness, and where I learned more of the beauty of the female character than was ever dreamed of in my philosophy. The third phase of the dream was that face, that face, way off in the past with the light of nearly four years and the shades of what seems to be twenty years between it and myself, yet with that well remembered smile upon it, that face of times so dear as it looms up through the past, its faults, if there were any, forgotten, its beauties intensified. Great God, how the memory of my conduct towards you burns me, I must not think of it, that way lies madness.

-The places of Walters' dream include both his native Holland and Norfolk where he had lived the last three years before the war. Walters never quite explains the face in his dream, although he does later mention a lost sweetheart named Fannie.

While Walters was in Petersburg recuperating from his illness, the Blues at long last were sent into battle.

After the fighting around Richmond, General George B. MacClellan pulled his army back toward the James River pursued by the Confederate army now under the command of General Robert E. Lee. The Union army stopped their pursuers at Malvern Hill, inflicting severe casualties, then paused while MacClellan regrouped around his supply port at Harrison's Landing (Berkley Plantation) on the north bank of the James.

On July 23, Lee assigned command of the Department of North Carolina to General Daniel H. Hill, and directed him to "endeavor by movable batteries, sharpshooters, and etc. to annoy and arrest, if possible, the transport of (MacClellan's) supplies." Hill's department controlled everything south of the James River, and included seven batteries of light artillery: Grandy's (the Norfolk Blues), Branch's, French's, Graham's, and Ruffin's Virginia companies, Coit's South Carolina, and Lloyd's North Carolina companies. At Lee's suggestion, Hill delegated direct command of this mission to Brigadier General Samuel G. French, ordering him to move quietly on the night of July 29 with three days' rations. We can imagine the Blues were very excited by the order to march, since a deliberate rumor was being spread (again at Lee's suggestion) that this force was to attack Suffolk and perhaps even Norfolk! However, their hope of liberating their homes was soon put aside when their force joined the Reserve Artillery under the command of General William N. Pendelton and took sheltered positions near Coggin's Point on the night of July 30. The force remained carefully hidden from the Yankee observation balloons the next day while the artillery commanders scouted the river bluff. This time, they found no gunboats defending the Union ships and army; these had moved three miles upriver to intercept ships from Richmond. The Confederates began quietly moving their cannons into position after dark.

About 30 minutes after midnight on August 1, the Confederate artillery opened up on Harrison's Landing. The cannon fire was randomly aimed at the few lights seen on the ships and in the camps; in fact it was unusual for artillery of this period to be allowed to fire without a clearly visible target. Nevertheless, the batteries had their intended effect. The Union troops were surprised and confused by the shells which began exploding in their camp in the middle of the night, their operations at the docks were interrupted, 10 men were killed, 12 wounded, a half dozen horses were killed, a wagon was smashed, and supply vessels around the landing were driven off. The Blues and others fired for about half an hour until their available ammunition was used up, then withdrew well beyond the range of the guns which had begun to return their fire. The next day, a Union force came across the river and occupied Coggin's Point. They cut down the trees which had sheltered the batteries from their lookouts, posted a strong force to prevent their return, and burned one of the houses of the Ruffin family. (Edmund Ruffin, an ardent secessionist born nearby at Evergreen Plantation had been given the honor of firing the first shot at Fort Sumter.) French's troops returned to camp near Petersburg without harassing the Federals any further, but they had helped to convince MacClellan to quickly withdraw his army back to the safety of Fort Monroe. The Blues themselves were very proud of their part in this event, and many of them, including Walters, would later list this as one of their company's major engagements.-

October 13, 1862 It is just seventy-one days since I made my last entry in this book for which seeming neglect many reasons can be advanced. As I anticipated at last writing, I reported to camp at Oak Grove, where I spent the day in overhauling and repairing my wardrobe, many pieces of which sadly needed it. Next day, I joined our company which I found some two miles from the city on City Point Road, in an open field where it was almost too hot to live, and where we were obliged to go nearly a mile to get water to drink, and where people charge only twenty-five cents per quart for buttermilk, and everything else in proportion.

On the next day, the 7th of August, one of our young fellows, W. A. Wilkins, died in the Bollingbroke Hospital of typhoid fever. He was a most admirable young fellow, very popular and greatly regretted. From this time until the 19th of August, we remained stationary, very pleasingly exercising our talents in devising ways and means to evade officers and orders, in running the blockade to town, in which agreeable division I succeeded in gaining an enviable reputation among our boys. On the 19th we received orders to strike tents and take up our line of march, to reinforce Stonewall Jackson, and about 11 o'clock am we started, and about dark encamped for the night at Drewry's Bluff, about a mile from our old camp ground. Early next morning we again took up our beds and walked to Rockett's old field near Richmond by way of the Pontoon Bridge. We got there at an early hour in the afternoon, and much to the regret of our boys, who were all eager to push on, were ordered to pitch our tents. We remained here three days and on the 23rd of August again struck tents, but instead of going forward, returned by the road we had come to within a mile of the Pontoon Bridge. Here we encamped in the midst of a drenching rain, on a hill where the soil was a red clay and very soft at that, so that it was impossible to keep our clothing, tents, guns, or anything else clean. Everything was full of clay. We remained here four days. On Tuesday the 26th of August, we received orders to strike tents and accompany the brigade to which we were attached to, as it was reported, Charles Town, Jefferson County, but as two of our gun carriages were in Richmond being repaired, the order was rescinded, though the brigade went on. This pleased us all very much as our boys had no particular liking for General Ransom, and did not wish to be in a brigade not from our own state. Not that the brigade was not all that it should be, but it is perfectly natural that we should wish to be in a brigade of our own. Next day the 27th, we struck tents and moved to within about two miles from Richmond, where we encamped on the ground once occupied by the celebrated Washington Artillery of which we have strong evidence in the scents, which are not at all "Gales from Araby the Blest", which arise from the defunct horses that are laying about in all directions, and though it is, in every other respect, a very fine place, it is full of inducements to melancholy thoughts, for here we see some old garment, the owner of which may be among the things that were. There are some leaves from a Bible, or a stray knave of spades, dread reminder of the one who performs the last sad offices for poor humanity, elsewhere we see a rude arbor or rustic table, or an old muster roll containing the name, perhaps of many, "A Cromwell, guiltless of his Country's blood" who ere this has paid his debt to nature.

In the evening of this day, I paid a visit to the family of Mr. J. L. Ege, the latter a brother of my dear and valued friend in Petersburg. I found them all worthy relatives of so worthy a gentleman as he of Petersburg, and spent a most agreeable evening there. From that day to the present, we have led a rather monstrous life, varied by but few instances worthy of being noticed. Every afternoon when the weather permits we have a drill which for the last three weeks has been very interesting, from the fact that Lt. Col. Lightfoot drills us in the battalion drill, in company with two other artillery companies which are encamped in our neighborhood, in which, and I can say without vanity, we are becoming very proficient.

Since our arrival here I have become accustomed to spend the Sunday afternoon and evening at Mr. Ege's house and sometimes spend an evening during the week there. I am always received there with the most gratifying kindness and strange as it may be to those who know me better than they have had time or opportunity to do, they seem to take a pleasure in my company, which I can only attribute to their kindness of heart manifested towards one who has but little to recommend him to the kindness of strangers.

Last Thursday, the 9th of October, I attended the wedding of Lama, the eldest daughter of Mr. Ege, who was married to a Mr. Brooks, a brother soldier from Charlottesville, Virginia, who has by this act obtained a very sweet, intelligent wife. The party was a brilliant and joyous affair, and one well calculated to live long in my memory, but the most pleasing feature of it to me who was, of course, "a looker on in Venice", was the presence of my friends from Petersburg, whom I had not seen since we left there. I met them and found their smiles as bright, their words as kind, and their looks as happy as formerly, all of which being contagious made me very happy. There seems to be something in the air which I breathe while with them which dispels gloomy thoughts from my mind. What is it? It cannot be that the essence of charm is contained in the person of their daughter Eddy, for she is ten or eleven years my junior, a very bright, sweet girl, added to which I have a very strong suspicion that she is reserving a large portion of her sweetness for a young fellow of my acquaintance named R., and who I am very partial to, he being a young fellow of fine personal appearance, good address, and excellent principles. But though I do not like to own it, even to myself, I fear that he will not make her happy as he has but little decision of character, a great deal of which will I think, be required should things terminate as I cannot but think they will. Let no one suppose that I write this because the grapes are sour, God knows that no grapes of this vintage can ever be sweet for me while ───── lives, and should the affair between ───── and myself be forever at an end, why then, why then for me "chaos has come again".

One amusing incident connected with my going to the wedding may as well be mentioned here. Wishing to appear as well as it was possible for me to appear, I applied to all who had anything to wear in the shape of wearing apparel, the result of which was that when I got to the house I had on one man's coat, the vest of a second, the white shirt of a third, the collar of a fourth, neck-tie of a fifth, shoes of a sixth, and as the last were rather tight, a thin pair of socks from a seventh, all of which enabled me to present a very credible appearance.

At the commencement of this rather long day's journalizing I said that many reasons might be advanced for my apparent neglect in permitting seventy-one days to elapse between the two last dates but did not advance any; let me do so here. In the first place, for nearly a month after leaving Petersburg, we were without tents or knapsacks (my saying in sundry places that we struck tents having reference to the flys which we had, our camp equipage having been left at the latter city) for which reason, conveniences for writing were almost out of the question. Another reason was that though almost constantly moving, nothing occurred of any interest, and the last reason was a distaste for everything which I began to experience. Consequently upon the neglect of my friends in Norfolk in not writing to me, notwithstanding the number of letters that I was constantly sending there, but this cloud is lifted, for last week I received a letter from home which assured me of the qualifying fact, so dear to the heart of every wanderer, that I was still held in the kindest remembrance by those who are so inexpressly dear to me.

October 15, 1862 (Wednesday) Today we see the sun the first time since last Friday, for we have had heavy rain incessantly. Last Monday evening I went to town to call upon Mr. and Mrs. Ege from Petersburg who are stopping on Grace Street for a few days before going home. The walk to and from there was very unpleasant as the mud was over my shoe tops, and though it did not rain going in, yet on coming out to camp at twelve o'clock at night, it came down in torrents. While it was so dark that I could hardly see to find my way through the woods (which in the daytime are gloomy enough but at night are doubly so) however I was received so kindly that the thought of a long walk and wet skin did not deter me from promising to come again on Thursday evening, which may be the last time for a long while as they return to Petersburg next Saturday.

(**October 15, 1862** As I wish to make a private memoranda which I may wish to destroy in the course of time without injuring the course of this diary, I will write on this slip of paper. This evening, while in conversation with Miss Eddy on the subject of matrimony, I jestingly remarked that she would be married before three years had elapsed, an assertion which she laughingly contradicted and dared me to a wager, whereupon I offered one which she accepted, which was that if she married within three years, her first act of authority would be to order her better half to present me with a gold watch, and in case I lost the wager, I was to give her a watch and chain. I am somewhat anxious to know whether there are any of the prophetic elements in my composition, and three years is a long time, but I fear the question cannot be answered in a much shorter length of time.)

October 23, 1862 (Thursday) Last Friday night, I paid a visit to Mrs. and Miss Ege and as the weather had cleared up, I had a fine though dark walk, and spent a few hours most agreeably in the company of my dear friends from Petersburg, and on leaving them, I bade them good-by for, as I thought, a long time, though the length will be determined tomorrow morning by the route we shall take, for this afternoon, just as I had commenced a letter to them, I heard some of our boys shouting and among the shouts I heard the words, "We're off!". On going out to learn the news I was informed that we were ordered off early tomorrow morning, to where, we could not learn. If towards Suffolk, which is possible, then I shall perhaps see them sooner than I expected, if the other way which is also possible, then I shall see them when I get back.

Last Sunday a friend and myself walked down about seven miles from camp to the battlefield of Seven Pines. There remains but little of the wreck and ruin of a great army to point it out as a field of terrible slaughter, which it really was, though its rays are but dim in the full glare of the after battle, or of battles, though many evidences of the battle remain in the almost endless line of earthworks, the massive batteries (in the ditches of which, covered by but little earth of the ramparts lie hundreds of the victims of this unholy crusade), the bullet riddled houses, and the many mounds which denote the last resting place of those who came to desecrate the glorious old soil of Virginia, but found the air to be heavily impregnated with leaden vapors. Immediately in the rear of a strong, eight gun battery are two wooden houses, well riddled, in which soldiers from both armies have written everything usually written on such occasions. Here can be seen names of men from every state in both confederations, while many instances are given of the perfection of doggerel talent, one or two specimens I give:

> Adieu! Adieu! to the stars and stripes
> Once an emblem of Liberty,
> One thought of thy present bearer,
> Wipes away all allegiance to thee!
> The bright stars that shown from it are dim,
> And the stripes into serpents have turned,
> An appropriate emblem for him,
> Who the rights of our company has spurned.
> Co. B, 18th Georgia Vol.

The next specimen shows the most decided talent in abbreviating the last word in the first line so as to make rhyme, and a rich imagination in supposing that anyone can sleep in that place where the fire is never quenched unless indeed, he should happen to be a salamander, though a special arrangement might be made for the unfortunate subject of the lines. Here they are:

> Abe Lincoln, Abe Lincoln, I'll tell you, old fell,
> In less than two years you'll be sleeping in Hell.
> Verily, cerily "is Saul also among the prophets".

October 25, 1862 (Saturday) Early this morning I packed up everything and strapped my knapsack to the caisson awaiting the order to march which did not come, but towards the night we were informed that we would start early tomorrow morning. Our destination, I believe, is Brandy Station on the Orange and Alexandria Railroad. This order to move ends all our pleasant anticipation of comfortable winter quarters here. Tomorrow I must bid a long farewell to the friends that I have made here, farewell to the kindly smile of the Matron, the blithe laugh, and light hearted tones of the maiden, the innocent prattle of children. War, not women, must be my future theme. Last night a number of our boys serenaded Colonel Lightfoot, under whose command we have been. He was greatly pleased with the compliment, expressed regret at our leaving, as he had hoped to lead us into battle himself, and trusted to hear good accounts of us, of which latter he had no doubt. God grant that we may not disappoint him. Good night.

> -On October 23, General Lee had written Colonel John R. Chambliss, Jr., commanding the forces along the Rappahannock River, and suggested that he get more artillery support from Major General Gustavus Smith, commanding the forces around Richmond. As a result, the Blues and the 61st Virginia Infantry were transferred to Chambliss, and as Walters mentions, they left Richmond on October 26. On November 5, Smith asked Lee to send the Blues back to his command. Lee responded that the Blues would be sent back as soon as they could be replaced, but before that could happen, a turn of events convinced him to order the Blues and the 61st Virginia to Fredericksburg instead.-

October 26, 1862 (Sunday) Early this morning a drizzling rain set in which towards daylight changed to a good, steady shower, but this did not prevent us from striking tents and starting upon our journey. 'Tis true the prospect overhead was not very cheering, but it is time for us to make a start if we expect to make a winter campaign like men. Before the battery started, I went ahead to bid good-by to my friends at Mr. Ege's. As the day promised so badly, his kind daughter, Mrs. Lama Brooks, at the instigation of her equally kind hearted mother, prepared me a deliciously strong whiskey toddy while Mr. Ege himself filled a pint bottle of the precious fluid to last me through the day. This kind thoughtfulness for others is a pleasing characteristic of the family, so it need not be wondered that on leaving them, I felt that I was leaving friends. May heaven be kind to them.

We passed through the city and encamped in the afternoon about eight miles from it. On receiving the bottle, I partly determined to keep it for my own private use, but on looking around me upon our boys and seeing them wet, and judging from my own feelings, I took one good pull at the bottle and passed it around, making three or four hearts glad which done me more good than if I had made my own heart glad three or four times.

I was much amused at a remark made by one of us named Freeman. In the afternoon, I had lagged behind so that the battery had

got a mile or more ahead, and while stepping briskly along, overtook him plodding along slowly, every now and then shaking the
water off his hat. On coming up to him I said, "Come, Freeman.
Step up. It is getting late! What time do you suppose it is?" On this
remark, he looked at me and answered, "Time! Time! What do I care
for time? Time was made for slaves, not Freeman!" I left.

> -Private Joseph M. Freeman, Jr.'s distaste for marching
> evidently grew, as he transferred to the Confederate navy on
> May 12 the following year, taking his wit along with him.-

October 28, 1862 (Tuesday) We laid over yesterday as it rained all
morning and when it cleared off, it was too late to do much that
day, but this morning the sun came out bright and clear and we
made an early start of it, and by night had traveled about twenty-
two miles to Hanover Junction. This was more than we should have
done as some of our horses were badly galled owing to the rain of
the two previous days, but our Lieutenant in command was anxious to make Hanover so as to obtain forage and provisions. He
found the former, but not the latter, as prospects are extremely
bright for short rations for a couple of days. In the course of the day
one of our boys and myself started ahead of the battery and stopped
at a house to get dinner. We got a very fair one for fifty cents and
here I saw two of the most beautiful children that I ever saw, girls of
seven and nine years of age, the youngest especially reminding me
of paintings that I have seen of the Madonna, and strange too was
that both the father and mother were course featured and if anything, ill-favored people.

> -The "Lieutenant in command" mentioned was Lieuten-
> ant William T. Peet. Captain Grandy, an attorney prior to the
> war, had stayed behind to participate in a court-martial.-

October 29, 1862 Started about ten o'clock this morning and a
little before dark we arrived at Beaver Dam on the Central Railroad,
which was the scene of a Yankee raid last spring. The damage done
by them was not great. The road has been very good today, a very
marked improvement on that of yesterday.

October 30, 1862 (Thursday) Early this morning two of our boys
and myself started off to hunt up a breakfast as our haversacks
present a most consumptive appearance. After walking about two
miles we came to the house of a Mr. Carter who kindly furnished us
refreshing remuneration. The breakfast was substantial, elegant,
and plentiful. We found both Mr. Carter and his wife people of education and refinement. They have lost much by this war, for where
in former years he saved at least three hundred bushels of wheat,
this fall he could only save thirty, and did not know whether he

would be able to get that in. Just before sundown we halted at Fredrick's Hall, a station on the Central Railroad. The road today has been very bad, it seemed as though we had all hills to go up and none to go down, besides which it is in bad order, full of deep ruts in which our wheels frequently went down to the hubs, and as our progress was of a necessity slow our boys had the more time to pay their respects to the apple orchards and persimmon trees, numbers of which we passed and in nearly all cases finding the fruit delicious. At night, a party of eight, myself one of them, went to a house where supper had been engaged, and had a most excellent one for fifty cents apiece.

October 31, 1862 We got under way this morning and in the afternoon halted for the night at the village of Louisa Court House. This is a very neat little place of some four or five hundred inhabitants, and containing some very fine residences. We here found some very good apple brandy which we obtained with but little trouble at sixteen dollars per gallon. At night about eighty of our boys took supper at the hotel, and here we were most outrageously swindled, as all we got was bread without butter, coffee without milk, sweetened with molasses and weak enough to require strengthening tonics, and ham on which the fat was ad libitum and the lean the reverse of it, for which we were charged one dollar apiece. After supper I got a number of our boys together and under the guidance of the village postmaster, whose acquaintance I made for the occasion, we went and serenaded four or five houses at all of which we were pleasantly entertained for the few minutes that we went in and stopped at each. One old gentleman and his daughter were very pleasing in their invitation to take supper, and upon our refusal, passed cakes and preserves all around.

-The Blues go trick-or-treating!-

November 1, 1862 Early this morning we left Louisa bearing many pleasing remembrances of the place and its people with us, and at night fall pitched our camp about one mile beyond Gordonsville in Albemarle County, I think. The road from Louisa here is very good. Just before entering Gordonsville on the left hand side of the road is a field in which we saw a large number of pieces of plank stuck in the ground, which on examination proved to be headboards, pointing to the last resting place of many of our brave soldiers who left their homes in the full flush of health, but found a shallow grave and a cheap monument in the Old Dominion whose sacred soil they came to defend from the polluting tread of Northern hirelings. May Heaven receive all who die in their country's cause, though this prayer is an economical one as I myself am in the service. The village lies nearly at the foot of the north western mountain, a spur of the Blue Ridge in sight of which we have been traveling for the last two days. The mountains present a beautiful appearance, decked as they are in all the beauty of Autumn foliage, where the bright green of the pine forms a fine contrast with the yellow of the chestnut and the many shades of red of the oak. The houses of the village, as of most country villages, are straggling. It contains three churches, only one of which however is used for its legitimate purpose, another being used as an army storehouse and the third standing idle, possibly for want of a preacher. There is also a seminary for ladies, the windows of which were beautifully illuminated as we passed by. The scholars, many of whom are very fine looking, were in the building. A large number of long wooden houses were in the course of construction for hospital purposes for the coming winter. With proper enterprise in time of peace, it might be a thriving place, as two railroads have depots here, the Virginia Central and the Orange and Alexandria.

The Exchange Hotel in Gordonsville, Virginia was a busy place during the Civil War. It served for a time as a hospital, and the graves of Confederate soldiers have been found nearby. The Norfolk Blues passed by this building many times.

November 3, 1862 As some of our horses required shoeing and all require rest, we laid over until this morning. Yesterday morning I went to the village for the purpose of hearing a sermon, but got there a little too late as I found the church full, which afterwards pleased me much as I found the preacher, though a Presbyterian, would have put to the blush many of the sensation preachers of our protracted meetings. His remarks reminded me greatly of a passage that speaks of the labor of a mountain to bring forth a mouse.

We traveled this day over very fair roads, passing through the village of Orange Court House which is by far the neatest village that I have seen since I left Norfolk. It contains some two or three hundred houses, many of which are very fine buildings, four or five churches, all with the orthodox style of country church steeples, a couple of hotels, and a very substantial court house building. Here martial law is not in effect, and liquor only twenty-five cents per big drink. While passing through the village I noticed an old gentleman who seemed to look in the face of every one of our boys with considerable satisfaction. As the gun to which I am attached, and which is the last of the battery to pass him, he remarked in a loud tone, "Well you are all a d——d fine looking set of men. You must be from some city". I told him we were from Norfolk whereupon after a little more conversation he gave me a pressing invitation to take supper with him in case we halted near there. As we did not, I did not. Late in the afternoon we crossed the Rapidan River and encamped that night about three miles from the shore in a fine hickory grove where the next morning I filled my haversack with hickory nuts to eat on the way, as our rations are growing very scarce.

November 4, 1862 (Tuesday) This morning we started and by sundown encamped within a half mile of Culpepper Court House, passing on our way over the battlefield near Cedar Run. There is nothing here to remind us of a battle save a few Yankee graves. About two miles before we got to where we halted, we passed through a portion of Longstreet's Corps, and what men we saw were certainly hard looking ones, dirty, unwashed, uncombed, with their clothes in rags and many without shoes. They presented an appearance which filled me with gloomy anticipation for the future. However I have, thank fortune, sufficient soap, towels, and toothbrushes to last me some time and water is plentiful in this section.

While here I had an unfortunate difficulty with one of our men which, though it resulted in nothing very serious, is still the occasion of much unpleasant feeling, not so much on my part as on his, as my knowledge of him leads me to believe that among many fine qualities he yet has sufficient littleness of mind to harbor resentment.

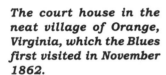

The court house in the neat village of Orange, Virginia, which the Blues first visited in November 1862.

The circumstance is this; while engaged in cooking our rations he, by an act of carelessness, spilled some water on my hands which, though not scalding, was yet hot enough to be very painful for the moment. Unthinkingly I called him a fool, whereupon he flew in a violent passion and made use of a very harsh expression, which he had no sooner done than I jumped into him and striking him once was about to repeat the blow when we were separated by some of our boys. Though separated by force, I should have taken an early opportunity to finish the job by whipping him had he not retracted the expression. I am very sorry that it occurred as I have no wish to be thought either a fighting man or a bully.

November 5, 1862 We were underway again early this morning and by midday arrived at a house about half a mile beyond Brandy Station. There we took up our quarters. We found here a section of howitzers whom we relieved and who left shortly after our arrival, and I must say that I never saw a finer looking set of men and very gentlemanly on their dress and address. Among them as a bugler, I found Mr. Crouch, formerly of the Richmond Grays, whose acquaintance I had made in Norfolk. The war has not reduced his jolly rotundity nor the music of his rich bass voice.

November 7, 1862 Nothing worth recording took place yesterday, save that the weather late in the day became cold and damp (either snow or rain soon). This morning while engaged in writing a letter home, in answer to one received while in Gordonsville, I was startled by the sudden order to "hitch and fall in" as it was reported that the enemy was crossing the river about three miles distant in large force. Shortly after two of our pieces, supported by Colonel Chambliss' 13th Virginia Cavalry, moved forward to meet them while the rest of the battery was placed in position on the hill on which the house stands where we are quartered. At night our pieces returned and reported the advance of the enemy was a false report.

November 8, 1862 This morning another section of our battery was ordered down to the river to guard a ford. Shortly after reaching their position they opened a slow fire upon the enemy and continued it for two or three hours, with what result is not known. They returned our fire but without effect.

November 9, 1862 Two hours before day all were again called up and our two rifled pieces and one howitzer ordered off to the river. In the afternoon, I was ordered off with a wagon after forage for the horses. After going about five miles I came to a house where I got forage and an excellent supper for myself. I returned to camp about nine o'clock at night and found the two rifled pieces returned, the howitzers having been left to guard the ford.

November 16, 1862 (Sunday) Since my last entry nothing very remarkable has taken place. Every day three pieces are sent to different points to relieve the others. The gun to which I am attached is doing picket duty at Beverly Ford, where we were within plain sight of the enemy, one of whom I should liked to have taken a shot at, with a fine rifle owned by a cavalryman, but could not get the permission of our Lieutenant in command, as he said that picket shooting was prohibited. This however, did not prevent one of the cavalrymen from shooting at a sentinel on the opposite side of the river. Whether he struck him or not I do not know, but he came so near it that we saw two of them come down and take him away.

This morning early, having previously received orders, we left our comfortable quarters and took the road to Fredericksburg, and at night we halted about two miles beyond the Rapidan River which we crossed at Raccoon Ford. We found the ford a bad one, though people living on both sides say that it was about the best on the river. If this is so, what must the worst one be? Heaven preserve me from it!

After we halted, a couple of fellows and myself went out on a supper hunt, and in our wanderings came to the house of an old gentleman named Mallory where we were kindly entertained, and had an excellent supper for which he refused remuneration.

November 17, 1862 We started this morning and at night halted within about ten miles of Fredericksburg. A portion of the road we traveled today was the worst that I ever saw, frequently requiring all the men that could get around a gun or caisson to assist the horses up the hills, and in other places compelling us to lock the wheels. The last three miles of our road we traveled on a plank road which we struck on entering Spotsylvania County and which we expect to find all the way to our journey's end, a short distance from where we halted for the night. I found a house where thirteen of us got an excellent and plentiful supper for one dollar. Being very hungry, I think the people of the house earned their money. Both yesterday and today the weather had been disagreeable, being damp with frequent showers of rain, which makes trodding unpleasant.

November 18, 1862 (Tuesday) At an early hour this morning we got underway, and by twelve o'clock we came in sight of the church steeples of Fredericksburg, where we halted for the day, as it would be necessary for us to take up our positions under cover of night. We spent the remainder of the daylight in uneasiness from the fact that we were all anxious to be at the post of danger, for I have noticed quite a change in our boys of late. While around Richmond or Petersburg enjoying good quarters, comfortable living, and comparatively easy times together, with frequent opportunities of pleasant social intercourse with the people of those cities, they were loathe to quit, but since leaving these things behind, and mixing almost daily with the heroes of many a well fought field, they are all eager to flash their maiden swords and have some memorable day in the past to point to. After dark we again started, and on arriving within a quarter mile of the city, the two rifled pieces stopped to allow the other four pieces to pass them, as the former were to turn to the left to occupy a hill in the rear of the city so as to draw the enemy's fire from one of the other pieces which was to be stationed at the fords within two hundred yards of the enemy, who occupied a commanding position across the river. As our four pieces passed the others, many a kindly "Goodby, God bless you" was uttered by those who thought that the next day would be big with events, and the last day for many of us. On the way to our post we passed through a portion of the city, and everywhere met with expressions of joy by such of the citizens as we saw, as they all stand in dread of Yankee rule under which they have before suffered. We arrived at last near the place. The pieces were unlimbered and placed in battery in front of the house by hand, while the limbers were placed in the rear of the house to be under cover as much as possible. The guns were loaded, guards placed, and the remainder of the men laid down to get what sleep they could.

November 19, 1862 At a very early hour this morning I went out to see how we were situated, and found the post assigned us, and which we were ordered by a telegraph order from General Lee to hold even at the sacrifice of every man, was full of danger. The ford at which we were is called McGrath's. About one hundred yards in the rear of it is the large and once beautiful, still fine residence of the late Mr. Fitzgerald, whose widow occupied it til a few days ago. This is where our pieces were placed. Directly opposite on the other side of the river (which is only about one hundred yards wide), on a hill some thirty feet higher than our position, the enemy was posted, and from the appearance of their camp fires, they must be there in very large force, and some twenty pieces of artillery can be seen distinctly, some bearing on the city but nearly all pointing our way, and the sight of which is by no means soothing to a man of weak nerves. The day before our arrival Captain Lewis's Battery from Halifax County was stationed where we are now and was fired into by the enemy. Many of the shells fired at them passed through the house and played sad havoc with it. They also killed one of his men named Snead. A shell struck his head and knocked the top nearly off. He was put in the ground where he fell, and taken up this morning to be buried in the cemetery. I saw him after he was exhumed and found him a horrid sight. In the course of the morning I took a spade and buried the brains, pieces of scalp, and skull which were lying about.

November 21, 1862 Nothing was done yesterday by either side. In the course of the day some of our men went down to the edge of the river and held a long and amusing conversation with some of the Yankees. Both sides were in the best of humor and many witty sallies passed. Some of them freely acknowledged that they were tired of the war, a sentiment which we reciprocated.

This morning a flag of truce from the enemy came to the city and demanded the surrender of it, threatening bombardment in case of refusal, and allowing but sixteen hours grace for the removal of women, children, and sick, which time however was lengthened a few hours on the representation of the Mayor of the grace being too short. Feeling that the threat would be carried into execution, a great many of the citizens immediately left, taking few such articles with them as could be carried. At night we were ordered to leave our position and retire up the road by which we came. This was a very just order, as we were in a position from which in case of a fight none of us would have been able to get away, as in retreating we would be exposed for more than a mile to the fire of the enemy, besides which, the immediate necessity of our remaining to hold the ford is removed, as yesterday and today Longstreet's Corps has been arriving and it is more than probable that by tomorrow we will have in the neighborhood of forty thousand men here. This will, I think, be quite sufficient to hold in check whatever force the enemy may send over. We went about three miles up the road where we halted; the men taking possession of a church nearby.

One good result of our march here is that I found an excellent pair of heavy boots, which I greatly needed, as my shoes were so dilapidated that I could only keep them on my feet by the understrap of my leggins. The Mrs. Fitzgerald who owned the house at which we were, is a descendant of the Washington family, being a granddaughter of a brother of Washington, at least I think that is the relation she bears to him "whom God left childless that all the nation might call him father". She is also related to the Thornton of Revolutionary War fame. Last fall while the Yankees were here, she lost fifty valuable Negroes, and is therefore by no means well disposed towards them.

November 22, 1862 At an early hour, our lieutenant commanding told me that the crew of one of our rifled guns was short handed, and asked me if I wished to go and act on that gun, stating that it was not probable that my gun would be called into action. As we all expected the fight to commence today, I of course went, but evening found me disappointed in my expectation as nothing of moment occurred. The weather has been clear and fine today, being the first clear day we have had since we left Brandy Station.

November 28, 1862 I am still with the rifled gun, and nothing has taken place except that we have been engaged at night in entrenching our guns, which I find to be hard work as the soil here is a heavy clay. All around us entrenchments are being thrown up, which partly leads me to think that the army will soon retire from here. We have had a couple of very rainy nights lately but beyond that, nothing to relieve the monotony of the times. Quite an excitement reigns among our men on account of news being received that General Lee had received an order from the War Department to send this company to Richmond to be changed into a horse or flying artillery company. I hope it may be so. Today I received a letter from home in which in the midst of the good news of the good health of my folks, I learnt of the probable loss of a number of articles for which I had written; among them were some shoes. This loss will perhaps amount to some thirty dollars. Well!

December 10, 1862 (Wednesday) It is seven months to the day since we left Norfolk, seven months! How short the time seems, yet how long during these severe months. What pleasant days I have spent, what valued friends I have made, friends whom a lifetime of grateful feeling on my part will not repay the kindness shown to me. What dear moments I have spent in their society, and what pleasant moments have I passed in reading letters from home, and then how many times have I turned away sick at heart, with empty hands, while others have received these missives so dear to the heart of the wanderer from home. And during these seven months how much have we, as a company, to be thankful for. While others have met the enemy on the battlefield, have made long and hard marches and harassing retreats, while others mourn the loss of soldier brothers in large numbers who breathed their last sigh amid the tumult and carnage of the battlefield, we have enjoyed the comforts of a camp life near or in a city. We have lost but four out of one hundred and thirty, and they died while sympathizing friends stood around, and where the sweet voice and soft hand of women soothed their last moments. Seven months already, and how many more? Heaven only knows, yet while it is absurd to prophecy of the future, I feel almost certain that while we will eat our Christmas dinner this year upon the banks of the Rappahannock River, next year we will eat it at home, and may God grant it.

-The four of the Blues who had died of illness were Lieutenant Nimmo, who died at Sewell's Point, and Privates J. S. Sterrett, Walter A. Wilkins, and W. H. R. Rogers who all died in Petersburg hospitals.

On December 1, the Blues were officially assigned to Anderson's Division of Longstreet's Corps, joining the Donaldsonville Battery, Pittsylvania Battery, and the Huger Battery (the Norfolk Light Artillery) as a part of the Army of Northern Virginia.-

December 11, 1862 At about four o'clock this morning, while on guard, I was startled by the report of two field pieces, fired in quick succession. As I know this to be the signal of battle, I lost no time in rolling up my blankets and repairing to my gun. Shortly after the enemy's opened; most of their pieces being directed against the city and a portion of the Washington Artillery posted in a grove in the rear and to the east of the city. A few hours after daylight I learned that the cause of the firing was to cover their throwing over some pontoon bridges into the city. We did not fire on them while crossing, as that might possibly have stopped them, but contented ourselves with answering some of their artillery force. About ten o'clock pm heavy volleys of musketry from the direction of the city told of the near approach of the enemy. It was not long continued. I afterward learned that a regiment of Mississippians, who were on picket duty, fired into the enemy as they were landing and after checking them for the moment, were ordered to retire. They lost a few men killed and wounded, but the loss of the enemy was considerable. During the morning I was ordered from the rifle to my own gun, as that might be called into requisition at any moment. This did not please me at all, as I was certain that the rifled pieces would be engaged (but I was very delightful about my own gun being called on) and the result of at least this day's work proved that I was right, though our rifled section did nothing til just before dark, when they, together with about forty other pieces, opened on the Yankee batteries across the river. After firing some forty rounds they ceased, and shortly after the enemy also stopped as it was becoming too dark to sight the guns. Frequently during the day the firing was very heavy, much heavier than any artillery duel that ever has taken place since the war. I am told that it is utterly impossible for me to give any idea as to the losses on either side, but that of the enemy must have been very heavy. In the early part of the day a dense fog prevailed which cleared up about noon.

December 12, 1862 (Friday) At an early hour this morning the battle recommenced on both sides, with more infantry fighting than on yesterday, owing to the fact that the enemy during the night threw a large force (report says twenty thousand) into the city. Our rifled section and Lewis' battery, having received orders not to fire unless the enemy came in sight, were only engaged three or four times, and each time succeeded in driving them back. Our other two sections all this time were held in reserve behind a large hill where we have nothing to do but watch the progress of the fight from the top of the hill. The shells that are falling around us are quite sufficient to keep up all the excitement necessary. The early part of the day was again obscured by fog which lifted about two o'clock pm.

- The hill Walters speaks of here is Taylor's Hill, which lies on the south bank of the Rappahannock across from Falmouth, and to the northeast of old Fredericksburg. The left of the Confederate defense lines extended around this hill.-

December 13, 1862 Again at an early hour the fighting recommenced and soon became very hot. The heavy booming of artillery was incessant, and the sharp rattling of musketry a continuous sound from early dawn until long after dark. As far as the eye could see down the river the combat raged hotly, and though we yet know nothing, it is the general impression that Jackson is engaged there. If this is so, the battle front must be some eight or ten miles long, employing our whole army. This afternoon one of our rifled pieces bursted (without damage to the men) and was ordered to the rear, while the gun to which I am attached was ordered up in its place.

A 12-pounder field howitzer. The bronze barrel for this particular gun was cast in 1862 at the Tredegar Iron Works in Richmond for the Confederate artillery. It is seen on display at the Casemate Museum, Fort Monroe.

On coming up to the front we found the enemy's skirmishers thrown out about eight hundred yards in front of us. They had probably seen the rifled gun go to the rear, and presumed upon it. Four or five well directed shells from our gun dispersed them, and we saw no more of them. Later in the afternoon the shells from the enemy killed three of our horses, wounded five others, and dismounted one of our howitzers, but with the aid of our spare wheels we soon had it ready for service again. At this time one of our young fellows had a most narrow escape, for the shell which in exploding did nearly all the mischief passed between his legs, tearing away a portion of the bottom of his coat. The fighting in our vicinity has been heavy and uninterrupted today; three times did the enemy form in volume of regiments and charge the hills on which our first line of batteries were planted, and each time they were driven back with great slaughter. In comparison to which our loss was insignificant.

December 14, 1862 At midnight while on guard a very sudden rattling of musketry caused me to jump to my gun, though nothing was done. It was continued for about five minutes, when silence again reigned undisturbed. We expected a renewal of the battle but were disappointed, and light opened and closed the day filled with nothing but flying rumors.

December 15, 1862 Very little was done by us today. Rumors were momentarily received of the fighting on our right, but none are worth recording owing to their indefiniteness, though the reported deaths of Generals Cobb and Gregg come from a good source. The loss of these two generals will be severely felt by us as they were both soldiers of undoubted courage and discretion and the most distinguished gallantry. In the course of the day an address from General Lee was read to the army in which the usual amount of stereotyped congratulation was dealt out, with the presumed assurance that if the battle shall be resumed tomorrow, which is probable, and we be victorious, which is to be expected from the gallantry of our soldiers, it will be most likely the last battle of the war. Fine talk is very cheap.

December 16, 1862 Contrary to all expectation, the enemy did not open on us this morning, and when their artillery did, it was only in answer to some of our guns. We were all greatly surprised at this as from the tenor of General Lee's address we looked for a desperate fight, but much greater was our surprise when about eleven o'clock am we learned that the enemy had evacuated the city, that the 16th Mississippi Regiment of our brigade were on duty there and had taken some eight or ten prisoners whom they found secreted in houses and who seemed pleased that they were taken. Wishing to see in what condition they had left the city, in company with some of our boys, I went there and knowing very well that sentinels had been posted, we executed a flank movement and entered it in the rear of the lines of sentinels. I found the city a wretched sight, three or four squares burned to the ground, churches and dwellings riddled by shot and shell and many of the latter entirely demolished, while the streets were full of destroyed furniture, books, papers, and dead horses. While in many of the gardens, lanes, and house porches were lying dead soldiers in every conceivable shape and position, some recently dead, while many, possibly those slain the first day of the fight, were far gone towards decomposition, the whole presenting an appearance such as I never care to see again; not that the sight of the mutilated corpses was too much for my nerves, but the destruction of the beautiful and thriving city is enough to call forth the causes of a man less tender hearted than I am. After looking around for some time I went to the field from which the troops charged our batteries, and here the sight was horrible. 'Tis true the wounded had been removed and were not there to fill the air with those oft written about shrieks and groans, but six or seven hundred lay strewn around, from whom our men were busily engaged in removing the clothing and other articles of value. I did a little in that line myself and got an excellent knapsack (empty), a haversack, a canteen, and four one pound bars of yellow soap. While looking about I saw a good pair of boots on a man's feet and as they looked to be about my size, I concluded to appropriate them, to which end I began to pull at them, but while lugging away with a perseverance worthy of a better pair, the leg came off with it just above the knee. As this was more than I bargained for, I left the boots. I had been on the field about half an hour and should have stayed longer but became disgusted on seeing two women stripping the dead men of their underclothes.

December 17, 1862 The enemy was busy all day in removing, and sent over a flag of truce to bury their dead. At night from the large number of camp fires, I should judge that they had not gone far away.

December 25, 1862 (Thursday) Christmas Day! Since last writing, nothing of importance has taken place. The day was spent by me in washing and mending my clothes, a pleasant pastime for this time hallowed day. As the commissary had given the men one ounce of sugar, I made a few fritters and ate my sugar with them. Towards evening I felt out of sorts, possibly the introduction of sugar (that stranger!) astonished my inward economy.

December 27, 1862 This morning we received orders to prepare to leave as did some twelve or fourteen other batteries. We are, I believe, to go some twelve or fourteen miles from here in the direction of Richmond for winter quarters, and to be where we can get food for the horses without sending thirty miles for it as we are doing at present. After dark we moved our guns out of the earth works and went up the road some three miles to the church where we had been before. At night a most melancholy affair occurred here. While sitting around a large bivouac fire, I suddenly heard a loud "Halt! Halt!" uttered in quick succession, and immediately the report of a musket startled us all, followed by an agonizing cry of "Oh, my God, my God!" On running up to see what it meant, I found that the Provost Guard had shot a man who belonged to our brigade, who they said had been arrested for being out of his camp limits and who was trying to run away. The ball entered his right arm at the elbow joint in front and frightfully shattered the bone, and then passing around it, entered his side, penetrating to the kidney. Now it seems to me that a man to be running away would be apt to have his back to his pursuer. The men were not ten yards apart, and the one that was shot was, from all accounts, too good a soldier to trifle with a guard whom he knew to have his musket loaded. All these circumstances led me, with my usual proclivities for attempting to solve things by causes, to turn the affair over in my mind, but I do not think that the problem would have been solved had it not been that a bright mulatto girl who lived in a cabin near at hand told me that both men had been prowling about her cabin for an hour or more previously. With a muttered

"Eureka!" I returned to the fire and soon forgot, in pleasant dreams, the events of the last few moments.

December 28, 1862 At an early hour we were called up and were soon underway, and by night halted within two miles of the first ford on the Mattaponi River, having crossed three fords of the same, which fords or branches are named by the syllables of the river. There being four fords, and coming from Richmond they are named thus: Mat-ta-po-ni, a rather singular, yet comprehensive fancy. The road for the most part was very good except at the fords where it was muddy, rocky, and very hilly. Before we left the church the poor fellow who was shot last night breathed his last. He had been in sixteen battles without receiving so much as a scratch and died here in a miserable negro hut, a victim of the worst passion which can animate a man. God grant that if I am to die by the bullet it may be on the battlefield.

December 29, 1862 We started at daybreak and soon afterward crossed the Mat, being the first ford we expected to cross, and at night halted in a dense pine woods three miles from Chesterfield Station on the Richmond and Fredericksburg Railroad in Caroline County. In the early part of the day, a party of us strayed off from the battery and took a shorter road, by which we saved some four miles walking, and found a mammoth persimmon tree loaded with most delicious fruit.

December 30, 1862 As it was late last night before we halted and our horses were very tired, we did not pack our battery, so this morning, our lieutenant in command found a spot farther in the woods better adapted for a winter camp. We cut a road to it and hitching up, soon had our battery packed in a very fine place, where let the wind blow as it will around us and overhead, we feel but little of it. On arriving here we immediately made ourselves as comfortable as circumstances will permit until our tents shall arrive from Gordonsville in a few days (where they were sent from Brandy Station, and where they have been ever since). We sleep in the mountain stables with the horses, for the houses must be built of pine and cedar brush which will take some time, more especially as the poles cannot be gotten within a half a mile from camp, and they all must be carried on our shoulders.

January 10, 1863 Today, while busily engaged in building a fire place and chimney to our Sibley tent, which arrived and was pitched a few days ago, a budget of letters was handed to me, one signed E. M. E., another C. R. E. (in which was a note from I. L. E.), and one signed W. G. E. The perusal of these afforded me infinite pleasure as they are all from dear friends. They were filled with kind expressions and all contained expressions of regret at my absence from their hospitable Christmas boards, with earnest expressive hopes of my presence at the next. Little worthy as I am of so much kindness from those to whom I was a total stranger a few months ago, yet a knowledge of their kind feelings towards me is wonderfully pleasant. God bless them during this new year, may they know no sorrow.

-We can assume that these cherished letters were from the Ege families; however, in this and several other places, Walters uses only the initials of his subjects, a popular custom of the time.-

January 16, 1863 This morning, very unexpectedly while I was busy oiling harness (having been detailed as a driver in place of one of our men who was sick), orders came to camp to have the battery ready to move to the front at a moment's notice, and while the bustle incident to such an order and the eager "What's the meaning of this?" were circulating about, the order came to hitch up and take the road to Fredericksburg without delay. We were soon ready and took up our line of march in company with some twenty or twenty-five other batteries. The weather was intensely cold and the wind keen, of which I got a full benefit, as I was seated upon my Rosinante, with my long limbs dangling loosely on each side of him, and my equally long body above swaying from side to side perfectly regardless of the rules of gravitation. At dark we halted for the night and soon the cheerful blaze of our campfires dispelled the cold and wind, which died down about ten o'clock. I passed as comfortable a night as circumstances would permit.

-Oiling harnesses with neat's-foot oil or some other conditioner to preserve them was a necessary chore, as leather goods of all types were growing continually more scarce in the Confederate army. Painting gun carriages and polishing brass uniform buttons also helped the artillerists to pass their time.-

January 17, 1863 At an early hour this morning we started and at night halted at Massaponax Church, having made only about fourteen miles, caused by the bad state of the roads, which was not at all improved for our traveling by our battery being in the rear of some ten or twelve other batteries. During the day I gave my horses up to another man, and as the weather had moderated considerably, I found the walk a very pleasant one, especially as I took to the fields where the roads were bad.

January 18, 1863 This morning we again started to find a camp as we had orders to remain in that neighborhood til further orders, and proceeding up the road two or three miles we turned off and came to a halt between two hills, where there was plenty of water at hand and oak wood within a hundred and fifty yards. We remained here four days. During two days and nights we had heavy rains and as we had neither knapsacks nor tents, our situation was disagreeable in the extreme, though a portion of the gloom of these two days was dispelled by the receipt of a letter from home, approving me of the continued good health of my dear friends, though the news of the nonarrival of Fred Clark, who has been absent on his way to Norfolk nearly a month, troubles me greatly. However I trust he will arrive there safely.

January 22, 1863 This morning we again hitched up and in the course of a few hours halted at that church from which we started on the morning of the 28th of December, with no thought of returning to it in so short a time, if at all. From what I can learn, the reason of our being ordered up here is an advance movement of the enemy, seeming to have for its object a crossing of the river at two fords called Banks and United States; the first some three miles and the last about eight miles above the city. We have learned that General Featherstone, to whose brigade we were attached, has been sent to Vicksburg, and his place supplied by the ranking colonel of the brigade. Featherstone, though a man of the most dauntless bravery so as to appear entirely careless and unconcerned under the heaviest fire of the enemy, has less the appearance of a soldier, much less a general, than any man I ever saw. He was never seen in uniform, and it is doubtful whether he owns a sword (never having been seen with one), and is as apt to head his brigade while charging at a double-quick with his hands in his pockets as to have them in any other posture. Let me now see him, pictured in some illustrated humbug at the head of his troops in some heroic stage position with his sword over his head, and I shall immediately protest against such a representation as being untrue to life. He was very popular with his men and only complained of partiality when some other brigade was allowed or ordered to do more than his own. During one of the days of battle, he moved his brigade up to within easy supporting distance of our battery and told us to fight our guns until the enemy were upon them, and he would take care that our guns were not taken from us by the enemy, an assurance well calculated to make men fight as long as they are able to do so. The officer who succeeds him is a dignified, gentlemanly man, brave to a fault, and who promises to become very popular with his men.

January 26, 1863 In accordance with orders received last evening, we got underway this morning and in the course of an hour took up a position on a high hill opposite the road which the enemy must take to come down to Banks Ford. Our position is about two hundred yards from the river, which is only some sixty yards wide at the ford. We found here some well put up breastworks into which we placed our guns, and then went to work to make ourselves comfortable, a not very difficult job from the fact that on the slope of the hill in the rear of our battery, we found a number of log huts with good fire places, and at the foot of the hill within twenty yards of our cabins, there is a run of excellent water, large enough to supply both men and horses.

January 28, 1863 At an early hour this morning it began to snow, which continued all day without intermission; clothing everything in winter's spotless garb. The picture presented was beautiful in the extreme, covered as the ground and bushes were with snow, while the trees bent and broke with the weight of their burden. All afternoon and night could be heard the crash of falling pines, some of them huge old fellows, while the limbs of cedars bent to the ground, all their thousand little sprigs and limbs pointing downward.

January 29, 1863 Before daylight this morning it ceased to snow, and as the clouds rolled away, the stars lit up the heaven's vault and rendered the landscape more beautiful than during the day. The weather was not cold and I managed to keep myself very comfortable while on guard duty by the battery, with the aid of a good fire. The sun came out this morning and the snow is fast disappearing under the influence of its rays. During the day the men belonging to Captain Lewis' battery (which arrived here a day or two ago) drew up in a line on a hill between their camp and ours, and gave us ten minutes to collect our forces and prepare for battle, or secure a snow balling. Our boys were quickly out, and forming a line of battle, advanced to the charge, but as they approached the hill a perfect storm of snow balls caused them to halt and at it they went with such good will that we could see the enemy's line waver, though they still showed a strong determination to hold their position. After a brisk engagement of some fifteen minutes, some ten or a dozen of our boys fell back for the purpose of executing a flank movement. Shortly after the signal was given, our boys loaded themselves with ammunition and advanced to the charge. When about halfway up the hill, the flanking division broke cover and poured a well directed volley into the enemy, who broke and fled to their tents, leaving the battleground in our hands. We remained there some time, but as the enemy showed no disposition to renew the engagement, we retired.

Banks' Ford on the Rappahannock River, a few miles upstream from Fredericksburg.

-The cannoneers' adaptations to the winter weather often took a pleasant or humorous turn in many companies. T. J. Macon of the Richmond Howitzers recounted this incident in his "Reminiscences":

"During the winter, when we were at the Dunn House, a good joke was played on the guard. It was extremely cold weather, and the order was passed from one sentinel to the other, to blow in the vent of the gun to see if it were clear. In doing so, it was necessary to put one's lips on the gun over the vent, when it took nearly all the skin from them, of course. One cannoneer, being fooled thus, he was not apt to disclose the trick to the next one, and so it turned out that the whole guard of six men got very sore lips for a while. Since no such order had been really given, it was but one of our boyish pranks."

Unfortunately, the cold weather would more than outlast the soldiers' playfulness.-

February 5, 1863 Another day of snow, but much more disagreeable than the last as the weather was very cold and disagreeable, though but about five inches of snow fell where the previous one fell to a depth of twelve inches.

February 17, 1863 Another heavy fall of snow. I am becoming tired of this place. Too much snow here to suit me. 'Tis true it does not last long, but then it comes down too often. A day or two ago, we received orders to prepare to march from here. Report says that we are to go to Richmond; the whole army is under marching orders, probably owing to the fact that the enemy is moving away. Most likely, Fighting Joe Hooker has got enough of this place. I fear that we will have a hard time of it getting to Richmond, due to the present state of the roads, unless they send us down by the railroad.

February 22, 1863 (Sunday) More snow, this time it fell to a depth of seven or eight inches. The weather is very cold and disagreeable! Two of the men belonging to General Perry's Brigade were frozen to death last night. The poor fellows were from Florida, and found our Virginia winters too much for them. We are still waiting for orders to leave.

March 4, 1863 Nothing new of any moment has occurred since my last writing. The health of the men remains most excellent. My own is fair, though a severe cold in the head and an acute rheumatic pain in my left shoulder troubles me greatly while it does not prevent me from discharging my duty. The weather today is very fine. The sun shines brightly while the air is just keen enough to render outdoor exercise pleasant. Considerable excitement is manifested in our company regarding the action of the North in investing Lincoln with dictatorial powers, and the probable effect this proceeding will have upon the war. Many of our men think that this shuts the door of hope towards peace while he remains in office. I differ with them, and my views upon the subject are these (though they must be taken with the largest allowances from the fact that I am not yet gifted with any prophetic visions, nor do I lay claim to pre-eminent diplomatic splendors). I look upon his being vested with the powers of a Dictator, not so much for the purpose of carrying on the war, as for the purpose and power it gives him of making peace, should the latter be the wish of our government. Who can doubt Congress, by its appropriations bills and its conscription acts, had or has already provided all in its power for the prosecution of the war, and Lincoln has already assumed the right of arbitrary arrest and the suspension of assemblies or newspapers hostile to his administration. What more could he require until the next meeting of Congress in December? Now the Constitution provides that the President of the United States can neither make war nor conclude peace without the advice and consent of the Senate. To conclude peace then, before the next meeting of Congress, would compel him to call an extra session, a thing which History teaches (and in no case more strikingly than in the case of Charles the First of England) all rulers to avoid, if possible. As a dictator requires no authority superior to his own, Lincoln could, therefore, conclude a peace without calling an extra session of Congress. Now it may be advanced against my theory that Lincoln has already called one extra session of Congress, and that also he did make war without the required advice and consent of the Senate, but I answer this by saying that while a president has or had no right of his own to make war, he yet has the power to call out the troops to suppress a rebellion, which disguise it as we will, ours was at its outset, and his calling the extra session, which he did, was necessitated by the high proportions presumed. Now I shall not defend the position which I have taken by calling this war a rebellion at its outset. Let those who understand the Constitution of the United States better than I do answer whether the South was constitutionally right by seceding.

March 15, 1863 For the last ten or twelve days nothing worthy of note has occurred, except that I sent two letters home, one accompanied with $40.00. I trust the same will arrive safe. This morning, very unexpectedly, the order was given to hitch up and pack up, and in the course of an hour we were on the road bound to the United States Ford in company of the brigades of Mahone and Posey. I learn that the reason of our move is the report which was received of a Yankee cavalry raid, which was to be made by way of the ford. At night we halted within about four miles of the ford, and as I was on guard that night, I had the questionable pleasure of standing it in as heavy a hail storm, which lasted nearly all night, as I ever saw.

March 17, 1863 Yesterday, just as we had gotten all ready for a forward move, orders came to wait til today. At one o'clock this morning we got ready, according to orders, and started and then began the hardest day's work that I ever did. We were until two o'clock (thirteen hours) making a distance of four miles. I really thought that I had seen bad roads, but these beat all that I ever saw. In some places, the horses were in mud up to their girths and entirely unable to pull the guns, when all that remained was for us to unlimber, put all the men at the prolong, and pull it out. At length we got to the position assigned us which is about five hundred yards below the ford. We found here some strong breastworks in which our pieces were placed and then we went to work to make ourselves comfortable, a thing not very difficult to do as there is plenty of wood in the immediate vicinity to where we pitched our tarpaulins.

March 26, 1863 Nothing of note has transpired since my last writing. On our first arrival here, and for some time after, the Yankees had a picket post across the river from our battery at the distance of about eight hundred or one thousand yards, but they have been withdrawn within the last few days. It is highly questionable whether we will ever have a fight here, but if we do, I should not be surprised if we got largely the worst of it from the fact that in front of us on the opposite side of the river is a high bold hill which entirely commands our position, while above and below us the river bends so that the enemy could, by placing batteries at both points, completely enfilade us, and should we be forced to retire, we could only do so through an open field, without shelter, exposed for a mile or so to all the fire of the enemy; and I learned from high authority that in case of a fight our general in command is satisfied that we must lose at least two of our pieces (mine one of them), as it would be useless to attempt to defend them. This is very mortifying to us. In front of our earthworks is an infantry breastwork of good proportion and well defended by traverses, from which our troops could pour a fire which would render the crossing of the river a rather difficult business.

This afternoon, one of our letter carriers from Norfolk came up and brought me a letter from home dated July 12, 1862. Where this letter has been all this time is a mystery to me. It was written by E. P. S. and contained a most earnest request for me to write them, as the report was being circulated in Norfolk of my being killed in one of the fights around Richmond, which report he doubts, hence his inquiry. As I had been anxiously looking for a letter from home, the receipt of this only made me feel miserable as it was a perfect burlesque. But the cloud which settled so dully over me was dispelled later in the afternoon by a late letter from home, brought by another carrier. This cheered me greatly and was answered by eight pages of large letter paper. This letter contained most anxious inquiries regarding F. W. C., who left Petersburg some time about the middle of December to go to Norfolk, but has not been heard from since that time. Rumors have from time to time reached me regarding his absence, but with them a number of seeming good reasons for the cause. But of late these reasons have been attended with hints of foul play, but situated as I am, I have no power to trace these rumors to their source and therefore can only wait for the future to develop the present mystery. Meantime, God grant that he may be safe.

-F. W. C. is most probably Fred W. Clark, Walters' former partner in his book business in Norfolk. Walters was doubtlessly worried that his friend had been caught and imprisoned for trying to "run the blockade" or cross the lines into Union-held Norfolk. The defenselessness of their families and homes must have been as tremendous a burden to the Norfolk soldiers as their separation from them.-

April 26, 1863 For the last month we have done nothing but eat and sleep. For some time back, the Yankee pickets have again occupied the shore opposite us, and two or three times we were ordered to be ready for a fight, but each occasion passed without result. Rumors are frequently coming in of preparation of the army to cross, but as I have learned long since that "sufficient for the day is the evil thereof", I have said nothing of them, but remain calmly confident of being able to make a good stand. Today I received a letter from home which contained but little more than any letter of last month, but it confirmed the suspicions of foul play in the case of F. W. C., which information I received from J. O. G. some days ago had caused me to entertain. From all I can learn, he left Petersburg in company with Peter, a letter carrier, and four or five others. He and Peter are lost, while of the others some returned to Petersburg and one or two got to Norfolk, where one of the latter was arrested on a charge of setting fire to some buildings used as government store houses. Thus the finger of suspicion points most strongly to those who started from Petersburg with poor C. and Peter.

April 29, 1863 While busily engaged today in manufacturing a garlic, or rather wild onion stew, orders suddenly came for our drivers to harness up and for all to be ready for a fight, as the enemy had thrown two pontoon bridges across the river below Fredericksburg, and that Jackson's Corps were hotly engaged with them. We were soon ready, but I continued my agreeable occupation until its completion and dined heartily, determined that fight or run, as the case may be, I would do it on a full stomach. In the course of the afternoon, General Mahone rode to our position and ordered our lieutenant in command of our gun to pay no attention to the enemy as far as returning their artillery fire was concerned, but if their infantry attempted to cross, then to hold our position as long as we could. At present, we are patiently, and as far as I am concerned, quietly awaiting further developments, though it is the general impression that we will have a fight here before many hours. All the afternoon the booming of artillery and the sound of volleying musketry from Jackson's position, though some miles distant, has been plainly heard. Night is now closing in and the rain with which we have been threatened all day is beginning to fall, though present indications above seem to point to a clear day tomorrow. I am sorry for our poor horses who will be compelled to stand in harness in the rain all night.

April 30, 1863 (Thursday) About dark last night, news was brought to us that the enemy had succeeded in starting a march on us by crossing a large force at a ford some six miles above us, and were making rapid way to our rear, so feeling that today would be a busy if not eventful one, I went to sleep. About an hour before daylight we were called up and ordered to retire with all haste possible. We soon had the horses put to the guns and started to take positions on a plank road some five or six miles from the city. We had left our position but a short time when we were joined by the other two pieces which had been stationed on the river, and then began a struggle for progress the like of which I have never before seen. The rain was falling heavily, the snow was more than ankle deep, we were obliged to carry our knapsacks and blankets, the horses were still too poor and weak to drag the guns over these roads, and the cannoneers were compelled to constantly work at the wheels and push the pieces along, and to add to all this, after traveling in this way some three hours, during which time we did not make more than two miles, a carrier rode along who informed us that the enemy were only a mile in our rear and pushing vigorously on! This did not add much to our piece of mind, as it rendered the prospect of our being taken very bright. Soon after this we saw the 19th Mississippi Regiment of Perry's Brigade, who had been left in our rear as skirmishers to hold the enemy in check, coming up at a double quick and just at this time some of our pieces were stuck in the mud so that it required more than six horses to pull them out. The times were becoming very critical. The lieutenant in command of our section ordered two horses to be taken from the caissons and put to the guns. While the caissons were unlimbered, the four horses were sent forward with limbers, and the rear chests of the caissons were left in the road to fall into the hands of the enemy. Our boys disliked to see this done, but the necessity was imperative. About this time a number of our boys began to throw away some of their knapsacks and others their blankets, but as I had all my present worldly effects on my back, I made up my mind to struggle along as best I could. My possessions were not so very heavy, but the road was bad and I was nearly broken down with the labor of pushing our pieces along.

At about eleven o'clock am, we came to a halt and soon after took a position at the intersection of some roads. Our two smooth bores were placed on one, and the others close by the plank road, and while Wright's Brigade was placed in a piece of woods in front of us, Perry's Brigade threw up a line of breast works on our right flank; their right resting upon the center of Mahone's, who occupy a position nearly at right angles with Perry. On Mahone's left, Perry's Brigade took position. Both of the last supported our rifled gun and howitzers. After taking our positions, we were ordered to load our guns and stand in place. At about half past one pm, heavy volleys of musketry from the direction of Mahone and Perry told of the advance of the enemy, but this was of short duration. We learned soon after that a large body of the enemy's cavalry made a sudden dash, but dashed back as quickly with many empty saddles. This was repeated two or three times in the course of the afternoon with like results, and now as the evening is closing in, we are making preparations to cook a little something, as many of us have only eaten a dry biscuit or two the whole day. While writing, some of the artillery is passing that has just arrived from the camp of reserve artillery in Caroline County. I have no doubt that tomorrow will be a long day. I had the pleasure of shaking hands with our captain when I saw him today for the first time since we left Richmond. He came up here about a week ago and is looking well and hearty.

May 1, 1863 (Friday) I have heard much and read more of the night before a battle, of the serious brow or the laugh that was not as it might seem, of the emotions, hopes, and fears, or rather forebodings induced by the occasion, of the exchange of perhaps last letters, of reminiscences rendered peculiarly sweet by the near approach of an eventful moment, but the reality of a battle eve is entirely different from what I had conceived it to be. Just before dark last night, we were cheered by the arrival of a battery from the camp of reserve artillery, which took position on our immediate left. After dark the infantry began throwing up earthworks for our pieces and during this labor, many a light jest was uttered, many a hearty laugh given vent to, while all were eager for the morrow as we were all confident that the genius of Lee is more than sufficient to outwit Hooker, while no one who looked for a moment in the flushed faces and flashing eyes of our brave soldiers could be doubtful of the result. At three o'clock this morning we were called up, and while the artillerists took their places at the guns, the infantry formed in line of battle and calmly waited for the advance of the enemy, for that they would advance was the belief of everyone. Soon the sun rose but was nearly obscured by a most dense fog, which cleared away about nine o'clock, and then every eye was stretched to the directions from which we expected the enemy, and every ear strained to catch the sound which would tell of the beginning of the battle. At about half past eleven o'clock General Stonewall Jackson came up on the field in which we were, accompanied by several generals and a number of couriers and orderlies. Soon the long black hair of A. P. Hill is seen floating on the wind as he leaves the group and dashes across the field towards our right where his division is. Rodes soon follows him. The burly form of McLaws is seen for but a moment and then disappears as he speaks to his command. Couriers arrive from Anderson, who is in a distant part of the field, to his several commands. One comes to us, we limber up, and soon are on the turnpike road towards Chancellorsville in pursuit, preceded some little distance by the battery of Captain Jordan. On gaining the pike road we are halted some time to allow the different brigades to take their place in line until that of Simms comes, who is to support us and in whose rear we fall. The order is then given and we proceed, but hardly have we done so when the rapid cracking of muskets in our front tells us that our skirmishers are engaged with the enemy's. Soon the battery of Jordan opens, the troops in our front advance at a double quick, strewing the road with knapsacks, blankets, overcoats, haversacks, and other articles. Our horses are urged forward at a gallop, the excitement of battle gives our tired boys strength to keep up with their pieces. In this way we cover a distance of nearly, if not quite, two miles. Engineers are hurriedly called to the front to break down a fence. This done in a moment, and again the horses are put to their best speed for about five hundred yards when the order is given, "Action front!". The guns are unlimbered and we await the shock of battle. While thus waiting, several brigades pass us at a double quick to our right, and shot, shell, and minie balls plough up the ground all around us, and the enemy can be seen not more than six or seven hundred yards in front of us. Soon after, Jordan's Battery is heard no more and while speculating upon the cause, we see them falling back to take up a position on our right and left. The reason for this retrograde movement being a movement of the enemy, which their captain thought was intended to flank his battery. Our captain, forming a different opinion of the movement, takes our rifled gun from our right and gallops up to the position left by Jordan and opens on the enemy with canister, he being only about four hundred yards from them. In about half an hour word is sent to our guns to send him some of our spare men as he has one man killed and four wounded. All this time he and our first lieutenant are working at the gun to supply the places of those disabled. Soon after, the enemy's guns are withdrawn and the firing ceases, our guns are limbered up, and we move to the road and rest until the infantry returns to take up their positions for an advance. At about an hour before sundown we move forward, and halt for the night on the road about three quarters of a mile from Chancellorsville, where the enemy is posted in heavy force. Thus ends the busy day.

After being two years in the service, our company has at last sealed their devotion to the country in the blood of their best and bravest. Our casualties are: W. C. Land, killed; J. W. Floyd, right arm shot off (he will probably recover); J. H. Watters, wounded in the right wrist and two fingers of his left hand shot off; M. C. Keeling, shot through his foot; Lieutenant Peet, wounded in the left leg slightly; and C. K. McKeown, in the back very slightly.

I shall relate one incident to show the good spirits of our men. While the enemy was firing their heaviest at us, a young fellow named Walker, attached to the same gun with myself, who was not with us at the battle of Fredericksburg, remarked that he had always been anxious to be in one battle at least, but if he came out of this one safe, he thought of writing a book, the title of which would be, "Battle, or Walker Satisfied."

May 2, 1863 (Saturday) Before daylight we were up and again all ready, but waited for the enemy, as I heard orders had been sent not to press the front, as Jackson wanted time to attack them upon our left. About nine am, our artillery opened on the enemy who were advancing, to which their artillery replied and heavens how their shot and shell did rain! I never saw nor heard the like. One shell struck a caisson belonging to a battery placed about thirty yards on our right, exploding it, and killing one man and wounding several. After remaining under this fire about an hour, our battery (which was in a very exposed position), was ordered to retire out of range, together with all the short range guns of other batteries. We fell back about a mile, and unhitched the horses to allow them to graze as they were nearly used up. About three pm orders were received to report our battery to General Lee on the Plank Road. We found him after traveling about three miles. On reporting to him, he seemed surprised that we were still in the front, as he was under the impression that our company had gone to the rear some time previous to recruit the horses. On being told that we had been to the front the whole winter, he told our captain that he expected to make a vigorous campaign, and that he could not take a battery whose horses were not in good condition. He therefore ordered us to our old camp. At about 4 o'clock pm we started on the back track and at two o'clock next morning halted at Spotsylvania Court House, both horses and men thoroughly used up.

   -Lee's position on the Orange Plank Road where he reviewed the Blues was also where he held his last meeting with Stonewall Jackson.

   These two days of the Battle of Chancellorsville would prove to be one of the greatest moments in the history of the Norfolk Light Artillery Blues. Captain Grandy's report of his company's action in this battle was later included in the official records of the War Department, the only one of Grandy's letters to be so preserved. His report to Lieutenant Colonel Garnett follows:

May 15, 1863

SIR: In accordance with Major-General Anderson's order, I removed my guns, in position at the United States Ford, as quietly as possible on the night of April 29, and fell back with Mahone's brigade to the wooden church. The lieutenant in charge of one section (owing to the weakness of the horses by being fed on nothing but corn during the winter, which they had to haul 14 or 15 miles, having no serviceable mules, over roads hardly passable with an empty wagon) had to leave the rear chests of his caissons about a mile below Child's house.

On May 1, I moved from the intrenchments at the wooden church with Mahone's and Semmes' brigades, and engaged the enemy with one rifled gun, in connection with one gun from Jordan's battery, at a distance of 300 yards on the turnpike, with canister principally, for more than an hour. The Yankee battery, according to the accounts of prisoners, was Weed's Regulars, supported by two brigades of Sykes division, which were drawn up in line of battle, and, after annoying us with their sharpshooters, attempted to charge us, while we gave alternate discharges to the infantry and to the battery until the enemy retired.

I suffered as follows: Private W. C. Land, killed; Lieutenant William T. Peet, slightly wounded; Private J. W. Floyd, lost an arm; Corporal J. H. Watters, wounded in the hands and wrists; Privates C. K. McKeown, John H. Day, and T. J. Wilkins, very slightly wounded. During the sharpest of the engagement I had only two men and Lieutenant Peet to work the gun.

Saturday I was in position in front of Chancellorsville and under the shelling of the enemy, but as my guns were of too short range to reach the enemy, I was withdrawn. Saturday at 6 pm, I was ordered to report to General Lee for position on the Plank Road, who ordered me to Chesterfield, in Caroline County, with the remark that my horses were unfit for service. On reaching Chesterfield, I was ordered to Hanover Junction by General Pettigrew, in order to guard the bridges at that point.

Very respectfully,
CHAS. R. GRANDY
Captain Norfolk Light Artillery Blues

Weed's Regulars (5th U.S. Army, Battery I) was commanded by Lieutenant Malbone F. Watson at this time, since Captain Steven H. Weed was temporarily acting as Chief of 5th Army Corps Artillery. The Union battery reported it lost a limber from a direct hit, suffered two men wounded, and had one horse killed and four wounded during its exchange of fire with the Blues. Weed's Regulars withdrew with Sykes' Division back to the Chancellor house after this engagement.-

May 3, 1863 About eight o'clock this morning we started, and at four reached New Market where we halted til nine to rest both men and horses. Here our men were enabled to get something to eat, of which they stood in great need, as we had received no rations for some sixty hours, and many of us had eaten nothing for thirty-six hours. At nine o'clock pm we again started, and by twelve had only gotten to Chilesburg, a distance of four miles, where we halted for the night.

May 4, 1863 We began our march this morning a little cheered by the prospect of reaching camp today, where we could rest after our severe labors of the past week. After making about seven miles, and while building a bridge over a small stream, some of our young fellows from camp arrived with seven or eight pairs of horses. These were soon hitched on and in about two hours we halted at our camp where those whom we left nearly four months ago were very glad to see us. Shady places were soon found and in a short time nearly all the newcomers were asleep. For myself, I went down to the branch and took a bath, changed my apparel, cooked some supper, smoked my pipe, pitched my tent, and said good night. I hope I feel well enough to write a couple of letters tomorrow, but if I do not, W. T. E. and another friend must wait until another day.

May 6, 1863 Feeling considerably refreshed today, I have written my letters and shall dot down a little in this, and while doing so, let me take a slight retrospection. We have been gone from this camp three months and a half, during which time we have seen many a wet and weary day and cold night, and though those who remained behind enjoyed a comparatively good and comfortable time, yet I would not exchange my hard bought experience with them were it to be done over again. My ideas of a battlefield are entirely different from those which I imbibed at the battle of Fredericksburg and while I cannot but regret those whom we lost, I yet feel that with every new loss the feeling of pride with which our friends and families look upon us will be increased, and it is pleasant to feel that when this company shall return home, even though I may not live to return home with it, that the sigh or tear of regret will be hidden behind the proud feeling which will swell the bosom at a recital of our deeds and achievements.

Another circumstance from which I derive a peculiar pleasure is that I was enabled to see Stonewall Jackson, the man whom of all others I most wished to see. God grant that his wound, the news of which we have just received, may not be attended with a fatal result.

I have one cause of regret and that is that I have lost a true old friend, none other than my old gray cap. Having forgotten to put it in my knapsack until it was too late, I put it in the rear chest of our caisson, and in the hurrying of abandoning our chests I forgot to take it out. I had fondly hoped to have carried that old cap back to Norfolk with me. I was greatly attached to it, much more so than to any other article of apparel of which I am or was possessed, and I blame myself greatly for my forgetfulness in leaving it behind. Possibly long ere this, the coward heel of some Northern rascal has thrown my old friend in the mud of the road. Well, farewell old friend, regrets are unavailing, but yet I am truly sorry that I could not carry you back with me, a souvenir of two battles at least, and many a wet day and blistering day.

May 11, 1863 Today, the Richmond papers come to us draped in mourning and bearing the sad tidings of the death of Jackson, the matchless hero, one of Virginia's noblest sons, the South's stoutest champion. Well may we mourn, and though it is impious, question the motive that offers this bitter chalice to our reluctant lips. 'Tis true our loss is his gain, for who can doubt but that this noble soldier and true Christian is with the blest. But who will take his place here? Who is so shrewd in the field, so sagacious in the council, so beloved by his men, so able to lead where death saw wildest riot (and where victory was sure to follow), or who is so capable of being followed to that point where the possible joins the impossible and man, mere man, can go no further? One star has been erased from our Southern constellation, and that of Virginia should be enlarged as a testimony to all future ages of her irreparable loss. May not the cry of "Eli, Eli, lama sabachthani" be ours.

> -"Eli, eli, lama sabachthani" or My God, My God, why hast thou forsaken me? From the Gospel of Matthew, 27:46.-

May 15, 1863 About ten o'clock this morning we got underway and about sun down we encamped near the Po River where we found the other companies encamped who belong to our battalion; viz the Huger, the Lewis, and the Donaldsonville Artillery from Louisiana, all under the command of Lt. Col. Garnett.

> -A month previous to this, Pendleton had issued orders which officially reorganized the artillery of the Army of Northern Virginia. Individual batteries had at first supported and accompanied infantry regiments, but experience soon showed that the "long arm" was more effective when battery operations were coordinated and guns were fired en masse. Under Pendleton's order, from three to six batteries were grouped together within a single battalion and from this point, these battalions would take precedence as fighting units within the army.

Lieutenant Colonel John J. Garnett's Battalion was equipped with a total of nine rifles and six smooth bores, manned by the four batteries which had been assigned to Anderson's Division the previous autumn; the Norfolk Light Artillery Blues under Captain Charles Grandy, the Norfolk Light Artillery (Huger Battery) under Captain Joseph D. Moore, the Pittsylvania Battery under Captain John W. Lewis, and the Donaldsonville Artillery under Captain Victor Maurin. These four companies would remain in close association for the rest of the war.-

June 4, 1863 Nothing worth recording has taken place since my last entry, except the sending home of a long letter a few days ago, though I did not receive one in some time. Today we broke up our camp and moved to within about a mile of Fredericksburg. From the way our troops are moving I am inclined to think that our present idle life will soon be exchanged for a more stirring one, for which I shall not be sorry.

June 5, 1863 This afternoon, while in conversation with the Rev. Leroy Lee, who had come from Lynchburg on a visit to his son, two guns were fired from the direction of the river below the city, and a minute or two after, the artillery from both sides opened on each other and continued until dark. The firing was very heavy. During its continuance we received orders to hitch up and prepare to move, to which Dean, who was talking to his father, paid no attention. In a moment, the old gentleman turned to him and remarked, "Go my son, and get ready, your duty is first to your country and then to your father". I took part of that to myself, and left him to get ready, which I did in a few minutes. At ten o'clock at night we received orders and moved to the old Telegraph Road near Mayre's Heights, where we awaited daylight in the confident anticipation of having a fight.

June 6, 1863 Contrary to expectation, no fight took place today and but little firing, though the enemy are on our side of the river with quite a large force, a report says one corps at least. This morning some of our horses were sent after a 12-pounder Napoleon gun which is to replace one of our 6-pounders and to which I am attached.

-Both of the 6-pounders were eventually replaced by 12-pounder guns. The Blues also manned two 3-inch ordnance rifles.-

June 14, 1863 Up to this time, nothing of importance has occurred. Occasionally there has been a little firing from one side or the other, with no apparent results on either side. The enemy during the past week has thrown up some two or three miles of artillery and infantry breastworks, but judge our surprise this morning to learn that they had recrossed the river during last night and in such haste as to leave a large quantity of stores and arms behind, besides all their advance pickets who were taken prisoners. Further observation during the day showed that they have not only left their position on this side of the river, but the whole army has gone from the other side also.

June 15, 1863 This morning, I was sent down with a squad of men to where the enemy had crossed the river and where they had left a number of their pontoon boats, to secure a picket rope for our horses. On our return, we found the battalion had gone, so we followed on and overtook it about sundown a mile below Chancellorsville, where it was packed for the night. Having walked about twenty miles today and it being very hot, I was pretty well used up at night. Near where we packed is a house that the enemy used as a hospital during the last battle, and I did not learn until it was too late that they had thrown the amputated arms and limbs of their wounded in the well. It is true that while drinking I thought the water had a peculiar smell and flavor, but I did not attribute that to the right cause until I saw an arm fished up. However I must confess that as thirsty as I was and not knowing what other water was to be obtained, a full knowledge of what was in the well would not have deterred me from drinking the water. I have learnt that this disgusting practice is common with the enemy.

June 16, 1863 We started at sunrise and packed about two o'clock pm, having made about fourteen miles. The road was very good, but the weather was very hot.

June 17, 1863 We started again at sunrise and about twelve, stopped at Culpepper Courthouse, having made some ten miles. After pitching my tent I went in town and got a pint of whiskey of a very poor quality, for which I was obliged to pay six dollars. After that, I went to a hotel and got my supper which was a fair one, though it cost two dollars. The town is filled with rumors of Ewell's fight with Milroy. From what I can learn, it must have been quite a victory, but a small battle. Large quantities of artillery, arms, wagons, and quartermaster and commissary stores were captured, besides several thousand prisoners.

June 18, 1863 We left about seven o'clock am and after making about fifteen miles, came to a halt for the day. The heat was so intense that it was almost impossible to go any further. During the march, as short as it was, eighteen men of Pettigrew's Brigade, which was just ahead of us, died from the effect of the sun. In the course of the evening a heavy shower of rain fell, which was very grateful.

June 19, 1863 Owing to the rain of last night, marching was a little more tolerable today. In the evening we halted about eight miles from Front Royal, having made some sixteen miles. During the day we passed through the village of Flint Hill (rather a poor looking place) where I saw quite a number of very fine looking young ladies and also a couple of mustachioed highbreds, who dressed in broadcloth and played agreeable to the ladies, and seemed to have no ambition beyond that. Tired, foot-sore, and muddy as I was, I could not but pity them, and I replied to their looks of pity with those of scorn at their want of manhood in being content to stay at home in these times of war.

June 20, 1863 We started at sunrise and found traveling very disagreeable as our road lay through the Blue Ridge by Chester Gap, where we were enveloped in a most dense fog, which shut out all those fine views on which I anticipated feasting. Besides this, the heavy rain of last night filled the road with mud which, in many places, was over our shoe tops. About eleven o'clock, we passed through Front Royal. This place, previous to the war, was quite thriving, but now its frequent occupation by both armies has killed business and now it looks about as stagnant as a Quaker settlement. However I saw many a pretty face whose owners showered sweet smiles upon us, and many a Confederate flag fluttered in the breeze. About two miles beyond this place, we came to two branches, the North and South Shenandoah River, both of which we crossed by fording. They are not very deep at the fords; the water seldom reaching above the waist. In crossing, we were greatly delayed by the division of Heth and his wagon train. We packed at night about four miles from the river, having made about fourteen miles. During the day I saw something which from its extreme rarity is worth mentioning. The feet of one of the men of Heth's Division were so galled that he could not walk, whereupon a surgeon, belonging to his division, mounted the soldier upon his horse and then took the man's musket and carried it for him about two miles, until they came up with one of the wagons, into which the man got while the surgeon remounted his horse.

-Garnett's Artillery Battalion at this time was attached to General Henry Heth's Division in General Ambrose P. Hill's Corps.-

June 21, 1863 Off again at sunrise, and when within about ten miles from Winchester where we thought we were going, our column turned to the right, and at night camped three miles from Berryville in Clark County. We passed on the way through the beautiful village of White Post. In the center of the village stands a large sectional post painted white, the top of which is ornamented with

The interesting white post at the intersection in the village of White Post, Virginia.

an urn-looking affair painted green. Now the question arises; does this post designate the name of the village, or does the village derive its name from the fact that the post is there? The citizens seem to be divided upon the question. As it is, there I found it, and there I left it. The Winchester Turnpike is a fine road in good condition, but after leaving that, we had a hard road to travel, it being very rocky and muddy. We made about sixteen miles today.

-Many years after Walters' visit, a brass plaque was affixed to the post to inform both villagers and passersby that the original white post had been erected in 1750 by George Washington as a guide post to the home of Lord Fairfax. The village later grew up around it.-

June 22, 1863 We remained camped today to rest both men and horses. This afternoon, very unexpectedly, I received a letter from home dated May 24th and it is the first that I have received for nearly three months. Thank God all are well there.

June 23, 1863 We were in the road shortly after sunrise this morning, but for some reason, ordered back. After repitching my tent, I began a letter to send home and had written about a page, when the bugle sounded the hitch call. In a short time we were again ready, and at night packed three miles from Charles Town in Jefferson County. Passing on our way through the village of Rippon, everyone turned out to see the soldiers, which they could do only at the expense of a vast amount of patience, as one column consists of the divisions of Heth and Pender, numbering some eighteen thousand men, and three battalions of artillery having about fifty pieces and about two hundred wagons. The people are ardent secessionists, and greeted us with many a pleasant smile and kindly word. After our battalion was packed, I went to town and called upon Dr. Steath, a kinsman of my dear friends in Norfolk. I was very kindly received by Mrs. S., the doctor being from home for the moment. Almost immediately from my arrival, the hospitality of the house was made manifest in the shape of a most excellent supper, to which I did ample justice after my eighteen mile walk. After being there a short time, a couple of charming ladies came; one the doctor's daughter, the other her friend. As both had the gift of speech well and sensibly developed, conversation ran riot for the short time they remained. Shortly after, the Doctor came in and gave me a kind reception and reiterated the hearty welcome of his wife. He was pleased with my news from Norfolk and we sat up til twelve o'clock, when, as he would not hear of my going away, I retired and enjoyed the luxury of sleeping in a bed, this being the first time that I did so since leaving Petersburg last August.

June 24, 1863 I arose at half past four this morning and on going from my room, met the Doctor in the hall. After making the inquiries customary to a hospitable host, he proposed that as my stay was necessarily very limited, that we should go to see his mother who lived some squares off, and who would be pleased to hear from Norfolk. Accordingly we went there and were received by the old lady in bed, she being too unwell to leave it. Like the Doctor, she was pleased with the news and wished me to mention her in my next letter home. On returning to the Doctor's house we found breakfast ready, of which we partook. On its conclusion, Mrs. Steath insisted on filling my canteen with milk while her daughter, Miss Rose, a sweet one of some fifteen summers, put up some excellent ham sandwiches, with which I regaled not only myself, but several hungry ones of my company during the day. About eight o'clock our column passed through town and as our company passed, I rejoined it, bearing away many pleasing recollections of the place and its people. Charles Town is without exception the rankest rebel hold in this section of the state. There seems to be none but old men there, and the ladies, of whom there are many and handsome at that, are perfectly enthusiastic upon the war and soldier question. They have but just been relieved from the hated sway of Milroy, whose name is anathemised in every tone of the garment. At night we halted about a mile from Shepherdstown, having made about sixteen miles. Shepherdstown is a very poor place indeed, and though in Virginia and but a few miles from Charles Town, yet it is full of Unionists.

The Jefferson County Court House in Charles Town, now West Virginia, where John Brown was tried for treason in 1859. The Norfolk Blues passed by this site on June 24, 1863.

June 25, 1863 Early this morning we started, and about nine o'clock crossed the Potomac while a band, which was the first to cross, played "Maryland, My Maryland". The men crossed in columns and as the water was about waist deep, it was quite a sight. At night we camped a mile from Hagerstown, having passed through the villages of Sharpsburg, Tilghmantown, and Jones Crossroads, the three latter small affairs. Many houses in Sharpsburg still bear the marks of last year's battle. In passing through these places we saw many a long face and frowning brow and heard many an insulting remark from that sex whose strength lies in weakness, to all of which, when addressed to myself, I made no other reply than a pleasant smile while raising my cap. Hagerstown is a very fine town (or city?) of some five or six thousand people. It contains many fine residences, churches, hotels, and other buildings. From what I could learn, the people are divided; about half being Union while the other half are Secessionists, though there are many of the latter who dare not express themselves openly. I never was in a place where there was such a mania for soldier's buttons. Nearly every boy you meet in the street would ask, "Please, Mister, give me a brass button", and sometimes ladies sitting in their doors or by their windows would ask for them, in an indirect but perfectly plain manner. No one knowing my weakness can doubt for a moment but that I depleted my jacket of an article so much in demand. Here we came up with Anderson's

Division which had been a day or so in advance of us and which completed our corps. Longstreet with his corps is just behind us and as all their troops are going to pass through town tomorrow, it is more than likely that a good impression will be made. In the field where we camped for the night I found, for the first time in my life, a sprig of four-leafed clover, and subsequently another was picked up by one of our young fellows. I regret that I did not save it as such things are, I believe, very rare. We made about eighteen miles today.

June 26, 1863 After dark last night it began to rain and has continued to do so all day in no gentle shower, which has made marching very unpleasant. In fact, since the evening of the 18th not a day has passed that we have not had more or less rain. During the evening, after making an early start, we passed through the village of Lettersburg (or Lydersburg), a place of some four hundred people. At four o'clock pm, we crossed the line into Pennsylvania and packed for the night two miles from Waynesboro. Just before we stopped we crossed a small river on a substantially built covered bridge, where the word commissioners is spelled "Comisoners". As there is a well built school house within two hundred yards of the bridge, comment is unnecessary.

-Evidently, the "commissioners" had also not erected a sign with the correct spelling of Leitersburg.-

June 27, 1863 We made an early start this morning, passing through Waynesboro, Quincy, Frankstown, and Fayetteville, packing a mile beyond the latter place. Waynesboro is quite a large place of about a thousand people, where the ladies expressed many a kind wish for our complete overthrow. The last three places are small but rather neat villages.

June 28, 1863 Today, we remained camped for rest, of which I took advantage to hunt around a little and found abundance of things good to eat and drink such as bread, butter, milk, apple butter, honey, fowls, pigs, mutton, lard, cherries, whiskey, and all of which we got very cheap, as we have no Federal money and the people do not want Confederate. Possibly the people do not care to have us about their houses, and give us what we ask for to get rid of us, a very reasonable proceeding, as who wishes to remain after getting what he wants? The country through which we have been passing for the last few days is thickly settled, while the fields are filled with the finest crops of wheat and clover that I have ever seen. A person need only see the huge, well built houses to see that the country is rich in all those things which go to make up the wealth of a farmer. I heard that in passing through here, about a week ago, our cavalry pressed in the neighborhood of three thousand horses. The horses which we get here are excellent drought, but too heavy for saddle horses; well adapted for artillery service, that is as a general thing.

June 29, 1863 Last night we received orders to move at four o'clock this morning, but owing to the reception of other orders, we did not start til about twelve, and after going but about eight miles we packed. We passed through Caledonia, where Ewell last week destroyed the large iron works of Thaddeus Stevens, involving that distinguished Northern Congressman in a loss of several hundred thousand dollars, and also passed through Cashtown, a small town of little account. Near where we camped resided an old farmer, who with his wife are of that very class who, while wishing success to their own side, are yet pleasant and accommodating to our men. While in conversation with him on the afternoon of our arrival, I spoke of the probability of a battle being fought here, when the old man in his simplicity remarked, "I hope General Lee will go a little farther off to do his fighting, because Betsy (his wife) is so nervous". Possibly a knowledge of this fact may influence General Lee in his selection of a battle ground.

June 30, 1863 We remained camped today, during the whole of which it rained. This afternoon I went out and bought some prime butter at eighteen cents per pound, lard at twelve, and eggs at sixteen cents per dozen. At the house where I got these things were some very handsome girls, who expressed themselves heartily tired of the war, and one went so far as to say that she did not care which side whipped, so that the war would end. I cried a ready amen to the latter part of her wish.

July 1, 1863 (Wednesday) As everything last night wore the appearance of battle, we were called up at four o'clock and everything made ready. At nine o'clock heavy artillery firing was heard in our front. At twelve, we were ordered forward and went up the road at a double quick, the horses in a lively trot for about six miles, where we halted until some of the artillery who had been in came out, having used all their ammunition. Then six or eight of our rifled pieces were ordered forward, and shortly after the remainder of the battalion was ordered forward, but we were not placed in position as about the time we were ordered forward, the artillery of both sides ceased firing in great measure, and the remainder of the day was spent in skirmishing. This also ceased and we packed on a portion of the battlefield, the enemy having been driven about two miles, where they took ground upon a range of hills from which I

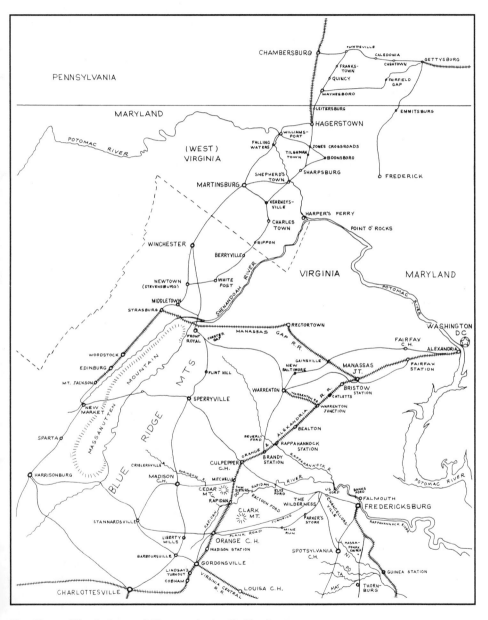

Northern Virginia and the route to Gettysburg.

think we will experience some difficulty in driving them. After firing ceased and up to eleven o'clock at night, I employed myself in carrying water to the wounded and binding such wounds as did not require the knife of the surgeon, not confining myself to our own wounded, but helping the enemy after our own men were removed from the field. In my human exertions I used up two handkerchiefs and as I have but one now, I shall save it as I may need it for myself. Due to my exertions on behalf of the wounded, I owe the fact that I did not get any battle plunder, and I sadly need a pair of pants and a pair of shoes, and besides, some underclothes would not come amiss.

-Walters neglects to mention that this day's fighting occurred near a small crossroads town named Gettysburg. The rifled guns of Maurin's, Lewis', and Moore's batteries replaced those of Pegram on a ridge just west of Herr's Tavern.-

July 2, 1863 (Thursday) At two o'clock this morning we were called up, and at four the rifled pieces of our battalion went forward to take a position in a piece of woods in front of us. At the same time, all the long range guns of our, and part of those of Longstreet's Corps, took the best position they could get so that their guns could bear on the range of hills where the enemy were posted most advantageously, and where they had about a hundred guns of their heaviest field caliber. Skirmishing was heavy and continuous until about four o'clock in the afternoon, when Longstreet on our right opened his artillery. Our line followed, and soon Ewell on our left (where he tried to flank the enemy) joined in. To this, the enemy replied most vigorously, and soon the noise and din of battle became truly infernal. Add to this the volleying of musketry which could be heard during the occasional lulls in cannonading. The shouts of the enemy and yells of our own men, and the groans of the wounded as they were borne past where I sat and the whole made up a scene such as I never before heard. Even some of our oldest soldiers say they have never heard or witnessed the like before, which is not surprising when it is known that at least three hundred guns were vomiting at each other, as fast as men could work their guns. This continued until after dark when the firing gradually ceased.

-The piece of woods where Garnett's rifled guns were posted was around the MacMillan House on Seminary Ridge. Maurin's and Lewis' guns were to the left of the house, while Moore's and Grandy's guns were to the right.-

July 3, 1863 (Friday) Before daylight this morning the cannonading recommenced, but was not very severe until about ten o'clock when last evening's awful work was repeated and lasted from two to three hours. After that, it slackened, and volleying musketry told that the infantry were at it. This, and the artillery firing was continued at intervals till after dark. Our loss up to this time must be heavy. Among the generals Heth, Hood, and Pender are wounded, Barksdale is killed, and Archer is prisoner. We also hear of several of the enemy's generals killed. During the last three days we have taken some twelve thousand prisoners; among them several hundred officers from colonels down. One rather singular feature of this battle has been the carrying off of our wounded by Yankee prisoners, and those men who one moment were doing their best to kill each other could be seen almost the next, helping our wounded with all the care and tenderness of old and tried friends.

-Although Walters was in reserve with the shorter range smoothbore guns of the battalion and not in a position to see it, the greatest and perhaps the most desperate Confederate assault of the war had just taken place. Shortly after the long range artillery fire slackened, Major Generals George Pickett and Pettigrew led their men on a direct charge at the center of the lines on Cemetery Hill, "where the enemy were posted most advantageously." The infantrymen pushed just into the Union lines, reaching a point since known both geographically and figuratively as the High Water Mark of the Confederacy. They were then forced back, retreating across the mile wide field to their positions with heavy losses. Lee met his men as they returned, and told them, "It is all my fault." He then prepared his army for an expected heavy counterattack which never came.-

July 4, 1863 At an early hour a very heavy shower of rain fell which lasted a couple of hours. When it cleared off, the sky gave promise to more ere long. About eleven am, the remainder of our battalion, which had been held in reserve, was put in position eight hundred or a thousand yards from the enemy. We all expected this to be the heaviest day's fighting of the battle, notwithstanding the terrible work that has already been done, but in this we were, I must say pleasingly, disappointed. Early in the afternoon it again began to rain very heavily and continued with more or less violence till late in the night. At dark, great was our surprise to see all the troops in motion, and all taking the back track. We were wondering what this movement meant, when we learned that the enemy had fallen back during the day, most probably with a view of coming up in our rear and holding one of those mountain gaps from which we would have met with much trouble. We marched all of that night over one of the worst roads that I ever saw and at five o'clock in the morning, packed at the foot of South Mountain, having passed through the small but rather neat village of Fairfield where I found a fine breakfast, which some kind soul must have put away for me. As it was very early, I did not wake the folks up, but put the plates back in the cupboard. This breakfast was greatly needed as I had eaten nothing for twenty-four hours.

A 3-inch Ordnance Rifle aimed at Cemetery Ridge marks the position of the Blues' rifled pieces on the Gettysburg battlefield.

CHAPTER THREE

On the Defensive

July 5, 1863 We remained packed until three o'clock this afternoon when we once more took the road, and at four next morning we halted at the village of Frogtown, a mean affair, having in all this time made but about seven miles, which was owing to the horrible state of the road, which was through the mountain by way of Fairfax Gap. I have seen bad roads, but this was without exception the worst that I have ever seen. One moment we were up to our knees in mud, and the next, lying full length in the mud, having tripped over a rock which we could not shun, owing to the total darkness in which we were enveloped. The rain also fell, sometimes in perfect torrents which added greatly to our discomfort.

July 6, 1863 Oh, you who read, and reading, believe the fancy sketches of the march of a grand army, the firm and martial tread of the men, their neat and tidy appearance, the unspotted whiteness of their gloves, the luster of their well polished shoes, and the glitter of their arms, the music of the bands, prancing of gay horses, nodding of plumes, and all those things that go to make up the "Pride, pomp, and circumstance of glorious war!" You should have seen our army as it emerged from that mountain gap this morning. War has unquestionably its poetry, but this is its plain, unvarnished prose.

While here, some seven or eight thousand prisoners passed on their way to Richmond, in the charge of the remains of Pickett's Division, which suffered greatly in the last fight. Shortly after, General Lee

79

passed, who was saluted in that silent, respectful manner which the glorious old man so much admires. After him passed Extra Billy, our Governor Elect, who received hearty and prolonged cheering to which he did not seem at all adverse. At three pm we again got underway and at three am, packed three miles from Hagerstown, having re-passed through Waynesboro and Lettersburg, and in both of which places the people seem jubilant over what they suppose to be our defeat. Now it is true we did not gain a victory, but we are far from being defeated. A great part of our want of success is attributed to our falling short of rifle gun ammunition, immense quantities of which were fired by our army.

July 7, 1863 At four o'clock we were again called up and in a short time passed through Hagerstown and camped a mile on this side of it, where it is likely that we will be for some days, at least until the enemy develop their plans which will probably result in another battle.

July 11, 1863 Yesterday, there was considerable fighting done on our right in the direction of Boonsboro, which place I understand, was burnt by our troops. This morning we hitched up and moved to within a short distance of the Sharpsburg Turnpike, where our troops are drawn up in line of battle on a splendid range of hills, and as we have received a large supply of ammunition, I think we will give the enemy a big whipping, notwithstanding the large superiority of their numbers. Everything seems to indicate a large battle in which it is necessary that we should prove victorious, as our rations are running low with but little chance of our getting more, until we take them from the enemy.

July 12, 1863 Nothing was done today beyond picket firing. Part of our battalion is in position, the remainder is held at hand ready for orders.

July 13, 1863 (Monday) This afternoon, the Napoleon gun to which I am attached went to the front and took a position in the first line of the battle. A large number of other pieces were in this line, and why they were sent there except for a blind, I cannot imagine. As soon as we got to our position we were kept til dark, when we limbered up and left. Just as we started, it began to rain, and our way lay through the woods for about five miles. We had hard work to get along. After traveling about an hour we were compelled to light some port-fires to enable our drivers to see where to drive.

During the night we passed through Williamsport where a portion of our army were crossing, but our column, consisting of Hill's Corps, turned to the left and at half past nine Tuesday morning we crossed the Potomac on a fine pontoon bridge, having made but about twelve miles. I think the horrible condition of the road equaled, if it did not surpass, that through the Fairfield Gap. The only thing in our favor this time being that until we were about two miles from where we crossed the river the road was comparatively level.

July 14, 1863 After crossing the river, four pieces of our battalion, together with guns from other commands, took positions on the hills to protect our infantry while crossing, which for the protection of our artillery and wagons formed in lines of battle by divisions. While thus in line, the enemy's cavalry began to show themselves, a battalion of which attacked Mahone's Brigade, who captured, or should I say killed and captured one hundred and ten out of one hundred and thirty who charged. While Heth's and Pender's divisions were crossing they were constantly annoyed by the enemy who dismounted from their horses and acted as sharp shooters. Our artillery put a stop to this in a great measure, and at about one o'clock the bridge was loosened from the opposite shore and taken up on ours. Picket firing across the river was kept up by both sides until dark. The pieces of our battalion remained all night, where we were entirely unsupported by infantry and almost by cavalry, there being but one hundred of the latter on picket. Had the enemy been aware of this it is more than likely that a dash would have been made by them from the direction of Williamsport, where I hear that they have been crossing for the last three days.

The south shore of the Potomac River as seen from Williamsport, Maryland. The Blues crossed the river near this spot on their return from Pennsylvania.

We have had but little to eat, nothing in fact but four ounces of bread and about two pounds of beef with no salt. I am very hungry, and the attempt to fill up with unripe apples I find to be a miserable future. If they do not give us something soon, I do not know what I shall do. This is not the case with our battalion alone, it is so with the whole army. I saw one man who paid one dollar and a half for a loaf of bread, weighing perhaps two pounds and a half. Last night, while struggling through the mud, wet, footsore, and weary, I made use of an oath. This is the first time that I have done so for over four years, and while it sounded strangely to myself, it also caused some surprise to those of our boys who heard me. What makes me more ashamed of it than I would otherwise be, is that it was not an involuntary oath, but one uttered with the utmost deliberation. God in his mercy grant that I may never repeat it. During the afternoon we had a very heavy shower of rain which lasted about two hours.

July 15, 1863 Early this morning we left the hill on our way to Martinsburg, eight miles distant. The turnpike road all the way was very good but we were greatly delayed by the passing of divisions with their wagon trains, so that it was four o'clock in the afternoon before we got to Martinsburg. This is quite a large place and contains a bank, several churches and mills, and once contained a large railroad depot, but this has been destroyed. There are but few secession people there, in consequence of which we could not get anything to eat there, though we stand in great need of it.

After passing through it we made about four miles more and packed. During the latter part of the afternoon, the major of our battalion named Richardson who was with us (and who by the way, is a fine gentleman and a good soldier who pays more attention to the comfort and welfare of his men and horses than to his own case) succeeded in getting a barrel of flour. He exchanged sixty pounds of which for thirty loaves of bread, which gave us nearly a third of a loaf to each man. He was also enabled to secure a small quantity of ham and middlings sufficient to give every man about three ounces. Hungry as we were, this was insufficient to supply us, but with the flour we did very well. My feet are becoming very sore, owing to my shoes being nearly worn out. They both have holes in the bottoms which cause my toes to touch the ground and let in rocks and gravel. These have ground the skin off my feet in several places, and makes walking very hard indeed.

-Major Charles Richardson was serving as temporary commander of the battalion in Colonel Garnett's absence.-

July 18, 1863 We are still lying, idly awaiting further developments. I heard that a council of war was held in Winchester yesterday at which President Davis was present. What will result from this is impossible to imagine. The sad news of the fall of Vicksburg has reached us. This must have a great effect in Europe, especially when they learn that our men held out with such Spartan firmness that the enemy were obliged to feed our men ere they had the strength to stack their surrendered arms. This, if nothing else, shows that we will hold out to the last extremity and that it is utterly impossible to subdue us. I now begin to think that fighting will never end the war.

Our battalion has been considerably exercised for the last day or two by the report that it was to be broken up and perhaps merged into other battalions. Should this be so, it will be owing to the fact of our having lost several guns, horses, and men since leaving Gettysburg. The reason of our losing them being the breaking down of our horses which have not been sufficiently fed for the last three weeks. In fact, you see horses lying by the side of the road dying from exhaustion and literal starvation. Our company, though losing no guns, has lost some twelve or sixteen horses, and three men who were taken prisoners. If this rumor should prove true, rather than go into the infantry, I shall ship to the navy.

> -This idea was not unique to Walters. At least seven members of the Blues left the company for service in the Confederate navy. Charles Borum and Otey Bradford became navy lieutenants, Henry Cornick became a master, and Joseph West, John B. Brown, Ames Johnson, and Joseph M. Freeman (the private who was not concerned about time) became engineers.

> The three men of the company who were taken prisoner at this time were Julius Elliott, Thomas H. Elliott, and Robert Reynolds.-

July 21, 1863 We have been lying idle up to this time, faring very poorly. For the last eight days, we received nothing but four pounds of flour, three pounds of fresh beef, and one pound of fresh mutton. This we were obliged to eat without salt, as none of that article is to be obtained. There are but few farm houses around here and they have nothing to sell. Our horses are in very bad condition owing to the want of forage.

We have just received orders to hitch up, but cannot even conjecture where we are going as there are so many points which can be made from this place. It is possible that Richmond may be our destination as I hear that a large force of the enemy is making head there. At eleven o'clock we started and by sundown we camped about a mile beyond Newtown on the Staunton Turnpike. Newtown is a singular looking village of seven or eight hundred people, and is nearly a mile long, all the houses being on the main street. There are no side or back streets in the place. It contains two churches, one built by the Methodists (the fish on the steeple tells us) in 1825. The other is a Lutheran Church. It also contains a hotel where I obtained an excellent supper for a dollar.

During the march we passed through Winchester which is crowded with soldiers, sick and wounded. The latter are from the fatal fields of Gettysburg. They have every possible attention paid them by the citizens of both sexes, and are loud in praise of Winchester kindness and hospitality. It is much to be regretted that our army still continues their retrograde movements, as it again exposes the people of this place (and in fact the whole valley) to the tyranny and oppression of the enemy. I could not see much of the city owing to the conditions of my feet which rendered walking painful in the extreme, for which reason I was allowed to ride on a caisson.

Just after passing through Winchester, we were overtaken by one of our Norfolk mail-carriers, who has lately arrived from there. He brought a large number of letters for our boys, but none for me. This nearly filled up the measure of my misery. I wonder if I am forgotten.

We made twenty-one miles today, which is owing to the splendid condition of the Turnpike road, which is as smooth as if it were flayed. I believe it has the reputation of being the finest road in the world. After our battalion was packed I went to a barn, which was a short distance off, for the purpose of getting some straw to sleep on, and on my way found an old pair of boots, which someone had probably lost. Being number tens they were not too small, and though of little value, are in my present condition a perfect godsend.

-In a way, it may have been fortunate that Walters did not get a letter from back home. The news was not good, at least for those who supported the Confederacy. The Union army under General Egbert Viele had established martial law in the cities of Norfolk and Portsmouth and anyone who did not swear an oath of allegiance to the United States was subject to search and seizure of property. Federal troops took up residence in most of the public buildings, and high ranking officers moved into private homes. Fort Norfolk and the Customs House on Main Street became prisons for those caught running the blockade. A Confederate flag was placed as a foot mat at the ferry terminal. Business licenses, taxes, and a two dollar fee for each pet dog were levied at the whim of the military commander, General Benjamin "Beast" Butler, who took over in November of 1863. In February of 1864 the Reverend S. H. Wingfield, a Portsmouth minister, was sentenced to sweep sidewalks for three months for refusing to pray for President Lincoln during a service.

Probably the greatest annoyance to the Southern Sympathizers was the recruiting and drilling of local blacks into the occupying forces. This resentment culminated in the infamous case of Dr. David Wright, a hero of the local Yellow Fever epidemic of 1855 and the father of Private Minton Wright who had enlisted in the Blues. On June 17, 1863, Dr. Wright became involved in a dispute with a white lieutenant named A. L. Sanborn who was marching a company of black Union soldiers, and in a fit of anger, he shot and killed the lieutenant. He was held in the Customs House, tried and convicted of murder, and sentenced to be hung. He attempted an escape during a visit by his daughter when the two disguised themselves as each other, but an alert guard noticed "Miss" Wright's peculiar gait (caused by the leg irons the doctor still wore) and the attempt was foiled. Dr. Wright was publicly executed the following October 23 and was buried in Elmwood Cemetery. He was never told that his son, who had transferred out of the Blues to accept the rank of lieutenant in the North Carolina infantry, was missing and presumed killed at Gettysburg during this time.

Through all of this, the men of Grandy's Battery remained faithfully on duty far from home, powerless to come to the immediate aid of their families and friends.-

July 22, 1863 We started at daylight, and going back to Newtown, turned to the right and made for the Winchester Turnpike on which we expected to go to Front Royal, but when within about six miles of that place (after traveling nine miles) received orders (which should have reached us last night) to make for Gordonsville by the nearest route. To do this we were again obliged to take the Staunton Turnpike, which we did after traveling seven or eight miles or more. We struck the pike at Middleton which is just five miles from where we stopped last night.

During the day I suffered greatly with my feet which are full of blisters. Owing to this, I fell into the rear of our battalion, and at ten o'clock at night, being still some four or five miles in the rear and completely broken down, I laid down in a house porch and went to sleep in company with five other unfortunates of our battalion. But while we suffered in the manner stated, we fared like lords, as we met with ready accommodations at almost every house at which we stopped, and the charges were in nearly all cases very reasonable. We got supper at the house of a Mr. Grayson, whose wife is a splendid specimen of the Virginia lady, and whose two daughters, young ladies of about eighteen and twenty, I found to be pleasant, entertaining, intelligent, well educated, and with all very pretty.

July 23, 1863 At daylight we started and after walking about two miles, reached Middletown where we got an excellent breakfast at the village tavern, to which we did full justice, for though weary and footsore, our appetites were in prime condition. This village, like Newtown, is a long line of houses, all pointing on the principle street which forms a portion of the Turnpike. After leaving this place, we walked five miles and reached Strasburg where we rested til dinner, which we took at the hotel for two dollars apiece. I had to sell my silver watch for fifteen dollars (which by the way I had won at a raffle from one of our young fellows while we were at Camp Anderson in the latter part of May). After dinner we pushed on as well as we were able, and by eleven o'clock at night laid down on the porch of a house near the village of Woodstock, which is twelve miles distant from Strasburg. Just before lying down for the night we learned from a wagon that our battalion was still some five miles ahead. During this day, the road led us through some of the finest scenery of this most beautiful section, frequently giving us views from an elevated position of the winding Shenandoah, but the pain attendant upon my locomotion blunted my perception of the grand or beautiful.

July 24, 1863 At daylight, "Company 2" of which I had been appointed captain again pushed on, but owing to our exertions in walking seventeen miles yesterday, we were so thoroughly used up that we were obliged to rest after almost every two or three hundred yards, and it was sundown before we reached Edinburgh, which is nearly six miles from Woodstock. In this village of about five hundred inhabitants, the houses are not quite so much confined to one street as in those previously passed through, though it has nothing to distinguish it from the average of country villages beyond a fine, large flour mill. After getting supper and resting about an hour we went on, but could only make about a mile when we were fain to take advantage of an excellent porch in which we soon forgot our troubles.

July 25, 1863 "Company 2", which has been reduced by desertion to two men beside myself, began their limping shortly after daylight and had made about two miles when we were overtaken by some empty wagons belonging to Early's Division, into which we were permitted to get, and which carried us as far as New Market, a distance of about ten miles. We passed on the way through the village of Mount Jackson at which place a large number of our sick and wounded are in hospitals, having been brought there from Winchester and other places. The buildings used for the purpose are two large wooden ones, full of windows and therefore well adapted.

The fine mill at Edinburg, Virginia built in 1848, which John Walters saw in 1863.

Everything about the buildings looked clean and tidy, and the poor sufferers no doubt received all the care and attention it is possible to bestow. A hundred or more ambulances were unpacked close by the village, from which I imagine the invalids will soon be removed to Staunton or elsewhere. New Market is the finest village I have yet seen on this road and contains some four or five churches. From the number of stores here, I should judge that it was quite a business place. At a drug store, I purchased a lotion with which to bathe my feet. In the window of this store is an article of great interest to the people of this valley, neither more or less than the vertebra of the horse which was killed under Turner Ashby in one of his fights in the Valley of Ashby. It is a great favorite with the people of this section, who in speaking of him always call him "Our Ashby", and never seem to grow weary of sounding his praise. At New Market we left the Staunton Turnpike and turned to the left, taking the Madison Turnpike for Gordonsville, some sixty-four miles distant. After walking four miles we reached the top of Massanutten Mountain, just as a heavy shower of rain began to fall. As it was nearly dark, we took shelter in the porch of a house which stands on top of the mountain. Close by the house is a well of water, as cold as any ice water that I ever drank and clear as crystal.

July 26, 1863 Our feet being much better, thanks to the lotion which I procured in New Market, we started long before the sun tipped the peaks around us and instead of keeping the road, took short cuts to the Blue Ridge across which our road lies. After walking about fifteen miles and by our short cuts saving at least six, we arrived at New Market, a small post village at the foot of the Blue Ridge where we stopped for the night. During the day a rather laughable event occurred. "Company 2" came to a large stream, the only means of crossing which was by fording, and as the water was about waist deep we were debating the question when a darky came along mounted on an ancient mule. We soon made a bargain with the darky to take us across, whereupon one of the members of my company mounted behind and they started. While the young fellow who remained with me and myself were congratulating ourselves on the easy solution of what a few minutes before was a difficult problem, we heard a shout and on looking, found that the mule had turned both his riders off in about the middle of the stream, wetting them completely. On seeing this, we who had remained behind quietly and quickly removed our clothing and crossed, while our friend was busy wringing the water out of his clothes and bitterly cursing his ill luck.

July 27, 1863 Being much refreshed by the frequent rests taken yesterday and the day before, and our feet also being much better, we started early to cross the Blue Ridge, and being well furnished with information regarding the short cuts, evening found us on this side of the mountain, having made a distance of at least twenty-four miles. In reality, we did not make more than sixteen or eighteen miles, and this will be readily realized when I mention that at one point we saw the road three times with no more than two or three hundred yards between. This was owing to the steepness of the mountain which causes the road to wind in one continuous string of S's. I was informed that the road occupied two years in building across the mountain and cost eighteen hundred dollars per mile. It is a magnificent evidence of the perfection of engineering skill, being as smooth as a floor though already twelve years old and much used. During the latter part of the afternoon a very heavy shower of rain fell, and as there were no houses or shelter of any kind near, we were obliged to take it all. At night we reached the house of a Mr. Bohannon where we got supper and permission to sleep on the porch, and as the night was warm, we suffered but little from our clothes being wet.

July 28, 1863 After eating a very hearty breakfast, we set out and in the course of a couple of hours came up with the battalion, which we found camped by the Robinson River, and about a mile from Criglersville, a small, six house affair. On arriving in camp, I of course, resigned my position as captain of "Company 2" and most sincerely trust never to have command or be in a company of this kind again. At four o'clock this afternoon the battalion got under-way and at dark, packed about a mile this side of Madison Court-house, having made about nine miles. Madison is a bright, thriving looking place of perhaps five hundred inhabitants, having a couple of churches and a Masonic Hall, besides the courthouse and other public buildings.

July 29, 1863 Off again shortly after daylight and in the evening, packed close by Gordonsville, having made about fifteen miles. So ends the campaign undertaken by our best general, with the finest army that was ever in Virginia, which opened so admirably with the defeat of Milroy (that children's terror), and which, though it does not close disastrously to us, yet leaves us no better off than we were before it began.

Except for the utility lines, the Masonic Hall and the Court House with its domed cupola stand in Madison, Virginia just as they did when John Walters passed.

A slight review will not be out of place here. The campaign occupied about fifty days, during which time the corps of Hill and Longstreet made about four hundred miles, while Ewell's Corps and Stuart's Cavalry marched much more. Without doubt, our army destroyed a large amount of property, captured first a number of guns and a large quantity of stores together with about two thousand prisoners from Milroy, secondly thousands of horses and cattle in Pennsylvania, and thirdly, Stuart captured about two hundred and fifty wagons with their mules and harnesses. Per contra, we lost on the march back about a hundred wagons and two guns, together with a large number of men who, unable to keep up with the main body, fell in the rear and were picked up by the enemy. Now during that march, both the advance and the retrograde and in the battle, we lost many hundred horses and mules and though the number taken far exceeds what we lost, still are we losers for the fact that the Pennsylvania horses are far inferior to ours, nearly at a rate of four to one. But our greatest loss is in prestige and this leads to the question, why did we not whip Meade's army at Gettysburg? Our men fought as well as they ever did. The enemy fought no better. 'Tis true that after the first few hours of the battle they fell back to a position from which we could not succeed in facing them, but they should never have been allowed to make a stand on that line of hills. From prisoners captured the first day, we learned that they had been marched eighteen miles, and without a minute's rest formed into line of battle and pushed forward, showing that Meade was in extreme want thus to put men into battle who had been nearly broken down by forced march. These prisoners also stated that but two corps were engaged and that three or four were hurrying forward and would most probably join Meade during the night. Now, while it is not very advisable to trust to the statements of prisoners too implicitly, yet many of their statements may be received as of value by allowing margins. Thus I hold that if our advantages of the first day had been pushed up the battle would have resulted largely in our favor. Again a general advance of our line was ordered to be made on the second day (why was it not brought up on the first day?). Initiatory to this, all our artillery opened, which was replied to most vigorously. After this had been kept up for some time the infantry was ordered to charge, but there seems to have been something "rotten in Denmark", for while we hear of brigades charging under the most galling fire with a heroism bordering on desperation, yet these noble brigades on gaining the crest of the hill (and in many instances driving the enemy back and compelling the gunners to leave their guns) found themselves unsupported and were compelled to fall back, frequently losing more men than they did while advancing.

The third day was a repetition of the second, terrific artillery work with no apparent or material results, and the close of the fourth day saw us turn our backs on that fatal field. I do not pretend to assign any reason why Longstreet was not up to participate in the first day's fight, nor why our advantage of that day was not pushed up, but believe if we had been up and the other pushed, at least two corps if not more would have been bagged. I shall look for General Lee's official report with much anxiety. What further remains to be done by this army this year it is difficult to conjecture. Possibly a portion of our army will be sent to Bragg to enable him to do something with Rosecrans, instead of standing eternally on the defensive. Or the whole army may await an advance of Meade, but this I think hardly probable. I have an idea, though I can give but little reason for it, that we will again assume the offensive in the course of six weeks or two months.

-It is interesting to find that Walters' analysis of the Gettysburg Battle, written so soon after the fact, places part of the blame on General James Longstreet. In the years to follow, a great many other soldiers and historians would also question Longstreet's performance in this crucial battle.-

July 30, 1863 This afternoon we moved camp to a field about three miles from Gordonsville on the Charlottesville Road. In the field about four hundred yards from our camp our boys dug a splendid spring, which yields water enough to supply a large brigade.

August 26, 1863 Today we moved camp to a field belonging to a Mr. McMutton on the Harrisburg Turnpike.

September 18, 1863 About three o'clock this morning we were called up and after getting ready, marched to Orange Courthouse where we camped. I understand this movement is made in consideration of a supposed advance of the enemy. Possibly they have got information of Longstreet's departure and hope to find Lee too weak to withstand them. I should not be surprised if they were to find themselves in error.

-Longstreet had taken part of the Army of Northern Virginia on an expedition against Union troops at Suffolk, which although not a great success, kept these forces on their guard.-

September 19, 1863 This morning we again moved our camp, passing through Orange Courthouse and camping about two miles from Rapidan Station on the river of that name.

September 24, 1863 This afternoon I was made glad by the receipt of a letter from Norfolk, accompanied by Fannie's picture. I have

Railroad bridge across the Rapidan River near Rapidan Station.

looked for this so often and so long without receiving it that I had despaired of seeing it until I got back to Norfolk, and coming as it did while least expecting it, almost caused me to make a fool of myself. I felt a moisture gathering in my eyes on looking at those loved features, but was enabled to force it back.

October 8, 1863 At an early hour this morning our battery received orders to hitch up, which we did. We proceeded to the Rapidan, which we crossed at Rapidan Ford, and relieved the battery of Captain Marmaduke Johnson which has been doing duty there for some time. Later in the day Lander's (later Wilcox's) Brigade was relieved of Walker's, a thousand or twelve hundred yards from our guns. They can be plainly seen, as they are in a level plain some feet lower than the slight elevation on which our battery is placed. Our own picket line is about three hundred yards in advance of our guns. About three miles from us arises a couple of peaks, which from their peculiar shape have been very appropriately named the "Maiden's Hearts". From what I can learn, we will soon have a battle, though unless our battery is ordered elsewhere, I think we will hardly be in it, for though this is at present the center of our position, I believe either Hill or Ewell will fall upon Meade's flank and force him upon the other, by which movement this position becomes either of no value or untenable, according as Meade is pressed from right or left.

October 9, 1863 During last night, three men belonging to Archer's Tennessee Brigade deserted to the enemy. They are said to be conscripts; whether what information they can give the enemy will injure us remains to be seen. Nothing of importance occurred today. We were anxiously listening for indications of battle to our left, but received none. Though it is rather too soon, yet tomorrow the ball will most likely open. After dark, the gun to which I am attached was withdrawn from its position and a Quaker mounted in its place. We recrossed the river and halted for the night behind the first hill that screened us from the elevation of the enemy. What this movement means, tomorrow will inform us.

-This "Quaker" was a dummy cannon, so called because those who belonged to the Quaker religion refused to fight. Quakers, Dunkards, Mennonites, and other faiths made up the conscientious objectors of this era. Quaker guns generally were roughly shaped tree trunks, painted black to look like cannon barrels. They were often quite convincing decoys.-

October 10, 1863 At early daylight this morning our gun detachment was called up and soon got under way, taking the road that leads to Robinson's Ford, which is about three miles from our position of yesterday. By the road which we took it was about five miles, and as a portion of the road was a new cut one through the woods, and on the side of Clark Mountain and other spurs, our horses had rather hard work of it. In the course of about three hours, we put our gun on a high hill which commands the ford where we await further developments. While thus waiting, let me give a sketch of the beautiful view that meets the eye, though I can give but a faint outline of the most prominent landmarks, leaving the imagination to fill the picture with all that is beautiful in nature. Our gun is in position on a sort of plateau near the top of Clark Mountain, which lies nearly due east of Blue Ridge, which latter stretches to our right and left in front of us, distant about five miles, until its tops and peaks are lost in the distance. Directly in front of us rises the twain peaks known as the "Maiden Breasts", continuing which to the right and left rise numerous slopes and peaks, all spurs of the Blue Ridge, some of which are under cultivation while others remain as nature found them, in all the beauty of autumn foliage. Between this range and ourselves lies an almost level plain through the center of which the Rapidan runs its tortuous course. Its banks are lined with trees, while here and there breaks in this screen of trees reveals the water, its silver here beautifully contrasted by the red and green of the leaves, the yellow corn fields and the deep green of the meadowlands. To add to this here and there can be seen the manories of wealthy farmers, surrounded each by its groups of barns, houses, and Negro quarters. Some of these stand in the midst of a fine growth of shade trees while others, without as much as a bush about them, relieve what otherwise would be a monotony of treeless fields. But now behold a singular feature of this magnificent panorama; across the river far as the eye can reach can be seen groups of three or four men at intervals of fifteen or twenty yards in the Confederate uniform, while in front of them not more than a thousand yards are similar groups of the enemy, each being, or purporting to be, the advanced pickets of their respective armies. While viewing this picture of present comparative peace it is saddening to think how soon it all may be changed to a perfect Golgotha, where the groans of the maimed and dying will pierce the wounded air, while high over all the din and smoke of battle, angels may be hovering while dropping a tear over "Man's inhumanity to Man". Ha! There goes a gun! The battle must have commenced, but as it is already five o'clock but little will be done today.

October 11, 1863 With daylight, artillery firing again commenced, but so distant as to render it impossible for us to determine from whence the sound proceeded, but the general impression prevailed that it must be from Germanna Ford on the Rapidan. If this is so, it must be cavalry fighting, but what the enemy are doing up there I cannot imagine. Certainly they cannot think of attempting to flank us. As soon as daylight was sufficient we discovered that the enemy had withdrawn all his pickets from our front, but this did not surprise us much as we anticipated that last evening. About five o'clock pm we received orders to move forward which we did in company with the infantry who were guarding the ford with us. We crossed the river and after traveling about seven miles reached Mitchell Station on the Orange and Alexandria Railroad where we found the other portion of our battery and also the remainder of Walker's Brigade to which we are attached for the present.

October 12, 1863 We were called up before daylight and were on the move before the sun rose, and here let me enter my solemn protest against this early rising. Of all the disagreeable features attending a march of troops, I think this is the most disagreeable, for we frequently have but time to roll up our blanket before the order "forward" is given and as to cooking anything, he is fortunate indeed who has a cold biscuit or two to fall back upon.

In the course of the day we passed through Culpepper Courthouse and the many expressions of joy were uttered by the ladies while tears of pleasure rolled down their cheeks, convincing us that Yankee sympathizers are scarce there. Near sunset we packed about

The view from atop Clark Mountain on an October day. The two dark hills in the center are Twin Sisters Mountain, known to the soldiers as the "Maidens Breasts." The Rapidan River flows from left to right through the wooded valley before them. The hazy Blue Ridge Mountains lie beyond.

A manor house and fields with Twin Sisters Mountain in the background.

nine miles north of Culpepper, having made about sixteen miles. At Culpepper, we found about three hundred Yankee prisoners who had been captured the day before by our cavalry.

October 13, 1863 We were called up again before daylight, but did not start until about nine o'clock owing to the passing of Ewell's wagon trains which moved but slowly as the head of it was crossing the Hazel River, about two and a half miles from here. After awhile we started, and reaching the Hazel crossed it, but as the ford was a very rocky one, some of our pieces stalled in the river which compelled some of our men to get in the water to work at the wheels. As I looked for some such a piece of work as this, I went down and stripped, crossed, dressed, and seated myself on the opposite bank, viewing the labors of those who thought to cross the river on the limber chests or caissons. About two pm we crossed the Rappahannock at Warrenton Springs Ford, and after dark packed about two miles east of the town of Warrenton after passing through that place. It is a sad sight to see the ruins of the large hotel and other buildings at the springs, and in fact the whole country around here is one scene of desolation and destruction. The land is overrun with weeds and pine brush springing up all around, and chimneys stand lonely and gaunt to mark the place where houses once stood. All these bear unhappy testimony of the unhappy state of things. The road over which we passed bore many evidences of yesterday's skirmishing in the number of dead horses, with here and there an unburied Yankee.

October 14, 1863 We were again called up before daylight, but owing to the whole corps being in the artillery, we did not move for some hours, and it was nine o'clock before we passed through Warrenton, taking the road to Manassas by way of Bristoe. Everything appears to indicate another life struggle upon those plains already so deeply stained with glorious blood, and possibly thy bones, immortal Bee, pure Barton, gallant Fisher, with those of other kindred spirits, will rattle in their far off sepulchers as we again pour the deadly showers into the bosoms of the foe, or drive them before us with the bayonet. About six miles from Warrenton, we passed through the village of New Baltimore, a mean, insignificant affair, but just beyond it we passed by a group of some ten or a dozen ladies who were there viewing the passing troops and uttering those pleasant nothings, with which the dear sex know so well how to cheer weary soldiers. While stopping a moment to answer a question addressed to me by one of the ladies, I suddenly heard a shout and on looking around found that the artillery was flying down the road at the utmost speed of the horses, while the officers were all urging greater speed. With a hurricane salute, I left the ladies and after a hard run of about five miles, I came up with my gun. Just as I did so, the order was given for cannoneers to mount, and then commenced a scramble to get up for there was no time to stop. Up at last! And such a scene; six battalions numbering about a hundred guns, all thundering over the road while conjecture runs riot as to the meaning of it all, though we all feel sure that battle is not far distant. On we go, through the sweet little village of Greenwich, all around which last night's campfires of the Yankees are still burning. On still, over roads and through fields, catching every now and then the sound of Ewell's cannon far off in our right. At last after keeping up this mad race for ten or twelve miles, the artillery column comes to a halt, while the sound of cannon not far ahead tells that the head of the column is engaged. The firing is rapid but not heavy, showing that perhaps one battalion is engaged, and no musketry is heard as our battalion is next to the last in line. I do not think it probable that we will be engaged today, so I am sitting by the roadside, resting and writing this.

About two hours before sunset we again moved forward about a mile, and all turned into a field on the right of the road when we packed, but did not unhitch as the firing still continued ahead. It ceased about dark, after the fighting was over, the horses were unhitched and fed, and I went off to gather points. Just across the road from where we packed is a large field, where a field hospital and a depot for prisoners has been temporarily established. I went there and found quite a number of wounded. Among them were Generals Cooke and Kirkland, the former with a limb shattered, the latter wounded in the arm. All the wounded, with the exception of a few from Poague's and McIntosh's battalions, were from their brigades. At the hospital I learned that the day's fight was much against us, as we had lost largely considering the small number engaged. We also lost five pieces of artillery from McIntosh's Battalion and all owing to the unfortunate haste of Cooke and Kirkland. It appears that across the road by which our infantry advanced is a cut perhaps six feet deep made for the Orange and Alexandria Railroad. In this cut, the enemy had a brigade or two concealed, while their first line of skirmishers were on the high ground in the rear of them. As I understand it, this trick was suspected by General Hill, and Mahone's and Posey's brigades of Anderson's Division were ordered to make a detour to the right through the woods, to flank and cut off this line in case there was one there. To effect this object, the remainder of the division moved to the right for support, all going at a double quick. Anderson's move to the right uncovered Heth's

Division, who continued to advance and support the artillery of McIntosh, who was posted on the edge of a piece of woods about three hundred yards from the cut. The infantry, on leaving the woods, immediately formed a line of battle, and Cooke and Kirkland ordered a charge upon what seemed to be the enemy's first, but which was in reality their second line of battle, and here occurred the unfortunate mistake; first of advancing without throwing out skirmishers (which while it is seldom done in charges, should have been done here), and second not giving the brigades of Anderson time to arrive at the point from which they would have unmasked the concealed line. The result was that when our line arrived to within thirty yards of the enemy, the enemy rose and poured in a withering fire of musketry while their second line moved quickly up to their support. About this time, Cooke and Kirkland were both wounded, and sent to the rear, and their brigades fell back. This move uncovered McIntosh, who also fell back, but owing to the fact of his having twenty-five or thirty horses killed, he was unable to bring off all his guns. He left five which were taken by the enemy, who, instead of pushing their advantage, fell back to their former position, and so ends the day.

October 15, 1863 At half past two this morning we were called up, and hitched up in accordance with orders received from General Anderson, to whom our colonel was ordered to report late last night. Just before daylight it began to rain, and soon it fell in torrents, to all of which we were exposed. As we were expecting orders every moment, we did not pitch our tents. About ten o'clock, word was brought that the enemy had fallen back and soon after, we received orders to cook up two days' rations which were served out. About four o'clock pm we were ordered forward, and the battalion was placed in position near a railroad bridge over Broad River, a short distance from Bristoe Station.

October 16, 1863 The rain poured down incessantly all day, but the weather cleared up about ten at night. The infantry were engaged all day in destroying the railroad track; hard work from which artillery are exempt.

October 17, 1863 At half past three this afternoon we were suddenly ordered to hitch-up, which we did, and took the back track towards the Rappahannock. We marched about ten miles and packed for the night. Our road was along the line of the Orange and Alexandria Railroad which is, or is being, destroyed, and a more complete piece of destruction I have never seen. The ties are all taken up and burnt, rails heated in the middle and bent double, bridges torn down, (the woodwork of which is burnt while the stone tiers were torn down and burnt up), embankments dug down, and deep cuts through hills first partly filled with felled trees, and then filled up by cutting down the banks on each side. The sight was a novel one; far as the eye could stretch in front or to the rear, there fires were burning brightly ten or fifteen yards apart, while at each, men were at work keeping up the fires or bending the rails. As it was late before we packed, and with the prospect of an early start in the morning, I was soon in the land of dreams.

October 18, 1863 We made an early start this morning and about four pm packed near the river, where they are busy in putting down a pontoon bridge as the river is too high to admit of fording. The weather today has been beautiful, but there are lines in the sky.

October 19, 1863 We were called up at half past twelve this morning for no earthly reason that I can discover, than to be ready to move by sunrise, a thing which we generally do in half an hour. About five o'clock a cold, drenching shower fell from which we had no protection, as our fires were put out by it. It ceased and cleared off finely about eight, and shortly after the wagons having all crossed, the artillery moved to about two miles from Brandy Station where we packed.

November 7, 1863 (Saturday) For the last eighteen or twenty days nothing beyond ordinary camp routine has occupied the time, but today our camp quiet was disturbed by the sound of artillery firing across the river to the left of Brandy Station. After packing we learned that the brigades of Hays and Hoag, which were on the other side of the river, had quite a fight with the enemy, and owing to the want of support, got the worst of it. Some ten or twelve hundred were taken prisoners, though not before they had succeeded in laying over nearly that number of the enemy. The Louisiana general also lost two of his guns.

November 8, 1863 At midnight we were called up and moved to within a couple of miles of Culpepper Courthouse, where we halted early in the morning. The infantry fell back to where the artillery were in line and formed a line of battle, hurriedly throwing up a timber breastwork. During the afternoon a heavy artillery firing was heard on our extreme left, where Wilcox with his division rests on the Hazel River. This looks as if the enemy were attempting to turn our flank. About four pm all the artillery was ordered to move to the rear to make the Rapidan at the nearest crossing points, while Stewart was ordered of towards the right to protect Ewell against a flank movement. While falling back, this retrograde move is no evidence of Lee's weakness for while I feel satisfied that we could whip the enemy here, yet the position to which we are going is so much superior to this, that it would be criminal in General Lee not to take it in preference. The bugles are just sounding the drivers' mount call, and we have all night before us.

November 9, 1863 After a long, cold, dark, and dreary march, we crossed the Rapidan about eight o'clock this am, and in a short time packed about two miles from Orange Courthouse, all being very tired and also hungry. There being no rations for us (though they were due yesterday morning) we will get some tomorrow perhaps, and as a man forgets his hunger in pleasant dreams of plenty, I shall sleep all day and leave the night to take care of itself.

November 10, 1863 About ten o'clock am we hitched up and in the course of a couple of hours we packed at the place that we left on the 8th of last month.

-Walters refers to Rapidan Ford.-

November 25, 1863 Nothing worth writing about occurred up to this date, and we were not expecting anything of the kind, when about seven pm the bugle suddenly sounded the "boot and saddle call". We were soon ready and underway, and in about an hour took a position between Rapidan and Robinson's River. I feel satisfied that we will not have a fight here. Our position is such a fine one. We occupy hills to get at which the enemy must expose himself for nearly two miles to our fire, while the position does not admit of our being readily flanked.

November 26, 1863 We remained in position all day doing nothing, and at about seven pm as I expected, we received orders to move, though I do not think we will move before morning. Reports today represent Meade as having crossed the Rapidan.

November 27, 1863 At three o'clock am we received orders to hitch up, which we did and were soon on the road, and after traveling all day halted about nine pm, but though we were about eighteen hours on the road, we did not make more than as many miles owing to the bad condition of the road.

November 28, 1863 We were called up before daylight, but did not move off until eight o'clock. Just after starting it began to rain, and continued to do so very heavily until towards evening. This rendered the roads, bad enough before, very bad indeed. After making only about fourteen miles, we packed at ten o'clock at night near the village of Verdiersville on the Fredericksburg Plank Road. The last three hours of our march was on a road through a piece of woods, and owing to the mud in the road, and the vines, undergrowth, and tree limbs on the side of it, we had anything but a pleasant time of it.

November 29, 1863 At early daylight we again moved forward, but only went two miles when we halted for orders, which however we have not yet received, and it is now about six pm. The weather is clear but very cold. There has been considerable firing on our extreme left during the day. Report says that Johnson's Division of Ewell's Corps was engaged, but the results have not yet reached us. Everything promises fair for a battle, though I cannot think that Meade means to fight us, as he has only about two and a half to our one.

November 30, 1863 Early this morning we were ordered into position on the extreme right of our infantry line with Scales' Brigade to support us. Our position is not a very enviable one as our guns are on a hill, at the foot of which is a dense woods. The enemy's skirmish line is in position not more than five hundred yards off; a convenient distance of picking us off at their leisure. Shortly after placing the guns in our battery, we were ordered to throw up breastworks for our guns, which are so well advanced already that we expect to finish them early tomorrow morning. The weather is intensely cold and we have nothing but pine to burn.

December 1, 1863 We all expected the fight to begin with the first approach of day, but contrary to expectation, hardly a gun was heard during the day. The enemy have been in motion all day, but with what object, I cannot divine. A couple of hours before day our right was extended and strengthened by the brigades of McGowan and Lane, together with a brigade of cavalry. At an early hour we finished our breastworks and now await the movements of the enemy.

December 2, 1863 About three hours before day, Anderson's Division, which had been on the left of Hill's Corps, passed us to the right followed by a portion of Heth's Division. This move puzzled me considerably, but I soon learned that it was a move preparatory to a charge along our entire line. As soon as the day should break, this latter event was looked for with great expectation, but soon a rumor began to circulate that the enemy had fallen back, which was shortly after confirmed by a prisoner who was brought in, who reported that Meade had made a hurried retrograde movement at two o'clock. Anderson and Wilcox were immediately sent in pursuit at a double quick, which they kept up until within about six miles of Chancellorsville. When learning that the enemy had recrossed the

Rapidan, they halted. During the morning the artillery withdrew their guns from position and went back to Verdiersville, were we all packed for the night.

December 3, 1863 Early this morning we hitched up and after making about sixteen miles arrived and packed at the camps which we left on the 25th of November.

-Between the Rapidan River and Robinson's River-

December 14, 1863 This morning we left our camp and at night halted about three miles from Gordonsville in Albemarle County. As I always try to keep one eye open to any advantage, I started about two hours before the battalion and took breakfast at the house of a friend in Orange, J. Y. G. After which, I got on the train and rode to Gordonsville, where I waited for the battalion, by which I saved a ten mile walk.

> -Although Walters does not provide the name of his host, this could be the same "old gentleman" whom he met on his first visit to Orange on November 3 of the previous year. Walters had evidently not forgotten the man's kind invitation to supper.-

December 15, 1863 We moved about three miles this morning and halted at the place where we expect to spend the winter. The place is a good one, as wood and water are abundant, and we are only about one mile from Lindsey's Turnout; a station on the Virginia Central Railroad from which we get our rations and forage. On our arrival the order was published that stables for all the horses should be built before the men would be allowed to build their quarters. This is hard as the nights are very cold and it will take some time to build the stables, as we are obliged to cut and hew all the timber and rive out boards for the roofs, but it is perhaps best that the horses should be sheltered as soon as possible, from the fact that they are becoming scarce, and they will require the best of care to render them serviceable in the spring.

December 25, 1863 (Friday) Having received permission, I this morning went to Orange to eat my Christmas dinner at the house of my friend, J. Y. G. I was received with the greatest kindness, ate a fine dinner, and closed the day with a glorious bowl of Egg-nog.

December 26, 1863 After an excellent night's rest in a feather bed, without that daily incubus, the Reveille roll call, I was called up to help at the emptying of another bowl of egg-nog. A fine breakfast followed, and then I once more took the train and in the course of three or four hours, I was back at my camp. On my return I received a bundle and a box. The former was from Richmond containing a present of an elegant pair of gloves, a neat little pipe, and a tobacco bag, the latter a present from Miss Lizzie J. The box was sent to me from Petersburg and contained a fine large turkey, some corned beef, potatoes, biscuits, cakes, pies, and a very neat silk tobacco bag, the last a present from Miss Eddy Ege. Thus it will be seen that I am still blest with the kind regards of friends. God bless them.

January 16, 1864 Today, after many disappointments, I received a furlough of fifteen days to go and visit my friends. It did not take me long to shake the camp dust from my feet, and after a brisk walk of about five miles I reached Gordonsville, from whence I expect to take the night freight train to Richmond. As my furlough dates from tomorrow, if I can get there early in the morning I shall make a day.

January 17, 1864 After a most fatiguing ride in a freight car, I arrived at Richmond at half past five o'clock. From the depot, I went to the Ballard Hotel, and in the luxurious warmth of a bath soon forgot my fatigue. About eight o'clock I went to the house if Mr. Ege in Broad Street, where my reception was all that I could ask, as all expressed themselves greatly pleased to see me. I remained at home during the day, fighting my battles o'er again and at night accompanied the ladies to church, but owing to my having been so long without sleep, I found the greatest difficulty in keeping my eyes open.

January 18, 1864 I spent the day in executing several commissions from our boys and in calling upon one or two acquaintances. Surely this being away from camp and its influence, and associating with ladies of refinement and education is a delightful thing, especially in a house like the one at which I am, where their every thought seems to be a kind wish towards me. May they long be spared to enjoy the richest of God's blessings.

January 19, 1864 This morning I made a call upon a young lady from Petersburg, whose acquaintance I made while I was there. I spent a couple of hours in her company very agreeably, and have I trust, left a good impression behind, as I behaved myself remarkably well for as careless a devil as I am. The day closed with a sociable game of Euchre at home.

January 20, 1864 Today I went over to Chimborazo Hospital to see a sick friend. After that I went home where the ladies played and sang for me, and again closed the day with four games of Euchre.

January 21, 1864 I idled the day away by walking through the city and at night went to the new theatre that played "The Lady of Lyons", but it was most wretchedly performed. The only credible performer being a Miss Bridges, who did very well, and exhibited an earnest desire to do better. The theatre is a very fine one and the scenery and appointments first class.

January 22, 1864 This morning I wrote a letter home. This afternoon I called upon Miss M. R. and Miss Josey L. with whom I went to visit a Mr. A. on 9th Street, where I took supper and had a most delightful time. The evening was passed with music, both vocal and instrumental. One feature of the evening was the handing around of pineapple, among other things, a rarity which I have not tasted for two or three years.

January 23, 1864 After idling away the day till five pm I got on the train, but was obliged to ride on top, and in about two hours and a half arrived in Petersburg. In a short time I reached the home of my friend John B. Ege, whose family I had hoped to take by surprise, but on arriving at the house, I found Mr. E. standing on the porch looking out for me. Their reception of me was all that heart could wish. A few minutes after, supper was announced which I learned had been delayed in anticipation of my coming. After which several young ladies from the neighborhood came in, among them Florence P. and Katie B. who sung and played so charmingly that the first minutes of Sunday almost caught me indulging in weekday entertainments.

January 24, 1864 On awaking this morning and finding the sun streaming brightly in at the window, I arose anticipating a happy day, but great was my disappointment when about ten o'clock I began to feel very unwell, and though I strove to combat the feeling to such a degree as to walk some distance with the family to church, yet I was obliged to turn back and make the best of my way home. On arriving there I could hold back no longer, but shook till the glasses on the sideboard rattled. The chill continued about two hours after I got home, when the fever set in which lasted nearly the remainder of the day.

January 25, 1864 After an uncomfortable night I awoke this morning feeling wretched, and not withstanding all the kind endeavor of Mrs. E. I got but little relief, till towards nine o'clock at night when after taking several pills, I retired.

January 26, 1864 Feeling much better this morning I attempted to eat some breakfast, but could not succeed. During the morning I walked down the street and the fresh air and bright sun did me much good. On coming home to dinner I found that Mrs. E. had prepared a rich soup wherewith to tempt my appetite. I have no doubt but what it was excellent, but could not eat it. Feeling much better at night, I ate some supper and retired at an early hour.

January 27, 1864 Richard is himself again. During the evening I went to Mr. E.'s place of business and in the afternoon took a long walk with some young ladies. The weather continues most beautiful.

January 28, 1864 This afternoon in company with several ladies, I went about two miles from town to a flower garden, and returned after dark. I found the walk very pleasant but ladies all complained of excessive fatigue. In the evening we had a quiet game of Euchre at home.

January 29, 1864 I have been miserable all day in view of the near approach of my departure. All the folks at home are kind enough to express regret at the shortness of my stay. After supper we all went to the house of a neighbor where we were regaled with some fine music until ten o'clock, when I was compelled to leave to sit up by the bedside of one of our company who is dangerously ill with typhoid pneumonia.

January 30, 1864 At six o'clock this morning I got home and laid down to take, as I thought, an hour's nap, but did not wake up until after ten o'clock. Luckily Mrs. Ege had ordered the servant to put breakfast away for me. This dispatched, I went out to bid some friends good-by, which occupied me until nearly time to take the train for Richmond. I then bade the family at the house good-by, which I hurried as much as possible, not wishing to exhibit my regret at parting too plainly. After a tiresome ride of two hours and a half I arrived in Richmond, and in a short time arrived at my home in good time for supper, and closed the day with a lively game of Euchre.

January 31, 1864 I went to church with the ladies from the house, but this morning, in the afternoon, and at night busied myself by getting my passport and transportation ticket, not being able to get the former until I had procured the latter. This system of compelling furloughed men to get passports is a vexatious one as it involves a great loss of time to those who have but a few days at their disposal. Naturally they wish to make the most of them, and it seems to me that a properly drawn furlough should be sufficient to pass a man anywhere within the limits of that furlough.

February 1, 1864 Wishing to lengthen my engagement as much as possible, I determined last night not to leave till Tuesday morning, though my time is up tonight. The day was spent as the others have been, in pleasant idleness, and closed with a brisk game of Euchre.

February 2, 1864 (Tuesday) At five o'clock I woke up and hurriedly dressing myself, went down to the depot in company with Mr. E., who is one of the guards of the 2nd class. I was well provided by the kindness of Mrs. E. with a snack as she called it, but which I found sufficient for the whole day's consumption. At six the train left, and by two pm I was in camp with nothing but a recollection of the past wherewith to face the future. Though I would not under any consideration have been deprived of it, yet my furlough has done me but little good as the time was so short, and I am constantly reminded of minutes and even hours that I almost threw away, that I might have used much to my enjoyment, but as usual, all such regrets are unavailing.

February 7, 1864 Last night our camp was greatly disturbed by the sudden order to make ready to leave in a moment as the enemy were advancing. We received no further orders till about two o'clock this morning, when we were ordered to hitch up. In about twenty minutes we were ready and the companies ordered off in different directions. We were sent to Cobham Station on the Virginia Central Railroad, only about three miles from here, and halted in a piece of woods while, as there were no infantry about here, some of our young fellows were mounted and sent off as scouts. I do not think this amounts to anything.

February 8, 1864 While waiting this morning until something should turn up, we received orders to return to camp as the enemy had recrossed the Rapidan, being somewhat closely pushed by Lee's boys. Today's papers contain the news of an unsuccessful advance on Richmond by way of the Peninsula. Possibly these movements had the same object in view.

February 10, 1864 Today an interesting affair occurred which as it will afford pleasure to look back to, I shall give in full. At a meeting of the Norfolk Light Artillery Blues, Captain C. R. Grandy commanding, Lt. Col. J. J. Garnett's Battalion of Light Artillery, held in their camp near Lindsay's Station, Albemarle County, Virginia, February 10, 1864, the following preamble and resolutions were unanimously adopted.

Whereas, organizations like ours, enlisted for the war, have expressed this unmitigated determination to uphold our country's cause by unrelinquishing zeal and patriotic devotion, therefore be it

RESOLVED, that we grant such manifestation with the most pleasurable emotions and recognize in them a spirit which we feel proud to emulate.

RESOLVED, that we pledge our sacred honor never to relinquish our arms while an armed foe threatens our constitution and liberty, and until all nations have acknowledged the sovereignty of our states by the recognition of the independence of our beloved confederation.

RESOLVED, that our commanding officer be requested to forward a copy of these resolutions to our esteemed and gentlemanly battalion commander, Lt. Col. J. J. Garnett.

To this immense affair the following was returned.

General Orders
No. 24
In response to the patriotic resolutions adopted by the Norfolk Light Artillery Blues, Company "C", declaring their determination never to relinquish their arms while an armed foe threatens our constitution, our homes, and our liberties, the Lt. Col. commanding deems it his duty to record in General Orders from Battalion Headquarters an action so credible to themselves and the beloved cause they honor in defending. To the Heroic Patriot who, forgetful of self, has only the interest of his country at heart, the need of praise, while impotent to nerve to greater efforts, is none the less done. Friends and relatives at home will at least appreciate the high resolve and noble patriotism you have evinced on this, as on many other occasions, and will treasure up until your return, words and acts of love, enhanced if possible by this crowning act of your loyalty. When peace, lovely in her smiles, shall return to bless the land, how proud will be the reputation of your old battery, and how much sweeter and more proud will be your emotions when another generation will recall to their veteran fathers their valor and endurance, but above all this action, the best calculated to incite them to like deeds of devotion and patriotism. O! That the craven few who linger at home in the engagement of ease and safety would profit by this severe rebuke administered by men whose homes are in the hands of the vile invader, and are now, many of them, rendered desolate by pillage and the torch.

(Signed) Lt. Col. J. J. Garnett

February 23, 1864 Up to today nothing of interest to disturb the monotony of camp life has occurred, but at evening roll call a letter was read to all the companies of this battalion of which the following is a copy:

"To the officers and men of Garnett's Battalion

It is with feeling of no ordinary sorrow and regret that I bid you good-by. After a companionship with you for nearly a year during which time I have been with you in your trials on the march, on the battlefield, and in your camp, I have been proud of the honor of commanding such men, and sharing in their trials and privations. I would do injustice to my own feelings were I to leave you without a parting word—it is to you that I look for a justification of my course, it is to you who have witnessed the interest and untiring zeal in your behalf and in behalf of the cause of our country, to whom I look to vindicate my character as an officer—your interests have been mine; your hardships mine; your dangers mine; if I have failed in any particular to gain for you all the comforts and to place your organization upon an equality with those of the army, it has not been from want of desire, or from want of energy or activity on my part, but from the inability of the government to supply them.

In leaving you I ask you to accept from me as a token of my high regard and esteem the flag which was presented to me last summer. I shall always entertain toward you the liveliest emotions of friendship and regard.

(Signed) Jno. J. Garnett,
Lieut. Col. Commanding"

This separation between ourselves and our Colonel whom we all respect highly and greatly admire is due to the sentences adjudged against Col. Garnett by a Court-Martial before which he lately appeared, on charges made against him by a person of superior rank, but of largely inferior abilities, and who was possibly afraid of Col. Garnett's influence. On the reading of this letter a committee of three from each of the companies were appointed to draft a suitable address in reply. On a meeting of the committees, a general request was made by the others for the one from our company to draw it up, which after some demure was acceded to. The committee appointed from our company was as follows: Sergeant William E. Taylor, Jr., Corporal William D. Montague, and Private John Walters. We went to work immediately and the following crude affair was turned off. All I can say for it is that we might (?) have done better if we had more time, but it was proposed to present it to the colonel at tattoo roll call, which gave us only about an hour to draw it up and copy it.

Beloved and Respected Sir:

It is with feelings of sincere and deep regret that we, the members of Garnett's Battalion, hear of your departure from us, and listen to the reading of your farewell. Your regret at leaving us, however painful, is equaled by our own distress at parting from one on whom we have ever looked with feelings of friendship and perfect satisfaction, and in whom, independent of the man we recognize and acknowledge, the able and kind commander.

Without flattery to ourselves we feel well assured that were your feelings only consulted, you would not be called upon to utter the word farewell, but in our parting we can readily trace the malign influence of those who possibly can trace their feelings to a source of base envy.

With unfeigned pleasure we accept at your hands that noble flag, fully understanding and appreciating the motive that entrusts to our keeping the glorious emblem of our present hour and future freedom and greatness. Our hearts being all fixed on the same purpose and our sympathies being similar, we can truly say that it shall live while we live, and fall only with us, and that whatever our trials or triumphs, the name inscribed upon it shall ever be held in dear remembrance as that of a perfect gentleman and pure patriot, however ruthlessly and maliciously it may have been assailed. Be assured sir, that in the future on many a long march, or by the cheerful light of the campfire, your name will often be mentioned by us and many a kindly wish will be wafted toward you wherever you may be and that your lines may be cast in as pleasant places as we feel that you richly merit.

In conclusion we earnestly and sincerely wish that your separation from us will at least accrue to your own advantage, and that the evil genius which at present seems to preside over your destiny will ere long be ignominiously put to flight by the Angel of Truth, and like the diamond from the hands of the lapidary, your fortune may shine the better and brighter for its past rough treatment.

(Signed) by the committee from all companies.

The flag spoken of is a beautiful one of white satin with the battle flag in the corner, and was made by Col. Garnett's sister or sister-in-law out of a portion of her wedding dress on the field, and the words

Garnett's Battalion

A

Light Artillery

in heavy gilt. Some of the men are sanguine that he will be sent back to us, but I fear not.

> -John Jameson Garnett had joined the Confederate army in 1861, just before he was scheduled to graduate from West Point. He served as a lieutenant with the Washington Artillery, and was promoted to major, chief of D. R. Jones' Division Artillery in June of 1862. He served as the 1st Corps inspector of artillery for a few months before taking command of the artillery battalion of Anderson's Division in February of 1863. At the recommendation of Pendleton, the chief of artillery for the Army of Northern Virginia, Lee suspended Lieutenant Colonel Garnett from duty on February 18, 1864, and he was transferred to Hicksford, Virginia where he was given command of an insignificant post. Walters' belief that Garnett would not return was borne out, as he served for the rest of the war as inspector of artillery for the Army of Tennessee. He died at his own hand at the age of 63 in New York City on September 10, 1902.-

February 29, 1864 Just before dark we received orders to hitch up as the enemy are making another raid, and there is some fear that they may pay the artillery camps a visit. Shortly after we started, it began to rain and continued to do so during the night which made our situation extremely interesting, especially as we have no tents with us. We went as far as Gordonsville by way of Mechanicsville, a distance of about eight miles. We were halted for the night in a field adjoining the government hospital sheds, under which we crawled and went to sleep, and though it was very cold under there, it was at least dry.

March 1, 1864 The rain poured down incessantly all day from which we had no shelter. At eight o'clock pm all the artillery was ordered off in different directions. Our battalion took the road to Liberty Mills on the Rapidan, and arrived and packed about half a mile from that place between twelve and one o'clock at night. The march there was a very severe one, as shortly after dark the rain changed first to snow and then to sleet. The night was an intensely dark one and the mud deep. A short time after we packed the sleet ceased falling and the stars came out, so that by daylight with the aid of good fires, we had our clothes and blankets dried out and all hands went to sleep to make up for lost time.

March 3, 1864 Early this morning we were ordered to hitch up, as it was reported that the enemy intended to attempt to force their way out of our line at this place. We remained in readiness all day and by dark, learned that they were all going by another route. We received news today that Sergeant William E. Taylor of our battery, who was off on furlough, had met with a serious accident on the Virginia Central Railroad near Charlottesville, involving the probable loss of both his limbs. As first rumors are nearly always exaggerated, I trust it is so in this case. Much sympathy is expressed in the company for him.

March 4, 1864 Nothing doing today. We have heard that the enemy had made their way out of our lines, having done but very little damage.

March 5, 1864 Early this morning we received orders to hitch up and return to quarters, where we arrived about four o'clock pm. We learned there that the accident to Sergeant T. is not as severe as first reported. One of his limbs is broken and the other much bruised. His father is with him and he is as comfortable as could be expected.

April 28, 1864 Up to this time but little of interest has occurred, but I make a note of this day as this morning we bade adieu to our winter quarters, or to come down to first principles, that is a camp in the woods with tents for shelter. The campaign will soon open and it is very advisable that the army should leave their winter quarters as the inertia engendered there might prove fatal to us on the battlefield.

A glaring evidence of what some might call insubordination was exhibited this morning. Our Major in command had heard that it was the intention of the men to burn their cabins before leaving, as the person on whose land we were camped had on several occasions acted in a very ungentlemanly manner toward us. To prevent this, he had issued orders that nothing should be destroyed, but early this morning one of the cabins in Company D was discovered on fire and as everything was very dry, the fire spread with the greatest rapidity and soon communicated to the cabins of our company. Here we had a striking evidence of how very active an element fire is, for while some of the men under order from officers would endeavor to extinguish the fire of one cabin, it would soon break out in a fresh place several cabins off, and soon all the intermediate ones would be in a bright blaze and at last, after much useless labor, it was allowed to burn itself out. Our new camp is in a grove of oaks within about two miles of the residence of William C. Rives.

> -The "Major in command" was Major (soon to be Lieutenant Colonel) Charles Richardson, who had begun his career as a second lieutenant in the Virginia Artillery in 1861 in Aquia. He had taken Garnett's place in Battalion A and now commanded its four batteries: the Norfolk Light Artillery Blues (Grandy's Battery or Company C), The Norfolk Light Artillery (Huger's, now Moore's Battery or Company D), the Pittsylvania Battery (Company A) now under Captain Nathan Penick, and the Donaldsonville, Louisiana Battery (Company B) now under Captain R. Prosper Landry. The total strength of the battalion at this time was 14 guns. Richardson's Battalion A was one of five artillery battalions assigned to the 3rd Corps of Lee's Army.-

May 1, 1864 Today we had a very fine sermon preached to us by Brigadier General Pendleton. His appearance was rather unique, as instead of the gown peculiar to Episcopalian ministers, he stood before us in his uniform coat with the three stars of his rank upon the collar, and cavalry boots reaching above the knee.

May 4, 1864 This afternoon (little expecting it) we received orders to send as many guns as we could to the front, and as our battalion had not been fitted up yet, the Huger Battery and ours took all the horses that were fit for service and all the Napoleon guns were ordered off. All that we could fit up was six guns, of which the Huger's had three Napoleons, while we had the remaining two and a ten-pounder Parrott. We marched about seven miles and packed for the night by Gordonsville. During the march about twenty of our boys marched in front of this company, and enlivened the way by whistling, occasionally varying the performance by all striking up some glee chorus or other.

May 5, 1864 We were called up at three o'clock this morning and were on our way by the first tinge of daylight in the east, and halted at five o'clock pm within five miles of Chancellorsville, having made thirty-two miles. The march was a very distressing one as the day was intensely hot and the road dusty, and in some places the road led through the woods which, being on fire, almost suffocated us. On approaching the place where we halted, evidence of battle became apparent in the wounded cavalrymen who were coming to the rear. From them we learned that Rosser with his brigade had been fighting a large cavalry brigade of the enemy all day and held his ground amid heavy loss till some of our infantry came to his relief, when he fell back. During the day Ewell, whose corps holds the left of our line, did some heavy fighting, though his loss was not great owing to the fact that the enemy made the attack. We however lost Brigadier Generals Jones and Stafford and Col. Thompson Brown, Chief of Ewell's Artillery.

A 10-pounder Parrott Rifle displayed at the Chancellorsville battlefield. The reinforced breech makes the Parrott gun one of the easiest to identify.

-On this day, the "Battle of the Wilderness" began. It was fought in much the same area as the Battle of Chancellorsville the year before. During this action, the guns from Richardson's Battalion guarded the roads at Parker's Store on the plank road just behind the main Confederate line. Lee soon found General Ulysses Grant, his new adversary, to be far more tenacious than Joe Hooker had been. Whenever Grant found he could not force his way through the Confederate lines, he moved his army and tried again. Thus the fighting would remain fairly constant for the next few months.-

May 6, 1864 For the fun of the thing, I shall now do what I have never done before, and that is to dot down the rumors from the front as they reach us, and as I shall write the items in pencil and not enter them in this book for two or three days, I shall, on entering them, make such remarks as may apply to each.

Before daylight we were called up and got ready to move to the front when wanted, and in the interval I walked around to get items. The first was, that on yesterday, Ewell on our left had had a very severe engagement with the enemy. They attacked him with seven lines of battle, but they were repulsed with great loss, though his own was very heavy. He captured some say two, some three, and others four thousand prisoners, together with several guns. As near as I can ascertain, he took some fifteen or eighteen hundred men and no guns. Not long after it was reported that Pickett was on his way up with his division via Fredericksburg. Several days after I learned that Pickett had not yet left Petersburg. About an hour after, we were somewhat startled by the news that Beauregard with some twenty thousand men was on his way up from North Carolina. This proved to be true, though he remained with his force around Richmond. On the heels of this came the news that Hampton with his division of cavalry was making the circuit of the Yankee army to destroy a portion of the Orange and Alexandria Railroad in their rear. All these reports admitted of and received much discussion, and it is a great pity that General Lee could not hear and thus profit by the admirable plans of battle which some of our military types drew up under the inspiration of the moment. The next report was that Ewell was moving his lines so as to intercept Hooker from getting to Germanna Ford. This report is decidedly rich when it is recollected that Hooker has a corps in the Western Army that is opposed to Johnston. With this came the stereotyped report that a large body of the enemy were cut off from the army on our right, all of whom would undoubtedly be captured. As this is a usual battlefield report but little faith is attached to it. The next item is a sad one but true for all, that General Jenkins is mortally wounded while charging at the head of his brigade, and Longstreet is shot through the left lung while unnecessarily exposing himself at the head of a brigade. It was reported that he was wounded by our men, but he himself says this was a false report. As a set off to, we heard shortly afterwards that Generals Hays and Wadsworth of the enemy were killed, the former by Ewell's men, and the latter by our corps. Also, that two other brigadier generals and nearly one thousand men were captured by Ewell. These reports proved true. All this time heavy firing has been going on all along the line, but it is nearly all infantry work on both sides, as the immense growth of pine and brush in the Wilderness where the battle is being fought precludes the extensive use of artillery. And now the report comes in of a general driving of the enemy by our army, and much speculation is afloat as to whether Grant will fall back or renew the fight tomorrow. Many incline to the former conjecture. For obvious reasons, I shall not venture here an opinion. That the fighting has been very heavy in our immediate front is attested by the long string of ambulances that are constantly going to the front empty and returning loaded, beside the large number who are going to the rear with bandages on and who being able to walk, are not allowed to ride, owing to the great demand for ambulances. Becoming wearied and the sun not being an hour high, I was on the point of ending my task when news was brought that General Hoke with his old brigade, together with the brigades of Ransom and Clingman, had reached Gordonsville from North Carolina and was on his way to the front. This report was decidedly premature. At sunset our battalion was ordered forward to relieve Poague's. We went and placed our guns in position in the second line with the brigades of Cooke, Kirkland, and Davis, while those immediately in front are held by Mahone, Wright, and Harris (late Posey's) Brigades.

May 7, 1864 The day passed off very quietly. About noon, the enemy tried on center but ran afoul of Harris' Brigade, each man of which had from five to seven loaded muskets lying at hand and they poured in such a heavy and continuous fire that the enemy fell back. In the evening all the artillery in our corps went up and took position in the advance line.

May 8, 1864 Early this morning the pickets reported, "no enemy in our front". Further observation confirmed this report and about three pm we took the road to Spottsylvania Courthouse; the infantry also moving that way. From this I conclude that Grant first thought to overwhelm us by numbers and the bayonet, but finding himself foiled, has sought a more open country where he can use his artillery. But as our army is well supplied with that material, he is apt to again be brought to grief.

May 9, 1864 Early this morning we took the road and in the course of a couple of hours passed through the village of Spottsylvania Courthouse and packed close by, ready to go in position at a moment's notice. We remained here all day and expect to do so tonight. There has been considerable fighting along our whole line today, but with what result I do not know. Our troops are in the best of spirits.

May 10, 1864 Early this morning our six guns and two belonging to the Crenshaw Battery were sent with Heth's Division to the left to prevent a flank movement, said to be made by Hancock's Corps. We marched about seven or eight miles when the infantry were hurried to a double quick while we dashed off at a hard gallop. Soon the divisions were thrown in line of battle and advanced while we went in position in advance of the line and opened on a heavy column of the enemy who were advancing. With the aid of the infantry we soon drove them back and advanced up the road, with Moore's Battery in front. In a short time, our guns and Crenshaw's were halted and Moore's sent forward to act with Heth's skirmishers. They had not been gone many minutes before we heard them open on the enemy. While under cover of his fire the division pushed forward and soon had the enemy on a run, driving them out of three lines of breastworks. Shortly after this Moore fell back, having used up all of his available ammunition and having four men wounded, two slightly, one left arm off, and the fourth's leg was cut off by a shell. (This man died during the evening.) On Moore's falling back, we were ordered up and were soon in to it hot and heavy, and by our own exertions, united with that of the infantry, soon drove the enemy across the Ny River. On the banks, our skirmishers took up a line while the main line fell back out of artillery range. It was not deemed advisable to follow the enemy across owing to the fact of there being no troops at hand to support the division. During the fight the enemy were compelled to abandon one of their guns which fell into the hands of our company. It is a beautiful three-inch U. S. regulation gun. Just before dark Anderson's Division came up, but little more was done today.

The affair of today has been credible in the extreme to our troops as we, with a force of some eight thousand and eight pieces of artillery (the latter not being engaged all at one time), drove back some four or five miles a corps of the enemy numbering from twenty to thirty thousand with at least twelve pieces of artillery. On falling back, the enemy either through accident or design, fired a piece of woods in which a large number of their men lay dead and wounded who were burnt up in consequence, and it was distressing to hear the shrieks and groans of the poor wretches as the fire enveloped them, and we could do nothing for them as the service of our guns demanded all of our energy. When the fighting had in a great measure ceased, some of us went there but it was too late, all had gone to their account, and the odor did not invite to a protracted stay in the vicinity. During the fighting Brigadier General Walker received a severe wound in the foot.

May 11, 1864 Contrary to general expectation the enemy made no demonstration until towards morn when they opened a furious cannonading upon our position with long range guns, but with no effect, to which our officers did not think it worthwhile to reply. After this had continued about two hours they suddenly advanced a line of battle, which was held in check by our sharpshooters long enough to enable the artillery, which was considerably in advance, to fall back to the main line which had been run in a skirt of woods. We took position supported by the brigades of Mahone and Harris and awaited the approach of the enemy, but in vain. Our sharpshooters did a little too much fighting and the enemy did not seem to wish to do more than hold the line that they first took, though it was of no value to either side. Late in the afternoon it began to rain and continued to do so throughout the night. Appearances indicate that the enemy are on our center and a heavy battle must soon be fought.

May 12, 1864 At two o'clock we were called up and moved to the right as the enemy were making a demonstration on the center of our lines, which run along by Spottsylvania Courthouse. After moving about a mile, heavy musketry caused us to hurry back to our old position. We remained here an hour or more when we again moved to the right and took the road to the courthouse, up which we went some three miles when we halted for orders. In about an hour we were sent off to cover a ford of the Po River, at which Wright's Brigade of Anderson's Division were placed to guard against our line being flanked on the left. We soon arrived there and remained all day. The fighting has been the heaviest of the war. During this day from what I can learn, one line formed on an angle at which General Johnston's Division were placed. This was a weak point of which Grant took advantage. As early as three o'clock he threw his troops against it in overwhelming numbers and succeeded in getting possession of the works, capturing Major General Johnston, Brigadier General Steuart, about two thousand men, and some fourteen pieces of artillery. Such of the division as were not taken fell back and formed a new line with our other works, rectifying the error of the Angle. Upon this line the enemy threw column after column in an endeavor to break it, as by so doing they would cut our line in two. The fighting here on both sides was splendid, all in fact that could be expected of the most determined courage. As the enemy came up they were literally mowed by our lines, but their numbers were proving too much for our gallant few. Our line waivers, slowly but surely it is breaking, the enemy rush forward with a shout, but at this critical moment when the fate of the day is so evenly balanced that a hair will turn the scale, Gordon, that paragon of soldiers, comes up at the head of his gallant brigade at a run, throws his men in line of battle so as to allow our shattered line to rally in his rear, which they do, gives the order to charge, and falls upon the front of the enemy like a thunderbolt. Amazed, they hesitate, halt, give way! On presses Gordon, the enemy crowds back in confusion, volley after volley is poured into them, oh! for some artillery! The enemy turn and fly for life, our line is saved, other troops come up to reinforce, and the day is ours, as far as it can be to an army whose entire policy is defensive. At other portions of the line we hold our own without difficulty. The heaviest fighting was done at the Angle and here, while our own loss was heavy, the enemy lost at least four or five to our one. From four o'clock in the morning until about two in the afternoon the roll of musketry was incessant and the heaviest ever heard in our army, while the artillery was not behind time with its thundering. After two o'clock it slackened off but did not cease till long in the night. During the day Brigadier Generals Perrin of South Carolina and Dales of Georgia were killed, and Brigadier General Gordon was promoted to Major General for his gallant charge. Heavy rain all day.

May 13, 1864 We remained in position until about midday when we moved up a by-road and packed our pieces in a piece of woods, the enemy having fallen back a short distance from our front. It rained heavily all day. Late in the evening a report reached us of the death of General J. E. B. Stuart, in a charge on the Virginia Central Railroad.

May 14, 1864 About ten o'clock am, in the middle of heavy rain, we were ordered off and in an hour, after passing through Spottsylvania Courthouse, we took position in the line of battle formed here, immediately supported by the Alabama Brigade of Anderson's Division, of which Colonel Sanders is in command. Shortly after we got there quick volleys of musketry in our front were heard. It proceeded from Wright's Brigade who made a sudden charge on a portion of the enemy's line for the purpose of feeling his strength. The affair was very short but brilliant. It occupied but a few minutes. Our loss was only ten or twelve, while we took eighty or ninety prisoners and two stands of colors, besides killing or wounding some twenty odd of them. At dark all received orders to lie down in their places and the whole line to be awakened at three in the morning as it is thought very probable that Grant may make a night or early morning attack. Sunset clear.

May 15, 1864 This pleasing anticipation of fair weather in which I indulged, predicated upon a clear setting of the sun last evening, was not realized, for about midnight the clouds began again to gather and today it has been raining at intervals the whole time. No attack was made today, nor can I hear of any fighting being done on any part of the line. Today a congratulatory order from General Lee was read to the troops regarding the successes of Kirby, Smith, and Price in the Trans-Mississippi Department, and Imboden, James, and Morgan in the Valley.

May 16, 1864 During last night the weather cleared off and it has been fine and warm all day. About four o'clock pm, a brisk cannon-ading took place which lasted about two hours with no apparent results. Heavy musketry was also heard on our left; said to be a flank movement of Ewell's to feel the enemy's force. Later reports confirm this, and state that he destroyed about one hundred of the enemy's wagons and then fell back to his original line; the enemy appeared to be in heavy force in his front. Another order from General Lee was read to the army regarding the victory of Breckenridge over Sigel in the Valley. It is more than probable that Breckenridge will now be ordered down to us, though I fear it will be found a bad policy to take our troops from the Valley, as it is more than likely that the remains of Sigel's command will be given to some other general, who receiving new troops or forming a junction with the troops in the Kanawhas Valley under Averell, will overrun Staunton, destroy Lexington, capture Lynchburg, destroy the Central Rail-road, and coming down perhaps destroy our noble old University at Charlottesville, and being unobstructed, possibly may come down to reinforce the already large army of Grant, but pshaw! What have I to do with all of this? If Uncle Bob orders Breckenridge down it must be all O.K.

May 17, 1864 But little was done on our part of the line today, though there was a brisk exchange of compliments on the left. About four pm the enemy made a dash upon the line of sharpshooters in our front and the artillery opened, but the enemy were driven back and the artillery, after amusing themselves for about two hours, ceased firing. It is a standing order now for half of the men to be up and ready all night.

May 18, 1864 At early daylight the artillery on both sides opened on each other, and for a couple of hours the fire was very hot. It then slackened off for a short time, but they soon got into it again for about an hour longer. Then our artillery was ordered to cease and the enemy soon after followed suit. At one time infantry were engaged on our left but I cannot learn the result. The remainder of the day passed off very quietly. Late in the evening we were cheered by the intelligence that Grant intends to make a good charge along our line tomorrow, and active measures are being taken to give him a proper reception. During the shelling, as my gun was not engaged this morning, I amused myself by a lively game of Euchre.

May 19, 1864 There was nothing done on our part of the line today. Late this afternoon heavy firing was heard on our left. We heard later in the day that Ewell had made another attack upon the enemy's flank, but with what result is not yet known.

May 20, 1864 Nothing done today beyond brisk sharpshooting along the whole line. We can get no reliable information as to Ewell's operation on yesterday. One thing is certain, which is that he again occupies his original line.

May 21, 1864 Everything was very quiet this morning, but about four o'clock pm, Wilcox's Division moved to our front to feel for the enemy, as it was reported by scouts that they were sliding off to our right. About two minutes after clearing our breastworks his skirmishers became engaged with those of the enemy. Wilcox immediately advanced his line of battle and drove them through their first and second line of entrenchments, when having learned what he wished (which was that he was engaging only the enemy's rear guard), he fell back to our lines. Soon after our lines began to show signs of moving. Some artillery, our battalion among it, was ordered off; where to we do not know, but I think it very probable that the section around Hanover Junction will bring us up. We have had considerable rain during the day and the prospect for an all night rain is decidedly brilliant. For the last few days I have been very unwell owing to a severe bilious attack, and can get no medicine to relieve me.

May 22, 1864 We marched till two o'clock this morning and halted until five when we moved off again, and about twelve o'clock we packed ten miles from Hanover Junction, after crossing the North Anna River.

May 23, 1864 If Grant gains the battle it will be for want of strategy perpetrated by our battalion. Last night, we were called up in the greatest haste at twelve o'clock, hitched up, moved off four miles, and then packed again until eight o'clock am, when we once more moved off to within three miles of the junction, where we packed for the remainder of the day. Later in the afternoon, heavy cannonading was heard on our right and front, not far off. We later learned that it was Pegram's and Poague's Battalions who had engaged and driven the enemy back. At ten o'clock pm, our battalion moved to the front, took position, and in about an hour the whole line fell back to Anderson's Station on the Central Railroad. During the day several trains passed us with portions of General Breckenridge's command. Among the rest were the cadets from Lexington who, though very young, are a fine looking body, numbering some two hundred and fifty. I understand that they are to be sent to Richmond as a prison guard.

May 24, 1864 Early this morning we went back about a mile where we found our fresh line of battle, in which we were placed in position. My gun was in the 6th Virginia Regiment. The rest of our battery was in Harris's Brigade on our left. About four pm the enemy advanced against our sharpshooters, who held them back an hour or more, when fearing a flank movement, they fell back. A regiment on our left was thrown forward as support, and they held their own well. Soon the artillery opened and work became brisk; the enemy enfilading our line with his artillery. In about an hour two regiments of Harris's Brigade moved to the front, charged the enemy, drove them to the North Anna River, captured a stand of colors and about one hundred prisoners. During the afternoon a heavy shower of rain fell, which continued well into the night.

May 25, 1864 The morning passed off very quietly, but this afternoon, while indulging in the luxury of a cup of coffee with I. G. B. in the line of the 41st Virginia Regiment, the enemy opened a brisk artillery fire on our line. We did not reply to this as our doing so might have proved dangerous to our line of sharpshooters, who were about a mile in advance of our line. The enemy continued their fire about two hours, doing no damage. Skirmishing has been very heavy in our front all day and it has been raining in torrents nearly all day.

May 26, 1864 Skirmishing in our front was brisk all day. Several times the artillery opened on us without doing any damage, to which we did not reply. About ten o'clock at night, heavy infantry firing was heard on our right for about half an hour, then it ceased. Probably one side or the other attempted to advance their skirmish line. We also heard considerable artillery firing in the rear of the Yankee line, supposed to be our cavalry. More rain during the day.

May 27, 1864 At an early hour today it was ascertained that Grant had left our front during the night, moving to our right, which confirms us in the pre-supposition that the Peninsula or the south side of the James will be the final field of this singular battle. Twenty or thirty prisoners were brought in, some of whom report that Grant has taken sick and gone to Washington, leaving Meade in command. No dependence is placed on this report, but if it is so, I shall begin to think that he has been greatly overrated, and has not the moral courage to do what a really great mind should do under the circumstances, which is that when at last becoming convinced that but one more chance was left him, to put himself at the head of his column, and in a desperate effort to regain his laurels, pluck victory from Lee's grasp or be mourned by the North as one who whatever his mistakes did nobly at the head of his column; but pshaw, I am writing as if the wretch was possessed of chivalric feelings. About ten o'clock am we took up our line of march towards Ashland. The march is a very fatiguing one owing to the fact of our being in the rear of seven or eight miles of wagon trains. Night finds us still on the road, having made but eight miles.

May 28, 1864 At two o'clock this morning we went into pack, very tired and very hungry, and received orders to be ready to move at five. We were ready at that time, but owing to the passage of infantry and wagons, we did not start till dawn, and after many halts on the road, packed about dark two miles from Mechanicsville on the road of that name. During the day our cavalry had a heavy fight with the enemy a short distance from here and would have used them badly, but that the enemy brought up a column of infantry, before which our cavalry was forced to fall back with considerable loss.

This morning, General Finegan came up with ten or twelve hundred Floridians and more are looked for in a day or two. They will be attached to Anderson's Division. The remnants of Perry's Brigade will be incorporated with them, and thus we will once more have a good sized Florida Brigade in our army, and better fighting men never stepped.

May 29, 1864 We remained quiet all day and for the first time in ten days got enough to eat, as our wagons came up to our park and in them we found some clay peas and shad, enough of both for a good, full meal. At sunset we took the road and marched about four miles when we packed for the night. We expect to take position early in the morning as we are near our line of battle.

May 30, 1864 At three o'clock am we were called up and as soon as we could get ready were moved forward and took position in our line of battle. Two of our pieces are supported by Wright's Brigade, the other two by Davis's, while the other pieces of our battalion are distributed along the line to our left. After dark the enemy shelled a portion of our lines well on our right with mortar. This is a new and rather novel feature in field fighting.

> -Walters was serving on the crew of one of the Blues' two Napoleons. Their other two guns were a ten-pounder Parrott and the 3-inch rifle captured on May 10. Being shelled by mortar would soon become a routine part of Walters' life.-

June 1, 1864 During this morning heavy artillery and infantry firing was heard on our right and in the course of the day, some of our cavalry got in somewhat of a box on our extreme left. They were however, enabled to withdraw without serious loss. On our portion of the line everything was quiet. I was not able to learn what was done on the right today.

June 2, 1864 Early this morning it was discovered that the enemy had again left our front without offering battle. Shortly after we all moved to the right to within a mile of Gaines Mill, the scene of a former conflict. During the latter part of the day, a sharp fight took part on a portion of our line not far from where we packed. This was continued till some time after dark. Everything promises fair for a battle tomorrow.

June 3, 1864 Considerable rain fell during last night and this morning, but about midday the weather cleared off. As I anticipated last night, heavy fighting commenced at early daylight by an attack on Hoke's Division. This was repulsed, as also were five other charges. The fighting then worked its way to Longstreet's Corps, where every charge of the enemy was repulsed. The whole of it resulted with but trivial loss on our side, as our men fought behind breastworks which they threw up last night. The enemy lost heavily; their dead, towards the last of the battle, lay three and four deep in some places. This certainly shows desperate fighting, but it must not be taken as an evidence of superior courage, as the men were more than half drunk. In one instance, they approached to within fifty yards of our line and when they received a volley from our line they stopped, and without firing or even attempting to do so, shouted out, "Show the d——d rebels no quarter!" Of course they were mowed down as with a scythe. A few prisoners were taken who expressed entire confidence in Grant's final success.

About twelve o'clock meridian, the heavy fighting ceased, though skirmishing continued briskly throughout the day, frequently participated in by the artillery of both sides. In the afternoon, all the Napoleons of our battalion were put in position about two miles to the left of the new bridge over the Chickahominy. Just before dark the enemy made a break on our portion of the line but were driven back. They came up again shortly after, and were again driven back when our troops made a charge which drove them from their line of rifle pits and advanced our whole line to that point. It has been estimated by several officers that the enemy's loss will amount to not less than twenty thousand in killed, wounded, and prisoners, while our loss is not more than two or three thousand. But from what I have heard from different sources, I do not think that the enemy have lost more than ten or twelve thousand. I understand that Kershaw's (late McCaw's) Division sustained twelve charges.

A Napoleon gun and limber on display in Richmond, Virginia. This type was considered by both sides to be the workhorse of the artillery.

June 4, 1864 As far as I can ascertain, but little beyond sharp-shooting was done today. About ten am the enemy gathered in our front as if for a charge. Immediately the artillery on our right, left, and our own opened such a tornado of shell in their midst that they sought cover in a hurry. Just after dark the enemy attempted a charge on our part of the line, but we soon got them out of the notion. Quite a number of Yankee dead are lying in front of our works, the result of a part of yesterday's fighting. Some are lying but a few feet from the breastworks.

June 5, 1864 Considerable sharpshooting was done today and several of the infantry who are supporting us were killed or wounded. Just after dark the enemy again made a feeble charge on our line of skirmishers in our front, and soon the artillery took a hand in and continued to play it about three quarters of an hour, when both sides threw up the game.

June 7, 1864 Ever since our guns have been in position at this place we have been greatly annoyed by the enemy's sharpshooters, who have kept a perfect shower of bullets flying over and around us, but without doing us any damage until this morning, when one of the young fellows at my gun, Ignatius Higgins, was struck in the left shoulder. The ball shattered the cap bone and going downward, it is said by our surgeon to be in or have passed through the left lung. As the ball cannot be found, it is feared that the wound is a mortal one. Sharpshooting was continued throughout the day, but by about six o'clock pm, white flags met between the lines to enable the enemy to bury their dead, who had become very offensive. At eight o'clock the flag returned to the line and though we anticipated an attack, none came.

June 8, 1864 Sharpshooting was very briskly kept up all day. The enemy showed a disposition to advance on our works by trenches, on which our artillery opened and kept up a slow fire all day without reply, till about sundown when shelling took place on both sides which lasted about an hour.

June 9, 1864 The usual sharpshooting was varied this afternoon by the enemy throwing six or eight mortar shells in uncomfortable proximity to our position, but no one was hurt. These missiles are very demoralizing as we have no mortars at hand to reply with. Artillery is but of little or no use, and we can construct no protection against them.

June 10, 1864 Nothing beyond sharpshooting was done today. I should not be surprised to wake up some morning soon and find the enemy has again left our front, as I do not think that Grant will again try this line. Should he leave here, he will most probably try the south side of the James, and by attempting to capture Petersburg will cut off our communication by the Weldon and the Southside Railroads. We received the news today that Higgins has been attacked with pneumonia. This in connection with his wound will, I fear, prove too much for him, though he has a most powerful constitution.

June 11, 1864 As on yesterday, nothing but sharpshooting was the order of the day. After dark, on our left, some of our troops opened twenty-four pounder Howitzers on the enemy as mortars by sinking the trail of the guns. What damage was done we could not find out.

June 13, 1864 At daylight we discovered that during the night the enemy had abandoned. In a short time we received orders to move, which we did, and after a long march and many halts, packed at two o'clock on the morning of the 14th, about two miles from Malvern Hill.

June 14, 1864 We remained in pack all day and the relief which we experienced in being able to walk around without being shot at is the most grateful feeling imaginable. A sad affair occurred in Colonel Cutt's Battalion this afternoon. Two men got to quarreling and from that to blows, and in the end one was stabbed by the other in the back and breast. The wound in the back is slight, but the other one was in the left breast in dangerous proximity of the heart, and is supposed to be mortal.

June 15, 1864 We were called up at two o'clock and in the course of a few hours packed about four miles from Richmond on the Darbytown Road.

June 16, 1864 The greater portion of this day was devoted to sleep by our boys to make up for lost time.

June 17, 1864 As on yesterday nothing was done, though about dark it was reported that we are to move early tomorrow morning.

June 18, 1864 At three o'clock AM our bugle sounded the "Reveille" and soon after we moved off, taking the road to Drewry's Bluff. About nine we reached the pontoon bridge, which we crossed, and near sundown packed on Dunn's Hill, opposite Petersburg, having made about twenty-five miles. Soon after packing I ran the blockade to town and was received by Mr. Ege and his family with their usual kindness. I remained there until about eleven o'clock, and not knowing but what we might be ordered into position, returned to the company. The arrival of General Lee with his army has relieved the citizens greatly, as Beauregard has but a very thin line of troops around the city, and they feared that the city would fall into the hands of "Beast Butler" and his Negro troops, a fate from which our arrival will save them.

> - General Benjamin "the Beast" Butler was a well known figure to the Norfolk soldiers. He had commanded not only Fort Monroe, but also the district of Norfolk for a time during its military occupation, and did his best to make life miserable for the Southern sympathizers of the city. He now commanded the Federal forces advancing on Petersburg from Bermuda Hundred, but his troops were kept bottled up and away from the city by a well placed Confederate force. Lee's army arrived and took positions around Petersburg before Grant could bring the main portion of his army into the fight, and thus the long Siege of Petersburg began.-

June 19, 1864 We remained packed all day and though I went in town last night under the friendly cover of darkness, I did not think that I could face daylight as my clothes are rather dilapidated, and owing to the scarcity of soap, not as clean as I could wish them. At sunset we were ordered to hitch up and move into position, which we did, passing through the city on our way. Our position is in a salient which the line makes on the farm of Timothy Rives, Esq. about two miles from the city. Our position is a horrid one owing to the incessant shower of bullets that the enemy are constantly sending over, and to which the night gives us but little sleep. In this respect it is worse than Gaines Mill where night at least usually put a stop to the sharpshooting. As soon as we placed our guns in position for immediate use if necessary, we went at the usual business of digging, at which I expect to spend the night.

-The Rives Salient (sometimes spelled Reeves) lay across the Jerusalem Plank Road, one of the main entrances to the city. It marked the point at which Batteries 26 and 27 of the original "Dimmock" defense line around Petersburg connected with the new line of defenses built after the Union attack from the east. The Blues would find their stay at the Rives Salient to be a long one.-

A commemorative marker at the site of a battle on the Jerusalem Plank Road near Petersburg. It reads, "This stone marks the spot where the old men and boys of Petersburg under Gen. R. E. Colston and Col. F. H. Archer, 125 strong, on June 9th, 1864 distinguished themselves in a fight with 1300 Federal cavalry under Gen. Kautz, gaining time for the defeat of the expedition. Placed by the Petersburg Chapter UDC May 1909." After this battle, the area became part of the Rives Salient of Petersburg's defense line.

CHAPTER FOUR

The Siege of Petersburg

June 20, 1864 At daybreak we were obliged to discontinue our work as the sharpshooters made it too hot for us to expose ourselves. At about eleven o'clock young Lee, one of our members, was struck in the head by a bullet. The wound is not of necessity dangerous. About ten minutes after, C. T. Joynes, another of our boys, was shot in the knee while lying under a tree close to the breastworks, inflicting a painful, though not dangerous wound. About six o'clock pm an artillery duel was opened between our line and the enemy. It was kept up for about an hour and was very heavy, the enemy having at least two guns to our one. Our second Napoleon, which is about ten yards to our left, was disabled towards the close of the engagement by being struck in the muzzle, and several of the men were slightly wounded. As soon as it was dark, spades were again trumps.

June 21, 1864 Sharpshooting was very heavy today. Heavy cannonading was heard both on our right and left, but I cannot learn what it is about.

June 22, 1864 Nothing was done till about three o'clock this afternoon, when Mahone with three of his brigades flanked the enemy on our right and in a short time succeeded in capturing fifteen or eighteen hundred prisoners, four guns, and five or six stands of colors. He came upon them so suddenly that they could make no resistance, which is proven by the fact that he lost but two men, one killed and one wounded. He also held the portion of the line from which he made the capture, which the enemy attempted to regain during the early part of the night. They were repulsed three times, losing heavily. After this our brigade fell back to their original line. Mahone deserves, and will undoubtedly receive, great credit for this affair, as it was executed with much of the dash for which Stonewall Jackson was so greatly celebrated.

June 23, 1864 Having received permission to do so, I went to town early this morning and returned to my gun about ten o'clock at night. My friends, Ege and his family, are considerably exercised as to the propriety of leaving town, in view of the danger to which they are exposed in consequence of the daily shelling to which the city is exposed. As their house has a finished basement four feet below the line of the street, I advised them to remain.

June 24, 1864 Late last night we received orders to be ready to open fire on the enemy at three o'clock this morning, to cover a flank movement which was intended to be made on our right and left, but though ready at three, we did not receive the signal till about seven o'clock when the whole line opened up. For about two hours and a half we had a hot time of it. After that, it slackened off and then ceased altogether, and then we learned of our casualties which were: killed, A. M. Watters (a shell struck him on the left shoulder and came out under the right arm, his death was instantaneous), wounded, J. B. Roberts (severe wound in the heel, he is probably crippled for life as the leader is entirely severed, he also received several slighter wounds), J. Rainier, wounded in the head (not severe), and Smiley and Saunders severely burnt in the face. The four lost were all wounded by the explosion of one of the enemy's shell in their breastwork, which before exploding struck the muzzle of their gun, disabling it for the time. After dark it was sent to the rear for repair and our other Napoleon, which is again fit for service, was put in the place of it.

June 25, 1864 Nothing was done today beyond a brisk sharpshooting. After dark the enemy made a feeble attempt on our line but fell back in a short time without accomplishing anything. The city was heavily shelled during the day and great damage done, though no lives were lost.

June 26, 1864 Today passed off very quietly, there being but little sharpshooting done. The city was again shelled today and several people killed, though singularly enough they were all colored people.

June 27, 1864 We have had a very pleasant day of it, as the sharpshooters on both sides have entered into an agreement to cease firing at each other. This is a most excellent arrangement and relieves our men very much. This afternoon we had a delightful shower of rain, but it lasted so short a time that the crops will derive but little benefit from it.

June 28, 1864 It again being my turn, I went to town and spent a very pleasant day. On going in I was the bearer of an obituary on young Watters, which had been written by one of our members for publication. By request of the author, I revised and made some additions to it, but it is rather a lame affair at best.

> To our late Comrade, A. M. W.
>
> Farewell dear comrade, sweetly rest,
> Where angel voices greet thee,
> In the happy land of spirits blest,
> Where thy comrades hope to greet thee.
>
> Falling in the spring of life
> In youth's bright, joyous bloom,
> Nobly serving in the strife,
> Which brought thy early doom.
>
> We'll hear no more that tuneful voice,
> In our evening's pleasant song,
> No more in our country's weal rejoice,
> Nor struggle against her wrongs.
>
> Though young in years thy heart ne'er knew,
> The pang of craven fear,
> Alas! That thus our brave and true,
> Should fill a soldier's bier.
>
> Flowers sweet the coming year
> Will gather round thy tomb,
> Watered by the comrade's tear
> An offering pure shall bloom.

June 29, 1864 Everything was very quiet all day. At night, two detachments of Company "B" of our battalion came to relieve our boys, but as they did not bring their guns with them, our boys refused to give their guns up to them, so Company "B" returned to their guns, not at all dissatisfied with the stand taken by our company. The weather has been remarkably pleasant all day.

June 30, 1864 The day passed off very quietly and the weather was cool and pleasant.

July 1, 1864 One of the enemy's sharpshooters on our left annoyed us very much by his practice at our heads. Towards sunset Hood's old Texans returned his fire by volleys of five or six, and every time they did so would shout to him, asking if that would satisfy him. After a while he ceased, whether wounded or not I cannot say. During the day the city underwent a severe shelling which is being continued at intervals of fifteen minutes during the early part of the night.

July 2, 1864 No a single word was heard from the fellow on our left who disturbed our quiet of yesterday. Probably he got enough of it last evening. Early this morning my friend E. sent for me to come and help him pitch some tents, as he was going to leave town with his family; they having been demoralized in consequence of the constant shelling to which the city was subjected. On asking permission of our captain, after stating the circumstances, I was refused, an act which I shall be at some pains to remember, as the service of my gun would in no way have been impaired by my absence. It is not the first time that simple requests have been refused to me, while similar ones have been granted to others. Tomorrow is my regular turn to go, when possibly I may be able to make up for not going today. As it is, I shall anticipate the morning by going tonight.

July 3, 1864 I got in town after dark last night and on going to Mr. E.s house found that the family had gone, but I found friend Tom there with whom I spent the night. Early this morning I went over the river and, with a little search, found my friends camped out in tents on the lot of a Mr. Davis. They were in company with the families of Messrs. Booth and Pucie. I remained with them all day, repitching their tents and making them comfortable against rain or shine. On returning to camp, I found that orders had been received along the line for great vigilance to be observed, as a charge is anticipated. I trust this may be so, as I am becoming very tired of doing nothing.

July 4, 1864 (Monday) Fourth of July has come and gone, and still is that halo of glory, which the Yankee nation fondly thought would encircle the brow of "Unconditional Surrender Grant" as the crusher of this "rebellion", held back by the potent hand of Lee, backed as it is by the smile of Providence and his army of "Ragged Rebels". Two months of alternate fighting and maneuvering with the loss of eighty or ninety thousand men has been insufficient to demonstrate to that deluded people that Richmond with Lee and Vicksburg with Pemberton are terms not at all synonymous. "Whom the gods destroy, they first make mad".

It was a general expectation both with the army and with the people that in consideration of the day a general opening of artillery on our lines would take place, even if we were not charged at one point or another (which later was not considered improbable). But as far as

I could learn or my observation extended, the day passed off remarkably quiet, in fact more so than usual. To what to attribute this I cannot imagine, unless Grant intends to let this campaign drag its weary length along until after the meeting of the Democratic Presidential Convention, which is to meet on the 29th of August. But if this should be his intention, I think that General Lee will ask him out of it, as we are looking daily for news that Johnson has defeated Sherman, in which case we will undoubtedly receive sufficient reinforcements from him to assume the offensive and then, alas poor Grant! Farewell, a long farewell, to all thy glory.

An amusing incident occurred on our portion of the line which is well worth recording. About sunset, several Yankee bands were playing up their line. Among other patriotic airs, one band struck up "Yankee Doodle", and on its conclusion a large number of their men started to give three cheers, but the first cheer had hardly cleared their lips when our line set up a yell of derision that effectually drowned out all the cheering of the Yankees, and though one or two of their bands afterwards played the same air, no cheers followed it.

July 5, 1864 The day passed off very quietly with us, though the enemy still continue to shell the city. For some days past, rumors of a rather startling character have been circulating among our troops regarding the movements of General Early, who has command of Ewell's Corps, and today the rumor reached us that he had captured Harper's Ferry. What credit to attach to the rumor I do not know. All that is known is that about the tenth or the fifteenth of last month Early and Breckenridge left us, taking their commands with them. Of course, nothing was known regarding their destination, though it was conjectured that Breckenridge had gone to the valley to look after General Hunter who, having succeeded Sigel, and being reinforced by Averell and others, was playing wild pranks in the valley; capturing Staunton, destroying the Institute buildings at Lexington, threatening Lynchburg, and thus making his way down the Central Railroad, possibly with the intention of forming a junction with Grant. For some time nothing was heard from these corps until the papers contained the news of the defeat of Hunter near Lynchburg, his hurried retreat, his almost rout up the valley, and the necessity he was under of destroying his trains to expedite his movements. But what troops were engaged on our side was not known. After this followed rumors of the capture of Martinsburg and large quantities of stores of all kinds, and the crossing of the Potomac by a large Confederate force, while another force captured Harper's Ferry. From all this, I am led to the conclusion that both Early and Breckenridge are together, and that after defeating Hunter and uniting to their force all the valley troops (consisting of the cavalry of the late General James under Ransom, the Buttermilk Rangers of Imboden, and the partisan rangers of Mosby and Harry Gilmore), they crossed into the enemy's country for the purpose of foraging for the army, or possibly with the intention of threatening Baltimore and Washington and by this means relieving the pressure on our lines by compelling Grant to withdraw a portion of his force from our front to protect his own capital, but all this is for future consideration.

July 6, 1864 The enemy, during the night, have thrown up a heavy earthwork directly in front of our guns and distant only about six hundred yards, but whether it is for infantry or artillery cannot yet be determined. It is probably for the latter, and as a set-off for some works which we have thrown up about two hundred yards in the rear of our line and where we have seven or eight Napoleons in position.

July 7, 1864 At daylight this morning it was discovered that the enemy was endeavoring to advance a portion of their line by throwing up an earthwork a short distance to the left of us. Our artillery opened a slow fire on them which, though it was returned at the rate of three shots to our one, put an end to their digging for the day. I think we threw our ammunition away to little purpose, as they will finish their work under cover of the night in spite of us. Had sharpshooting not been discontinued, I do not think the enemy would have advanced their work, exposed as they would have been.

July 8, 1864 At three o'clock this afternoon all the artillery received orders to open on the enemy at five o'clock, and to fire three rounds from each gun for the purpose, I suppose, of feeling for the enemy's artillery. At the appointed time we opened and received a very hot fire in return. On the left of the line near the river we heard heavy musketry, which I learned afterwards was caused by a charge made by the enemy on our line, from which they were repulsed without much loss on either side. After the firing ceased I went to town on a twenty-four hour permit, and on reaching there found that the city was on fire in three places in the vicinity, and also on Sycamore Street. These were caused by the incendiary shell that the enemy were throwing, and as the smoke of these fires rose in the air they presented an excellent mark for the enemy, and they were not slow to avail themselves of it. But though the shell fell thick and fast, I did not hear of anyone being hurt, and after several hours of exertions the fire brigade succeeded in mastering the fire at all points. I went to all the fires and must say that the men worked with a disregard for danger but seldom seen in those who, in many cases, seek these positions for the sake of keeping out of the service.

July 9, 1864 To those who have seen Petersburg when her business places re-echoed with the hum and din of commerce, and her streets were bright with the smiles of her lovely ladies, the appearance presented now is sad in the extreme. In the lower portion of the city not a body is to be seen in the streets, stores and places of business are all closed, and it needs but the hollow rumbling of the awful death cart and the citizens seen hurrying along with handkerchiefs to their face to imagine oneself in one of those plague stricken cities of the Southern latitudes, where Death holds such high command. While viewing the scene, the unchristian hope will rise that, should our armies succeed in capturing any of the Northern cities, a full retribution may be meted out to them, for only by that means can they be taught the horrors through which this glorious old Commonwealth is struggling to her freedom. In the afternoon I paid my usual visit to my friends over the river, and at night returned to my gun.

July 10, 1864 At early daylight our pickets, who had formed the foolish idea that during the night the enemy had left our front, advanced, but soon found out that they were mistaken by coming on the enemy's picket line. They however continued advance until they had driven the enemy back to their main line, when they fell back to their old position.

During the day we received the sad news of the loss of the *"Alabama"*, but Semmes is one of the inexpressible men impossible to whip, and I should not be surprised if in less than three months he was out in a larger and better vessel.

July 11, 1864 The day passed off very quietly. Late in the afternoon we had a slight shower of rain and the clouds bid fair to give us more during the night. Rain is much needed in this section and though in wet weather I am always miserable, yet when I look at the corn and sugar cane fields I am tempted to pray for copious showers.

July 12, 1864 The rain fell but lightly during the night and the sun rose this morning in unclouded splendor. The weather was intensely hot but towards sunset the clouds gathered as if for rain, but in this we were disappointed as the moon, on rising, dispelled all the clouds. After dark the enemy opened on our line with mortars, and though our boys are mortally opposed to work, they yet are quite willing to build a bombproof. In a day or two they will have become accustomed to these visitants and then, with the usual recklessness of youth, they will not care to provide against the evil day.

July 13, 1864 We worked all last night under a heavy mortar shelling. Fortunately none were struck. About daylight the enemy ceased shelling, which enabled us to work with much greater comfort, so that by night we were well advanced with our work. Our work is very fatiguing as the clay is almost hard as a brick, and the weather intensely hot and no air stirring.

July 14, 1864 We again worked all last night and today, and by evening placed the logs on which are to form the roof. It is expected that we will finish the job by daylight tomorrow, as all that it now requires is to throw earth on the logs to the depth of three and a half or four feet. As tomorrow is my turn for a trip to the city, I anticipated it by going this evening and spending the night with friend West.

July 15, 1864 During the morning several shells were thrown into the city, one or two of which fell on Old Street, near the house of my friend Mr. Ege, though they did but little damage. In the afternoon I went over the river to the family camp and spent a few hours very pleasantly, as usual. In the evening I was regaled with a fine dish of ice cream, a delicacy that I have not tasted since I left Norfolk.

July 16, 1864 This morning we had an assembly of rare military talent in the persons of Generals Lee, A. P. Hill, Anderson, Fields, M. L. Smith, Heth, and Mahone just in the rear of my gun, and who were viewing the operations of the enemy and discussing their movements. I felt uncomfortable the whole time they were there, fearing that the enemy might discover the group and throw a shell into it, but this did not occur. The day passed off very quietly. The enemy are as busy as beavers in strengthening their works, though we send a few shell among them occasionally to disturb the monotony of the day.

July 17, 1864 Several men belonging to the 64th Georgia Regiment, Wright's Brigade, who were on picket in our front, deserted to the enemy during the night. This is getting to be somewhat of a common practice with this regiment, who are mostly of the new issue and have but lately joined the brigade. During the day it was rumored that Field's Division, which occupies the line on our immediate left, has orders to charge the enemy in their front at three o'clock tomorrow morning. Should this rumor prove true, I feel satisfied that they will take the enemy's works as it is one of the best divisions in our army, containing among others, Hood's old Texas Brigade. But in taking it they will loose heavily, as the works are strong.

July 18, 1864 At last after a most protracted drought, a most delightful rain has been falling, to the relief of vegetation and the strengthening of our works. It began about daylight and is still raining though already six o'clock pm. The clouds are somewhat lighter so that it may not hold out much longer, but we have already had enough to be very thankful for. At early daylight we saw that the enemy had been crowding their works on our left with men during the night, and learned subsequently that four men of Field's Division had deserted to the enemy, in consequence of which it would have been a difficult thing (if not impossible) to take their lines. Nothing occurred during the day.

July 19, 1864 But little rain fell during last night and none today, though it did not clear off until near sunset, when blue sky appeared. Nothing in the way of fighting was done that I could see or hear of.

July 20, 1864 Nothing was done on the lines til this afternoon when the enemy opened a brisk artillery fire on our position, during which they wounded two or three of the infantry who hold our line. Our artillery opened in reply and shortly after, both sides ceased. This afternoon I went to town on a forty-eight hour permit, and in the evening went over to "Camp Davis" where I found my friends all well. I had partly determined to go over to Richmond tomorrow evening, but found on arriving at Camp Davis that Mr. E. had gone there a short time before I arrived, and as I expected to get a passport through him, I shall be obliged to go some other time.

July 21, 1864 Today we received news of the death of young Higgins who was wounded on the 7th of last month. This evening, Mr. E. returned from Richmond bringing Miss Eddy with him. She seems to be enjoyed at being with her family again, even though her being so compels her to taste the disagreeable realities of a camp life.

July 22, 1864 As this book is nearly full, I employed myself today in making one to replace it, and found that I am growing very rusty in my business. I spent the afternoon at Camp Davis and returned to my gun at night.

July 23, 1864 A great excitement was created by the issue of a newspaper "extra" announcing a great Confederate victory at Atlanta in which it is said we captured many thousand prisoners, a great many pieces of artillery, twenty or thirty stands of colors, and killed, among others, General McPherson. Even if all this is true, the latter event is worth all the rest for McPherson is, or was, without exception the most able general the North has, or had, though it has always been his misfortune to be subordinate to some favorite of Lincoln's of inferior talents and abilities. And not content with all this, the papers say that Hardee with his corps is on the enemy's rear while Hood is pressing on his front. Now all this is splendid news, if true, but I always wait for the news of the second or third day when I hear of Georgia victories, as the incorrectness of the first dispatches from there has almost passed into a proverb with our army.

July 24, 1864 Between midnight and two o'clock this morning, very heavy cannonading was heard on our extreme left, but I am unable to learn the reason of it. Probably one side opened to prevent the other from working. Everything is very quiet on our portion of the line, so much so that to me at least, this quiet is ominous, and one from which we may be rudely awakened one of these fine mornings; though in what manner Grant will next come at us, it is impossible to imagine.

> -Walters was being somewhat of a prophet on this day, as the Confederate line was soon to experience an unimaginably rude awakening on July 30.-

July 25, 1864 The day passed off very quietly, with nothing being done on either side that I could see or hear of.

July 26, 1864 I wonder what Grant is up to? For the last day or two he has been sending troops up the James River. They went as far as Deep Bottom where they were met by Kershaw's Division, the latter of whom got rather the worst of it, losing four pieces of artillery. But this movement cannot seriously affect Richmond as troops have been sent to the assistance of Kershaw, and if it is an attempt under cover of which he hopes to capture Petersburg, it is a poor thing, as we have more than enough men here to hold our lines. Nothing was done on our lines today.

July 27, 1864 Today the enemy again amuse themselves by opening a heavy artillery fire on our portion of the line, without doing other damage than wounding a few men. Our artillery did not reply. This afternoon I went to town and in the evening I went over the river to Camp Davis where I found my friends as well as usual. At night we had some most excellent vocal music.

July 28, 1864 Through the kind influence of my friend Ege, I got a passport to go to Richmond and return, of which I availed myself by taking the four o'clock train up; arriving at Richmond about half past six this afternoon. Mr. Ege and family expressed themselves much pleased to see me, and did their utmost towards my enjoying a delightful evening, in which they succeeded to a charm.

> -From a century later vantage point, it is difficult to comprehend that a twenty mile train ride would last some two and a half hours, and that a soldier would need a passport to visit his friend's brother. Such was Virginia in 1864.-

July 29, 1864 At an early hour this morning, I accompanied Mrs. Ege to market which I found exceedingly well supplied with meats, fruits, and vegetables, all of which were selling at reasonable prices with a downward tendency. Beefsteak was selling at three dollars per pound, cimblins [*sic*] at four dollars per dozen, tomatoes at five dollars a quart, eggs at seven dollars per dozen, butter at nine dollars per pound, and large watermelons from seven to ten dollars each. After breakfast I started out and having considerable business to attend to, I was on a trot till three when I dined, after which I bade the ladies of the house good-by, went down to the depot, by dark reached Camp Davis where I stayed a short time, and then went to my gun, where I arrived between ten and eleven o'clock, much pleased with my trip.

July 30, 1864 (Saturday) Just before daylight this morning, hurried orders were passed along the line for the men to fall into their places in the breastworks. It required but a minute for all to be ready and waiting for developments. As day brightened all eyes were strained to discover the movements in the Yankee lines, but scarcely a man could be seen there, though this was anticipated as they would be likely to show as few heads as possible previous to the advance, hoping thereby to lull suspicion. In this suspense, the minutes glided by until a quarter to five o'clock when a dull noise and heavy shock of the earth caused us to look around, when a singularly horrid sight presented itself about three quarters of a mile on our left, which was no less than the going upward of a huge mass of earth, together with logs, guns, wheels, limber chests, muskets, and men. The enemy had sprung a mine on us! At the moment of doing so they opened a furious cannonading all along our line, while their sharpshooters and skirmishers rained over a shower of bullets. At the same time they threw forward heavy columns of their troops on the portion that they had breached, who succeeded in taking possession of our shattered breastworks and portions immediately adjoining the opening, from which they poured an enfilading fire on our men who held the works, and who were soon forced to fall back to a second line which we had there. From this, they kept up such a heavy fire as to prevent the enemy from advancing beyond our first line. Up to this time the mine was a most perfect success for the enemy, and gave them fair promise of cutting our line in two. But Mahone who is never satisfied unless he can be in at the death, hurried up three of his brigades; his own, Wright's Georgians, and Sanders' Alabamians. The moment he arrived at the scene of action, he threw forward Wright's and his own brigades, who succeeded in driving the enemy out of a portion of the works, killing a great number of them and capturing several stands of colors. As the weather was very hot and sultry, each side contented itself with what they held, till about two o'clock in the afternoon, when Mahone threw forward Sanders' Brigade, who rushed forward with a fierce yell and drove the enemy out of our line. They advanced so as to cover the hole made by the mine, and formed on Mahone and Wright, on the right and left. We thus held our own again while we captured twelve stands of colors, eight hundred or one thousand prisoners (among them General Bartlett and staff), and killed five or six hundred, wounding a great many.

A portion of the assailing column consisted of two brigades of Negroes, who charged with the cry of "Remember Fort Pillow!" and we did, for when our men got in among them, they clubbed them with their muskets. But a few were left alive, and these all tell the same pitiful lie of having been pressed into service and add, "but master, I didn't fire my gun". I'll wager that if the enemy had got the upper hand of us, they would have sung an entirely different song. Thus ended the fight.

It is true that they kept up their fire on our line till nearly sunset, but the main business of the day closed soon after the charge of Sanders. Our loss all told will probably count up as high as eight or nine hundred men, two hundred of whom were killed by the explosion. In fact, I understand three South Carolina companies are missing, and Pegram's Battery which was blown up lost twenty-four men killed beside many wounded. Among the mortally wounded is Brigadier General Elliott of Fort Sumter fame, whose brigade held a portion of the line which was blown up, and whose men, not withstanding the demoralizing influence of such an occurrence, nobly kept up the reputation that South Carolina soldiers have earned during the war. This afternoon, Robert Butler, one of our corporals, was instantly killed by a large shell striking him in the head, taking the whole top off from the tongue upward.

The affair of the day proves one thing conclusively, and that is that newspapers may talk as they will about the bravery and soldierly qualities of the Negro, but they are not to be depended upon at the moment which is perhaps to decide the fortunes of the day. In fact, a good soldier can never be made out of a Negro, and that the white officers who command them are afraid or ashamed to acknowledge the fact when captured is evident from the circumstance that of all the officers taken today, not one of them would own that he had been attached to the Negro brigade. After the fight, rather an amusing thing occurred. General Mahone, wishing to find some of the officers of the Negro battalion, ordered some of the Negroes who had been spared to point them out. On this, one of them, pointing to an officer said, "There is my captain". The captain thus spoken of turned hastily around and answered, "You're a damned liar, I never saw you", on which the Negro said, "O yes, you is my captain. I done walked wid you many a time". On marching the prisoners through town on their way to the depot, General Mahone put in practice the Yankee theory of a Negro being as good as a white man by marching them in alternate files of white and black. It is true that the Yankees, especially the officers, grumbled at this arrangement, but I cannot see what ground of complaint they can have when we adopt the theories which they publish to the world as theirs and seem to glory in. This is the second new and novel feature of field warfare that Grant has introduced. What he will try next remains to be seen.

-Walters had just taken part in what would eventually become known as the Battle of the Crater, one of the most unusual and spectacular events of the war. Pennsylvania coal miners of the Union army had tunneled beneath the Elliott Salient and filled the chambers they dug at the end with black powder. This gigantic mine was exploded just before daybreak. Strangely enough, Walters neglects to mention much of the action his own unit saw that day. At one point, shells ignited the roof of a powder magazine just in the rear of the Blues' position, and the infantry around it began to scatter. Private J. Theodore Taylor of the Blues quickly grabbed two buckets of water and extinguished the blaze, saving the magazine and perhaps his company's position as well. The Blues remained under fire most of the rest of the day.

The battlecry "Remember Fort Pillow" refers to an infamous event which occurred April 12, 1864, when General Nathan Bedford Forrest's troops captured Union-held Fort Pillow, Tennessee on the Mississippi River. Stories widely circulated in the North told of the killing of many of the fort's 300 black soldiers after they had surrendered. These reports had prompted General Grant to immediately halt all exchange of prisoners. The tales of massacre were doubtlessly also on the minds of those Union officers at Petersburg who refused to admit command of the Negro brigade. Although the Confederate government occasionally discussed proposals for establishing its own units of black soldiers, the idea would never have been taken seriously by its troops in the field, as the strong opinions recorded by Walters attest. As far back as any of these soldiers could remember, the economic benefits of slavery had been accompanied by the constant fear of a slave uprising. This threat was often fueled by lurid stories of bloody insurrections in the West Indies and other places. White Southerners agitated themselves for so long with the specter of a grisly slave revolt that the mere sight of a black man with a gun (or any weapon for that matter) was enough to provoke an irrational and inordinate response. These smoldering fears had been fanned to new heights by Nat Turner's Rebellion in Southampton, Virginia in 1831, in which 57 whites were murdered by escaped slaves. The old Norfolk Light Artillery Blues themselves had responded to this event by disbanding the group of free blacks which the company had hired and equipped as musicians (though they were allowed to keep the instruments assigned to them). Elsewhere across the South, armed "patrollers" began wandering the countryside at night, searching for escaped slaves or "dangerous" blacks. Years later, John Brown's unsuccessful raid on the Harper's Ferry Arsenal convinced many Southerners that the Abolitionists were openly supporting the murder of white people by revolting slaves, and the ranks of militia companies quickly swelled with young men determined to protect their families and homes against this gruesome threat.

When war finally came, Massachusetts Governor John Andrews and others pursuaded the North to accept black men into the armed service, and the eventual appearance of armed blacks on the battlefield incited the soldiers opposing them into a vengeful frenzy. U.S. Colored Troops bore the brunt of generations of pent-up fear and hate at places like Fort Wagner, Fort Pillow, and at the Crater. In spite of Walters' statements to the contrary, it will ever be a tribute to the courage and soldierly qualities of these men who stepped forward into combat knowing full well ahead of time that they would find no chivalry; they would either win, or die at the hands of an enraged foe.-

July 31, 1864 The day passed off very quietly though there was quite a brisk picket fire kept up on the lines in the vicinity of yesterday's battleground. About midday, a two hours suspension of hostilities took place to allow the enemy to supply their wounded, who are lying between the lines, with water, though they were not allowed to remove any. During the day in digging over a portion of the earth that was blown up yesterday, three or four men were dug out who were still alive, though some of them died almost immediately after.

August 1, 1864 Another suspension of several hours took place today to allow the enemy to bury their dead and carry off the wounded from between the lines, and a horrid job it was, for though so short a time dead, yet the stench was almost sufficient to sicken soldiers, and in nearly all cases decomposition had arrived at such a stage that but for their hair and differences of features, the whites could not be distinguished from their colored brothers.

August 2, 1864 About two o'clock this morning a sudden volley from our picket in our front 'roused everyone along the line, but it proved to be a false alarm, though I have not been able to learn the cause of it. Beyond this, there was nothing to disturb the monotony of what is becoming a very monotonous life. Oh! for a long march through the valley or somewhere else where the same objects will not be the alpha and omega of each day's existence.

August 3, 1864 Nothing beyond picket firing and a little mortar shelling from both sides took place today.

August 4, 1864 Today's paper contains the news, copied from Northern papers, of the burning of Chambersburg, Pa. by our forces, and a horde of indignation goes up at what they are pleased to term our vandalism. These wretches seem to forget their destruction of Fredericksburg, their attempt at Charlestown, ignore their raids made against Richmond for the purpose of sack and plunder if captured, and lately, conveniently forget that their troops shelled Petersburg while it was filled with women and children. I am glad that at last our generals are laying aside a little of their Christian forbearance, and by inaugurating a stern system of retaliation, are fighting the enemy with weapons with which they have fought us for the last three years. Possibly the blazing roofs of Chambersburg may induce the people of the North to look at this war in an entirely different light from that wherein they have been accustomed to view it. Well done, General Jubal A. Early! Oh! for the power to whisper in your ear that Pittsburgh is also in Pennsylvania.

August 5, 1864 It having been discovered that the enemy were approaching our works on front of Gracie's Brigade, we ran a countermine under them and this afternoon exploded it. The enemy, most probably anticipating that this would be followed by a charge, reopened a previous cannonading to which we made no reply. We accomplished all that was intended and therefore made no further demonstration. We are running several other galleries intended as countermines, one of them about five hundred yards to the right of my gun. I wish to heaven that our officers would do the same for our battery, for though I do not show it, yet I am becoming terribly demoralized at the thought of finding myself going up some fine morning or other. Not that I have such a slavish fear of death, but the possibility which exists of being buried alive and dying in that condition, while the panorama of my last life passed before my eyes in all its startling hideousness, this thought is terrible and almost unmans me. Great God in mercy, protect me from such a fate.

August 6, 1864 At an early hour this morning, I went to town where I remained til about three o'clock this afternoon, when I accompanied my friend Ege to Camp Davis where I found the family well as usual, but growing very tired of camp life. In the evening, Sergeant R. from Drewry's Bluff came out on his way to the early morning train for Richmond. I was greatly pleased to see him as I had not done so since last January when I was in furlough. He is one of the few men whom I like very much and yet who bores me to death after the first five minutes after we meet, but he is a splendid fellow and that is an ample mantle.

August 7, 1864 On waking this morning I found R. gone. If he had yielded to my persuasions of last night to share my bed, he would have overslept himself and then I would have had his company today. In consideration of it having been Mr. E.s birthday one day last week, the ladies regaled him with ice cream for dessert after dinner. I had a share, and none but soldiers can properly appreciate such a rarity after the course of fat meat and corn bread to which they are subjected. In the evening I left Camp Davis and after one or two calls made in town, returned to my gun.

August 8, 1864 This morning's papers come freighted with news from Mobile which is not of a very cheering nature, though things may not be as bad as they are reported. The news is that three of our vessels there were sunk or destroyed, that Admiral Buchanan had a leg shattered and was captured by the enemy, and that the Yankee Fleet had passed Fort Morgan, while Fort Gains had been surrendered in consequence of the treason or cowardice of its commander. Considerable fears are entertained for the safety of Mobile. Everything on our lines was very quiet today.

August 9, 1864 Yesterday's news from Mobile is confirmed by today's reports, though the authorities do not entertain very serious apprehensions from the water approaches to the city, as the bar which is nine miles out will prevent the nearer approach of larger vessels. The channel has been carefully obstructed, which obstructions are commanded by strong water batteries which if properly officered and manned, ought to be sufficient for smaller vessels. The enemy's fleet numbers seven hundred and twenty guns, while ours numbered but thirty-two, a sufficient difference to account for our getting the most of it. The surrender of Fort Gains is to undergo a thorough investigation.

August 10, 1864 An unusual quiet has prevailed for several days along our lines and conjecture runs riot as to the probable movement which Grant will next make. The Northern papers still howl over the slaughter of their troops at the mine, some blaming one general and others another, among which Grant is by no means spared, and many papers are becoming clamorous for peace. God grant that they may soon become satisfied.

August 11, 1864 A little artillery firing from both sides relieved the monotony of the day in a slight degree. The enemy did no damage, nor can I see that we did any.

August 12, 1864 For several nights past, the Washington Artillery, Cutts, and our battalion have been sending details of men to throw up works for heavy guns, all of which are approaching completion. One ten-inch Columbiad was brought up last night and will be mounted in a short time, two others of like caliber are to be mounted, three thirty-pounder Blakely guns are daily expected up from Wilmington, and several thirty-pounder Parrotts are already in position. What is to be done when all these are ready I cannot imagine, but trust that the results will be commensurate with our labor at the works, which is very severe, especially as the heat and flies prevent our sleeping enough during the day to recover from our fatigue.

August 13, 1864 Everything was very quiet until this evening when the enemy opened a short but brisk cannonading on our lines, during which a piece of shell struck C. A. Newton of our company on the left leg just above the ankle, rendering amputation necessary. I trust this wound will not involve his life, but regret to say that he is very much frightened and low spirited in consequence, which is a bad feature in his case.

August 14, 1864 Newton bore the operation of amputation very well and seems to be endeavoring to raise his spirits. He has been sent to Richmond and will, no doubt, receive excellent attention.

All appearances promise fair for a heavy rain very soon, which is very much needed.

August 15, 1864 Considerable rain fell during last night, and the earlier part of today seemed to be set apart by the sun to make everything drier than before, but about midday it again clouded up and soon after the rain came down in perfect torrents and continued to do so for several hours, flooding everything and filling ditches, trenches, bombproofs, and covered ways, to the damage of a large quantity of ammunition for which limber chests were no protection. I think that without exception it was the heaviest fall of rain that I have seen since I have been in service, against which our tents were but little protection. Towards dark the storm passed over, and the moon and stars at present give promise of a clear night.

August 16, 1864 Early this morning I went to town and on getting to Mr. E.s house, I found his folks busy in cleaning the house preparatory to a return to town, during which I assisted them in moving some of the heaviest articles of furniture. After dark I returned to my gun, my permit being for one day only.

August 17, 1864 More rain fell during the night, but the day has been intensely hot. In the midst of this we have been very busy in cutting ditches to drain the water off, and in overhauling our ammunition.

August 18, 1864 At two o'clock this morning we were called up, and taking the cue from the guns on the right of our line (according to orders) opened a very heavy cannonading on the enemy's lines which we continued for an hour or more, and to which the enemy replied but feebly. After this we quieted down and did nothing more for the rest of the day. What the object of this can be I do not know, unless it is to cover demonstrations on other parts of the line, or to attract Grant's attention and prevent his moving under the fear that we may attack his lines.

August 19, 1864 We were again called up at two o'clock and opened for half an hour when we stopped for a like space of time, and then opened again for about an hour, to all of which the enemy made no reply. This silence does not for one moment induce us to believe that they have no guns there, even if that is the object of their quiet. Now it is possible that all of this firing may produce immense results, but it is a decided bore being called up as early as that, especially as we are compelled to work til twelve o'clock. I most earnestly hope that the powers that be will defer all future shelling until a more reasonable hour.

August 20, 1864 Another repetition of the artillery work before day. The enemy are making a demonstration on the Weldon Railroad in large force, and I have no doubt our work is in connection with counter movements made by our troops.

August 21, 1864 We were again called up to give the enemy the morning dose, but this time they kicked against the infliction and gave it to us in return both hot and heavy. Fortunately, no-one was hurt on our side that I could hear of. As mentioned in yesterday's notes, the enemy made a demonstration on the Weldon Railroad and showed an anxiety to tamper with the integrity of the Southside Railroad, to check which Mahone with three of his brigades and other troops were sent there, but on their arrival they found the enemy too strong for them. Nevertheless, our troops, though in some cases at a discount of three or four to one, went in with their characteristic "pitching in" propensity, and though they were severely handled, succeeded in capturing between twenty-five hundred and three thousand prisoners when they fell back to their original lines. At night, troops were sent out to their assistance and this morning we were ordered to listen for the sounds of battle and open on our line at the same time, though this did not interfere at all with our little arrangement before day. After this we awaited in considerable anxiety until about nine o'clock, when the rumble of artillery on our left told that the issue was being joined. We immediately opened with a heavy fire, which was again well returned until about twelve o'clock when it gradually ceased all along the line. We now were all very impatient to learn the results, which came in by details, the result of which is that our troops in the front drove the enemy from two lines of entrenchments, but could not succeed in dislodging them from the third line, which was a formidable work (considering the short time they had to throw it up). While this was going on in front, Mahone, who had been sent with four of his brigades, viz Harris's, Sanders', Wright's, and Finegan's, to execute a flank movement, came up on the enemy's line where their skirmishers were thrown out at least a mile in advance. Throwing his troops in line, they rushed with a yell, but owing to the distance, and the fact that the rain the night previous had rendered the ground very heavy, the men are coming up with the line of battle too exhausted to do anything. A short halt was made. This enabled the enemy to bring up some artillery, who came in at a flying gallop and opened immediately. At this moment, the order "Charge" was given, and our gallant boys rose up and rushed forward, but were met by a storm of lead and iron. Yet on they pushed and the enemy began to waiver, when one of our brigades, the largest of the four, broke and fell back, nor was it possible to rally them, though great efforts were made. At one time their own brigadier, Lt. Colonel Pegram, young McCabe, adjutant of Poague's Battalion, and a sergeant belonging to the Crenshaw Battery from Richmond (whose name I could not learn) were all in front using prayers and oaths, menaces and entreaties, but all to no purpose. They could not be rallied and the whole line was compelled to fall back, thereby losing to us what would have undoubtedly have proved to us a great success. The only palliation for the conduct of this brigade is that they are nearly all comparatively new men. The results of today's fighting is about three or four hundred prisoners, while the enemy, among others, killed Brigadier General Sanders and Colonel Lamar of the 5th Florida Regiment, both of whom were known as soldiers of rare ability and most perfect gentlemen. I could not learn the amount of our losses, but fear that they are more than we can afford, and in the meantime, the enemy still hold the railroad, from which it will be necessary to dislodge him in a very few days to re-establish our communication with the South, to which end large reinforcements are being sent.

August 22, 1864 The day passed off very gently though we all expected to hear of some movement on the right. About sunset a heavy shower of rain fell which lasted about two hours.

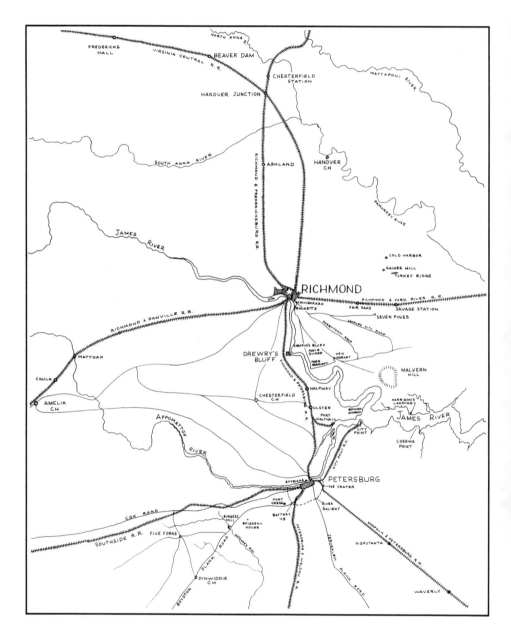

The Richmond and Petersburg area.

August 23, 1864 Considerable rain fell during the night but the day was very bright and warm. About three o'clock this morning, the enemy opened on us with artillery, to which we replied, but after about an hour's interchange of compliments, both sides ceased. After daylight I went to town on a forty-eight hour permit and found Miss Eddy very ill with bilious fever. From what I can learn, a change for the better must soon take place or there will be wailing in the house where God grant I may never live to see tears of sorrow. Owing to the interruption of travel over the Weldon Railroad, sugar has advanced two dollars per pound, flour twenty-five dollars per barrel, and other things in proportion. Who will say after this that the Yankees are our only enemies?

August 24, 1864 There is considerable improvement in the condition of Miss Eddy, so much so that with the care and attention which she will undoubtedly receive, she will get over it if no relapse occurs. At the dinner table today, while speaking of the probable duration of this war, I expressed a firm belief in an early ending of it, but Mr. E. and the family took a more gloomy view of affairs. At the close of the conversation a very one sided bargain was made, which was, that in one year from this day (provided the war was ended), Mr. E. was to give me a huge dinner and pay my traveling expenses to and from Petersburg. I certainly can lose nothing by this bargain, and the week following, Price is to do the same thing, paying the traveling expenses of Mr. E. and myself to and from Macon. Though my permit is not out till tomorrow, I had partly determined to return to my gun tonight, but it looks too much like rain so I shall not start till daylight.

August 25, 1864 At four o'clock this morning I was called up and left the house for my gun, which I reached shortly after daylight. But a light rain had fallen during the night, however the appearance of it caused me to enjoy at least one more night's sleep in a bed, a thing not to be despised, even though I have become so accustomed to sleeping almost anywhere. The day passed off very quietly, but about five o'clock a most terrific artillery fire was heard on the right in the direction of the Weldon Railroad. This was continued til nearly dark, with what results I have not yet learned. We have been looking for a battle in that quarter for some days and probably this is the opening chapter, but I fear that we have not troops enough here to dislodge the enemy from the railroad where they are strongly entrenched. It is probable that Early may be ordered from the valley.

August 26, 1864 Before daylight, an artillery duel occurred on our left in the neighborhood of the mine, which was kept up very briskly for about two hours. No damage was done that I could learn of. The rest of the day has passed off very gently. The fighting of last evening on the railroad resulted in our taking one line of breastworks from the enemy, which we hold, nine pieces of artillery, seven stands of colors, and from twenty to twenty-five hundred prisoners, besides killing and wounding a large number while our own loss was comparatively light. Most of the fighting was done by the North Carolinians of Heth's and Wilcox's Divisions, who fought with more than their characteristic gallantry. The prisoners are the most miserable looking set that I have ever seen, and many of them are too young to be engaged in the dreadful business of war, unless it is for the protection of their own houses and firesides from invasion.

August 27, 1864 The "Petersburg Express" of this morning contained the funeral notice of Alexander D. McCarrick, a member of our company who joined us about two months ago, and who died yesterday after a short illness, so short indeed, that but few in our company knew he was sick until this announcement of his death. He is greatly regretted, for though with us so short a time, yet that had been long enough to show him as being possessed of a most excellent disposition, kind and obliging in the extreme, and though not eighteen years of age, yet in the presence of the enemy he exhibited all those qualities which go to make up a man of the very best type. He died at the residence of a gentleman from the city, from whose family he received all the care and attention that it was possible to bestow, and attended to the last moment by a priest of his faith, at whose hands he also received much kindness and all the religious consolation that could be given.

-Private A. David McCarrick's remains were the first to be returned to Norfolk following the war. He was eventually laid to rest in St. Mary's Catholic Cemetery in his family's plot.-

August 28, 1864 Nothing was done on our portion of the line today. About dark, the enemy opened up quite a heavy fire on the city which was kept up a couple of hours, after which they threw mortar shell for the greater part of the night. What damage was done I have not learned. Gilmore came out to see me today. He talks about bringing his family down from Lynchburg.

August 29, 1864 The shelling of the city was resumed about dark. I wonder if this is not done to draw our attention from some other part of the line, against which they may have some design in the way of a mine or other devilish contrivances. Time will answer this question.

Today the Democratic Convention meets at Chicago and much anxious speculation is going on among our troops as to the probable candidate. Though I think that good will result from the election of either a war or peace man, nor would I be much surprised if both wings formed a compromise and worked together.

August 30, 1864 Quite an excitement was caused along the lines by an exchange of white flags between the lines, the object of which we could not learn, though later in the day it was rumored that General Lee had notified Grant that in case the shelling of the city was continued, our whole line would open an artillery fire, together with sharpshooting. I scarcely think that this rumor is the solution of the white flag business, for though Grant would lose more by it than we, yet it is a two handed game and a man of his stubbornness would not be apt to yield to such an ultimatum. But one thing gives the rumor an air of plausibility and that is that the shelling of the city was not resumed tonight.

August 31, 1864 News from the North comes in but slowly across the lines in our front, but such as we get leads to the belief that MacClellan and probably Pendleton of Ohio will be the nominees of the Democratic Party, and indications are that they will be pledged to a war platform. If this is so, we may well ask, "How long, oh Lord, how long?" I do not know what Pendleton's sentiments are, but I think it likely that he is a peace man and that the party may unite on a compromise platform, which God may grant.

September 1, 1864 I was greatly shocked this morning by hearing E. M. E. was much worse, in fact the doctors had but little hopes of her. As it was my turn to go to town, I waited very impatiently for the return of one of my detachment. As not to impair the effectiveness of my gun, we are compelled to wait til one comes out before another goes in. About sunset, I got in town and found that the condition of Miss Eddy was very critical, neither her family nor friends having any hopes for her. I used my best exertion upon the universal apophthegm that while there is life there is hope, and that she had the best medical talent, unweary attention, youth, and a good constitution all in her favor, but my endeavors met with but little success, I fear.

September 2, 1864 This morning the doctors reported but little change in the condition of the patient, but this evening they report a slight but yet decided improvement. Oh, God in mercy, continue thy good work to her complete restoration. Do not compel her parents and friends to drain this bitter cup to the dregs.

September 3, 1864 While there is but little if any change for the better in the condition of the patient, yet there is none for for the worse, from which we all derive some hope and consolation. About three o'clock this afternoon, I left town for my gun, and on arriving there learned that our line had engaged in an artillery duel with the enemy, during which a corporal of the Donaldsonville Battery (whose gun was about five yards to the left of mine) had his head knocked to pieces; scalp, skull, etc. flying in every direction to a distance of ten or fifteen yards. Also, one of the men of the Huger Battery (whose gun is about ten yards to the right of mine) had a portion of his left arm, involving the loss of that hand, carried away while serving vent at his gun. He was also wounded in the side, which latter may prove a mortal wound, as from the blood that he is constantly spitting, it is thought that the left lung is injured. No other accidents happened that I could learn.

September 4, 1864 This morning, half a dozen shots were exchanged, but with this exception the day passed of unusually quiet. In the afternoon the news reached us of the fall of Atlanta, but with what loss to us or the enemy in men and material is not yet known. The capture was effected by a flank movement and assault in heavy force by the enemy. Now while the possession of Atlanta, as a military question, is or was of but little moment to us as long as the army remains there, even amid large loss, yet I fear it will have a great effect upon the November election in the North, and that not all to our benefit, unless between now and then we can make a strike here with our army to which end I am somewhat anxious to see Early come back from the valley, especially as for the last two or three weeks I cannot see that he has been doing anything of sufficient importance to warrant his longer stay there. While writing this, the rather amusing question arises as to what General Lee would think of this criticism upon his actions by High Private Walters. I have no doubt but that he would feel highly flattered.

Late this evening, I learned that a slight improvement was perceptible in the condition of Miss Eddy, and that her family entertains hopes of saving her.

September 5, 1864 Though yesterday passed off so quietly, not so the night, for about midnight we were awakened by a heavy mortar shelling on our left and shortly after, the enemy opened a heavy artillery fire on our lines, which they continued for about an hour, and to which we replied by an occasional shot. Shortly after it ceased, they opened a lighter fire of cheers and shouts over the fall of Atlanta, while several bands struck up patriotic airs, by which we were led to believe that the firing was merely a jubilation over the fall of that city. I cannot say that I greatly admire their style of pyrotechnics, especially when the display involves an interruption to rather pleasant dreams.

During the day occasional shots were exchanged, but I cannot learn of any damage being done. Late in the evening a most absurd report was circulated to the effect that Atlanta was recaptured. This is so improbable that I place no faith in it.

September 6, 1864 During last night it began to rain, which increased at one time, to a heavy shower. It ceased before day, yet it has been one of the most disagreeable ones that we have spent on this line, being foggy and very chilly, with the wind from northwest. The enemy have been comparatively quiet today, though they threw a few light mortar shells over from immediately in front of our gun, though none of the shells exploded.

This morning I went down to Mahone's old Brigade to get some news from Mr. E.s family, but could not get any. I hope to get some tomorrow.

September 7, 1864 Early this morning, John Cockes came to see me. He has just come out from town, and reports no improvement in the condition of Eddy. I begin greatly to fear that we shall lose her after all. Poor John Gamage has just received news of the death of his father in Norfolk. This sad event leaves a house full of girls with no male protector, and is quite sufficient cause for all his sadness. The weather was warm and pleasant, and quiet on or between the lines characterized the day.

September 8, 1864 Today I ate my initiatory dish of Pussley, a weed that grows about here in great abundance. For camp use, I find it an excellent substitute for the greens which we eat at home. Farmers tell me that it is one of the best vegetable productions wherewith to fatten hogs, and as we Confederate soldiers have learned to eat almost any and everything, I do not see why we should not pitch in to pussley with our characteristic vim, especially as many of us have many inches of hide which sadly needs filling out, and as I count myself chief among the cadaverous crew, I contemplate eating it in considerable quantities.

-Pussley or purslane (Portulaca Oleracea) is a trailing weed with small yellow flowers, reddish stems, and fleshy leaves. It later became popular as an ornamental flower and is sometimes used in salads to this day. Another vegetable production which Southern soldiers converted from hog feed to culinary delight was the ground pea or peanut. According to one popular story, it had originally traveled to the South from Angolia, Africa, where it was known as nguba. This name became "goober," and Yanks and Rebs alike went home singing the praises of goober peas.-

September 9, 1864 Several unsuccessful attempts were made by the clerk of the weather to get up a rain last night, but it was no go and today has been remarkably pleasant. Yesterday and today passed off quietly on the lines, that is if I except a few shell which are sent over semi-occasionally by the enemy, and to which we sometimes reply (though it is more often the case that our batteries are silent). This is becoming disagreeable in the extreme as the shell pass over or explode in our midst when we least expect it; a circumstance which keeps us so constantly on the qui vive as to render our situation at times quite painful. This reminds me that last evening after writing up, Lieutenant Duncan of Cutts' Battalion was instantly killed by a piece of shell striking him in the face and entering while at his gun, which is about one hundred yards to the left of my piece.

September 10, 1864 About half past two o'clock this morning we were awakened by the rattle of musketry, and in a moment all were at their places. We soon learned that the enemy had advanced their picket line and in so doing, had captured a portion of the pickets belonging to Finegan's and Harris' Brigades. We soon reinforced our pickets and drove the enemy out of our lines, capturing fifty or sixty of them. All this time, the musketry firing was very lively. As soon as there was sufficient light to sight the guns by, the artillery took a hand in, and soon everything began to look a little more interesting than suited me, especially as there was a concentrated fire of six or eight guns on the one to which I belong. In a short time, the enemy closed up the embrasure through which we shoot, and to this circumstance I attribute my present ability of writing this, as after it was closed, we left the breastwork, being of no further use there. About five minutes after we had left, a shell came through the debris which filled the embrasure, and struck the gun cheek on the right side just under the trunnion, and bursting, tore away everything in the shape of woodwork and bolts. As this is the place to stand while serving the gun, it will be readily perceived that had I been there, my chances would have been very small. The Number 1 on the gun would also have been cut in two and other damage would probably have been done. Shortly after, another shell struck the left wheel, knocking it to pieces. Considerable firing of all kinds was kept up during the day though but little damage was done.

In the evening I went in town on a permit and was much relieved in learning that there was considerable improvement in Miss Eddy.

> -Walters served at the vent as the Number 3 man on his Napoleon. Each of the ten men serving a particular gun were assigned a numbered station and a specific duty. The Number 1 man stood to the right of the muzzle to ram the powder bag

and round down the barrel, and to occasionally sponge the barrel. The Number 2 man was at the left of the muzzle to place the charge into the barrel and to worm or clean out the barrel between rounds. The Number 3 man (Walters' position) covered the vent with his left thumb during loading, helped with aiming the piece, and steadied the friction primer (the igniter) while the Number 4 man stretched the lanyard tight. Number 4 attached the lanyard to the primer, slipped the primer into the vent (sometimes called the "touch hole"), and pulled the lanyard when commanded to fire. The other men of the gun squad prepared the charges, carried them to the gun, and tended the horses of the limber and caisson. Rapid, accurate firing of the gun demanded close teamwork between each man of the squad.-

September 11, 1864 (Sunday) My uniform came from Richmond! I borrowed a boiled shirt and collar from Mr. E. and went to Grace Church. After service I walked home with one of the fairest of the fair sex. This afternoon I called on J. Y. Gilmore and family who have just come down from Lynchburg. Mrs. G. is somewhat demoralized on account of the shell that continue to fly around, but I found her the same kind and gentle Maggie of old. I hope they will stay here some time. Two or three showers fell during the day, but they did not amount to much. The improvement, though slight, still continues in the condition of our friend.

September 12, 1864 I forgot to state that on Saturday evening, while some of the prisoners were being brought in, I exchanged hats with a sergeant who was among the lot. His was a very fine one for which I have since been offered one hundred dollars and mine was a shocking affair. He was not greatly disposed to trade but I persuaded him to do so, and would have insisted upon his giving me his haversack and canteen to boot, but that the guard who had charge of the squad were in haste to get under cover with them. I remained in town til about four o'clock when I returned to my gun, and found the sharpshooting going on very briskly.

> - With his new jacket and trousers from Richmond, and his new hat, Walters was no doubt quite a dandy compared to most of his more threadbare comrades. He was also fortunate that Lee was not nearby when he coerced the Yankee to part with his headgear. In at least one case when a prisoner complained to Lee that his hat had been taken, the general made the Rebel soldier give it back.-

September 13, 1864 I received a note from J. W. C. in which he informs me that the improvement in the condition of Miss Eddy continues. The artillery was very lively along the lines today, though we did not participate. After dark, we attempted to repair our embrasure but the picket firing was a little too brisk, though it must be done, and might as well have been done today as to leave it until tomorrow, especially as we have a 3-inch regulation gun here in place of our Napoleon, which has been sent to the rear for repairs.

September 14, 1864 This morning while walking in the covered way in the rear of my gun, I was struck by a "Minie" on the muscle just under my left ear, which took a little skin off and has stiffened my neck considerably. It did not give me sufficient pain to go to the rear, though I was strongly advised to do so by our boys, but I have long since determined not to go to the rear unless I receive a wound which will require medical attention, as I dread the ridicule of the surgeon were I to go to him with a mere scratch. During the morning there was a heavy artillery duel on the left of our lines. Many of the enemy's shell fell in town, though what damage was done I have not learned.

-Any soldier who was wounded was permitted to immediately go to the rear to seek aid. This standing order would prove to be of great benefit to Walters in the coming spring.-

This afternoon, I received two letters by the blockade, one from Albany dated June 28th, the other from Holland dated June 4th. The former, which was written by Herman, that heart of gold, informed me of the arrival of Brother Abelard, from whom we have not heard in fifteen or sixteen years. The latter, which was written by my darling Mousie, breathed nothing but forgiveness. What more could I say even were I to write a volume. The letters also contained the news of the marriage of Fanny D. which event occurred some two years ago, and so ends the only dream of romance in which I allowed myself to indulge, and with it vanishes all hopes and speculations for the future. The world may now come and go as it will and, but for my hopes and prayers to once more meet dear Mousie on earth, I might be silly enough to do something rash. However, this war may yet give me a soldier's grave.

September 15, 1864 And so Fanny is married. I can scarcely realize it. I have read the letter over and over again, but there it is, and yet I cannot realize that she, who for the last seven years was first and last in my thoughts, she whose dear picture I have carried, and which has cheered and comforted me during many a gloomy day and sad night, under the burning suns of summer or the chill winds of winter from which I had no other protection than such as was afforded by the wardrobe of a Confederate soldier, that her image must be banished from my mind. She must be thought of no more, or if thought of, only as the wife of another, and he, not having the inducements which I should have had for treating her with the utmost kindness, had she remained true to me, he may at times treat her harshly. This thought is agony, but thou art another's now, dear Fanny, and the place that thy image has filled must forever remain empty, for though I may in years to come be foolish enough to marry, there is no one who can be to me what thou hast been. Farewell dear, dear Fanny. May the choicest of heaven's blessings be your daily portion.

-And so Walters closes the door on a part of his past, and leaves us no further clue as to the identity of Fanny D. or the others he has just mentioned. We can assume that Herman, Abelard, and Mousie were his brothers and sister from Holland (which he left with some bad feelings evidently, based on Mousie's forgiveness), but time has washed away any further records of their attachments. Fortunately, Walters' gloomy spell would be short lived, and the years to come would indeed find him to be foolish enough to marry.-

September 16, 1864 This morning I was greatly cheered by the intelligence from town that Miss Eddy was considerably better. There is nothing new on the lines. The sharpshooting continues brisk as ever, with an occasional artillery duel. A great deal of gloomy feeling is taking possession of our soldiers in consequence of the uncompromising war spirit which breathes through the letter of acceptance written by MacClellan, and many fears are expressed that if Lincoln is re-elected (as is most improbable), from the symptoms of a split in the Democratic Party, that this war will be continued another four year term, in which case it is a matter of great speculation as to who will live to see the end of it.

Late this evening, some man of Davis' Brigade, which is just on our left, perpetrated a cowardly act unworthy of a white man. Since sharpshooting has recommenced, it has been customary for both sides to cease operations just after sunset for about an hour, of which both sides took advantage to relieve their pickets. It also allowed the men in the works a short respite at least during which to walk about without being constantly reminded of broken heads and shattered limbs by the whistling of "Minies". But this evening after the firing had ceased, and while all the pickets were out of their holes in the fancied security of each of the others honor, this man of Davis' Brigade deliberately took aim and shot one of the enemy, the ball striking him in the forehead, no doubt killing him instantly. Now while I believe in the abstract principle of killing a Yankee where even one is found on our soil, yet in such a case as this, it was not only brutal, but dishonorable in the extreme.

September 17, 1864 The enemy have taken revenge for the affair of last evening. This evening some fifteen or twenty minutes after the usual cessation, and while our men were walking about, a single shot was fired from the Yankee line which struck a poor fellow from Perry's Brigade in the left side below the ribs and passed entirely through him. He died in about five minutes. I have no doubt but that this was done in retaliation, and as it is usual in such cases, the innocent suffer for the guilty.

September 18, 1864 Nothing broke the dull monotony of the day, and even the sharpshooting seemed to yield to the influence of this day of rest, until after the sun went down when they made up for lost time by keeping up a fusillade that would have done us discredit to a regular line of battle.

September 19, 1864 The papers of today bring us the news of brilliant raid made by Hampton in the rear of the enemy's line, in which he captured twenty-five hundred head of cattle, ten or twelve wagons, a lot of horses, and about three hundred prisoners, all of which he brought safely into our lines. Our loss in this affair being only about forty or fifty men. The results of this raid are of great value to us and breaks through the dull cloud which has enveloped the two armies for some weeks past.

> -General Wade Hampton had led his cavalrymen out of their camp on the morning of September 14 toward a large herd of cattle the Yankees were keeping near Coggin's Point in Prince George County. They successfully made the fifty-mile trip around the Union lines without detection, crossed the Blackwater Swamp, and early on the morning of the following day, they surprised and defeated the small force guarding the herd in a two-hour fight. They retraced their route with only minor interference, and returned to the Confederate lines in triumph with their prize on the morning of September 17. Hampton's official report of the "Beefsteak Raid" stated that 2,486 head of cattle had been taken. The defenders of Petersburg would enjoy the taste of this victory for a long time to come.-

September 20, 1864 The enemy tried our lines with his artillery for a short time today, but no damage was done that I could hear of.

September 21, 1864 This afternoon I went in town on a forty-eight hour permit. I found the family greatly upset in consequence of symptoms in the case of Miss Eddy which led them to fear a relapse. I certainly trust that their fears may prove groundless. The city is filled with rumors of a defeat, attendant with great loss, said to have been sustained by Early near Winchester. Reports are so very conflicting that but little can be relied on. All we can do is wait for tomorrow's papers.

September 22, 1864 Though not quite as bad as we were led to anticipate from yesterday's rumors, yet the affair at Winchester is bad enough for many a secret misgiving regarding the integrity of Richmond. It appears that Sheridan, having been largely reinforced lately, made a bold push on Early with his infantry while he sent in his whole cavalry force against his flanks in a severe fight which lasted the whole day. Early was compelled to fall back to Fisher's Hill near Strasburg, losing about three thousand prisoners, besides a large number in killed and wounded, together with three pieces of artillery and three or four stands of colors, though he succeeded in saving all of his trains. Among the killed is Brigadier General Goodwin of North Carolina and Major General Rodes of Virginia. Both are a great loss to us, especially the latter, who was made Major General on the Chancellorsville battlefield by Stonewall Jackson, for the distinguished gallantry he there displayed. The position at Fisher's Hill now held by Early is a very strong one, but it admits of his being flanked from the Luray Valley, a fact of which I have no doubt that the enemy will avail himself, in which case Early must fall back still farther so as to cover Staunton and Lynchburg, and also Orange Courthouse and Gordonsville. Whatever he does must be done by his present force as I do not think that a single brigade can be spared from our lines at present. But the question arises, where is Breckenridge with his division? And what is Kershaw doing at Orange? Though both these questions will probably soon be answered.

September 23, 1864 Again a slight improvement in our patient, and no further news from Early. This evening, I returned to my gun where I found everything quiet with the exception of sharpshooting; though this is not as lively as it has been.

September 24, 1864 At an early hour this morning, word was passed along the line as it was expected that the enemy would open on us with artillery, which they did about daylight, firing one hundred shots in honor of Sheridan's victory over Early. We did not reply, nor did we sustain any damage that I could learn. Heavy guns have been heard all day in the direction of the river, probably at or near Dutch Gap.

September 25, 1864 The day passed off very quietly, there being no artillery and but little sharpshooting.

Quite a good thing was gotten off at the picket lines last evening. One of our pickets sung out, "I say, Yank, come over and try a little of Hampton's beef", to which the Yankee replied, "No, thank you, I don't like Early meals". I think he rather got us.

September 26, 1864 Early was flanked as I expected from the Luray Valley, and was compelled to abandon his position at Fisher's Hill, losing some eight or ten pieces of artillery though but few men. This was all owing to our want of an effective body of cavalry, for though we have some six or eight thousand there, yet they are all very much demoralized, while that of the enemy is very much effective. The papers do not say much as to where Early has fallen back to, nor can I imagine.

This evening we received news of the death of one of our company named Scott, who joined our company last winter. He died at home in Orange County of typhoid fever.

September 27, 1864 There are rumors today that Early had gained a victory over Sheridan. While this is not impossible, yet it is so improbable that it would be folly to build a hope upon. I heard today that our patient was a little better. During the evening's cessation on the picket lines, one of the Yankees told our men that a test vote was taken on the presidential election in the division who hold the lines, which resulted in MacClellan receiving seven votes to Lincoln's one. If this is a sample of the feelings at the North and the integrity of the ballot box maintained, the chances of the latter are slim indeed, though I do not think MacClellan is very strong with the western army.

September 28, 1864 The day was quiet enough and everything promised the same for the night, but about eight o'clock the pickets on the extreme right in the neighborhood of the Lead Works opened a fusillade which sounded somewhat like a line of battle affair. This was rapidly carried along the lines until it passed us and went down, and we could hear it rolling along for another mile or two. Soon the artillery and mortars of both sides joined in, and we all began to hope that Grant was at last going to charge our lines, but we were disappointed for in about an hour it died out, and the quiet that ensued was unbroken for the remainder of the night.

September 29, 1864 This afternoon, quiet orders were given to all the artillery on the line to get everything ready to be able to move at a moment's notice. This order caused many long faces to appear, more especially when news was brought out that the sick and wounded from the city were being sent to Danville and the hospitals broken up. All prognosticated the evacuation of Petersburg, and expressed the belief that in this case Richmond and probably the state would have to be given up next. I did not like to incline to this extreme view, nevertheless I cannot but yield to a gloomy feeling that has been stealing over me for the last two weeks. I do not think that this city will be given up, but what with the great disparity existing between the members of our army and that of the enemy, I fear we may be forced back in the next great battle, which cannot be far off. Though it is a melancholy satisfaction to know that we, in going back, will do so with our faces to the foe, dealing death to thousands, yet the results are the same. If we are forded from the state, the army will, I fear, lose many thousand Virginians. As for myself, not being "to the manor born", and having put my hand to the plow I shall finish the row, unless General Lee should leave the head of the army, in which case I should take a serious thought upon the subject.

September 30, 1864 This morning much of the excitement of yesterday had subsided in consequence of receiving no further orders in relation to our guns. About ten o'clock, I went to town for forty-eight hours and found our patient much better, though very weak.

This evening just before dark, heavy musketry and cannonading again began on the right and was carried along the line, lasting about three quarters of an hour. I imagine that Grant is feeling our lines. I think he will find them rather too strong for the health and comfort of his men.

Considerable fighting was done today at Forts Harrison and Gilmer, the former of which we lost, though the enemy was repulsed from the latter with heavy loss. These are small forts, or rather salients, intended to partly cover the batteries at Chaffin's Bluff from a land attack, and while their loss is a matter of small moment to us, their capture is, or would be, of but little advantage to the enemy.

October 1, 1864 Much excitement exists in the city in consequence of the "reserves" having been called out and sent to the "trenches", to fill portions of the line made vacant by the withdrawal of several brigades that were sent to the right, where the enemy were making forward demonstrations from their position on the Weldon Railroad, and this excitement was increased by the sound of heavy firing in that direction. Towards evening reports and prisoners came in, from whom we learned that Grant had advanced against our lines and driven our troops back, but with reinforcements coming up, we in turn drove them back, capturing from twelve to fifteen hundred prisoners and several stands of colors, beside killing and wounding a large number. Our own loss is not yet ascertained but is said to be light in comparison to what we inflicted.

Rain has been falling heavily all day, notwithstanding which I managed to call upon some ladies by whom I was most pleasantly entertained, and finished up by taking supper at friend Gilmore's, where I spent the evening.

October 2, 1864 On awaking this morning I found that the rain had ceased, though the whole sky was one mass of dull leaden clouds. However about twelve o'clock the sun broke through and the rest of the day was intensely hot, which leads us to look for more rain before long. This morning I attended Grace Church, and after dinner, returned to my gun.

Our patient had a narrow escape from what might have proved a serious accident this morning, by the plaster falling down in the room where she is lying. Fortunately though it fell nearly along side of her couch and none of it fell on her. Though she was greatly frightened for the moment, yet no apprehensions are entertained that the fright will injure her.

Our loss in yesterday's fighting is put down at about five hundred in killed, wounded, and missing.

October 3, 1864 Last night and today it was very cloudy but though appearances were very threatening and the weather very uncomfortable, yet it did not rain. About two o'clock this morning we were awakened by the rapid firing of the pickets, and everything was made ready in case of a charge, but in about fifteen minutes it quieted down to the usual standard and we went to sleep again. There was nothing done on the lines today that I could learn.

October 4, 1864 Today's papers bring us the news of the appointment of General Beauregard to the command of the Department of the Southwest. This, together with the rapid advance and injury of Forrest in Sherman's rear, leads us to look for good news from that quarter soon. Sherman is beginning to feel very uneasy in Atlanta, and is reported to have said that if he is compelled to fall back from there he will lay the town in ashes, a threat which he is quite heroic and noble enough to put into execution. Should he do so, we must send another division to Early who has already turned the tables on Sheridan in the valley, and by that means give the North the second edition of Chambersburg. In such the stern law of retaliation must be our only course.

The day has been remarkably pleasant and to add to it, early this morning the pickets agreed to do no shooting during the day.

October 5, 1864 About nine o'clock last night, after having written up and while everything was very quiet, very rapid musketry firing a short distance on our right indicated a row of some kind. Almost in a moment all hands were at their posts, and then the question, "What is it?" was asked, but cut short by the opening of the enemy's artillery. And now the firing becomes hot and heavy, passing us and gradually extending both to the right and the left, until the air became almost light with the bursting of shells from artillery and mortars, and the fire from the muskets. This continued nearly an hour when it gradually died out, and quiet again was restored. I have been unable to learn what it was about, beyond the supposition that it was a false alarm on the picket lines. During the disturbance, O. S. Benson, one of our members, was struck on the arm by a spent ball which inflicted a slight wound, and this is the only casualty of which I could hear. The lines were very quiet today.

October 6, 1864 The pickets of both sides have entered into a private arrangement to do no sharpshooting during the day (though with dusk of evening this truce ceases and then they go at it with a will). All day, little white flags can be seen flying from nearly every picket pit that is on the enemy's line, for they use handkerchiefs for that purpose. This thing is not quite as common with our troops; as handkerchiefs are not convenient, we do not hoist any. This is a very agreeable arrangement as it enables us to move about with considerable freedom, though it does not pay to be too exposed as both sides have a sly way of throwing an occasional bullet over which hurts where it hits. These shots are always fired from the main lines; the pickets preserve the purity of the white flag.

October 7, 1864 For some days past the enemy have been inching up to our lines on the north side of the James with a view probably to ulterior movements, to all of which our generals offered no opposition until this morning, when thinking that they had advanced far enough, they threw three or four brigades forward. After some severe fighting, they succeeded in driving the enemy back some four miles, capturing nine pieces of artillery, four or five hundred prisoners, and about one hundred and fifty horses, besides killing and wounding quite a number. After this, our troops fell back to their original lines, though the enemy did not attempt to reoccupy theirs. Our loss was not heavy. Nothing was done on our portion of the lines, though from the constant movements of our troops here it is very probable that something will be done here soon.

October 8, 1864 This afternoon I witnessed for the first time in my life a military execution. The victim was a private named Snow, belonging to Wise's Brigade, who was shot for desertion. It was his third or fourth offense; all his previous offenses in that line had been pardoned, they all coming under the limits of the pardon proclamation of the President issued last fall after the return of our army from Gettysburg. The unfortunate man met his fate with the utmost composure, much more indeed than was exhibited by the spectators. He expressed himself utterly resigned to his fate. I cannot comprehend the source from which men in such cases derive the nerve which they display, for though death is common to all, nevertheless to a man of some mind, come when it will, it is an awful moment and well calculated for the exhibition of nature's weakness. 'Tis true men rush to almost certain death in the discharge of duty, or beckoned on by that ignis fatuus of the soldiers fame with a light step and every pulse beating high with the excitement of the moment and defying the utmost efforts of nature to unman them. But here is a man who is brought before his comrades and associates in irons. He sees or feels himself the one object on whom all eyes are turned. He sees the stake to which he is soon to be tied, near it the coffin, and a step or two off the grave dug and only waiting its occupant. Then comes the dread preparation; his irons are taken off and his hands tied behind him, he is led to the stake, made to kneel, and tied to it, the chaplain goes to him for a last few words and perhaps a last prayer, he then is blindfolded, he has taken his last look of earth. Soon he hears the firm and measured tramp of the men detailed to cut short his earthly career. The proper officer is then heard reading his crime, the sentence of the court-martial, and the endorsement of the commanding general. A moment's silence, the signal is given, and the poor wretch is launched into eternity. What supports a man in such a moment as this no one can tell, and singular though it may seem, men who have been condemned to death for cowardice in the presence of the enemy have yet been known to die exhibiting not the least sign of fear, and not even assuming the air of the most distant bravado. This is our anomaly.

The weather last night turned very cold and today overcoats have been in great demand. As I am unfortunately without one, I took it out in an extra shiver or two.

October 9, 1864 The weather has moderated considerably, but is more cold than comfortable. This morning I was sent off on a detail to cut wood. After cutting a wagon load, and while passing through town on my way back to the gun, I stopped at Mr. E.'s where I spent the remainder of the day. I found Eddy much improved, so much so that while in a room next to the one she occupies, I heard her laugh, though the laugh was but a ghost of former efforts at hilarity indulged in by the same party previous to her illness.

October 10, 1864 During last night some fifteen or twenty deserters came in, who reported that Grant was massing troops in our immediate front for the purpose of charging our lines at daylight, for which reason we were all called up at four o'clock, and a couple of brigades brought up in the rear line to be at hand in case of necessity to relieve a pressure from any part of the line where it might be felt. But daylight came without the enemy making any movement, probably feeling sure that we, being warned by the deserters, would be all ready to receive them. That such a move was contemplated and in the process of execution I have no doubt, as the "Reveille" drums and bugles showed the presence of a much larger force than usual. Nothing occurred during the day worth noting.

October 11, 1864 This afternoon I went to town on a forty-eight hour permit and on arriving there I found a great commotion among the Negroes, both free and slave, as there were guards on all the streets arresting all the males. During the day they gathered up from fifteen hundred to two thousand. They were wanted to throw up some batteries to the right of our line and the usual method of obtaining them is too slow for emergencies.

This evening I was permitted to see our convalescent, whom I found looking much better than, in view of her serious illness, I had a right to expect. It was a pleasant, yet rather amusing sight to see her taking a little exercise by walking across the room supported by her father, and from his pleased looks I imagine that he assisted her feeble steps with more fond pride than he ever felt before, even in her first attempts in the days of her infancy.

October 12, 1864 In view of the large reinforcements which Grant is daily receiving, and the probability that he will attempt to make a grand strike before the November election in the North, General Lee is making every exertion to fill our lines at all points, to which end all detailed men not absolutely needed have been ordered to their commands. The hospitals have been emptied of their incubi, and even those who under less pressing circumstances would be allowed to remain have been ordered to their commands. In addition to this an order was issued today to the artillery chiefs to send half the drivers of each batttery and all the surplus men to the trenches where they will be furnished with muskets. As the latter order brings from two or three thousand good men in the field, its importance is very apparent.

October 13, 1864 Last evening, heavy cannonading and musketry fire occurred on the lines, which continued with more or less vigor for about three quarters of an hour. Once or twice I attempted to go out to my gun, but I felt satisfied that no charge would be made by either party on the main line unless at early daybreak, and the artillery seldom have anything to do with a charge on the picket line. But notwithstanding all this I felt quite anxious, till today when I learned that it was a false alarm which did not amount to anything. At nine o'clock pm I bade my friends good-night and good-by, and in the course of half an hour or so arrived at my gun, where I found everything as quiet as could be expected under the infliction of "Minies" from the enemy's sharpshooters. The weather has been very pleasant today, though the nights are very chilly.

October 14, 1864 Today's papers bring the news that the enemy attempted to make an advance on Richmond by the Darbytown and Charles City Road, but this met with such a stubborn resistance at our works on those roads that though they charged three or four times with large numbers, they were driven back every time with what General Lee reports to be heavy loss, while our own loss is slight indeed. This is gratifying to us who, holding as we do the city of Petersburg, and Richmond from this side, can now feel satisfied that the latter city is equally well defended at her other approaches, a circumstance which has heretofore given us great uneasiness. From present appearances and counting all sources, we will soon have from thirty to forty thousand more troops in the field, so if Grant will only delay five days longer he may then come on.

October 15, 1864 By an order received today, Sergeant Major, couriers, and all other staff incubi of the artillery have been ordered to the trenches. This will make the Adjutant's position anything but insecure, though it is but right that those who have been living in comparative ease for the last three or four months should bear a little of the heat and burden of the heavy day which we are looking for with the advent of every sun. After all this preparation, I certainly hope that Grant will make his attempt while we are in as good condition to receive it as we are (or will be in a day or two more), and I think that unless he can bring at least three men to our one, he will find that though he may say the "Rebellion is on its last legs", yet he has not power sufficient to throw it off of them.

This morning I was sent off on a detail to cut poles and logs with which to form a traverse on the right of our other Napoleon. After a day's hard work I went to town and spent the evening at Mr. E.'s house, and arrived at my gun about ten at night.

October 16, 1864 The day passed off very quietly but I cannot but think that it is the quiet that precedes the storm, and this state of suspense is to me worse than the hardest reality can be. That a great battle is imminent is the settled conviction of everybody. That it will decide this war is my firm belief and this being the case, the sooner we get at it, the better will I, for one, be pleased, though with each day's delay we increase in numbers. If in the coming battle we should be worsted, it will not be for want of care on the part of our glorious old chief in putting every available man in the field.

October 17, 1864 This morning I was again sent off on a detail to cut poles for our work, and returned to my gun about ten o'clock at night. On getting there I found the troops in considerable commotion, dodging mortar shell which the enemy were, and had been, sending over all day, eight and ten at a time. It was amusing to see the men watching the shell as they were coming over and running from them when they came too near for comfort, while shouts of laughter greeted the impromptu efforts of grand and lofty tumbling. Thus far, none have been hurt that I could hear of, but some damage has been done to the works in several places, which was however, repaired immediately.

There was a report in town today of a victory gained by Early over some of Sheridan's Division, but I could not learn any particulars. By General Order No. 81, published today by the War Department, all men between the ages of forty-five and fifty, who have heretofore been in the reserve forces, have been ordered into the field. This has occasioned a great deal of commotion among the dry bones.

October 18, 1864 Today, the mortar practice of the enemy was renewed, and I am free to own that they throw their shell a little too near to our gun to suit my idea of comfort, as I have no doubt that they are getting ready for the big fight which we are all looking for.

October 19, 1864 Everything on the lines has been very quiet today, though it is extremely dangerous to expose oneself, as the confounded Yankees seem to keep a most vigilant watch, and whenever a head is shown, shoot at it, and not infrequently with the most fatal effects, a practice which I think our troops might follow with great advantage, as it is no unusual occurrence to see the enemy walking in full view, and frequently in groups of from three to six or more. For our men not to fire from the main lines may be good policy, but I must plead guilty to the ignorance of not being able to see it.

October 20, 1864 This morning I was again sent on a detail to cut poles for the traverse which our company is building, though I think this will be about the last, as one wagon load more will be enough. After getting through with my work, I went to friend E.'s house and spent a few hours very pleasantly, though I found Mrs. E. suffering somewhat from neuralgia in the face and head. Eddy is getting along so well as to be able to walk across the floor without assistance.

I returned to my gun between eleven and twelve o'clock, having waited for the moon to rise. On arriving there I found that the enemy had been throwing mortar shell over in a very lively manner. One of which, striking the left wheel of my gun, knocked it to pieces, though no other damage was done, and this was soon repaired by putting up one of our spare wheels.

October 21, 1864 Last night all the troops on the line received orders to be in their places by half past three o'clock this morning, as a deserter had come in who reported that the enemy were making preparations to charge the lines. Accordingly at the hour named we were all called up and as the morning was foggy and very chilly, anyone can imagine what a pleasant time we had till daylight. But it is almost needless to say that no charge was made, nor can I for one moment believe that one will ever be made at this point. Perhaps they think to blind our generals by menacing this part while they really intend to strike some other portion of the line, but if this is their idea, let them pitch in. We are willing. As to these or other reports of deserters, we have long since learned that but little reliance is to be placed in them.

October 22, 1864 This morning, it being my turn on a forty-eight hour permit, I arrived at Mr. E.'s and found he had at last concluded to move his shop back to his old stand on Sycamore Street, as the place which he had been occupying on Old Street was too small and did not admit of the putting up of a stove. Repairing to the scene of operation, I went to work with a hearty will and by dark, we had everything moved down and the presses all cleaned and ready to put up, and as this had been no small job, I was not at all displeased when darkness put an end to our labors. I most sincerely trust that if the enemy recommence the shelling of the city that this place may escape being struck, as one shell might do sufficient damage to almost ruin Mr. E. who has already lost no inconsiderable amount by the presence of the Yankees in the destruction of presses and type.

October 23, 1864 Having borrowed a boiled shirt and collar from friend E. I went to Grace Church this morning where the Reverend Mr. Gibson held forth from a text taken from the twenty-second chapter of Numbers, and during this discourse, I could not but smile to think how often the miracle of the ass speaking had been reproduced in our day, though this reflection did not at all touch the speaker who is an honest hearted Christian gentleman of no mean talents, and one whom I greatly admire. On returning from church I found Miss E. quite indisposed, having had a very severe chill during the morning, and in the evening, Mrs. E. was taken down with neuralgia from which she suffered greatly. This afternoon I called on J. Y. G. with whom I spent several hours very pleasantly, and to add to the rarity of the sensation experienced this day, after supper, the Countess of Blessington favored us with her presence.

October 24, 1864 After an early breakfast, we all went to work, and by three o'clock had the presses and other machinery up, and everything in the best order that circumstances would allow us to put them. I then got my dinner, after which I went to my gun where I found everything very quiet.

Last night, Kellam arrived from Norfolk, bringing several letters for our boys from home but none for me, in view of which I am becoming very much discouraged as it seems my friends in Norfolk have entirely ceased writing to me. Though I have written twelve or fifteen letters to them this year, I have not received a single line in reply, and this is the more singular as many of my letters have been sent by flag of truce, a channel through which they could answer without at all compromising themselves. But their kindness to me in the past leads me to hope and believe that even if they do not write to me, it yet affords them some satisfaction to hear from me, so I shall continue to write, and shall start a letter today by flag of truce.

October 25, 1864 For the last two or three days we have not been troubled by the enemy's mortar shell, but this morning they had quite a lively time of it about a half a mile on our left. The enemy were engaged in throwing up a heavy breastwork in the rear of their main lines, upon seeing which our batteries on the left opened up on them, which of course elicited a reply, but as our guns seemed to do no damage, the firing gradually eased off until it ceased entirely.

October 26, 1864 Slowly but gradually the news comes to us of another reverse to our arms in the valley, and the whole is owing to the fact that in the midst of assured success, our troops forgot the great issue at stake, and in passing through the camps from which they had routed the enemy, stopped to load themselves with the rich booty that was lying about in all directions. During this fatal pause, the enemy was slightly reinforced, rallied, and succeeded in reversing the fortunes of the day in their own favor, recapturing eighteen pieces of artillery which we had taken from them early in the fight, and capturing twenty-three pieces of our artillery. It is true that we captured twelve or fifteen hundred prisoners, and killed and wounded a very large number of the enemy in comparison, but the prestige and material results of the fight remain with the enemy. It is a fact becoming more apparent every day even to the least observant that our armies are in a sad state of disorganization, which is not alone confined to the privates, but extends to officers of even high grade, and it is to this unfortunate state of things to which we may more often attribute our want of success than to the generalship or numerical superiority of the enemy. Should the war last two years longer, our armies must be entirely reorganized, and the rules and articles of war enforced and carried out, or all that has been done will have been done in vain, and ultimate defeat and consequently subjugation awaits us.

-It has been said by many that the Southerners were great fighters but poor soldiers, and Walters would seem to agree. The concern with personal interests at the expense of affairs at large were not confined to the army, but also occurred between the individual states and the central Confederate government. Of course, Walters and his fellows were still undaunted by the numerical superiority of the enemy, and obviously believed, even after three years of fighting, that one Rebel could whip ten Yankees.-

October 27, 1864 Shortly after daylight this morning, heavy artillery firing was heard on our right and supposed to be in the vicinity of the Boydton Plank Road. As the morning advanced, this grew heavier, accompanied by the roll of musketry. Soon Harris' Brigade, which holds this portion of the line, and Wilcox's old brigade were ordered out, and together with Mahone's, sent to the scene of action, while Bushrod Johnson lengthened out his line from the left to fill up the space from which the two first named brigades had been withdrawn. All this gave evidence of heavy works, as these are choice troops who always make their mark when engaged, representing three states of the Confederacy, the troops which have always been first among the foremost, viz Virginia, Mississippi, and Alabama. Towards night reports from the fight began to come in from which we learned that the enemy, early in the morning, had assaulted the right of our lines and by the vigor of his onset after considerable work, forced a brigade or two of cavalry back a couple of miles, when they were met by two of Heth's North Carolina brigades who checked and held them until Mahone came up, and as by this time Hampton with his cavalry was working briskly in their rear, the enemy fell back to the plank road where they made a determined stand. As the day was by this time nearly spent, they were left there while preparations were made to recommence the fight early tomorrow morning. Shortly after dark, the enemy charged our works at the Crater and as it was held by a brigade which has never been known to stand, they drove them out without difficulty, but in a short time Gracie's Alabama Brigade was moved up, and retook the line capturing about fifty prisoners.

About the time that this took place, a strong line of the enemy assaulted our picket lines just to the right of my gun, and after a stubborn resistance, drove our men out and took possession of about one hundred yards of our picket line. Immediately two hundred men from the Holcomb Legion were selected to retake the lines, which they did in gallant style, capturing some thirty or forty prisoners. They themselves sustained but a loss of one man killed, and thus our lines remained as they were. While all this was going on, the artillery and mortars on both sides were doing their best to add to the din and did a splendid business in the noise and pyrotechnic line. Some fifteen or twenty mortar shell would be seen in the air at the same time. As it was thought that these demonstrations in this vicinity were merely intended to draw attention from our right, and thought probable that more would be attempted, we were ordered to remain up all night, and as the weather was cold and the rain coming down in no very gentle showers, this was by no means pleasant. As I am writing in my tent by the flickering of a piece of light wood, cold shivers run through me, while an occasional anathema from without tells the fact that the rest of the gun detachment are awake to all the discomforts of their position, but I must get out of this as our captain is just now inquiring whether or not all our men are at their posts.

October 28, 1864 About three o'clock this morning the rain ceased and the stars came out, but the wind from the north and east was very chilly. After what I had written last night, nothing occurred to break the stillness. The enemy probably had enough of it. Soon after day it was discovered that the enemy had left the Boydton Plank Road and fallen back to their old line on the Weldon Railroad, upon which our troops also fell back to their old positions, which ends this affair. During this we lost from eight hundred to a thousand men, the majority being taken prisoner, while the enemy's loss will not fall short of three thousand. We also captured four pieces of artillery but could not bring them off for want of horses. There is one very significant fact connected with this fight which is that seven-eighths of the enemy's killed, wounded, or prisoners were decorated with the McClellan Badge. This is a decidedly novel method of electioneering, and one entirely original with the chiefs of the Lincoln Party. From the papers we learn that considerable fighting was done yesterday on the extreme left of our line, in which as on the right, we were also successful, capturing several hundred prisoners and seven stands of colors.

October 29, 1864 As it was thought possible that the enemy might make an endeavor on our line, we were called up at three o'clock this morning, but nothing was done. In fact, the enemy were remarkably quiet all day, so much so that our men exposed themselves with perfect impunity. I forgot to state yesterday that on Thursday (the 27th), we captured five stands of colors, which with the seven captured near Richmond, will do very well for one day's fighting.

October 30, 1864 (Sunday) Both sides seemed disposed to take a rest today as scarcely a gun was fired during the day, but tonight we are making up for the quiet. Shortly after dark a number of the enemy's pickets deserted and came into our lines, and on being carried before General Mahone, they stated that by their leaving a large space was made in their picket line, by which he if he chose, he could pass through and come up in the rear of their line and capture the whole of it. After many questions and some deliberate motion, General Mahone determined to act upon the suggestion, so taking one of them with him for a guide, and threatening to hang the rest should the information prove false, he sent General Finegan with three regiments upon the errand. Under the guidance of the deserter they passed from our works and on reaching the opposite picket line, found it deserted at this point. Passing well through it the column was moved by the flank and then "forward" was whispered, and soon the Yankee line was reached from the rear, and a more astonished set of men perhaps never were seen before, but not a word was allowed. They were ordered in line and the column moved to our works, which they reached just as the enemy discovered that their line had been emptied for the space of a mile. Upon this they opened a furious fire of musketry and artillery which was soon carried down the line and entered into by both sides without much damage to either side. By this maneuver we bagged two hundred and forty officers and men without losing a single man ourselves.

October 31, 1864 By a late order emanating from artillery headquarters, our pleasant forty-eight hour permits have been cut down to twelve hours, and as we have long since learned to be satisfied with small favors when we cannot get large ones, I went to town this morning, though with the full determination to remain until tomorrow morning. On arriving I found my friends all well. During the day I learned that Dean Lee, one of our best members, had been wounded dangerously by a Yankee sharpshooter. The ball struck him on the left side of the face, severed the facial artery, and passing down into his shoulder, lodged somewhere in the back. Just where had not been discovered up to late this evening. The wound is supposed to be mortal. His father was immediately telegraphed for and is expected down tomorrow night.

November 1, 1864 After spending a very pleasant evening and comfortable night, I left town shortly after daylight and soon reached my gun. I found sharpshooting going on very briskly which continued so throughout the day. In the afternoon I had a very narrow escape. While in a bent position, mixing some clay to build a chimney, a bullet passed within two inches of my face and spread through a tent beside which I was standing. I got away from that place in a hurry.

Accounts from Dean Lee represent him as being very comfortable, but the bullet has not been found yet.

November 2, 1864 Today set in cloudy and about noon it began to rain which continued throughout the day. This morning without any apparent reason, the enemy opened on our part of the line with several pieces of artillery. About half an hour after, some of our artillery in the rear line returned the fire. This caused the enemy to increase his fire and throw in a few mortars, which made a lively noise for an hour or so when both sides cooled down. During the shelling I was struck on the head by a bullet from one of the shell which however did not strike hard enough to even give me a head-ache. This afternoon both sides again indulged in an hour or two of shelling without apparent result, though a couple of our men of Harris' Brigade who hold this portion of the line were wounded, one of them mortally.

November 3, 1864 All last night and today a drizzling rain has been falling which, together with the mud in the ditches and trenches, renders us very uncomfortable. There was nothing done on the lines today, and no news of interest or importance from other quarters.

November 4, 1864 The rain which set in the night before last still continues, and the weather is becoming very cold. Should this continue but a few days longer, active operations in this section must cease, nor would I be surprised if both sides were to draw their picket lines soon, as it requires more than an iron constitution to withstand the exposure to which pickets are subjected.

November 5, 1864 This morning the weather showed signs of clouding up and at night there was every indication of fair weather tomorrow. Just after dark, H. C. Lovitt, a member of my company, was shot. The ball entered above the hip bone on the right side and, passing downward, made its way out between the bone and the femoral artery, about two thirds of the length of the limb above the right knee, making a wound thirteen inches in length, which though serious, is not necessarily fatal. Young Lee is still quite comfortable, but as the ball has not yet been found, I begin to fear that he will not recover. The impression of the surgeon is that the ball is lodged against the shoulder blade.

November 6, 1864 About eight o'clock last night, though no orders were issued, it yet became apparent that something was up, though what this something was we could not find out at the time. But we did soon after, for about eleven o'clock all hands were called up and a few minutes after, heavy firing, first of musketry, then artillery and mortar, began to the left of us, which was soon carried down by us and to the right. This continued for upwards of an hour when it gradually died out. At an early hour this morning, it began again but ceased before daylight. During the day I learned that Bushrod Johnson (whose division begins just on our left and extends down to the river) charged the whole length of the enemy's picket line and captured it, but this morning the enemy charged him in turn in heavy force and retook their lines. We got the worst of it as our loss will not fall far short of four hundred, while that of the enemy is not more than half that number. The object of the charge was a reconnaissance as it was reported that the enemy had withdrawn their forces from a portion of our left front, but it was discovered that they were in sufficient force still to hold their lines.

November 7, 1864 Whatever of interest this day might possess, it all yields to the two great events of tomorrow; the election at the North, and the meeting of publication of the President's message to Congress of the Confederate States, which assembled today at Richmond. The first will (I doubt not and certainly hope) result in the re-election of Lincoln. I think that peace is not so far off by that, as it will be by the election of McClellan. In the former event, there is a possibility of the Pacific States leaving the Old Union to form a Confederacy of their own, and in this case the Northwestern States will most probably cut loose from the Eastern, and this of itself would end the war (unless the South should carry the war into the Eastern States for the purpose of giving the "Saints" a taste of the war which they were mainly instrumental in bringing upon the people of this country). But should McClellan be elected, I fear hoping much, for his administration will furnish him with men and means in sufficient number and quantity to overwhelm the shattered remains of the past three and a half years of hard fighting.

November 8, 1864 President Davis's message is published today and gives much cause for dissatisfaction in one portion of it, in which he more than hints at the probable necessity of making soldiers of the Negroes at no very distant day. I shall not at this time enter into a discussion of this subject, but trust that this necessity may never occur.

November 9, 1864 At an early hour this morning, I went to town on a twelve hour leave. I found the family all well and Miss Eddy doing well. In the afternoon, I called on Mrs. J. Y. G. whom I also found as well as usual. As I had determined to remain in town all night, I was considerably disturbed about dark by the sound of rapid firing in the direction of my battery, and after listening to it for a short time, was on the point of going out when it began to slacken, and in half an hour thereafter it had ceased entirely to my great relief.

November 10, 1864 About daylight this morning I got up and made for my gun where, on arriving, I found everything as quiet as could be expected under the dispensation of a heavy sharpshooting fire. During last night, Mahone's Division was withdrawn from the lines, and B. Johnson stretched out so as to occupy a portion of the line just vacated, while Seales' Brigade of Wilcox's Division was moved up to the left so as to connect with the city battalion reserves and detailed men who hold the line between the two. What is to be done with Mahone's Division is not known, though there is a rumor that as Grant is extending his lines into North Carolina, they are going in that direction as a sort of counter movement.

November 11, 1864 This morning, Theodore Taylor of our company was shot by a sharpshooter. The ball entered in the upper part of the right breast and, passing through, emerged under the left shoulder blade causing death in about ten minutes. The deceased was a first class soldier, kind and obliging in all his actions among his associates, a very moral young man. Unfortunately, we have few like him and none better. He was carried to the city for interment, and will be placed for the present in the lot adjoining Grace Church, at which the funeral services will be held tomorrow.

During the day we were heavily shelled by the enemy's mortars, of which six and eight shell were frequently in the air at a time, and as their practice is rendering their aim very accurate, we were constantly kept on the qui vive to dodge them. Fortunately no one was hurt, though considerable damage was done to our breastworks, which however will be repaired tonight.

November 12, 1864 Today we had a renewal of the mortar shelling but not as heavy or long continued as that of yesterday. On both days our mortars replied to them, but the odds are largely against us as the enemy has at least five to our one.

It is generally believed that Lincoln has been re-elected, as all the states heard from thus far give him a majority, while those not heard from could not turn the scale in favor of McClellan. To judge the Yankee Army by the pickets in front of our line, they are not over well pleased with the results of the election, for as our men would in derision cheer Lincoln, they ceased and using all the strength of their lungs would shout for McClellan.

During the day our lines were visited by Generals R. E. Lee, Anderson, and others of lesser note.

November 13, 1864 (Sunday) The day has passed off unusually quietly. Hardly a musket shot broke the stillness, but we did not for this reason expose ourselves at all, as we have been here too long to place any dependence in such occasional lulls of sharpshooting.

November 14, 1864 By extracts from the Northern papers in the Richmond papers today, we see that Lincoln calls for the modest number of one million men wherewith at once to smash this rebellion. This is decidedly rich, that this little affair which was to be put down in three months with seventy thousand, should at the end of the fourth year require one million, and after that number have been already nearly used up. But let them come and they will find that the same spirit of resistance which nerved our men at First Manassas still animates us.

November 15, 1864 The time of our permits has been lengthened to twenty-four hours. I went to town today and enjoyed myself hugely, as usual, winding up the day by beating Mr. E. several games of backgammon, though I am sadly out of practice as I have not played more than two or three games for the last three years.

November 16, 1864 After our early breakfast, I returned to my gun and found two bullet holes through my tent. This is rather demoralizing as I thought that my tent was entirely out of harm's way. If this continues, I shall be compelled to stoop a little lower, though I am puzzled as how to accomplish that, as ever since I was struck in the neck I have moved about with my body at right angles. Well, if needs must, I shall try a little of the snake locomotion.

November 17, 1864 Everything has been very quiet on the lines today. Bushrod Johnson's Division has been stretched out to the right so as to occupy the line of two of Mahone's Brigades. The latter of whom has gone into winter quarters with his whole division and as things look now, I should not be surprised if the artillery would be compelled to remain on the lines the whole winter.

November 18, 1864 Today, we were again subjected to a very heavy mortar shelling. Really, this thing is becoming a terrible bore, as it keeps us dodging and tumbling about and in constant fear of having our tents invaded by one of the shell, and all torn and bursted up.

This afternoon, I went over to our mortar batteries to see our lieutenant in charge there, and on my return to the gun, a "Minie" pipped me in front of the right thigh, which though it did not go in has left quite a bruise.

November 19, 1864 Last night, it began to rain and has continued to do so all this day with no prospect of its clearing off, but notwithstanding this we were again treated to two or three hours mortar shelling. Beyond this, nothing was done. Today, an order was circulated to reduce the number of caissons of a battery by one half. This is done on account of the scarcity of horses.

November 20, 1864 The rain still continues and the mud in the trenches is over the shoe tops in consequence, which makes our life here almost intolerable.

November 21, 1864 It was my turn to go to town today, but having no overcoat and my blanket being soaking wet (as I stood guard last night with it on), I did not go. I will try to go tomorrow, unless the boys on my gun should hold me to my day, in which case I must wait until my day comes around again.

November 22, 1864 Up to nearly daylight, the rain came down incessantly, but shortly after it ceased. About eleven o'clock the sun came out, though his rays were very faint nor does it look as though it would hold fair long. This morning I went to town where I learned that Early's Corps had come down and were going in winter quarters in the neighborhood of Richmond, though the cavalry will still remain in the valley.

November 23, 1864 After dark last night the weather became very cold and this morning, ice was found from one to one and a half an inch thick, though it moderated considerably after the sun had been up a couple of hours. About ten o'clock I left town and soon got to my gun where I found everything very quiet. The pickets on both sides have agreed to a few hours cessation of hostilities to enable them to empty and dry their pits. At dark they recommenced sharpshooting.

November 24, 1864 This evening the officers in charge of the respective picket lines met midway under the shield of a white flag and mutually agreed to a cessation of hostilities every evening from sunset til dark, to enable each side to relieve their picket posts without being exposed to fire. This is a very happy management for both parties and can injure neither, and the moment it became known, loud and long cheering testified to the satisfaction of all.

November 25, 1864 It is rumored among the troops that Hoke's Division has gone to Georgia to lend a hand against Sherman, and that Kershaw's Division and Young's Brigade of dismounted cavalry are under orders for the same destination. This looks as though General Lee felt satisfied of his ability to hold his own, notwithstanding the boastings of the Yankee journals, and though all appearances would seem to indicate a battle at no very distant day, yet we have so often been deceived that it will not pay to prophecy upon the subject.

November 26, 1864 Nothing worthy of mention occurred today.

November 27, 1864 A very lively mortar duel was engaged in by both sides for several hours today, occasionally varied by artillery practice by the enemy during the afternoon. Cary B. Wilson of our company was shot through the left limb above the knee by a ball from a sharpshooter, which splintered the bone without shattering it. A short time after, John L. Reid received a similar bullet through the fleshy part of his left limb, also above the knee. The former wound is serious, but the latter is an excellent furlough wound.

November 28, 1864 This morning I went to town on a twenty-four hour permit where I found all well. John B. Ege went over to Richmond this afternoon and wished very much that I should accompany him and though I would gladly have done so, the fear of getting myself in trouble restrained me. But I was amply repaid for my remaining behind by the pleasant evening which I spent at the house.

November 29, 1864 I reached my gun about ten o'clock and found everything quiet, but in the afternoon we were again subjected to a heavy mortar shelling, during which some of our boys lost all they had by shell falling and exploding in their tents. Thus far I have escaped, but goodness only knows when it will be my turn, and as my tent contains all that I possess, an explosion in it would ruin me, though this is borrowing trouble.

November 30, 1864 News was received today of a brilliant though small cavalry affair in the valley in which two of our brigades captured two field pieces, several stands of colors, and some five or six hundred prisoners, and spiked two siege guns which we were unable to bring off, with a loss on our side of but two killed and less than twenty wounded. Our troops also tapped the B. and O. Railroad in two places. Our own lines were very quiet.

December 1, 1864 We were again subjected to a very heavy mortar shelling which was vigorously returned by our mortar. We are gradually increasing the number of our mortars, and I trust that in that particular at least, we will soon be able to compete with the enemy. A short distance in the rear of our line we have two eight inch and five Coehorn mortars, and expect soon to get some more of the latter. To the left of those are two more eight inch and places long prepared for two or three more. Of these mortars in the first battery, our company man two 8-inch and four Coehorns and will most probably man at least two more of these which they expect soon to receive. This, with the four guns which we have on the line, and a number of men who have muskets in the corps battalion of "Muskettors", fully occupies all our members, though I understand that we have at present one hundred and fifty-three names on our rolls, of whom about one hundred and ten are in the trenches. This is as fine a company record as can be shown by any company in service, and one of which we may well be, and are, very proud.

-By this time, Grandy's Battery had become one of the few companies in Lee's Army to keep a full number of men on its rolls, thanks to the steady enlistments of young men who "ran the blockade" from Norfolk and Portsmouth to join. The mortar battery detachment mentioned by Walters did eventually receive a total of seven Coehorn mortars and two 8-inch mortars. They were under the command of Lieutenant Henry V. Moore. The main body of the Blues, under the command of Captain Grandy, remained on the Petersburg lines with their two Napoleons and their two 3-inch rifles. In addition to the Muskettors, a few men of the company were assigned to staff duties and to the reserve artillery camp near Amelia Courthouse.-

December 2, 1864 This afternoon the enemy again opened on us with his mortars and as ours did not reply, he is keeping it up, and I should not be surprised if they continued to do so all night. As they are firing by intervals of ten or fifteen minutes, this will be no great inducement to a comfortable night's rest, as I do not think our tents are quite strong enough to resist a shell. However, I shall try it.

December 3, 1864 As I anticipated last evening, the mortar shelling was kept up all night, and though many fell in our lines, yet no one was injured. To guard against them, the men on guard kept a sharp look out and when they saw any which they judged would fall in the immediate neighborhood of their detachment, the alarm was given, upon which all hands tumbled out; to go to sleep again as soon as the shell exploded. About nine o'clock our mortars opened on the enemy and after about two hours of very heavy shelling, both sides ceased. During the firing W. D. Montague, one of our corporals in charge of an 8-inch mortar, was struck in the side by a piece of shell which broke one of his ribs, and it is feared that his injuries, being internal, may prove serious. Without any idea of depreciating anyone, it is the common remark among all who know Montague that there is no better soldier in the Confederate service.

December 4, 1864 (Sunday) Yesterday, in writing up for Friday, I forgot to state that General Gracie was killed by a shell from the enemy while looking over the works. Today passed off without any incident worth recording.

December 5, 1864 Everything is beginning to assume that state of unrest which usually precedes a battle. Hospitals are being broken up, brigades in line sent to the rear while those that remain are stretched out to cover as much space as possible, and all the troops have received orders to keep three days rations cooked. Other circumstances point to a battle at no very remote day, but at what point we are to look for it, no one with our very limited means of information can even conjecture, though if I were asked, I think I should say that for the purpose of drawing Lee's attention from the immediate vicinity of Richmond, Grant may make a strong demonstration on our right in the neighborhood possibly of Dinwiddie Courthouse, hoping thereby to draw enough of our troops, either from these or the Richmond lines, to give him hopes of success in the event of an attack. There are some who incline to the opinion that Grant may send a portion of his troops over land to help Sherman out, but I cannot entertain any such idea.

> -Walters guessed correctly as to where the Union army would strike, but it would be nearly four months before this "strong demonstration" would finally take place.-

December 6, 1864 Stillness reigns among our lines, but the work of "Indian Summer" is nearly at an end, and if Grant intends to do anything, I think it must be done soon.

December 7, 1864 This evening for some reason or other, the Yankee pickets would not cease their sharpshooting so that ours were obliged to relieve the line under fire, but no accident occurred in consequence that I could hear of. One reason given for this was that a new division had taken the place of those who held the lines when the truce was agreed on, of which I made mention some days ago.

December 8, 1864 Last night we received orders to call all hands at an hour before daylight as it was again reported that an attack would be made, but as usual, this was proved to be a humbug. This morning I went to town where I found Mr. E's family all well. In the afternoon, Mrs. Ege, at my request, called with me on Mrs. Maggie Gilmore and I was much pleased to observe that both ladies seemed to take a liking each to the other.

December 9, 1864 During the night the weather turned very cold and remained so all day, and if it does not snow tonight then no dependence is to be placed on signs. About ten o'clock I left town and soon got out to my gun where I learned that last evening, orders had been sent to the city for all who had permits to report to their companies immediately as an attack was expected. Fortunately, I did not get the order, though if I had, it is doubtful if I should have obeyed the order as the rumor of an attack is an everyday occurrence, resulting in nothing but the curtailing of our enjoyment of that hour between daybreak and sunrise, which I so love to devote to dozing and winking.

December 10, 1864 Shortly after dark last night it began to snow, which it continued to do till nearly daylight this morning. It was no light, flaky snow that fell, but a pebbly affair which was about two-thirds hail and froze as it fell, sufficiently hard to bear a man's weight. I was on guard during the night and believe that I suffered more than on any previous night since I have been in the service, and yet my sufferings were light in comparison with those of the poor fellows on picket, and I heard this morning that one was brought in from the picket line frozen, whose life is despaired of. During the day the weather moderated a little, but scarcely enough to do any good. All day we have heard the report of cannon and occasionally the rattle of musketry on the right, but I have been unable to learn anything in regard to it.

December 11, 1864 During last night it rained very heavily, which flooded many of our tents, for in this weather it is almost impossible to keep our ditches clear. Fortunately, mine was not of the number, and it was with many a congratulatory chuckle that I lay shivering under my blanket and listened to the anathema of those who were compelled to get up and bail their tents out. It was rumored during the day that Hampton's Cavalry had been engaged and made some captures on the right yesterday, but nothing definite has yet come to us. With the setting of the sun the weather is growing colder, and I think that we will have a very severe night of it. I trust that the poor fellows on picket will have wood enough to keep themselves warm, for if they do not, some of them will freeze to death.

December 12, 1864 The weather was intensely cold last night, freezing everything hard, and though the sun has shone brightly all day, its heat was insufficient to thaw even the upper crust. We have heard the reports of heavy guns on our left all day but do not know what it means.

December 13, 1864 The troops are all returning to their winter quarters and former positions on the lines. The affair on the right amounted to but little or nothing, and though the enemy succeeded in destroying about six miles of the Weldon Railroad together with the depot at Stony Creek, yet a couple of days will repair all this.

December 14, 1864 The weather has moderated considerably and it is very pleasant during the day, and as the moon is at the full, the nights are very fine. The enemy tried their hand at a little artillery and mortar practice today but did no damage.

December 15, 1864 Everything was very quiet today. Even sharpshooting was not indulged in by either side till after nightfall, but it seems that there shall be no rest for our company, for they have got us at building a large bombproof for the whole company. Nearly all the men would rather take their chances as they have been doing heretofore than labor at it, but unfortunately no attention is paid to their likes or dislikes. However I should not be surprised if spring found us still working on it.

December 16, 1864 This morning the 8-inch Columbiad in the rear line opened on the enemy which as usual cited a vigorous reply. Soon after, two of the 8-inch mortars opened to her assistance. Of course, the enemy did the same upon which all our company opened mortars, and then both sides went at it with a vim which was kept up till nearly dark, when both sides dried up. During the firing, Colonel Mosely, chief of Mosely's Artillery Battalion, had his head shot off. This is the only casualty of which I could hear, but considerable damage was done to our breastworks and our traverses, all of which was repaired as soon as night set in.

December 17, 1864 This morning the enemy made a slight demonstration with his mortars but soon dried up. This evening it clouded up, promising rain soon, which will stop work on our incubi as we have got down nearly six feet below the surface and there are no ditches deep enough by two feet to run the water off.

December 18, 1864 The weather has been very cloudy all day with an occasional shower, but from appearances I am inclined to think that if we do not have rain during the night that it will clear off after the sun shall be well up.

December 19, 1864 Things were unusually quiet on the lines this morning, but this afternoon without any apparent cause, our mortars opened on the enemy, to which they replied with their usual vigor which was continued for about three hours, during which several tents in our vicinity went up, but no other damage was done.

As it is my turn to go to town on permit tomorrow, I anticipated a little and went in this evening. At night, I went to Grace Church with the ladies from our house to assist in decorating it, but I did nothing.

December 20, 1864 Today was spent as such days usually are, by my doing a hundred and one things, all of which amount to nothing. I dined with my friend Gilmore.

December 21, 1864 On awaking this morning, I found that the rain was pouring down, which with the reflection that my time was up, was anything but pleasant. After breakfast, I went to the Bindery, and in awaiting for the rain to cease, the dinner hour overtook me. After this, I did an errand for Mr. E. and then returned to my gun, where I arrived at five o'clock, having been absent just forty-eight hours, which I think was doing very well on a twenty-four hour permit.

December 22, 1864 Last night the weather set in clear and cold, and today though the sun shone brightly, yet it was very cold and blowing a perfect gale, which I trust will blow strong enough to scatter the fleet which now menaces Wilmington.

> -Walters refers to Wilmington, North Carolina, where a Union fleet had sailed against Fort Fisher, the last major seacoast fort guarding the South's last uncaptured port.-

December 23, 1864 The weather still continues clear but intensely cold, though towards evening it moderated a little, which leads me to hope for better things tomorrow. The papers state that yesterday's gale compelled the fleet off Wilmington to put to sea.

December 24, 1864 The weather cleared off beautifully today and the night is clear and starlit, giving promise of a fine day tomorrow. Nothing was done on our lines and but little news of interest from other quarters, though there is a report gaining ground that General Lee has been appointed Commander-In-Chief of the armies of the Confederate States. God grant that his may be so, but it should have been done at least a year ago, as it is a general impression that our want of success in the campaigns of the Army of Tennessee are attributed to the fact of their being planned by the President, who however bright a statesman he may be, is but illy adapted to planning a campaign in which so much is required from small means such as those of Georgia and Tennessee. Should this rumor prove true, I have no doubt but that one of General Lee's first acts will be the replacing of General Johnston in command.

December 25, 1864 (Sunday) Christmas is here again and still does peace seem to be as far away as ever. Alas, how many there were in our army who on last Christmas, cheered themselves that on this day they would be with loved ones at home, enjoying in the sunshine of peace all those privileges and blessings for which they had fought and toiled so long and hard, but who now sleep their last sleep in unmarked graves, while still is heard from morning till night the sharpshooting, the sharp crack of the musket, and the loud booming of the cannon. I try to think otherwise, but sometimes I fear that we will never be at peace again.

At an early hour this morning, I went to town on a special permit for twelve hours. On arriving at the house of Mr. E. I found that none of the family were yet astir, in consequence of their having sat up very late the night previous. On their appearance, I was greeted with the salutations appropriate to the day, and was regaled with a brimming goblet of egg-nog, which Mrs. E. in her kind thoughtfulness had set aside for me the night before. At the proper time I accompanied the family to church at which there was a large congregation, among whom was General Lee. The music was excellent, the service very impressive, and the sermon good. We remained until after communion and then went home to as fine and as plenteous a dinner as I care to sit down to. On viewing the table which almost groans under the weight of good things, and comparing it with my usual coarse and scanty daily fare, a momentary feeling of envious repining took possession of me, but almost immediately after, the recollection of the unvarying kindness which I have received since my arrival here from this family and others, induced a better and more pleasant train of thought. Towards the latter part of the afternoon the sky again became overcast, so that it required but little persuasion to induce me to remain all night.

December 26, 1864 Shortly after daybreak this morning, I left the house and soon arrived at my gun without my absence having been remarked by my officers. The roads on the way out were very muddy, as it had been raining hard all night, though towards daylight it ceased. The lines were very quiet both yesterday and today.

December 27, 1864 The news from Wilmington today is very good. The enemy made a landing under cover of the guns of the fleet and attempted to carry Fort Fisher by land while the fleet bombarded it, but they were repulsed on both sides with considerable loss to themselves, while our loss was very slight, and but little damage was done to the fort. I feel very hopeful regarding our ability to hold the place.

December 28, 1864 I went to town this morning on a twenty-four hour permit (it being my regular turn) and as usual, spent a very pleasant day. In the afternoon and the first part of the night we heard quite a heavy cannonading in the direction of my gun, but the time has gone by when such a sound would induce me to return to my gun, though justice to myself requires me to say that no attack is at all anticipated and to go out merely for an artillery duel is unnecessary.

December 29, 1864 About eleven o'clock this morning I left town to return to my gun. On arriving there I learned that the cannonading which I heard last night was from mortars. During the shelling a piece went through my tent, making a hole large enough to put my head in, and as it had rained during the night, I found my bed and blankets soaking wet, and no sun out to dry them.

December 30, 1864 All has been quiet on the lines today, though we have occasionally heard the report of heavy guns on the left. This evening we finished the excavation for our bombproof and brought in the first logs for it. We are getting along with it much more rapidly than I thought we would, but it will take some weeks yet to finish it, unless the enemy should take it in their heads to open a brisk sharpshooting during the day, in which case we should be compelled to suspend all operations.

December 31, 1864 Between four and five o'clock this morning we were all startled by the rapid discharge of musketry on our right which continued for about half an hour, when it ceased and we all turned in again to finish our morning nap. Later in the day I learned that Scales' Brigade, who hold a portion of the line on the right and adjoining Johnson's Division, made a dash at the enemy's picket line, capturing about one hundred prisoners without losing a man. I could not learn whether the dash had any object beyond the above named result.

CHAPTER FIVE

The Last Battles

January 1, 1865 (Sunday) Hail New Year, and may God grant that it may be happier to all than the last year has been.

Early this morning I was awakened by a friend who had just returned from Richmond, and who brought me a small slice of cake and a big drink of excellent whiskey, both of which disappeared in a remarkably short space of time. This is all the New Year that I had, though we all revel in pleasing anticipations, for there is a big dinner preparing for the army in Richmond, to which the amount has already reached a handsome sum of nearly one hundred and fifty thousand dollars. It is expected that this dinner will be ready for distribution about the middle of this week.

The weather was cold and blustery all day, but towards night it moderated somewhat.

January 2, 1865 Nothing of importance occurred on the lines today. Our works on the bombproof progress but slowly. The weather was a little more comfortable today, but the nights are intensely cold.

January 3, 1865 "There is something rotten in the state of Denmark". I fear that all our pleasing anticipation of a big dinner will end in smoke. Today, Wise's Brigade drew theirs and as a sample I will give the statements of an officer of the 34th Regiment, whose company, numbering fifty-eight men, received "the leg of one turkey, eight pounds of beef, two turnips, two irish potatoes, one head of cabbage, and one pound of apple butter", and this gentleman assured me on honor that this and sixteen small loaves of bread was all that his company got. Another gentleman belonging to the Richmond Blues 46th Regiment told me that his company of forty men got the wing of a turkey and nothing else in the shape of meat. Judging from this I do not think we will get much.

January 4, 1865 This afternoon our company received their portion of the "Great National Dinner", which consisted of forty half-pound loaves of bread for the company, or about one third of a loaf per man. If this is, as it pretended, the nation's acknowledgment to the army and an evidence of the people's appreciation of our toils and suffering, let no one in the future say "republics are grateful". Heaven grant that the Northern papers do not get hold of it, for if they do we will never hear the last of it, and it is enough to be insulted by my own people without adding to that the ridicule of our enemies.

January 5, 1865 Today we received an order from headquarters granting seven furloughs to a hundred men. This measure is both wise and kind in that it is a relaxation in which men stand of so much need, and wise in that it has a tendency to discourage desertion, which is becoming a great and crying evil, and indulged in to an extent but it bids fair to leave but few of us to contend with Grant when the spring weather shall admit of active campaigning. Setting aside the question of honor, I who am a foreigner with no ties (except those formed by the grateful remembrance of past kindness received from a few, and interests such as a man must naturally acquire at the spectacle of a brave handful of men struggling with almost superhuman energy against an ungenerous and mercenary foe) cannot but think it strange and view with the utmost disgust, the picture of men, whose every tie and association is in and of the South, so far forgetting themselves and so reckless of their honor as to desert, and that at a period when more than at any other time their country needs them and their services most. Nor can I see that desertion is any remedy for the evils of hard and scant fare, insufficient clothing, and no pay.

January 6, 1865 At an early hour this morning the sun rose clear, and promised a beautiful though cold day. About eight o'clock I went to town on a twenty-four hour permit, but feel almost certain that I shall make it thirty-six at least. I found my friends as well as usual, and as usual, enjoyed myself hugely. During the day I weighed myself and found that I weighed one hundred and fifty-four pounds, being an increase of nine pounds in the last four months. But this nine pounds has cost me its weight in gold, even at the rate of fifty for one in Confederate money.

January 7, 1865 The weather promising to be very fine this morning, I concluded to stretch my permit, and to that end, went to Grace Church in the morning with the family. After dinner, I stayed for a couple of hours at Gilmore's, where I enjoyed a very good old friend, a glass of Black Jack, though instead of gin, apple brandy was used. I arrived at my gun about five o'clock this afternoon and found all quiet.

January 9, 1865 Today, J. O. G. received a letter from home by flag-of-truce, which contained a message for me to the effect that my friends were very anxious to hear from me, not having done so for nearly twelve months. Now the question arises, what has become of all the letters that I have sent during the last year? There were fifteen or sixteen at least, some by flag-of-truce and others by the blockade, and though I received none in reply, yet it was some satisfaction to think that they heard from me. Well I shall continue to write and hope that at least one may get there. The weather was fine today, but I am much mistaken if we do not have very bad weather soon though, as the moon is nearly at the full. I am in hopes that it will become settled and that in the moon's declination we will have a dry spell.

-J. O. G. most probably refers to Private John Gamage.-

January 10, 1864 Late last night it began to rain and it continued to do so until nearly sundown, and I have never seen such a heavy rain and one so long continued in my life. During the day, many and heavy peals of thunder were heard. Everything was flooded, and tents and chimneys were washed away by the dozen. While lying in my tent just after daylight, I heard a noise of falling earth near my head and had but time enough to crawl out of the way when my chimney came down, and with it, my tent, flooding myself and everything that I had with mud and rain. For the last two years and a half I have been accustomed to regard my life as belonging to the country, and for this reason can view the subject of death with comparative philosophy, but all my philosophy is insufficient to reconcile me to dying the inglorious death of having my brains knocked out by a familiar chimney.

January 11, 1865 There was so much mud floating around that it was impossible to do anything towards clearing up the wreck occasioned by yesterday's rain, and though the sun shone brightly, yet the heat from it was not sufficient to dry out our clothing or blankets.

January 12, 1865 All were enabled to dry their clothing and blankets today and those who had it to do began to clean away, to rebuild their chimneys, and repitch their tents. Among these, I was one and

I entered on my work with the full determination to fit myself up in a manner that would leave no room for apprehensions in future rain storms, even though it should occupy me a week to refit.

January 13, 1865 An order was received today granting four extra furloughs to our company, and to be given to meritorious men, in which category our captain was pleased to class me. I anticipate a very fine time in Richmond for eight or ten days and the relief which it will afford me from the fatigues of trench life and duty will be very grateful (and is much needed). I worked like a Trojan all day, but owing to the distance that I had to throw the earth, I get along but slowly. During my digging I came to a portion of the foundation of Rives' house, which will furnish me with brick.

January 14, 1865 By working till after dark last night and beginning again early this morning, I was enabled to nearly finish my digging and put up a portion of my chimney. Much as I dislike to do it, and condemning as I do the practice of working on the Sabbath (unless in a case of necessity), yet as I deem this is to be such a case, I think it no harm and shall therefore try to put up my tent tomorrow.

January 15, 1865 (Sunday) By working hard, I got into my tent this evening and though it is not yet finished, yet I am guarded against any cold or bad weather that may come. One thing from which I derive immense satisfaction is that my chimney draws well and does not seem inclined to compel all the smoke to find an exit by way of the door as my other one did upon many occasions.

During the day several rumors reached us regarding the mission of Blair to Richmond. One was to the effect that Lincoln had promised to recognize the independence of the Confederacy provided the South would abolish slavery, and I could not but smile while listening to some of my company, who four years ago were ultra pro-slavery men and ardent advocates of war for the protection of our institutions, heaping all manner of anathemas upon President Davis if he does not accept the proposal. Some of them did not hesitate to declare their intention of going home if these terms were not complied with, and as the thought is the father of the deed, I regret to hear the boys speak in this manner as it is a matter of grave pride with me that my company has never lost a member by desertion.

January 16, 1865 The weather being very beautiful this morning, I went to town on a twenty-four hour permit. Everybody that I saw was very gloomy on the subject of the state of the country, and rumors of every description were current. As it would be impossible to give them all, nevertheless those who circulated them all vouched for their coming from the most reliable source. From the rumors then, it would seem that a council of war is being held in Richmond to take into consideration the advisability of evacuating Virginia, and falling back through North Carolina to make a stand in South Carolina, but one gentleman has it from the very best of authority that General Lee is opposed to such a measure, and should he be overruled by the majority, he will immediately throw up his commission in the Confederate States Army. Upon this, Virginia will cut loose from the Southern Confederacy and declare herself a free and independent state, and in a proclamation of surpassing eloquence and natural pathos, call upon all the sons of the old Commonwealth, wherever they may be, to rally to her defense. This call, it is supposed, will bring into the field a large army, and to augment the members, the ladies will be called in to take charge of the hospitals, bureaus, quartermaster, and commissary departments, and in fact all departments which have been filled heretofore by men. As the standard of age will be over nine and under ninety, there is every reason to anticipate a large army. As the result of these vigorous measures, and in addition to this, the army will be reorganized, and all officers of whatever grade they may be who are thrown out will be formed into a corps de elite, on the plan of that corps of Titans which Napoleon formed on the retreat from Moscow. General Lee will be placed in command of this army of Virginia and there is not the least doubt but that with the army he will make villages and plains, now almost unknown beyond the Post Office guide, more celebrated than the plains of Marathon, while the deeds of valor which will be enacted at the passes of the Blue Ridge will forever after cause Thermopylae to mourn over its eclipsed glories. As to giving up the contest before Virginia is recognized a free state by all the world, this is not to be thought of for one moment, and even though we are reduced to the extremity of the last man in the last ditch, when that event shall transpire it is expected that General Lee will make a requisition upon the state for a band of firecrackers upon which he, together with the aforesaid man, will place themselves and then with a tear for Virginia and a glance of defiance at the foe, light the match, fire the train, and depart in a grand blaze of glory. As it is supposed that "Barnum" has the original mantle of Elija, the cape of which at least he obtained for an adequate consideration, it is earnestly hoped that the patriotism of the ladies will be sufficient to induce them to obtain it for the purpose of enveloping the head of General Lee in it, and thus protect his sacred whiskers from the foregoing. It will be perceived from all of this that the alarm and distress of the times has not interfered with the spirit of invention of good people. It is of course unnecessary for me to comment upon the rumors of which the above are a small portion.

January 17, 1865 The papers of this morning contain the startling intelligence of the fall of Fort Fisher. Few details are given, but these show that a slight attack was made by land and that the real attack was made by sea by a large force that came up in boats under cover of night. Though the fall of Wilmington does not of a necessity follow this event, yet there is but little hope felt of our being able to hold this place, and should it fall, I fear it will place this army in an ugly position, as it uncovers our most important flank.

I remained in town till about ten o'clock, when I returned to my gun where I found everything as I had left it.

January 18, 1865 This morning I went to town on a twelve hour permit to get my shoes repaired. I finished the latter and was charged only fifteen dollars for having the work done. This, for the times, is very reasonable. Though my time was up at dark, I determined to remain till morning as there is nothing doing on the lines.

January 19, 1865 Everything is quiet on the lines and the weather continues fine, but from the appearance of the clouds at sunset, it will not remain so for long. I arrived at my gun about nine o'clock this morning without my absence having been discovered by the officers.

January 20, 1865 A short time ago, Mr. Crenshaw of Richmond (but at present in England) sent a number of fine gray uniforms to Colonel R. Lindsay Walker, Chief of Artillery of the 3rd Army Corps, to be given to those who had distinguished themselves, or who by good conduct had merited an acknowledgment. Of these, four suits were sent to our company. In distributing them, Captain Grandy selected six men whose conduct, in his estimation, justified a testimonial of this kind, and to my great surprise I was one of the six, but the usual fortune attended me, for in the raffling for these I was one of the two unlucky ones, though it is a subject of considerable qualification to have been one of the six men, if I did not get one of the uniforms.

Late this evening it began to rain.

January 21, 1865 It rained all night and the whole of today, and we are again in mud up to the knees. The weather also is very cold without any prospect of better for a day or two at the least.

Today's papers contain the news of the resignation of the Honorable John A. Seddon, Secretary of War. Who his successor will be is not known, though from the fact of J. C. Breckenridge having passed through Petersburg on his way to Richmond a few days ago, he is most probably the man, and I think he would make a good one, though we can illy spare such men from the field.

January 22, 1865 But little rain fell during the day, but it looks overhead as though it requires but little provocation to pour down in a perfect deluge.

January 23, 1865 Considerable rain fell during the night and to-day, but the clouds are becoming thinner and it is probable that during the night or tomorrow morning it will break away. The spell of bad weather seems to exert itself over an immense space, for today's papers are filled with accounts from as far down as Georgia, and through North and South Carolina of damage being done of the rise in the rivers, which I fear will trouble us greatly, as many rail-road bridges are washed away and much track torn up.

As I am anticipating a furlough, I left the lines today, but when I arrived at our battalion headquarters I found that it had not arrived yet, but as there is a great probability of its arriving tomorrow or the day after, I went to town to await its coming.

January 24, 1865 During the night the weather cleared off and though it is very cold, yet it is so great an improvement on the weather of the past few days that no one feels disposed to complain. As I was not particularly anxious to get my furlough today, I did not go up to see if it had come, but will do so tomorrow. This evening I took tea with Mr. and Mrs. Gilmore, returning home about nine o'clock.

January 25, 1865 I had almost forgotten the fact that on last Saturday the 21st, I completed my thirtieth year. Really, I am beginning to feel my old age. This morning I went up to headquarters, but found (somewhat to my chagrin) that my furlough had not arrived yet, but as I have been waiting some time for a good opportunity by which to learn patience, I shall take this and wait till it comes.

January 26, 1865 This morning I again went up to our headquarters and found that my patience was likely to undergo quite a severe test, as my furlough had not yet arrived. I trust that my patience will meet with its perfect reward.

January 27, 1865 On going to headquarters this morning, I found that my furlough had arrived at last, so I had it dated from tomorrow the 28th, thereby giving myself five days in addition to my allowance. This I consider but a just reward for my patience.

This afternoon I accompanied Mr. Ege to Dunlop, as he expected his family down from Richmond. It was cold, and when we got there we were obliged to wait nearly an hour for the train. When it arrived, we found the ladies there, and putting them in a hack, we walked back and got home a couple of minutes after them, and spent the night until eleven o'clock in hearing the good news of Richmond.

January 28, 1865 After a very busy morning and an early dinner, I walked to the train and arrived in Richmond about six o'clock. From the depot I went to the store where I found Mr. E. and Mr. G., both of whom expressed much pleasure in seeing me. About half past eight, we went to the house, and from the kind of reception with which all favored me, it would be churlish in me to think anything but that I was heartily welcome. After supper all hands engaged in a game of "Muggins" till nearly twelve when we drew our chairs around the fire, and I by general request fought all my battles of the past year over again, a task not at all disagreeable to a man who likes to talk as well as I do. At two we retired.

January 29, 1865 Woke up this morning about eight o'clock and while dressing, a "toddy" was sent to me with the message that I must not fail to drink it, as all the ladies had tasted it. Apart from my fondness for the Creator, this message would have been sufficient to have induced me to drink a goblet of poison. After breakfast I went with Mr. E. to see the skating on the Canal Basin. After dinner I went with Mr. Y. on Franklin Street where I met Cousin Josie, with whom I spent the afternoon and went to old Saint John's Church (that memorable old pile). At night, after seeing her home, I returned to Mr. E.'s and retired about one o'clock.

January 30, 1865 The weather today was warm and beautiful. During the morning I called on a few acquaintances, and after dinner I accompanied Mrs. B. and Miss Lizzie in a walk, in the course of which we made a few calls, one being on Mrs. G. At night, a spirited game of Euchre engaged us till nearly two o'clock, when we retired, but we consumed an hour after the light was out in telling jokes.

January 31, 1865 Went to a hundred and one places today, among them to the house of Mr. Y., but did not see Cousin J. as she was out. Wrote a letter to Gilmore, and finished the day with Euchre and pleasant family conversation.

February 1, 1865 This morning it was very cloudy, but it cleared off about noon and remained pleasant for the rest of the day. About five o'clock I called for Cousin J. by appointment, with whom I went to Mr. Allen's where we spent the evening. A joke was got off, which though partly at my own expense, is so good that I must put it down. I was in conversation with a handsome, bright eyed witch of perhaps seventeen summers and in the course of it, while speaking of the soldiers and their almost omnipotent qualities, I jestingly remarked that I had no doubt that when she got to heaven she would find soldiers there, wherefrom she turned to me and with an air which I find it impossible to describe, she asked me "if I really thought so". About half past one we broke up and as I had to see Cousin Josie home, I did not get to my house till nearly three o'clock, when I found that all had gone to bed and locked the house up. By good fortune, I found a ladder in the yard, and I got in one of the windows and went to bed very well satisfied with the success of my exploit.

February 2, 1865 When I woke this morning I was greatly amused by hearing one of the servants giving the young ladies in the next room a huge account of the attempt of someone trying to break in the house. I made haste to dress and on reaching the dining room, I found all the ladies discussing the affair. I said nothing until Mr. J. came down, who the moment he saw me asked me how I had got in, whereupon I was compelled to acknowledge and he well laughed at me for the trick.

In furtherance of her desire to make my time pass more pleasantly, Mrs. E. invited some company to the house. Two of the ladies were quite pretty and the third was sufficiently interesting to pass a very critical examination. It is unnecessary to say anything of the gentlemen. The evening was spent in singing, dancing, and music. After the company left, the elders, that is Mr. J., Uncle Fayette, Willie, and myself adjourned to the dining room to discuss the affairs of the country over a pipe. This occupied us till two o'clock when we retired.

February 3, 1865 The weather has been very gloomy today and considerable rain has fallen, but this did not interfere with my sports. This morning I went to the House of Delegates and must say that I was not very greatly impressed with the vim which the House presented. I found limp and slovenly looking old men with scarcely a fine looking head in the whole number, and pert looking young messenger boys who fly around with an air of importance as if the weight of the Confederacy rested on their shoulders. In this chamber is that magnificent portrait of General Lee, painted for the State of Virginia. About dark I called by appointment on Mrs. A. who, with the family, I accompanied to the house of her sister, Mrs. R. where a party was given. I thought it was a small affair, but was undeceived when on reaching the house I was ushered into the parlor which I found filled with little ones, and on making my way through to the back parlor, I found it nearly all full of grown people. Being somewhat unaccustomed to party going of late, I felt some embarrassment on first getting in, but on looking up, I was greeted by the kind smiles of Cousin Josie, Miss A. and Miss V., Mrs. J., Mrs. Y., Mrs. R., and some other acquaintances. I soon made the acquaintances of some other gentlemen, then I got along very well.

Soon after I got there the dancing began and was kept up with much spirit. Several fancy dances were executed, among them a Sailor's Hornpipe by Master W. and a Highland Fling by little Miss R., the eldest daughter of the hostess. About twelve, the little folks went down to the table, and after they had finished the table was reset and the big folks went down. The table was supplied with everything that could be desired, and the rooms were very warm enough to make the ice cream very refreshing and pleasant. About half past two, the party broke up and I had the pleasure of seeing Cousin Josie home, which by the way was no short pleasure as the party was given on Main above Fourth Street, and Cousin J. resides on Franklin below Twenty-third. I got home about four o'clock and went to bed wonderfully well satisfied but very tired.

February 4, 1865 This morning the sun came out bright and the weather overhead has been very fine, thought the streets were in a bad condition owing to the rain of yesterday. This afternoon I called on Miss G., where I met with Miss Gertie M., a very charming young lady with whom I hope to be better acquainted before very long as I anticipate bringing her over to Petersburg with me when I go over. As it was announced that General H. A. Wise would speak in the chamber of the House of Delegates this evening at seven o'clock, about six Mr. E., Mr. J., Uncle Fayette, and myself went to the Capitol where we found a very large crowd assembled, among which we worked our way till we got to the stairs leading to the gallery. After waiting about half an hour the doors were opened, and without any volition of our own we were pressed up the stairs and forced into a seat from which we found it impossible to move until the meeting broke up. The old man was very hoarse and in bad condition to speak, but several times he seemed to forget or ignore this fact, and the hot blood of the old war horse rose and his clarion tones reminded me of the days of yore. We got home about ten o'clock and after supper, played Euchre till nearly twelve when we drew our chairs around the fire and spent a couple of hours in smoking.

February 5, 1865 This morning I accompanied the ladies to Dr. Moore's church. His sermon was one of a series which he is preaching from the Book of Job, and though it was an able, I cannot say that it was a happy effort. After dinner I called on Cousin Josie with whom I spent the afternoon, and at night I again accompanied the ladies from our house to Dr. Moore's church, where we had another installment on the miseries of Job. Owing to the impure state of the gas, the coughing in the church reminded me forcibly of a hospital for consumptive patients. Owing to the fact of its being Sunday, twelve o'clock found me in bed, though not asleep.

February 6, 1865 This morning Mr. J. and I went to the Senate where we saw Stevens and Hunter, regarding whom there is considerable curiosity, since they have but just returned from that Peace Conference which has of late been upsetting the minds of the good people of this Confederacy. Stevens is the same dried up, puny little giant, while Hunter looks larger and his face looks more genial and pleasant than when I saw him last year. After the House was called to order, Commander Simms, late of Alabama, who is privileged to a seat on the floor, came in. He is a small man, with rather an inferior face, but a fierce and most determined eye. During the morning Mr. Simms of Louisiana made a speech defining his position regarding a former question relative to the re-installing of General J. E. Johnston. In the course of his speech he bore rather heavily on General Johnston whom he styled, "that great general who never won a battle". He was replied to by Mr. Wigfall of Texas, who reviewed in a very able manner the course of Johnston from the beginning of the war to the time when he was relieved from command before Atlanta, and wound up by attempting to compare the present state of affairs with what they would have been had Gen. J. been left in command. At the close of his speech, the House went into a secret session and as our dinner hour was near at hand, we concluded to leave. At night I remained home and the hours were devoted to Euchre.

February 7, 1865 During the night some snow fell, which after daylight changed to sleet and rain, making the day very unpleasant. I was engaged to make a call on some ladies with Cousin J. and spend the evening, and though I was well satisfied that owing to the weather she would not go, yet I determined to redeem my word by going to her house. But on going down Franklin Street, I slipped and fell down, which made such a mess of my apparel that I quietly picked up my fragments, went home, brushed up, and remained there.

February 8, 1865 The weather was bright and beautiful, but the walking was bad. This afternoon I called on Cousin J. to explain my non-appearance of yesterday and learned to my great regret that I was just in time to bid her good-by, perhaps farewell, as tomorrow she takes the early train on the Danville Railroad to return to school, and many months must elapse before I can see her again. Even if the chances of war do not cut me off forever from the music of her happy laugh, it was a bitter thing to bid her good-by, but I was helpless in the promises, and therefore I hurried over, though I was unwilling for cogent reasons to display much feeling. One subject of great regret was that I was engaged to spend the evening at Mr. G.'s, and was therefore compelled to leave her at seven o'clock.

Cousin Josie wished to persuade me to break this engagement and spend the evening with her, but I could not do this, though I would like to have done so. After her, I went to Mr. G.'s where I met Miss Gertie, whom I found to be wonderfully pleasant. We had a fine supper and I left about eleven o'clock, seeing Miss Gertie home and then went towards my own home, but stopped on my way at the theatre where our whole family had gone to see the play of the Drunkard. When I got there they were playing some silly farce of which I could make nothing, so finding the folks, I got to their vicinity in time to help the ladies through the crush, and on reaching home, took the head of the table (Mr. E. having eaten his supper and retired before we got there). Two o'clock found us all on our way to bed.

February 9, 1865 It having been announced that there would be a mass meeting held at the African Church to take into consideration the state of the country, and as many good speeches were to hold forth, the ladies of our house determined to go and of course, I went with them. The hour for calling the meeting to order being twelve o'clock, and feeling satisfied that the house would be filled, we went at half past ten for the purpose of obtaining good seats, but though the hour at which we went was so early, yet on arriving there we found the house already more than half full, though we were fortunate enough to secure good seats. While waiting for the speakers, a band stationed in the choir gallery did the best they could with some very inferior instruments to beguile the time which would otherwise have hung so heavily on our hands, and between the pauses of the music, I found time to look around upon the audience which was largely supplied with the feminine element, and many a bright eye and handsome face met my gaze. In a seat near where the ladies from our house had pinned me up against the wall sat a lady whose face pleased me wonderfully, and whom I learned was one of our Confederate heroines, though I was unable to learn any of her history beyond the fact that some time ago, she was captured by the enemy and sent to Cincinnati where she was tried as a spy and condemned to death, but the sentence being commuted, she remained several months in prison and was finally released and sent South. On arriving in our lines she received a major's commission in Morgan's Command, which commission she still holds, though I do not know whether there is any pay attached. She wore a Confederate gray cloth coat, the seams of which are trimmed or corded with white velvet, and on the collar was the star, in gold, of her rank. On her head she wore a black velvet jockey hat looped up on the right side, from which loop a neat black plume was seen, and against the side of the hat was pinned a silver crescent on which was engraved the words, "Louisa Phillips of Morgan's Command".

She is a lady of medium height, and as far as I could see, of good form, a most decided brunette with beautiful black hair which hung in curls around her head, eyes black and very expressive. Her features were thin and firmly cut (though her face was rather more attenuated than agreed with my style of beauty) while keeping a sly look on her face. My mind involuntarily wandered off into the realms of romance and I was building up quite a fancy structure, when all was put to flight by the entrance of a long procession, of which many mounted the speaker's stand, while the remainder took seats in front of the stand which had been reserved for them. As soon as quiet was restored, the meeting was called to order by R. M. T. Hunter, the chairman, and a fervent prayer for guidance and support in this time of great trial was offered up by the Reverend Dr. Hoge. At its conclusion, large headed Hunter again got up and addressed the meeting. He began by explaining the object for which the meeting was called, then entered into a brief review of the origin of the war and the principles upon which it was carried on. He spoke at some length on the points touching the late mission upon which he was sent, in which connection he spoke of Lincoln's doubts, as expressed to the commissioners, that in case the South returned to the Union whether in consideration of the rebellion, we would be allowed the old rights of representation, but in case we did return, he, Lincoln, would use his best and kindest endeavors to make the terms as lenient as possible. The dear man! His remarks were short and very much to the point. He was followed by the Honorable Mr. Sheffey, Speaker of the House of Delegates, who presented a preamble and set of resolutions expressive of the spirit of Virginia to remain firm to the cause of the South, after which he made quite a lengthy speech which I would much rather have read than heard. It abounded in grand language and great thoughts, but to my mind his delivery was rather an unhappy straining after the dramatic. In speaking of Virginia's relics of the Revolution, in the event of the enemy overrunning the state and taking possession, he remarked that he would rather see the old speaker's chair of the House of Delegates, in which Pendleton and other grand men of the past had sat, burnt than that it should grace a Yankee triumphal procession. I found myself unable to take extended notes of any of the speeches, being unaccustomed to it, but one thing in his speech struck me, possibly more from the manner in which it was received by the immense audience than any other circumstance, and it was this; he said that God never created a people of whom Stonewall Jackson was a type, President Davis, a representative man, that greatest Roman of all, R. E. Lee a leader of their armies, who could consent to bend at the footstool of such low nature as the Northern people had shown themselves. When he came to the name of Jackson, a silence as of death pervaded the hall and many a head bowed, seemingly involuntarily, when he uttered the name of Davis, quite a respectable cheer was raised, but when he came to the name of Lee, such shouts and cheers were raised that it was at least five minutes before he could again make himself heard. On taking his seat, J. P. Benjamin, Secretary of State, rose. I must plead guilty to a strong inclination to dislike this gentleman, and the prejudice was so strong within me that though I had heard him spoken of as perhaps the finest orator in the South, I yet had made up my mind that he was vastly overrated, and sat down (for I had been standing all this time), fully determined to disagree with him on every point, and to dislike him as much as if not more than ever. He had spoken but a short time before I was struck with the beauty of his tone, which though somewhat labored at first, gradually became full and remarkably clear, but still I remained seated and as all stood up around me, I could not see the speaker, but as his beautifully sounded sentences came floating toward me I felt myself lifted to my feet, and though while standing I had an excellent view of him, it was only by means of severe cramps in my toes that I became aware that I was standing on my toes, and at this moment one of the ladies remarked that she had kept an eye on me, being determined to pull me back in case I attempted to get on the back of the pew in front of ours, an endeavor she said, which I showed every inclination to make. Gallantry compelled me to listen to her remarks, but the thought would obtrude that while Mr. Benjamin was speaking, I would gladly have dispensed with her remarks. Mr. B. is a warm advocate for the employment of Negroes as soldiers, but on this point I must disagree with him or anyone else. His whole speech, so redolent of the finished orator, and the man of grand intellect abounding in wit and pathos (the latter especially when he spoke of the noble dead of Louisiana), and all combined to make it an effort such as I have never before listened to, and though he spoke for nearly three hours, I would gladly have listened for three hours longer, and the man who could sit there and hear Mr. B. and not feel his blood stirred to its innermost depths must have been bloodless. He was followed by Mr. Gilmer of North Carolina, during whose remarks many left the church, probably at the calls of hunger, and while the hall was yet ringing with the eloquence of the previous speaker, I did not care to listen to the dry statistics of Mr. G. Fortunately, his remarks were brief to a charm and at their conclusion, the meeting adjourned till half past seven o'clock at night.

We arrived at home at nearly five o'clock and partook of dinner, and at six we again got to the church, but found that though the gas was not even lit that some hundred or two people had already arrived. The crowd at the church was more dense at night than during the day, if that was possible. At both periods, every seat and every available foot of the floor was occupied.

At seven o'clock the chairman introduced Mr. Simms of Louisiana. His opening was not a happy one as he seemed to be laboring under some restraint, but after speaking a short time he warmed up with his subject and did much better. In speaking of the policy of arming the Negroes, he said that he would express no opinion, as it was probable that the question would be brought up in Congress, and for that reason he did not wish to commit himself to any line of policy at this time. Speaking of the finances of the country, he remarked that before the close of the session, Confederate notes would be worth something, which likely event would be brought about by a system of close and rigged taxation. His speech was not greatly admired, though it was replete with practical, common sense observations, for instead of pleasing the ear and tickling the fancy with fine periods and grand bursts of rhetoric, he told the people that though they had undergone great trials and had suffered, much greater trials and suffering were in store for them, and it was the duty of everyone to gird up the loins for future efforts. In closing, he paid a just and beautiful compliment to Virginia, her heroic women, great chiefs, and gallant soldiers. He was followed by the "old man eloquent", Hensey of Tennessee, who began by saying that he was the worst used man in that assembly, as he had the mortification of hearing the previous speakers absorbing all the topics on which he wished to speak and on which he had prepared himself, and this had been carried on to such an extent that he had been led to beg that he might be saved from his friends. After some minutes indulgence in this strain, which elicited considerable laughter and cheering, he glided into a grand flow of eloquence, and during his speech his old Revolutionary blood rose to the surface, and it was to me like a voice of the past calling upon the present age to vindicate their right to enjoy the privileges for which the old heroes of '76 struggled. His speech fully entitles him to the title of the "Eagle of Tennessee". At the conclusion of Mr. Hensey's speech, J. Randolph Tucker of Virginia was loudly called for and took the stand. At his appearance I was fearful that the scream of the eagle would be lost in the noise of the barnyard fowl, but I was undeceived in a very short time as he electrified the audience with bursts of eloquence which, though they might sound somewhat spasmotic, were yet very fine. He spoke about twenty minutes, and when he sat down, the Rev. Dr. Hoge was called for who responded in a short speech, which however did not impress me very favorably, and at his conclusion the meeting adjourned. We went home to supper about eleven o'clock, all very much pleased with the events of the day.

February 10, 1865 This morning I employed myself in executing several commissions preparatory to my departure, and this afternoon, called on Mrs. G. and Miss Gertie M. (whom however I will see tomorrow). I called also on Mrs. R. and Mrs. A. to bid them good-by, both of whom were kind enough to express regret at my enforced early departure, and particularly impressed it upon me that I must not fail to visit them on my next visit to Richmond, a something which I shall be sure to do as I have the most pleasant recollections regarding the kindness of these ladies. As this was to be my last night in the good city of Richmond, we had determined to devote it to Euchre, to which end we began before supper and kept it up till after two o'clock when we retired.

February 11, 1865 I finished up with all my business and about half past one, bade Mr. E.'s family good-by, during which I repressed many a sigh of regret which struggled to my lips at the thought of leaving. I went to the house of Miss Gertie M. whom I was to have the pleasure of escorting to Petersburg and whom I found entirely ready. I make mention of this circumstance as it is so unusual with the dear sex. From her house, we called by the way on Mrs. G. and then went to the train where we arrived in time to get a good seat, and by five o'clock, arrived in Petersburg. On arriving there, I was somewhat set back on my inability to procure a hack, but entirely on Miss Gertie's account, for she is such a charming girl that a two mile walk in her company would be anything but a subject of regret. But the roads were in bad condition, for which reason I would gladly have spared her the walk. On learning the state of affairs, she, with a brave smile and bright eye, made light of it and we started, but we were soon overtaken by a gentleman in a buggy who inquired if the lady was going to the city, and in being answered in the affirmative, kindly offered her a seat, regretting the impossibility of accommodating both of us. As in duty bound, Miss Gertie referred the matter to me, and I did not hesitate to accept the offer for her, thereby perpetrating about as unselfish an act as I am capable of. On seeing her off I made rapid steps and arrived at Mr. E.'s about ten minutes after Miss Gertie had gotten there. We sat up until about eleven o'clock, though every minute, symptoms of a chill were increasing, and which I felt would culminate before many hours. Nor was I wrong, for about eleven, I was seized with a chill which caused me to shake for two hours with the most frightful energy. After this, the fever set in, which lasted until daylight, which left me in such a condition which entirely precluded the possibility of my getting up, so that to my regret, the whole of Sunday passed with my head bound up, while the voices of the family reached me, not greatly adding to my sense of comfort, though Mr. and Mrs. E.

came in frequently to sit with me, and after supper, Mrs. C. came in and sat with me some time.

February 13, 1865 My furlough expires today, but on getting up this morning I found it almost impossible to walk, owing to severe rheumatic pains in my limbs while my head ached sufficiently to induce me to believe that it would split. So yielding to the solicitations of my friends, I determined to remain a few days in hopes of improving my health.

February 14, 1865 Though my headache has left me, the pains in my limbs are still enough to cause me some trouble.

February 15, 1865 I feel somewhat better today and if the improvement continues, shall try to return to my company tomorrow, though I feel far from well.

February 16, 1865 During last night a heavy rain fell, and as the weather has not cleared off yet, I must of necessity, defer going to my company until it clears off. Last night my headache came back, in consequence of which I slept but little.

February 17, 1865 Feeling somewhat better today, and the weather being bright but cold, and much against the advice of my friends, I determined to go out to my company today, but in the walk from the house to the office, I fell twice from sheer weakness, so that I was fain to turn back again.

February 18, 1865 Today I have felt much better than I have felt for some time, and if this will only continue, I shall try to go to my gun on next Monday. I feel somewhat ill at ease at my long absence as I fear it may be misconstrued by some of the ungenerous ones who are always so ready to see the beam in the eye of their neighbor.

February 19, 1865 Today the weather was very beautiful, though slightly cool, in consequence I determined to accompany the family to church, but I had cause to repent of my rashness for during the service I had a severe chill. Fortunately it came on toward the close of the service so that shutting my teeth hard together enabled me to sit it out, but on coming out in the open air, it increased in volume to such a degree that it was with the utmost difficulty that I reached home. Though the chill was unaccompanied by a fever, it yet left me with such an immense headache that I was compelled to keep to the house for the remainder of the day. A short time after we arrived home, Sgt. J. R. W. and J. F. W. came to see me, having heard that I was sick. They were kindly invited to dinner by Mr. E. and spent a portion of their afternoon at the house, where they seemed to be well pleased with their reception, while the family expressed themselves much pleased by their appearance and actions.

-Sgt. J. R. W. would be Sergeant James R. Wright of the Blues, and J. F. W. is probably Private John F. Wilkins.-

February 20, 1865 My limbs are again full of rheumatic pains for which reason I must of necessity lay by for a few days longer. I. G. B. came to see me today. He has just been released from Point Lookout where he has been a prisoner for nearly nine months. He spent the evening with me, relating many hours of his prison life experiences. One of the ladies at our home did not seem to be over well pleased with him, for which I could readily account but do not care to enter into detail here.

February 21, 1865 Today I learned of the death of one of our company. He died two or three weeks ago at the house of an uncle, where he had been sick for some time with a disease contracted in the trenches, and which led to cancer in the stomach. In his death, our company experiences a great loss, as he was a most excellent soldier while in camp or on the march. He was a most agreeable associate and a perfect gentleman. Peace to his ashes, and I trust that the name of J. W. Hatton may long remain green in the memory of our boys.

I feel somewhat better today, and the weather remains fine.

February 22, 1865 This morning I walked to Mr. E.'s office, and on reaching there, I learned that our company was ordered to withdraw their guns from the line for the purpose of being held in readiness in case of a battle on the right, at which point Grant is expected soon to make a desperate and final effort for the possession of the Southside Railroad. As soon as I heard this, I left town and in an hour reached my gun where I had the satisfaction of being told by all that I was a fool for coming out looking as badly as I did. After considerable exertion I succeeded in getting my things together and then waited for night, under cover of which we were to take our pieces out. Towards nightfall I began to feel so bad that I deemed it advisable to remain on the lines all night, which I did, being accommodated with a good bed in the tent of the Donaldsonville Battery.

February 23, 1865 During the night, I suffered so much with pains in my limbs that I found it impossible to sleep. At an early hour this morning I got up and left the lines, and after great exertion and much pain, reached the house at which our company had quarters at the head of Harden Street. On reaching there I was so much exhausted that I took to the floor where I lay all day, unable to move.

February 24, 1865 After passing another sleepless night, suffering greatly, I yielded to the advice of many of my comrades and my First

Lieutenant, and sent for the surgeon of our battalion who, on seeing me, sent for the ambulance and had me conveyed to the hospital of our corps. It was not without much inward quailing that I was carried out of the house, as I have always had a most unaccountable dread of a hospital, but there was no help for it, as there are orders to send all the sick to Richmond and other places in anticipation of a battle at an early day, for which reason our surgeon could not give me permission to go to private quarters.

February 25, 1865 Last night, I was in such intense pain that I required all my nerve to keep many a shriek of pain, as the twinges of acute rheumatism seized me. Toward midnight, my condition became such that the attendant sent for one of the surgeons, who ordered mustard plasters ad libitum, which were applied and from which I received considerable relief, but I began to fear trouble from my bowels which the doctors find it almost impossible to move. There was considerable talk of moving me to Richmond but I cannot be moved at present.

February 26, 1865 Owing to the vigorous measures adopted last night, I slept a little towards morning, and have been much easier all day.

Houses on Harding Street, Petersburg, Virginia. One of these may well be "Aspen Hall" where the Blues were temporarily quartered.

There has been great excitement in the city today in consequence of the promulgation of an order to remove all the cotton and tobacco to places of safety in the interior, which has given occasion for a renewal of the absurd report that Petersburg and probably Richmond were to be evacuated. Without question, the removal of all government property looks rather ominous, but it is only an act of prudence, entirely in keeping with the known characteristics of General Lee who, while hoping for the best, prepares for the worst. I have no idea that either of these cities will be given up unless we are driven from them, and Grant will find this a big job.

February 27, 1865 I passed another terrible night, relieved somewhat towards morning by the application of mustard externally, and croton oil (to which they were obliged to resort) internally. I am growing wonderfully disgusted with the sights, sounds, smells, etc. of our hospital, and shall leave the first moment that I am able to walk, limp, or hobble out.

February 28, 1865 I slept considerable during last night and am feeling somewhat easier this afternoon. I crawled from my cot to a bench near the fireplace where I sat about an hour, but I was in much pain the whole time, and several times regretted having gotten up, but I am very anxious to get sufficient strength to leave here.

March 1, 1865 I feel somewhat better today and again I got up and went to the fire, but in a foolish endeavor to raise myself to my feet by the aid of the tent pole, I fell down and, but for the presence of the hospital attendant, would have fallen in. For a short time after, I suffered the most intense pain and could find no consolation in the thought that I deserved it.

March 2, 1865 My improvement continues slowly. Today I got up and by the help of a stick was able to walk a little. On ascertaining this fact, I tried it at intervals during the whole day and though it pained me greatly, yet I persuaded myself that I was doing remarkably well.

March 3, 1865 Having done so well yesterday with a stick, I tried this morning without one, and though it pained me greatly, I walked to the chief surgeon's tent and asked permission to leave the hospital and remain a few days in private quarters. He advised me not to leave the hospital for some days yet as I was not well enough, but on my insisting that I wished to leave, he told me to wait and see my own battalion surgeon. This afternoon the latter gentleman came over and on my repeating my request, he also advised me to remain a few days longer, especially as he had no power to let me go to private quarters. As I had fully determined to get away from the hospital, I reiterated my request for leave to quit, which he at last gave me, and a few minutes after, I bade adieu to the place without any fond regrets or a lingering wish to return to it. After much exertion, I got to the house of Mr. E., determined to take the responsibility of remaining until Monday. The family kindly expressed much sympathy for me and are determined that I shall not again leave their house until I am entirely recovered.

March 4, 1865 I felt so much better today that I cannot but think it is in a great measure attributable to my feeling of relief at leaving the hospital. How some wretches can go to the hospital and use every trick and means to remain there, I cannot understand. Even upon the eve of a battle, I could not so far debase myself as to go there, and certainly when no fighting is going on I want to give them a wide berth.

March 5, 1865 The weather being beautiful today, I accompanied the family to Grace Church this morning, where we heard a very fine sermon by the Rev. Bishop Levy. This afternoon the ladies went there again, but Mr. E. and I remained at home and blew a cloud. At night we all went to St. Paul's Church to hear Mr. Platt but were disappointed as Bishop Levy preached. The church was very full and the singing excellent.

March 6, 1865 This morning I went up and reported to my company, but yielding to the advice of my captain, did not report for duty and shall not for a week or so yet, or at least until I feel sufficiently well to perform duty and to attend to the daily drills of the company (which have been resumed after an interval of about sixteen months).

March 7, 1865 The weather being remarkably fine, I went to town this morning and invited some ladies to accompany me to see our company drill, to which they readily assented. At about three o'clock we started from our house. The party consisted of Mrs. and Miss E., Miss Gertie M., and a moment after we were joined by Miss Mollie W. and Mr. W. On our way down Old Street, we took up Mr. B. and Mrs. Mollie B., and on going to Market Street, called by for Mrs. G. The party being by this time complete, we took up our line of march for our company quarters and on arriving there, found the men forming in line. A large assembly of ladies was already there, and several groups could be seen coming up the different streets which lead to our quarters. The drill lasted about an hour and at its conclusion, we turned our steps homeward, where we arrived at the dark of the evening. The ladies were all very much pleased with the appearance and actions of our boys. J. F. W. came down with us and remained til about eleven o'clock when we returned to quarters.

March 8, 1865 The improvement in my health is slow but sure, and every day I feel better and stronger than on the day previous. If this fine state of things will continue, I hope to be able to report for duty in the course of a few days, though all of the boys advise me to defer doing so as long as possible.

March 9, 1865 The weather has been very wet and gloomy all day, which induced me to remain in quarters all day, and as time hung very heavily on my hands, I wrote a long letter to W. T. E. in which I gave him an account of my past sickness in extenuation of my long silence. I trust that he will be more edified by the reading of it than I was by the writing.

March 10, 1865 Today having been set aside by proclamation of the President as a day for fasting and prayer, I went to town and accompanied Mrs. E. to Grace Church. The weather not being very promising, there were not many at church, which was a subject of regret as Mr. Gibson preached a most able sermon and one well calculated to inspire renewed confidence and hope in the hearts of the people. This afternoon the weather cleared off and remained very fine. About eleven o'clock I returned to our quarters.

This stone next to the Boydton Plank Road marks the site of Battery 45, where the road passed through the defensive earthworks which encircled Petersburg.

March 11, 1865 Early this morning, news was brought to us of the death in our hospital of George O. Gaskins, one of our company. This took us all by surprise as scarcely any of us knew that he was sick. He died of diphtheria after an illness of about three or four days. Poor George. We could much better afford to lose a better man, for while no means a brilliant soldier, yet George was ready to do his neighbor a kindness always, and became endeared to us by many an act which springs entirely from a kind and social heart. On being notified of the fact, a meeting of the company was called and a committee of six (of which I was one) was appointed to make proper arrangements for his funeral. On our getting down in the lower part of the city, we met some of our boys who were busy in making all arrangements. He is to be buried in the lot of Grace Church, the pastor of which with his usual kindness will preach the funeral service. The whole company it is expected will attend the funeral under command of their proper officers.

March 12, 1865 Very unexpectedly we were called up at four o'clock this morning and ordered to prepare for a march. About seven, the horses came up from their camp and in a short time we were going up Halifax Street. We went as far as Battery 45 where we were ordered to halt. We remained til about four o'clock when we went back and the horses sent back to their camp. As soon as we were packed, the boys began to fix themselves up and in about an hour, nearly all were in town. Having an engagement with Miss Eddy to accompany her to church, I made tracks for the house. At the proper time we went to Saint Paul's Church which we found quite full, though we succeeded in obtaining good seats. Mr. Platt, the pastor, preached and his sermon was without exception the most eloquent one that I have ever listened to. The subject was: Woman—her moral and social influence, her importance in the economy of nature, her duty to her God, her country, her kind, and herself. The delivery of this occupied an hour and I would have gladly devoted several more hours to listening. During the service one of the boys, seeing me, came and whispered that we were ordered off at three o'clock tomorrow morning. After service I went home, stayed until about eleven o'clock, bade the family good by, reached my quarters, and so good night.

March 13, 1865 At three o'clock we were called up and about four, we started off and reached Battery 45, where we halted and remained til after sundown, when we again received orders to go back. When we started this morning we did not expect to return, as we thought that perhaps we would take up a position somewhere on the right of the line, and so far from the city as to preclude our visiting this fine old "berg", and this thought was not particularly agreeable to a large number of our boys. We have been making such good use of our time as to warrant the remark made in a spirit of fun by one of us, that nearly all of my company were laboring under the complaint of "gall of the brain". But while this rather shrewd remark applied, and the fact is sufficient to cause our boys regret at having to remove from this place, but as far as I am concerned I am ready to leave at any moment, for though I have met with much kindness from many and made many friends, yet the thoughts of the past prevent me from allowing myself to become interested in any one particular one of the dear sex, and for this reason I cannot but feel very lonely while seeing so many of our boys walking along the streets with a fairy pinned to their arm, and leaning on with every manifest of affection.

March 14, 1865 This morning I reported for duty and henceforth I must be a little more circumspect than I have been, for missing roll call subjects us to a tour of duty, which though it may not be much, is yet apt to restrict our liberties. This afternoon I went out to drill with my company suspecting no evil, but hardly had we begun, when I saw a party of ladies coming whom I soon discovered to be Mrs. E., Mrs. and Miss B., Miss Gertie M., Miss Florence P., Miss Fanny G. and Ella B., who wishing to see me drill, had come up under the escort of Mr. E. and Will Fenn. Not having gone through the drill for about sixteen months I felt very rusty, for which reason I declared that I would not drill when they were by and could laugh at my blunders, though fortunately in the present instance I made none. At the conclusion of the drill, J. F. W. and myself walked home with the ladies and remained at Mr. E.'s til about eleven when we returned to quarters.

March 15, 1865 The weather promised rain this morning which kept me at the house all day, but the sun set clear and bright and the moon and stars came out brightly, so I made a call on George B., and was introduced to his sister Miss Addie, and Miss Mollie B., the latter of whom is a really beautiful girl of some nineteen springs with very sweet manners. Miss Addie, while not being quite so handsome, has yet a sufficient amount of good looks to be well satisfied with nature's gifts, besides which she is a fair conversationalist and seems to have a very happy disposition. About half past ten I left, having spent a pleasant evening and made an engagement to call for the ladies on next Friday afternoon to accompany them to see our drill.

March 16, 1865 Today it being my turn, I took a twelve hour permit and went to town. As far as permits are concerned, they are almost unnecessary as we go down town as often as we wish, but having a permit relieves me from answering roll call. On arriving at the house this evening I found Sergeant J. R. W. and J. F. W. there making a call. Being invited to do so, they stayed to supper and spent the evening. The whole party engaged in a laughable game of Smelt and continued it until all but Mrs. E. paid the penalty, and I have no doubt but that she would have shared a like fate, but that I sat upon her right and played so as to run her out. On getting up to go we were much surprised and somewhat chagrined to hear that it was ten minutes of two o'clock. We made quick steps for quarters and after emptying a pipe, laid down as the guard was being relieved for three o'clock.

March 17, 1865 There was a strong wind the whole day, though the sun shone brightly. I secured permission from our lieutenant in command to be absent from drill and about three o'clock I went after Miss Addie and Mollie B., but as I expected they were somewhat afraid to venture out, for which reason they asked to be excused, proposing to go on the first day when the weather was fit to allow comfort in walking. I remained with them about half an hour and then, not wishing to return to quarters, took a ramble down town, intending to be back by roll call. Meeting Mr. E., he insisted on my going home with him, which I did, and remained til eleven o'clock. On going up Old Street, I met some of our boys with whom I went out to quarters.

March 18, 1865 (Saturday) As I missed roll call last night, I was put on extra guard duty today, but this is far from being a great hardship, as tomorrow would be my regular day for guard which would very probably prevent my going to church, but being on today throws me off tomorrow, and being on Monday again will enable me to go off in the afternoon after the ladies who were to have come out last Friday. This much good may be extracted out of a little evil. This afternoon between guard hours I took a stroll down town with some of our boys and met quite a number of my lady acquaintances.

March 19, 1865 Today the weather was as beautiful as any weather which I have ever seen, and the ladies all took advantage of it by turning out to church in large numbers. After breakfast I spruced up as much as my limited wardrobe admits, and went around to the house of friend E. but he had not come up yet as I went down Halifax Street to meet him. On getting down as far as the Market Street Church without having seen him, I went in and heard as fair a sermon by a country practitioner as I have ever heard. After dinner I went again and found Will at home, with whom I spent the afternoon. I wish I could do justice to my feelings in regard to this dear friend of mine. I have been acquainted with him nearly three years and in all that time never seen one single trait that I could condemn. He is of the strictest integrity, true to a fault, and always seeming to seek for an opportunity to do me a kindness. It is a matter of great surprise that with my looseness of character and so many selfish characteristics, he is so ready to hold out a helping hand to pure fellowship. Dear Will, may God grant me the time to show you that your many kindnesses are not seeds sown in barren ground.

After sundown roll call, I went down to accompany Miss Eddy to church. J. F. W. enjoyed the same pleasure with Miss Gertie. After service we remained until eleven o'clock when we returned to our quarters, and got there just in time to enjoy a hearty laugh at the expense of a couple of our boys who had just been "Garroled" by some of our boys, who did it in that spirit which forms so large a part in the character of our company.

> - Will Fenn was a bookbinder who had boarded with the Ege family before the war. He was later a partner in the "Fenn and Owen Printing Company" of Petersburg.-

March 20, 1865 At four o'clock we were called up and ordered to prepare for a march. We were soon ready and our horses soon coming up. We awaited orders but they were not received, although the horses were ordered to remain at the park until further orders. This afternoon I walked down town for the purpose of exercise and on reaching the Bindery I met Miss Eddy, Gertie, and Mollie B. with whom I walked as far as Poplar Lawn and then home, after which I went out to quarters.

March 21, 1865 Today the weather was very disagreeable, with strong winds and much rain. We are still awaiting orders which may arrive at any moment, but I trust that we shall not receive any until the weather clears off. This afternoon I went out, wishing to mail a letter to W. T. E., and on coming back the rain poured down, drenching me through.

March 22, 1865 Today the weather was clear and cold with a very brisk wind, which rained the dust in such clouds that walking in it was very unpleasant, nor would I have done so had I not been compelled to go over to our wagon yard to get some clothing. Coming from there, I stopped at Gilmer's and helped him until dinner time, when I went home with him. I remained there until about half past four when I returned to quarters. After dark I went up Halifax Street and spent the evening with Mrs. F. til about half past nine o'clock.

March 23, 1865 The wind still continues with all the vigor of which this boisterous month is so proverbially capable of, but towards dark it lulled down somewhat. J. R. W., J. F. W., and myself went down to Mr. E.'s, where we spent the evening and at bedtime, we left for our quarters.

March 24, 1865 The *Express* of this morning announced that the Rev. Mr. Duncan of Richmond would preach in the Market Street Church, so I determined to go as I had considerable curiosity to hear him, having heard much of him. After dinner, I went down to invite Miss Eddy and Miss Gertie to go to church, but as the weather did not look very bright, they concluded not to go. After roll call I went in company with several of our boys, and in the course of a short time I found our company well represented as there were at least forty in the gallery besides some twenty or more with the ladies in the body of the church. The text for the evening was from 2nd Timothy, Chapter 4, and 10th verse, "For Demas hath forsaken me, having loved this present world". From it, he preached an extraordinary sermon, the delivery of which took up an hour and forty-five minutes. When he first got up I feared that I would be disappointed in him as he seemed to be a very inferior looking man, but after he preached a little while he improved in appearance, and this continued to such an extent that before he finished, I thought him the best looking man that I had ever seen. On leaving the church we met one of our boys with word that our company had been ordered to move at three o'clock in the morning, so we hurried to our quarters and after getting things together, I laid down for a nap.

March 25, 1865 (Saturday) On laying down last night I calculated on at least four hours sleep, but in this I found myself an unfortunate victim of misplaced confidence, for about twelve o'clock orders came to hitch immediately. This was soon done and we bade adieu to Aspen Hall, named so by our boys because the lightest footstep would make it tremble. We went out Halifax Street and on reaching Battery 45, turned to the left and went out Boydton Plank Road about three miles, when we reached the right of McGowan's Brigade on the Boisseaux Farm, where we were held in reserve in a bottom, ready for action. About daylight a very heavy artillery firing was heard on the left of the lines, which we supposed (and afterwards ascertained) to be in the neighborhood of the Appomattox River. This continued for two or three hours, then it ceased. In the course of a few hours we learned that our troops had assaulted Battery 3 and captured it with some five hundred prisoners, including two brigadier generals, and also the horse and sword of General Warren, who is reported killed. He was one of the most valuable of the enemy's generals. On taking the fort, all of the enemy batteries that could bear on it opened, to which the assaulting troops replied by turning the captured guns on them, and they kept this up as long as the ammunition lasted. After spiking the guns and bringing off a few brass mortars, they fell back, for by this time Grant was massing heavily on that flank to retake the battery, and I do not think that we could spare the men to hold it.

At this time the sharpshooters in our front charged the enemy's picket line, drove them out, and then quietly fell back to their own. Shortly after, the enemy tried this but was repulsed. While this was going on a heavy artillery fire was opened on the right at or near Hatcher's Run. This continued for about two hours. Just before this ceased, the enemy advanced a heavy line of skirmishers against the skirmish line on the left of McGowan's Brigade, who were captured after a slight resistance. As soon as this was done, the enemy advanced a heavy line to reinforce the first, thinking no doubt but that we would attempt to recapture our line. The moment the second line left their works, orders came for us and we moved to the left about three hundred yards at a hard gallop, unlimbered, came into position, and fired upon the enemy, firing as rapidly as we could. But this did not prevent the movement of the second line, who reached the rifle pits from which several of the enemy's flags were already flying. As soon as this movement of the enemy was well completed, heavy columns of the enemy were seen leaving their works on our left, and moving farther to our left. A short time afterwards the guns from Batteries Gregg and 45 opened rapidly, showing that their works were being assaulted. As long as the enemy remained in range of our guns we kept up a rapid fire on them, and I think that we must have done considerable damage, as our shell was bursting above and all around them. All this time the enemy were keeping up a heavy artillery fire on our line, one of which passed within eight or ten feet of General Lee's head, who was riding by at the time. While we were thus engaged in our line, we could hear on our right in the neighborhood of Hatcher's Run, the heavy roll of musketry which was kept up for about two hours. As darkness was gradually approaching, the firing on both sides all along the line slowly ceased.

Our battery fired about three hundred and fifty times with no casualties, which is somewhat remarkable as we went into position under a heavy fire which was well sustained the whole time, and we were protected by nothing, unless we can call a small mound of earth which would scarcely turn a bullet protection. During the afternoon, three men belonging to the Crenshaw Battery were wounded, two mortally and one severely. The gun to which they were attached was in position about eight yards to the right of my gun.

-The section of the lines to which the Blues had been sent was a thin line of rifle pits and trenches, which ran west from Battery 45 roughly parallel to the Boydton Plank Road, in front of Forts Gregg and Whitworth, toward Dinwiddie Courthouse. Walters was mistaken in his report of General Gouverneur Warren's death. He was actually in action at Five Forks, to the right of the Blues' position, and was not wounded in this fighting.-

The Boisseau House, also known as Tudor Hall, near the Boydton Plank Road west of Battery 45. Grandy's Battery was posted just to the east of this house on March 25, 1865.

March 26, 1865 (Sunday) Contrary to all general expectations (which all looked to be a warm one), today passed off very quietly. Not a single report of artillery could be heard, and scarcely that of a musket, though both sides kept themselves well under cover of the works, as an occasional "Minie" would whistle through the air to remind the unwary that peace was not yet made. After dark, our two Napoleons were moved some seven or eight hundred yards farther to the left to be prepared to lend a helping hand to Battery Gregg or 45 in case the enemy should again assail these works.

March 27, 1865 (Monday) As the first faint tinges of day made their appearance in the sky, rapid musketry and rebel yells told that our boys were charging the Yankees in the skirmish line which was taken from us on Saturday. In less than a minute, every man was in his place awaiting developments. The firing was kept up with considerable vigor for about three-quarters of an hour when it tapered down to an ordinary picket line fire. While this was going on, we saw what seemed to be a disposition of the enemy to mass a force on their line in front of my gun. We sent a case shot among them which caused them to scatter. A short time after this some twenty or thirty Yankee prisoners were brought in, from the guards of whom we learned that our attack on the picket line had been successful, that we held the line, and the possession of which the enemy does not wish to dispute with us. During the day, flags of truce passed between the lines, the object of which I could not ascertain, though it was probably to enable the enemy to carry off their dead and wounded who had fallen on Saturday. We could see stretchers being carried, and picket firing ceased along the whole line.

March 28, 1865 (Tuesday) Everything remains quite still and therefore true to our usual custom (or at least, a custom very prevalent of late). A heavy detail was made from all of the artillery on this portion of the line for the purpose of throwing up a heavy advanced work for artillery. The work as laid out will have three fronts or faces, will be forty feet thick at the base and eight feet high, and the guns will be mounted on platforms and fired "En Barbette". I do not believe that we will remain here long enough to finish, for it will require near two weeks to build it. I believe that Grant will try us in less time than that even if General Lee does not take the initiative, though I scarcely think the latter will be the case. Reports are current in town today that Johnston fought two days with Sherman and the latter was badly worsted.

March 29, 1865 (Wednesday) This morning I was sent off on a detail of three men to get logs and poles for the inside of the new work. We worked hard all day long and had the satisfaction to learn, on going back, that the battery was ordered off towards dusk. This order was countermanded, or rather changed into one to be ready to move at a moment's notice. I lay no claim to prophetic powers, but I would not be afraid to wager all that I have that we will leave here before daybreak, and my reasons for thinking so are that I feel certain that Grant will try our lines somewhere soon to repay us for Saturday's work at Number 3, and another reason is that there is a report today that the enemy have taken Dinwiddie Courthouse and it is possible that Grant may make a demonstration on the left to draw our attention from his operations on the right. But as these are all perhaps idle speculations, and as the fire is dying out, I think it advisable to turn in, so as to get all the sleep possible whether we move or not. I greatly fear that it will rain before morning, though the new moon seen tonight had her horns well up.

March 30, 1865 (Thursday) About twelve o'clock last night we were awakened by a most terrific cannonading on the left of our lines, accompanied by the heavy roll of musketry. This was continued for nearly three hours when it gradually ceased, owing probably to a heavy rain which began to fall, and which did not cease until nearly sunset. Then it cleared off, with the wind to the southwest, though the banking of the clouds in the northwest betokens a change of wind if they do not move.

Shortly after the firing of last night began, our Napoleon sections were ordered to take position some seven or eight hundred yards further to the left, a position just vacated by a section of rifled guns belonging to the Crenshaw Battery. We reached there in the midst of the rain and as soon as our guns were placed in position, the horses were sent off to bring the guns of the Huger and Donaldsonville Batteries of our battalion out of the lines on the left of the Jerusalem Plank Road, but owing to the firing this could not be done. Col. James of the 2nd Corps, whose command relieves our guns, exchanged, giving his for those which our battalion left on the lines. As soon as this was effected, our batteries were moved to the vicinity of Burgess Mill, which is some four miles to the right of the position occupied by my company, where they took position. Though it has been raining incessantly all day to within a short time before sunset, heavy musketry firing with frequently the report of artillery has been heard on the right, which occasionally was carried down nearly to our part of the line, but I do not think this anything more than sharpshooting, varied by an occasional charge on the picket line by one side or the other. I cannot learn the meaning of the cannonading on our left last night, but I think it probable that it was nothing more than an attempt of the army to draw our attention from the right.

Having the time today, and the weather compelling me to stay indoors, I wrote a letter to Cousin Josie, but since sending it off this evening, I regret very much that I wrote it in the tone that I did, as in it I took pains to vent a portion of my sarcasm on a circumstance in which she was perfectly right. Had I taken a second thought I would have destroyed it, as I fear that the perusal of it will pain her greatly. Even if it does not invoke a spirit which will cause her to cease corresponding with me, should she reply to it, let the tone of her letter be what it will. When I write to her again, I shall clothe myself in the robe of humility and come into her presence as a penitent.

March 31, 1865 (Friday) About one o'clock this morning it began to rain again and continued to do so until about midday, when it cleared off with fair prospects for clear weather for some days. On the very first appearance of day the fighting again commenced on our right with more artillery firing than was heard yesterday. In the afternoon, we learned that the enemy had charged our picket lines near Burgess Mill in front of the position occupied by the Huger Battery, a portion of which they captured and from which, as it is only some three hundred yards in advance of the main work, they annoyed our artillery greatly, almost preventing the working of the guns. A short time after, we learned that the Huger Battery had lost three men killed and four wounded. The former were Sergeant Badgers and Privates Boutwell and Whitehurst. The wounded were Corporal Brown (flesh wound through the thigh, severe but not serious), Herbert (thumb shot off), Rye (through neck and face, severe), and the forth I do not know the name of. The latter three are privates. Lt. Colonel Richardson of our battalion was also wounded, the ball entering his right side above the hip, and is supposed to have lodged in the spine, though it has not been found yet. The wound is considered dangerous. Toward the dark the fighting ceased. I have been unable to learn anything reliable from today's fighting, but from such reports as I could pick up, I imagine that our loss in the last few days must have been heavy without much to show for it on our side. I understand that at one time we pressed a portion of the enemy's line back about two miles, but owing to the large disparity of numbers in the enemy's favor, we were compelled to fall back to our original position, during which we lost heavily.

April 1, 1865 (Saturday) All day we have heard the report of fighting on the right, but I could learn nothing definite about it, but one report on which I am inclined to place some reliance is to the effect that Pickett's Division and Pegram's Battalion were cut off today by the enemy, but were enabled to enforce their way through to our lines again, though the latter was attended with considerable loss. For several days past, the lines at which we are in position have been almost entirely depleted and all the troops that could be taken have been sent and massed on the extreme right of our lines for the purpose of being at hand to counteract any movement which Grant may contemplate on that flank. Now, while this might be right, it is apparent to the most common observation that a very small effort on the part of the enemy would carry the portion of our lines, and if this was done, our army would be cut in two beyond even the hope of reconstruction (in consideration of our small numbers), and though I have heard or seen nothing to lead me to the conclusion, yet I feel almost certain that if an assault is made, it will be at this point, and I cannot but think that the hour is not far distant when my doubts will be verified. But as Grant has shown in several instances that Sunday is no favorite fighting day, I shall be compelled to wait until next week to learn if my idea is the correct one, and as I like to be well employed on the Sabbath, I think I shall run the blockade tomorrow evening and go to church with the family. From the incessant whistling and screaming of the engineers, I am led to believe that Grant is moving his troops to some point in large numbers.

April 2, 1865 (Sunday) Last night about ten o'clock the enemy commenced another terrific cannonading on the left near the river which gradually extended to our front and passed along to our right, though that on our front and right was the merest trifle to that on our left. About one o'clock this morning the continuous roll of musketry added to the din on that point and soon the picket in our front took a hand in and kept it up at short intervals until about four o'clock, when rapid firing and loud cheering about three-quarters of a mile to the right of my gun, and the opening of our rifled section told us that our lines were assailed. In a short time thereafter, the infantry on our right gave way and Captain Grandy, who had been with the rifled guns, came hastily down to our Napoleon section, reporting the former captured together with all of the men attached to them. At this time we ran Number 2 gun out of the salient which it had been occupying and placed it in position to enfilade inside our own line, while Number 1 gun was turned for the same purpose, and also to enable us to obtain something of a crossfire on the enemy who were coming down on us in heavy masses. As soon as this was done we opened with one second fuse case shot, and here occurred a mistake which frequently occurs while fighting in the dark and which, though unproductive of any serious results, yet embarrassed us considerably. Just as we fired the first shot inside our lines, a colonel shouted out that we were firing into our own men, a few of whom were flying from the rapidly advancing enemy who by this time were not more than fifty yards from our guns. To pause now would have been fatal, so acting on the general principle that no great result should be risked for the sake of a few lives, we loaded with cannister. During this time our infantry were flying by our guns in a perfect panic and at a rate which promised in a few moments to leave our guns entirely without support. To prevent this, Captain Grandy and one or two others tried, and in a measure succeeded, in stopping a sufficient number to form a thin line, who stood their ground a short time but could not succeed in any time more than causing a momentary check. And now our boys began to drop. Gus Johnson was shot in the face and through the left arm, Broughton received a shot in the left leg above the knee, Doughtie also sung out that he was wounded, but as we had plenty of men, these casualties did not impede the service of the guns. One circumstance greatly against the effectiveness of our guns was that we were so cramped for room that only one gun could be fired at a time for fear of killing some of the men at the other, but the intervals, short as they were, were occupied by the men in assisting to rally our infantry. Seeing others engaged in this, I for the moment forgot that prudence for which I have always been remarkable during moments of danger, and did the same. While engaged in this, I received a bullet in my left shoulder which I at first thought had gone into my lung owing to a momentary difficulty in breathing, but subsequently found it had struck against the blade, and glancing on that, ranged upward, and was cut out some hours afterward about four inches from where it entered. The force of the blow, or something else which I did not have time to analyze, knocked me down, and picking myself up, I found that the enemy were within ten or fifteen paces from our guns, upon which I put out, making the best time that I could, nor did I feel safe from more bullets or capture until I got inside of Battery 45.

On arriving in town, I found at least half the people standing in the streets or in their doorways, and many and eager were the questions asked regarding the state of affairs, and great anxiety was expressed regarding the fate of Petersburg. In answering these I used my best endeavors to instill feelings of confidence with considerable success, though on so doing, I belied my own convictions. On my way down Halifax Street, I stopped at the house of Mr. Mingie to get my uniform jacket, and great sympathy was expressed for me and my company, and their offers of assistance were earnest and pressing. After leaving their house, I next stopped at Will Fenn's house and met with a repetition. From there I went to Mr. Ege's house where I had a wet cloth put on my wound, and ate breakfast, after which I went to the corps hospital to have the bullet cut out, which was done by the dullest lancet that I think was ever used. When my shoulder was dressed, the surgeon ordered me to take the ambulance train for Richmond and report to some hospital there, but at my request he gave me permission to remain in Petersburg til tomorrow when I shall go over. During the day I went twice to different portions of the line and found that we were holding our own, but the tobacco warehouses were being burned, and the quartermaster and commissary stores were being given away to all who chose to go for them. That showed that the city was soon to be evacuated, so not wishing to be caught there, I bade my friends good by with a smile on my lips, but such anguish at my heart as I have seldom before experienced, and crossed the pontoon bridge to Ettricks about eleven o'clock at night. I walked with the wagon train til about three o'clock when, after writing this, I shall try to get a couple of hours sleep.

-Walters' wound actually proved to be a fortunate occurrence, for it caused him to leave his company just before it was captured with its guns. His officers and most of his comrades were taken to prison camps, and were not released for two or three months after the surrender at Appomattox Court House.

These last moments of the Blues in action were also recorded by Westwood A. Todd, another Norfolk native, who was serving with the Petersburg Rifles, 12th Virginia Regiment. His observations of this moment are copied here from his journal "Reminiscences of the War Between the States".

The Norfolk Blues

The efficient service rendered by this company and their gallant conduct on the 2nd of April, 1865 deserves to be recorded. The command was divided, one detachment under Lt. Henry V. Moore manned the mortar battery in the rear of the Rives Salient, a detachment with two Napoleons under Lt. James W. Gilmer were near the Boisseau House on the right of Petersburg, and the remaining detachment with two rifled guns, under Captain Grandy and Lt. William T. Peet, were posted several hundred yards to the right of Lt. Gilmer. The four guns were supported by a mere skirmish line from Lane's Brigade. About daylight, the enemy broke through the feeble line on the right of the Blues and came pouring down upon their flank. After a gallant fight in which Lt. Peet was seriously wounded and some others killed or disabled, the two rifled pieces together with many of the men were captured. The enemy not advancing in Lt. Gilmer's immediate front, he obliqued his two Napoleons (in barbette) to the right, and swept the field in that direction. Captain Grandy with a few of his men escaped to Lt. Gilmer's guns, followed by the enemy. Lt. Gilmer then withdrew one of his guns from the rampart and, turning it to the right down our own line, poured grape and cannister with terrible effect into the advancing enemy, but the Federals soon came up in his rear and captured Captain Grandy, Lt. Gilmer, many of their men, and both Napoleons. The remaining detachment under Lt. Moore at the mortar battery fared better. The enemy captured the main line in their front a few hundred yards off, but strange to say, did not advance further, although the enemy could have gobbled up the mortar battery at any time during the day. In the meantime the mortars were kept actively employed by Privates Calvert Petty, Walter H. Doyle, Merritt Cooke, the Fitzgeralds, Smiley, and John Doyle of the cavalry (the last named was on a visit to his brother Walter, and got caught in the lines). About dusk they ran the gauntlet of the Yankee bullets to the covered way and escaped through

Petersburg, followed the rest of the army, and surrendered with it at Appomattox.

As of April 2, 1865, the Norfolk Light Artillery Blues ceased to exist as a fighting unit. However, those men who had not been taken prisoner remained true to their resolution to stay with the Confederate army, and made themselves available for service in whatever way they could.-

April 3, 1865 (Monday) About an hour after daylight I started off and soon got to the wagons of our train which though they had been going all night, had made little headway owing to the bad condition of the roads. As I intended to make for Richmond today I pushed ahead, thinking to strike across the country so as to come out at the halfway house on the Petersburg and Richmond road, but just before leaving the main road I learned that the city was evacuated and in possession of the enemy. This rather startling intelligence determined me to remain with our wagon train until we arrive at Amelia Court House, on which the enemy is moving, where I expect to take the train for Danville or some other point where my wound, which though not serious but is very painful, can be attended to. At dark, I halted for the night in a fine piece of woods about a mile to the rear of our wagon train. Today, I came up with that portion of our company who had charge of the mortars in the rear of the main line at Petersburg. They all came out safe and must have done well, as after firing til the friction primers were exhausted, they fired some sixty rounds more by heating the priming wires red hot and then inserting them in the vents. No better evidence than this is required to show that they did their duty. I learned today that Booth was killed yesterday morning at his gun, and that W. J. Taylor had one of his feet shot off, that Lt. Peet was shot through one of his limbs, and that Captain Grandy was seriously if not mortally wounded. God grant that these reports are false, for the army contained no better soldiers than the first two named, and the officers were worthy of their men. Taylor was in the act of sponging his gun when the enemy came up and took the sponge out of his hand.

April 4, 1865 (Tuesday) At daylight we started, and by night made and packed at Amelia Courthouse. The roads are in very bad condition, the horses and mules breaking down at every step, while the countenances of the men wear a look of despondency such as I have never seen before. What fate may have in store for us, I cannot imagine, but I fear that the last day for the Army of Northern Virginia is near at hand. Just as we halted for the night, I heard that a force of the enemy's cavalry had struck the railroad on the other side of the courthouse but had been driven back by Longstreet's forces.

April 5, 1865 (Wednesday) At daylight all were ready to move forward, but an hour passed and no movement was made. We became satisfied that something was wrong, and being anxious to learn what it was I went ahead and soon came up with a portion of Longstreet's forces who were drawn up in a line of battle, from whom I learned that the enemy were massing up in our front. As I did not care to know more, I went back to our wagons. On my way back I met the infantry, cavalry, and all the available artillery moving to the front, many of the men in apparently as good spirits as ever, but it seemed to me that the usual jest was constrained, while the laughter was evidently forced. I also saw General Lee sitting on his horse in a piece of woods just off the road, and wishing to take a good look at him, I worked around til I got a position from which I could see him without myself being seen. The good old man looked—I had almost said as good as ever, but this is not so. It is true that his thoughts are not written on his face, but several times I thought I saw a shadow pass over his face such as I did not care to analyze and it cannot well be otherwise in view of all circumstances. Poor, pitiful, I feel almost heartbroken. How must that great heart of his throb with anguish! I could not remain long viewing this sad picture as I began to feel decidedly womanish, especially about the throat and eyes.

On getting back to the wagons, I found them moving off towards a road on the left of Amelia Courthouse, which leads off to Farmville. After striking this road we had made about three miles when the train halted. This seemed rather singular, but we soon learned that a body of the enemy's cavalry had broken into the head of our train and destroyed about three wagons, but that Gary's Brigade of cavalry had driven them back, killing a few, whom we passed a short time afterwards. After many stoppages on account of bad roads, about dark we again passed the Appomattox River and packed about a mile on the other side. My wound has been very painful today.

April 6, 1865 (Thursday) We were again underway about daybreak and at noon passed through Cumberland Courthouse, where a halt was made, and some of the train artillery was moved to the front, as it was reported that the enemy, moving on a road running parallel with the one we were on, were only two miles off. This piece of information caused me to don a new pair of pantaloons which I had been carrying since I had left Petersburg, for I knew that if I was captured, I would have been plundered of all articles not actually on my person. Fortunately, it proved to be a false report and after about an hour's halt, we again moved off. After making about twenty-one miles, we packed for the night about ten miles from the town of Farmville. I understand that tomorrow we are to take a road that leads to Lynchburg by way of Appomattox Courthouse. I also understand that our final destination is Lincolnton, North Carolina, but if this army ever crosses that line, I shall be greatly surprised, as both men and horses are broken down and the rations which were served out today were two ears of corn per man. Tomorrow we will probably get a bundle of fodder. My wound has been very painful today, and as I have been compelled to walk all day, I am almost used up. Heaven grant that I may be able to keep up with the army, for independent of my horror of being captured is the feeling that ere many days General Lee will need the service of every man, and though one man can do but little, yet when the death struggle takes place, I should like to be there.

April 7, 1865 (Friday) We were called up about an hour before day but for some reason, did not start til about seven o'clock. We found the roads in very bad condition so that we made only twelve miles, though we did not pack til nine o'clock at night, which we did one mile from New Store, a small post village in Buckingham County. During the day the enemy broke into one of our trains capturing twenty-five or thirty guns, and destroying about two hundred wagons. It is reported that General Mahone and Colonels Huger and Taylor were killed in an engagement yesterday, but I am inclined to doubt the report, as I can find no one who can affirm positively that he knows it to be a fact, though if it is so, it is a terrible loss at this moment.

April 8, 1865 (Saturday) Having gotten some flour and a small piece of meat last night, though very tired, I went to work to bake some bread, but as I had several things to bother me, it was after midnight when I got through, and I was just on the point of laying down to take a nap when the bugles blew the hitch-up call. This elicited many an anathema from those whom it woke up, but I was rather glad of it, for I have often felt that a short nap after a heavy march is worse than no sleep. In about an hour we moved off and at four o'clock in the evening we packed three miles on the other side of Clover Hill, the courthouse village of Appomattox County, having made nearly twenty-four miles. The roads over which we marched today were as a general thing, very good. During the evening, we passed around a house, or rather hovel, at which I stopped to get a drink of water, and in which I found the most wretched family that I have ever seen. The father and the eldest son were almost useless from the fact of their hands being turned in at the wrists, so as to almost touch the arm. The mother was idiotic, the eldest daughter, who did not look to be more than eighteen years of age, was the mother of two children of more than doubtful parentage, the second daughter, who told me she was only seventeen "las birfday", had no arms, while a hand protruded from each shoulder, and one of the younger children was club-footed. Incredible as this sounds, it is nevertheless strictly true, and if necessary can be vouched for by several of our boys, whose attention I called to it. As might be anticipated, the house was a perfect den of filth. On packing, orders were issued for our trains to be ready to move at seven o'clock, as an endeavor would be made to reach Lynchburg, which was some twenty miles distant by daybreak. As this gave us three hours, many of us stretched out to take a greatly needed nap, but we had scarcely done so when a cry was raised of "here they are!" and sure enough, a drove of Yankee cavalry came flying in among our wagons and guns. Some of the men immediately unlimbered, put a number of guns in position, and loaded with cannister. In seeing this, the enemy dismounted and advanced in line of skirmishers, opening a fusillade under which our men were compelled to leave their guns. As we had no infantry support, when our men began to leave, such a putting out I never saw before, with everyone trying to do the best he could for himself. On the principle that "misery likes company", I got three or four of our boys together, and all agreeing to remain together come what would, we struck out for a piece of woods about a quarter of a mile off. On reaching it, we called a council of war at which, after many arguments pro and con, it was decided to make the best of our way to Clover Hill and thereafter to be guided by circumstances. As we know nothing of the country and could form no idea of the whereabouts of the enemy, we dodged about until nearly midnight, when we reached the village and found ourselves within our own lines, and being very tired, the boys laid down to get some sleep, an example which I shall follow in a few moments.

April 9, 1865 (Sunday) At early daylight our shattered ranks were arranged for battle and soon after, the fight began, but even to the most sanguine of us it was no difficult task to foretell the result as far as the pending battle was concerned, but such was our confidence in the resources of our old chieftain that few even dreamed how they would terminate. The enemy advanced against our lines in heavy numbers and with much boldness, apparently certain of an easy victory, but the glorious recollections of past days and past deeds nerved the heart and steeled the arms of our men, and with a shout of defiance, they stood their ground and checked the advance of the enemy. Soon after, two pieces of artillery, which had been captured with all their horses and men by some of our cavalry, were sent to the rear and this circumstance, slight in itself, infused considerable courage in our hearts. And now from the movement of our troops we could see that the enemy was pressing our left, even if they were not swinging around so as to double us up, and while this was going on, heavy masses of the enemy could be seen advancing away off on our right while we had no troops wherewith to confront them. All this time, heavy fighting was going on in our front where we still held the enemy in bay. Affairs were still in this condition at nine o'clock when General Custer and another Federal officer came into our lines bearing a flag of truce to General Lee, to whom they were escorted by a Confederate officer. This event caused considerable speculation among such of our men as saw it, but it caused a sinking of heart within myself, for I thought that this could bear but one interpretation. In a short time thereafter, the firing suddenly ceased and in the course of a couple of hours we learned that General Grant had demanded, and General Lee acceded to a surrender to save further effusion of blood, which could have availed us nothing in consideration of the fact that we numbered only about eight thousand muskets, two thousand cavalry, and about two thousand artillerists, while the enemy's army is estimated by their own officers and men at over one hundred and twenty thousand, who had us completely surrounded. All day there was a constant passing and repassing of officers between the armies, and about four o'clock Lee made a short speech to his troops, stating the necessity and motives which caused him to surrender and also the terms upon which it was done, which are extremely liberal, being that all private property is to be respected, officers to retain their side arms, and all to be paroled as soon as the necessary papers can be made up. At its conclusion, everyone crowded around the old general to shake hands with him and then ensued a scene such as I never before witnessed. Tears ran down the cheeks of the old man and his voice was so broken with emotion that it was scarcely possible to hear his frequent "God bless you", and as for the men, not a dry eye could be seen, while many sobbed aloud in uncontrollable anguish. How long this continued I cannot tell, as the moment I shook hands with him, I made my way out of the crowd almost blind of tears of which I dared not be ashamed, and it was not til some time after that I discovered that my shoulder had received considerable damage in the press, which had caused it to bleed, and made it intensely painful. But so far from regretting this circumstance on account of the pain, I would not have missed shaking hands with our beloved old chieftain even at the price of a broken arm.

Later in the day, all that remained of our artillery was packed together, preparatory to be given up, or rather turned over, which will be done in a day or two. Just before dark, several of the general officers made speeches to their commands. Among others was General Walker of Gordon's Corps, whose speech, while it did ample justice to those of his men who did their duty well, was a most scathing rebuke to such as had not done so. The following is a part of his speech: "This morning, I led into battle seven hundred good and true men. This afternoon, my muster rolls showed me fifteen hundred. Where were you all when the stern voice of battle pointed out to every man his place and post of honor? Where were you? Sulking cowards! You noble men of the seven hundred, go home with the consciousness that if the cause failed, it was from no fault of yours. You well know those who were not with you, and I advise you to beware of them. If you meet them in the social circle, avoid them, if on the walks of business, distrust them, and if at the altar of your God, turn from them. For the man who would forsake his country and her cause in the hour of greatest need would sell his God."

April 10, 1865 (Monday) Last night it began to rain, which it has continued to do all day, and as we have no tents or clothing to change in, we are all very uncomfortable. Early this morning we tore down an old log house and this, together with some rails, enabled us to keep up a fire without which we would have suffered greatly. This afternoon the artillery was again moved so as to occupy a position in advance of our infantry and cavalry, the latter of whom were all well marched up to within a short distance of the courthouse, where they delivered up their arms, after which they were marched back to await their parole which will probably be made out tomorrow. Today, an order was published to our army which will probably be the last one that General Lee will ever publish to the Army of Northern Virginia, of which the following is a copy:

Headquarters, Army N. V.

April 10, 1865

General Orders

No. 9

After four years of arduous service marked by unsurpassed courage and fortitude, the Army of Northern Virginia has been compelled to yield to overwhelming numbers and resources. I need not tell the brave survivors of so many hard fought battles, who have remained steadfast to the last, that I have consented to the result through no distrust of them, but from the ardor and devotion would accomplish nothing that could compensate for the loss that would have attended the continuance of the contest and a determination to avoid the useless sacrifice of those whose past services have endeared them to their countrymen. By the terms of the agreement, officers and men can return to their homes and remain until exchanged.

You will take with you that satisfaction which proceeds from the consciousness of duty faithfully performed. I earnestly pray that a successful God will extend to you his blessing and protection. With an unceasing admiration of your constancy and devotion to your country, and a grateful remembrance of your kind and generous consideration of myself, I bid you all an affectionate farewell.

(Signed) R. E. Lee

General

Here where our artillery was packed was a farmhouse occupied by Major General W. H. Lee of the cavalry with his staff, and as this promised at least shelter from the rain, the remnant of my company, some twelve or fourteen in number, concluded to quarter there. But as the house was small and the general and his staff were the first occupants, we concluded to let them remain in posession of the house while we got underneath. It is true that we were a little crowded for room and had to crawl in, but we had been in the service too long to be choice, and we would have done excellently well but for the fact that we were compelled to share our chamber with an interesting family consisting of a sedate and maternal looking sleet [*sic*] and a litter of peeps who kept up an infernal yelling nearly all night, besides filling us with fear.

April 11, 1865 (Tuesday) The rain continued all day and as the weather is very chilly and our clothes and blankets wet, our feelings can be better imagined than described. But amid the cheerless prospect and gloom of our position, one thought throws a gleam of pure sunshine over all and that is that ere many days, the loved tones of home folks will ring in our ears, while in the contemplation of their glad smiles of welcome we will forget much of the hardships of the past and gain strength to renew our battles with the world in the endeavor to rise above the low straits to which this war has reduced many of us. Today the cavalry all received their paroles and left for home, and toward dark, the artillerists were called up, but owing to the blanks running some three hundred short, we could not all leave, among which unfortunate numbers my company figured, though probably we will receive ours early tomorrow morning and then, hurrah! for home. I understand that we will have to walk to Burkeville Junction, a distance of over forty miles, from whence we are to get transportation.

I have seen more of the Yankee army by passing of endless lines of troops, artillery, and wagon trains than I ever saw before, and in view of their immense numbers, unlimited resources, and perfect and complete appointments in all that belongs to an army, my astonishment is not that we were all compelled to surrender day before yesterday, but that we were able to stand as we have for four years with our comparatively small numbers, lean cattle, and imperfect equipment.

April 12, 1865 (Wednesday) About daylight this morning, we were awakened by the glad intelligence that our paroles had come. We soon had them filled up, and with glad hearts at the prospect of soon seeing the dear ones at home, started taking the nearest route to the railroad. We struck this after walking about ten miles, at a point twelve miles from Farmville. On starting this morning, we took with us a mule which, not being branded, was claimed as private property, and which we intended to dispose of on the road for something to eat, for having no rations, we expected to be hungry before reaching Farmville, the nearest point at which we could draw rations from the Federal supply trains. We had walked about fourteen miles, passing many houses on our way, at which we could get nothing, owing to the fact of a raid having been made on these places two or three days before by Federal cavalry who had cleaned out all the houses on their route. Then we came to the house of a Mr. F. who, though having but little himself, gave us a plentiful dinner, thereby almost literally dividing his last crust with us, and doing it with a free hearted welcome that will ever leave a pleasant recollection of him in my breast. Nor did he wish anything in the way of remuneration, but as all his horses and mules had been taken by the enemy, we insisted on leaving the one we had with him, and though this repaid him far beyond the actual value of what we had consumed, yet a thousand mules would not compensate him for the kind feeling which prompted the act, nor his wife with the pleasant alacrity with which she bustled about and prepared the dinner for us. After leaving Mr. F.'s house, we walked about five miles and halted for the night, quartering up in an old deserted house, having made about eighteen miles.

April 13, 1865 (Thursday) During the night a heavy rain fell which continued till after daylight and delayed us somewhat. But on the clouds breaking away a little, we started and had scarcely time to get wet before the rain ceased and the sun came out, through the influence of which the walking soon became very good and the remainder of a day's journey very pleasant. About noon, we reached Farmville, the streets of which presented a very motley appearance, filled as they were with a mob of half satisfied and insolent looking Yankees, and also dirty, and ragged, yet proud and defiant looking Confederate soldiers. Farmville in the "piping times of peace" may have been a neat, thriving place, but at present it is under the influence of so complete an eclipse that it is difficult to discern even the traces of thrift or beauty, nor could I see the face of a single lady from which to form an estimate of that feature of beauty. We found the Federal Provost Marshal, from whom we received an order to draw rations, after receiving which we struck out and in a couple of hours, reached the "High Bridge" on the Southside Railroad over the Appomattox River. On leaving, our troops had destroyed four spans of this magnificent bridge on the side nearest Farmville, but beyond this the bridge is uninjured, but it is a question whether it will ever be repaired for railroad purposes, as I understand that a new route has been surveyed, which will not require the keeping up of this bridge and answers all purposes. While our party took a short rest on the bank of this end of the bridge, I, led by what I trust was pardonable curiosity, walked over about half the length of the remains, and was well rewarded for my walk, as no one can form a fair vastness of the structure by standing at the bottom and looking up. I regret that I am unable to give a particular description of it. On rejoining my party, I found them preparing to move on, which we did. Soon after getting about a mile from the bridge and the day nearly spent, our party which consisted of twelve concluded to divide, as six stood a better chance of farm house accommodations than the whole number. By request, I took charge of our party, and striking to the left of the road and after walking about two miles, we came to the house of a Mr. F. who received us very kindly and gave us an excellent supper, notwithstanding a raiding party had nearly cleaned him out the day previously. We also received permission to sleep in one of the rooms, on the floor of which my party is stretched while I am writing this, and the nasal sound which they emit sounds so provoking to me that I shall add my organ to the orchestra in a few minutes.

April 14, 1865 (Friday) We were up at early dawn and left before the family were up, leaving a heavy blanket (nearly new) as remuneration. I feel satisfied that the family expected nothing from us, but I trust that they will receive and think kindly of our gift, poor and humble though it may be. About an hour after leaving the house, we came up with the other party who were sitting around a fire by the side of the road and looking rather gloomy, which was accounted for by hearing them say that they had slept in a barn and had gotten nothing to eat. Shortly after coming up with them, we all pushed forward, and at ten o'clock arrived at Burkeville Junction, where we received the gratifying information that we could get transportation, and that the train would leave a two o'clock for Petersburg. We also learned that we could draw rations here, for which purpose I went to the Provost Marshal, and receiving an order for one day's rations for twelve, we attempted to get it filled, but owing to the immense crowd, I was unable to do this, so that we were compelled (very reluctantly) to get on the train.

-On arriving in Petersburg, Walters evidently parted with the rest of the men of his company. The brevity of his following entries seem to indicate the hurried pace at which his last goodbys were said on the long awaited trip home.-

April 15, 1865 (Saturday) At 7 am, stopped and was received by Mr. E.'s family with great kindness. It rained all morning but cleared up in the afternoon.

April 16, 1865 Weather fine.

April 17, 1865 Arrived in Richmond. Mr. Ege's family ruined, also Mr. G.s' family, and Miss Gertie is wounded.

April 18, 1865 Mr. T.'s family wounded very painful. Robinson Hospital.

April 19, 1865 As I had determined to start for home tomorrow morning, I went up for a passport but could not get one as they had stopped issuing them for a day or two. This was a sad disappointment, for though receiving the greatest kindness from my dear friends here, yet the earnest craving to get home is becoming such that, should the prohibition be long continued, I shall feel sadly tempted to attempt to walk home. Wound awful.

April 20, 1865 This morning, on going to the Provost Marshal's office, I found that the giving of passports had been resumed, and got one for Norfolk. As the boat leaves at 6 am, I finished up a little business that I had, called on and bade good by to Colonel Richardson, Mrs. G., Miss Gertie, and one or two others, and spent the last evening in that social game of Euchre.

-Colonel Charles Richardson had been wounded during the last of the fighting around Petersburg and had been sent to Richmond to recuperate. He turned over temporary command of his battalion to Captain Grandy just prior to Grandy's capture. He soon returned to his home "Willis Hill" in Fredericksburg where he married Miss Charlotte Blaine in 1869. He was the successful proprietor of a pickle factory there until his death in 1913 at the age of 78.

The long and bitter campaign around Petersburg had left the riverboats as the only transportation available to Norfolk. Scheduled steamers between Richmond and other ports along the James River were quickly restored, since the Federals had controlled most of the river for over a year. Train service would not resume until the following winter when General William Mahone rebuilt and restored the Norfolk and Petersburg Railroad which ran through the former Petersburg defense lines.

Petersburg itself gradually recovered from the long and arduous siege it had suffered. John Ege reopened his printing and bookbinding shop at 120 North Sycamore Street, and for a time also published an agricultural newspaper. He was considered to be a "well known" citizen and served his community as president of the Board of Overseers for the Petersburg Almshouse. At his death on August 27, 1886, his business was taken over by the Fenn and Owens Printing Company, run by his former boarder Will Fenn.

Grace Church, where John Ege's funeral was held, merged its congregation with that of Christ Church in 1953, and the building on the corner of High and Lafayette Streets was taken down soon thereafter.-

CHAPTER SIX

Reconstruction and Resumption

Although the Confederate military service of John Walters and most of the other men of Grandy's Battery ended at Appomattox Court House, their story was far from finished. The influence of the men of that company and of the company itself would continue to be felt in their home city for a great many years to come.

Walters and the other men of the battery made their way home from Appomattox or the various prison camps in which they had been held, defeated but proud of their record. They soon found that not only would the Military Commander of Norfolk not allow them to be re-established as a militia unit, but they were also forbidden to wear any trace of their old Rebel uniforms under threat of arrest. The men were also strongly urged to take the "Ironclad Oath" by which they renounced the Confederacy and promised never again to take up arms against the United States government. In spite of these restrictions they "pitched in with their characteristic vim," and served their city and each other as best they could, maintaining the brotherly bonds forged in war.

Walters himself found work for a short time as a clerk in the office of the "Norfolk Journal," then returned to his former trade by opening his own bookbinding shop at 54 Roanoke Square.

Soon after they had returned home and resumed their civilian lives, the Blues took up the sad task of laying their lost brothers to rest. On December 16, 1865, the bodies of Privates A. David

McCarrick and George O. Gaskins were returned to Norfolk from Petersburg where they had died during the war. The following day, McCarrick's family and former comrades in arms attended his funeral at Saint Mary's Roman Catholic Church. His body was then taken to Saint Mary's Cemetery at the northern end of Church Street, and was buried in the family plot. Gaskins was buried in his family's plot in Elmwood Cemetery by his parents.

Several members of the old battery began to see that some families were financially unable to properly bury their loved ones. They formed a mutual aid society to provide for this need, and to also keep the Blues together and preserve the records of the company until such time as a civil government was restored to Virginia and the company was allowed to reassemble. The new "Blues Memorial and Benevolent Association" met on March 16, 1866, and voted to bring home the fallen members of Grandy's Battery. They approached the members of the Norfolk Common Council with a request that a burial lot in the city's Elmwood Cemetery be donated for its needs, and with an informal nod from the council, the Blues Association began its grim work.

On March 31, 1866, a train arrived from Petersburg with members of the Blues Association and the remains of six veterans of the Blues. The bodies were taken to Norfolk City Hall and laid in state. On April 2, a funeral cortege was formed which included the Masons and volunteer fire companies, and the surviving Blues in their civilian clothes led by Captain Grandy. The coffins were then taken out for final burial. Private Ignatius Higgins, his casket covered by an ornate wreath made by the Sisters of Mercy, received the last rites of Saint Mary's Church and was then interred in the mausoleum of Saint Mary's Catholic Cemetery. He was later laid in his family's plot, close to the resting place of David McCarrick. Corporal Robert Butler was buried in his wife's family plot in Cedar Grove Cemetery with Masonic honors. The remaining four men, Privates A. M. Watters, J. S. Sterrett, W. C. Land, and W. A. Wilkins, were the first to be buried in the plot donated to the Blues Memorial and Benevolent Association near the center of Elmwood Cemetery. They were later joined by 14 other veterans, including Private James Wilkinson.

On April 9, 1866, in a formal session of the Norfolk Common Council, the burial plot in Elmwood Cemetery was officially turned over to the Blues' Association. In June of 1874, the association was chartered by the Circuit Court of Norfolk for the purpose of providing for the former members of the Norfolk Light Artillery Blues and their families. John Walters was one of the active members of this group and served as the secretary and later as treasurer of the Blues

Memorial and Benevolent Association. The group erected a chain fence with ornate wrought iron posts around the small plot and provided a decorative gate, representing crossed cannon, cannon balls, and a name plate at the top reading "Norfolk Light Artillery Blues, 1828." Unfortunately, a monument identifying the men whose remains rested within the plot was never erected, and except for the gate, the plot itself remained unmarked until April 26, 1992, when the United Daughters of the Confederacy and the Virginia National Guard dedicated a small memorial stone.

Just two years after the reburials, the veterans of the battery were surprised by the news of the death of their 33-year-old captain, Charles R. Grandy. On April 3, 1868, he passed away in his father's home on Bute Street of heart disease which had plagued him since his return to Norfolk. Some who had known him during the war as a healthy and stout young man blamed his illness on conditions at the Federal prison at Johnston's Island, Ohio where most of the Blues' captured officers had been held. Captain Grandy's funeral was attended by his family and former servants, by his comrades in the Blues, and by the United Fire Company and Masonic Lodge No. 166, in which he was also a member. He was buried in the Grandy family plot in Elmwood Cemetery.

The plot of the Norfolk Light Artillery Blues in Elmwood Cemetery, Norfolk, Virginia where 18 men of the company were laid to rest. The stone in the center was erected by the Pickett-Buchanan Chapter, United Daughters of the Confederacy.

Grandy had not lived to see the end of military rule in Virginia after the War Between the States. It was not until 1871 that an acceptable state constitution was adopted and control was finally returned to the citizens of the state. On April 24, 1871, a meeting was called to reorganize the Norfolk Light Artillery Blues as a militia company under the new government, and in just less than two weeks on May 4, the company was sworn into service. Its new captain was William E. Taylor, Jr. who had served the battery as a Confederate sergeant, and whose father had presided as an antebellum captain of the company. Several other former members of Grandy's Battery joined him on its new muster roll. On the Fourth of July in 1873, the reorganized Blues were presented with a new command flag by the City of Norfolk, and their old captain, Jacob Vickery, assisted at the presentation. Once again the Norfolk Blues proudly joined ranks under the flag of Virginia, and resumed its service to its state and country with the honor and distinction expected from an organization with such a proud heritage.

One record which the Blues Memorial Association was unable to pass intact to the re-established company was the original organization date of the unit. At some time during their service with the Confederate army, the Blues had begun to claim 1828 to be the year of their first meeting, and because they were separated from their home and their written records, this year was generally accepted to be correct. "1828" was later included in the decorative work on the cemetery gate and in the emblems adopted by the reorganized company. When the unit again began celebrating Washington's Birthday as their anniversary, February 22, 1828, was claimed as the birthdate of the Norfolk Light Artillery Blues, even though this date is actually two years before their first public appearance. Even some early surviving minutes of company meetings have been altered to support this traditional date.

Walters did not rejoin the Blues when the company was reorganized in 1871. By this time he was 36 years old and a family man. Evidently he had quickly lost his fascination with the ladies of Petersburg and Richmond, as he married Miss Virginia Phillips of Norfolk early in 1870. Their first child, Mary Lee Walters, was born later that year, their second child, William D. Walters, was born in 1872, and their third, Lottie L. Walters, followed in 1875.

With his bookshop providing his family a steady income and his military career complete, Walters took the position of clerk of the city market. He was also extremely active in a number of civic organizations. As previously mentioned, he served as an officer in the Blues Memorial Association and he also joined the Pickett-Buchanan Camp of Confederate Veterans when that organization was formed in Norfolk in 1883. He joined the Masonic Lodge in 1868, eventually reached the 32nd degree, and served as secretary for the Scottish Rite bodies for 24 years. For 9 years he was secretary of the Grice Commandery, Knights Templar, and served as its Eminent Commander; he served 13 years as secretary and as Master of the Atlantic Lodge, No. 2 A. F. and M.; and he served for an impressive 49 years as the secretary of the Norfolk United Royal Arch Chapter.

"Uncle John," as he became fondly known, was also active at McKendree Methodist Episcopal Church where he was a member of the men's bible class. He was frequently called on to serve as a pallbearer by the families of his many friends. On February 22, 1906, he was one of several surviving members of Grandy's Battery who were the special guests of the reorganized Norfolk Light Artillery Blues at their 78th Anniversary Banquet, when the Command Flag carried by the Blues during the War Between the States was returned to the unit.

Walters' wife, Virginia, passed away in 1892 at the age of 47. Walters himself lived another 26 years until January 11, 1918, when he died at the age of 82 at his home at 807 Marshall Avenue after a brief illness. He was buried next to his wife in the family plot in Elmwood Cemetery the following day with both Masonic and Knights Templar honors. His many years of contribution to the Masonic bodies was recognized in 1922 when "John Walters Chapter No. 68" was organized and was chartered under the United Royal Arch Chapter on October 25 of that year. Two hundred sixty-eight men were charter members of this unit.

Many years later, on August 22, 1956, Mary and Lottie Walters had the remains of their father, their mother, and their brother William (who also died in 1918), re-interred in a new family plot in Norfolk's Forest Lawn Cemetery. The two daughters lived together at the Ballentine Home on Granby Street until Lottie's death on October 2, 1959, and Mary's four months later on February 6, 1960.

The other former members of Grandy's Battery led similar lives. Some became founding members of Confederate veterans groups, others never again mentioned the time they spent as a Rebel soldier. Some became successful, renown citizens. Five former members of Grandy's Battery, namely William E. Taylor, Jr., James Gilmer, Samuel Hodges, R. Frank Vaughn, and M. C. Keeling, were elected to terms as the captain of the newly reorganized Norfolk Light Artillery Blues. Other veterans led more intimate lives or completely faded into obscurity. But each of them in some way contributed to the legend of the Blues until one by one, they passed from life. The last known surviving member of Grandy's Battery, Private Charles White, died on December 2, 1935.

This marker commemorates the Battle of Sewell's Point, the first combat action of the Blues. It is shown located on the Norfolk Naval Base at a site which in 1861 was in the water, several hundred feet from the shore. In the background across Hampton Roads lies Fort Monroe.
Courtesy of the Hampton Roads Naval Museum

The reorganized Norfolk Light Artillery Blues continued to be an important part of the official and the social life of Norfolk. They were called upon to participate in nearly every noteworthy event of the area from the time of their reorganization through the rest of the 1800s. No parade, grand opening, unveiling, or other gala occasion could be complete without an appearance by the Blues in their ornate uniforms. They were present for the funeral of Confederate General George Pickett who died in Norfolk on July 30, 1871; they welcomed the first trainload of "Pocahontas" coal to the Norfolk and Western Railroad docks at Lambert's Point in 1883; they paraded at the Philadelphia Centennial in 1876, the Yorktown Centennial in October of 1881, and the Jamestown Exposition of 1907; were present for the interment of Confederate President Jefferson Davis in Hollywood Cemetery in Richmond in 1893, and they attended the New Orleans Mardi Gras of 1895.

The Jamestown Exposition which the Blues helped to open was held at Sewell's Point, just north of Norfolk. The earthworks which the Blues and others had built here in 1861 and defended against Union warships including the *Monitor* were levelled during the building of the Pine Beach Hotel. In 1917, this land was purchased by the U.S. Navy and became the nucleus of the Norfolk Naval Base. A historic marker about the Battle of Sewell's Point was later erected on the base; an ironic reminder that the Navy had once tried to take this site by force.

The beginning of the twentieth century brought changes to the company as global tensions increased, and a World War began in Europe. Once again, the ornate uniforms and peacetime parades of the Blues would be traded for more somber equipment and serious training.

The first change occurred when the Blues were officially designated "Battery B, 111th Field Artillery" during the conversion of the state militia to the Virginia National Guard. In a show of its pride in its artillery company, the city of Norfolk donated land in its newly annexed section of Lambert's Point for a new armory. This imposing brick facility on Meyers Avenue (later Hampton Boulevard) was completed in 1914. (Interestingly, some residents of the area strongly objected to the large stable building which was later built on 47th Street behind the main gun room as unnecessary "militarization" of their neighborhood.) It was at this armory that the Blues were assembled to serve in the Mexican Punitive Expedition under General John "Blackjack" Pershing in June of 1916. The Blues were soon roaming the Mexican border, chasing the bandits of Pancho Villa and playing football with their comrades. They returned to Norfolk the following March, and had just three months of rest before they were called up for service in the American Expeditionary Force bound for France and the World War. The battery became part of the 29th "Blue and Gray" Division and trained at Fort Oglethorpe, Georgia before embarking on the Fourth of July 1918 aboard the *Aquitania*. In France, the battery was trained on the latest artillery piece, the French 75mm gun, and arrived at the front just days before the Armistice was signed on November 11, which effectively ended this fighting. They returned to Virginia the following May and were demobilized at Camp Lee.

While America celebrated the "Roaring Twenties," the Blues adopted a new coat of arms with the motto "Nunquam non Paratus" (Never Unprepared). Local headlines highlighted the champion polo team which they fielded for several years until their faithful artillery horses were finally traded for motorized trucks in 1935. As the lights of peace again began going out around the world though, the Blues began to take their new motto very seriously. They drilled with the latest available equipment, and were called back to active service on February 3, 1941, while the United States was still uninvolved in the Second World War. Re-equipped with 105mm howitzers in place of their old French 75s, the Blues trained for most of the next year and participated in the large scale Carolina War Maneuvers.

The Blues continued their training in the States after war with the Axis Powers was officially declared on December 7, 1941, then boarded the *Queen Mary* with the 29th Division and arrived in Greenock, Scotland on October 3, 1942. More training, marching, preparation (and occasionally football games) followed until June

6, 1944. On that fateful day, the latest generation of the Norfolk Light Artillery Blues and the other batteries of the 111th Field Artillery Battalion loaded their twelve 105mm howitzers into DUKW amphibious trucks, and became part of the Allied D-Day invasion of Nazi-occupied France. During the landings, most of their heavily loaded "Ducks" swamped in the rough sea. Only one of the battalion's guns survived the intense enemy fire and came ashore at bloody Omaha Beach. Those men who did make it to the beach were told by their commander, Lieutenant Colonel Thornton Mullins, "To hell with our artillery mission, we're infantrymen now!" Re-equipped with new howitzers in France a week after D-Day, the Blues spent the next year fighting their way across Europe with the famed "Blue And Gray" 29th Division. They were in heavy action at Saint Lo, Vire, Brest, and Julich before finally linking up with Soviet troops at the Elbe River in Germany on May 9, 1945.

In the years that followed the Second World War, the 111th Field Artillery Battalion was reactivated in the Virginia National Guard and was reorganized several times. In the 1950s, the battalion became racially integrated for the first time, and was also designated as one of the few Virginia Guard units authorized to carry the Confederate flag as an emblem of the service and sacrifices of Grandy's Battery and its other predecessors. The battalion flag was decorated with Civil War service streamers earned by the four batteries of Richardson's Confederate Battalion, creating some confusion as to exactly which units (the Norfolk Light Artillery Blues or the Norfolk Light Artillery) had served at what battles.

In 1962, the battalion moved into another new armory building in Norfolk on Virginia Beach Boulevard near the site of the old "Intrenched Camp" which had defended Norfolk at the beginning of the Civil War. The battalion took with it the old crossed cannon emblem of the Blues which had been mounted in the wall of its former home on Hampton Boulevard, and installed the emblem outside its new building. Within the new armory, treasured artifacts of former days were put on display in glass cases and on its walls. Pride in the battalion's past was strongly emphasized here and also at the monuments erected in Elmwood and Forest Lawn Cemeteries to its former members.

After surviving wars on numerous battlefields against a variety of enemies it seemed ironic that the Norfolk Light Artillery Blues could be threatened with extinction from the stroke of a pen, yet in March of 1992 it was announced that B Battery, the Norfolk Light Artillery Blues and the other batteries of the First Battalion, 111th Field Artillery Regiment would soon cease to exist, due to the extensive downsizing planned for the Virginia National Guard. Fortunately, just before the final formation of the battalion on September 23, 1992, it was decided that B Battery would not be terminated, but would instead be consolidated with B Battery of the Second Battalion, 111th Field Artillery and remain at Norfolk. After 163 years of service, the Norfolk Light Artillery Blues, one of the most ornate of the strands weaving throughout the rich tapestry which forms the story of Norfolk, had once again been continued when its end had seemed certain, and would remain as a proud example of the unselfish, colorful service of many of Virginia's finest citizens.

Armory of the 111th Field Artillery, Virginia National Guard in Norfolk which became the home of the Norfolk Light Artillery Blues when it opened in 1962.

The Men of the
Norfolk Light Artillery Blues
A Roster of the Company from
1861–1865

Name	Rank	Name	Rank
Allyn, Joseph Tyler, Jr.	Pvt.	Brown, Charles	Pvt.
Ashton, John Cocke	Pvt.	Brown, E. P.	Pvt.
Bagnall, Richard D.	Pvt.	Brown, H. C.	Pvt.
Banks, Richard B.	Lt.	Brown, James W.	Pvt.
Barraud, C. D.	Pvt.	Brown, John B.	Pvt.
Beale, H.	Pvt.	Browne, Joe S.	Pvt.
Bell, Albert S.	Pvt.	Browne, Victor H.	Pvt.
Bell, Norman	Pvt.	Buskey, Charles Henry	Cpl.
Benson, O. S.	Pvt.	Butler, Robert M.	Cpl.
Bishop, W. J. E.	Pvt.	Capps, Leonard O.	Pvt.
Blow, Walter W.	Pvt.	Carroll, William S.	Pvt.
Booth(e), William	Cpl.	Chamberlaine, Andrew E.	Pvt.
Borum, Charles	Pvt.	Clarke, Wm. T.	Sgt
Bradford, O.	Pvt.	Cocke, P. St. George	Pvt.
Branham, John B.	Lt.	Cocke, Wm. R. C.	Pvt.
Brickhouse, Benjamin D.	Pvt.	Collins, W. W.	Pvt.
Brickhouse, Smith N.	Cpl.	Cooke, John S.	Pvt.
Brock, Lysander A.	Pvt.	Cooke, Merritt Todd	Pvt.
Brooks, E. W.	Pvt.	Cornick, Henry	Pvt.
Broughton, Robt. S.	Cpl.	Cox, William R.	Pvt.

Name	Rank	Name	Rank
Cutherell, William S.	Pvt.	Higgins, Ignatius	Pvt.
Day, John Henry	Pvt.	Hill, Albert	Pvt.
DeFord, D. N.	Pvt.	Hodges, John M.	Pvt.
Denson, Alex J.	Pvt.	Hodges, Samuel	Pvt.
Doughtie, H. S.	Pvt.	Holmes, William H.	Pvt.
Doyle, Walter Herron	Pvt.	Hudgins, George C.	Sgt.
Drummond, Charles Henry	Pvt.	Hume, Richard Gregory	Pvt.
Drummond, R. Joseph	Pvt.	Hunter, J. Frank	Pvt.
Dunn, J. R.	Pvt.	James, Henry W.	Pvt.
Dunn, William H.	Pvt.	Johnson, Ames C.	Pvt.
Elliott, John W.	Cpl.	Johnson, Augustus W.	Pvt.
Elliott, Julius Augustus	Pvt.	Johnson, John W.	Pvt.
Elliott, Thomas E.	Pvt.	Jones, George	Pvt.
Elliott, Thomas H.	Pvt.	Jones, R. Henry	Pvt.
Evans, Richard	Pvt.	Joynes, Custis T.	Pvt.
Fitzgerald, D.	Pvt.	Joynes, Solon H.	Pvt.
Fitzgerald, Ed	Pvt.	Joynes, Wm. C.	Pvt.
Fitzgerald, W.	Pvt.	Keeling, John E.	S(QM)
Fletcher, Frank	Pvt.	Keeling, John L.	Pvt.
Floyd, Jos. W.	Pvt.	Keeling, Melville Cox	Cpl.
Freeman, J. M., Jr.	Pvt.	Kilby, William Turpin	Pvt.
Gamage, John O.	Pvt.	King, Warrington C.	Pvt.
Gaskins, George Oscar	Pvt.	Land, William A.	Pvt.
Gatch, J. A.	Pvt.	Land, W. C.	Pvt.
Ghiselin, Horace	Pvt.	LeCompte, John W.	Pvt.
Ghiselin, Richard	Pvt.	Lee, Frank Dean	Pvt.
Gilmer, James W.	Lt.	Lee, LeRoy M., Jr.	Pvt.
Goodrich, Alexander J.	Pvt.	Lovitt, Henry C.	Pvt.
Gordan, George Wash.	Pvt.	Lovitt, Robert C.	Pvt.
Gordan, Joseph P.	Pvt.	Malborn, Oscar L.	Pvt.
Gordon, Morton	Pvt.	Masi, Frank J.	Pvt.
Grandy, Charles R.	Capt.	Maupin, Geo. W. O., Jr.	Pvt.
Graves, Charles Mallory	Pvt.	McCarrick, A. David	Pvt.
Gwaltney, J. T.	Pvt.	McGuire, Jos. B.	Pvt.
Gwaltney, Richard H.	Pvt.	McKown, C. K.	Pvt?
Haines, Jas. M. D.	Pvt.	Montague, William D.	Cpl.
Hallett, William R.	Pvt.	Moore, Henry V.	Lt.
Halstead, Richard L.	Pvt.	Moore, John W.	Pvt.
Hatton, John F.	Pvt.	Moore, Joseph Porter	Pvt.
Haughton, Armistead J.	Pvt.	Morris, David P.	Pvt.
Higgins, Andrew	Pvt.	Morris, John Jesse	Pvt.

Name	Rank	Name	Rank
Morse, Burwell N.	Pvt.	Toy, Crawford H.	Pvt.
Nash, John H.	Sgt.	Vaughan, E. S.	Pvt.
Nash, Wadsworth	Pvt.	Vaughan, R. Frank	Sgt.
Newton, C. A.	Pvt.	Veale, Samuel	Pvt.
Nimmo, Powhatan E.	Pvt.	Vickery, Jacob, Jr.	Capt
Nimmo, William T.	Lt.	Walke, Isaac T.	Pvt.
Norsworthy, Joseph C.	Pvt.	Walker, R.	Pvt.
Norvell, C. R.	Pvt.	Walters, John H.	Pvt.
Peet, James D.	Pvt.	Ward, J. T.	Pvt.
Peet, William T.	Lt.	Watters, A. M.	Pvt.
Petty, J. Calvert	Pvt.	Watters, James H.	Sgt.
Porter, Robert T.	Pvt.	Webb, William T.	Pvt.
Rainier, John T.	Cpl.	West, Joseph S.	Pvt.
Reid, John Spence	Pvt.	West, William M.	Pvt.
Reynolds, J.	Pvt.	White, Charles E.	Pvt.
Reynolds, Robert E.	Pvt.	White, Nathaniel E.	Pvt.
Roberts, John B.	Pvt.	Whitehurst, Luke H.	Pvt.
Rogers, Crawford S.	Cpl.	Whitehurst, Steven T.	Pvt.
Rogers, John C.	Pvt.	Whiting, J. R.	Pvt.
Rogers, Theodore. F.	Pvt.	Whiting, John S.	Pvt.
Rogers, W. H. R.	Pvt.	Whiting, Thomas B.	Pvt.
Saunders, Smith S.	Pvt.	Whitmore, C.	Pvt.
Sebrell, N. C. H.	Pvt.	Wilkins, Charles L.	Pvt.
Segar, Thomas F.	Pvt.	Wilkins, George W.	Pvt.
Simmons, Bains A.	Pvt.	Wilkins, John F.	Pvt.
Simmons, J.	Pvt.	Wilkins, Thomas J.	Cpl.
Smiley, C. D.	Pvt.	Wilkins, Walter A.	Pvt.
Smith, Charles A., Jr.	Pvt.	Wilkinson, James	Pvt.
Smith, Elbridge C.	Pvt.	Williamson, Clarence H.	Pvt.
Smith, J. E.	Pvt.	Wilson, D. C. B. (Cary)	Pvt.
Smith, John W.	Pvt.	Wingfield, R. C. M.	Pvt.
Smythe, William	Pvt.	Woodhouse, John	Pvt.
Steever, Edwin	Pvt.	Woodhouse, Philip D.	Pvt.
Sterrett, J. S.	Pvt.	Woodward, W. W.	Pvt.
Swank, Wm. A.	Pvt.	Worrell, J. R.	Pvt.
Taylor, J. Theodore	Pvt.	Wright, Edwin L.	Cpl.
Taylor, William E.	Sgt.	Wright, James R.	Sgt.
Taylor, William J.	Pvt.	Wright, Minton A.	Pvt.
Thomas, Benjamin D.	S(QM)	Wright, William S.	Pvt.
Thomas, Jesse D.	Pvt.	Zills, Alexander C.	Pvt.
Thompson, E., Jr.	Pvt.	Zills, Julius A.	Pvt.
		Zills, John M.	Cpl.

Roster Biographies

JOSEPH TYLER ALLYN, JR.

Joseph Allyn, Jr. was a prominent Norfolk lawyer who served as a private in the Norfolk Light Artillery Blues. He was born to Joseph and Elizabeth Allyn on August 9, 1840, in the Allyn family summer home in Westfield, Montgomery Township, Massachusetts. His English ancestors had originally settled in that area in 1630. His father was a member of the Norfolk hardware firm of Allyn, Rose, & Co. with Dr. A. Rose and Mr. Washington Capps.

Allyn grew up in Norfolk and attended Miss Serena Holden's school in 1848, before attending Norfolk Academy. He enrolled in Washington University (later Washington and Lee) and was a student there when Virginia seceded in April 1861. He left college to become a drillmaster in July of 1861 in Floyd's Brigade at Wythville, Virginia. Allyn also served at the Camp of Instruction at Raleigh, North Carolina, then transferred to Norfolk, Virginia where he fell ill from typhoid fever. On March 26, 1862, after recovering his health, he enlisted as a private in the Blues at Sewell's Point. He served in all the company's engagements and became 6th corporal in the autumn of 1862. Allyn was eventually promoted to sergeant and on May 25, 1863, he was transferred to Lane's Battalion, where he served for the remainder of the war as lieutenant of ordnance. On furlough when Petersburg was evacuated, he attempted to return to his battalion, finally rejoined it the day before Lee's surrender, and was paroled at Appomattox Court House. He had been promoted to captain in the last days of the struggle, but the orders with his promotion were lost during the evacuation of Petersburg. Many years later, they were found in the National Archives.

After the war, Allyn attended the University of Virginia where he completed his degree in law. He was admitted to the bar, and returned to Norfolk to set up his practice. He became quite well known as an expert chancery and real estate attorney, served two terms on the City Council, and served as president of the Norfolk-Portsmouth Bar Association. His honesty and fairness were highly regarded in the community, and according to one story, he returned after the war to a farm where he had once "foraged" for necessary supplies, and repaid the owners in full.

On December 16, 1868, he married Miss Mary Russell Bell, the 24-year-old daughter of Russell and Mary E. Bell of Norfolk. Allyn was a member of the First Presbyterian Church, but was married at St. Paul's Episcopal Church by Reverend Nicholas A. Okeson and continued to attend St. Paul's after he was married. The Allyns eventually had three daughters and one son.

Allyn served on the executive committee of the Blues Memorial and Benevolent Association, and was elected 2nd lieutenant when the Norfolk Light Artillery Blues were reorganized in May of 1871. He was later a member of the Pickett-Buchanan Camp of Confederate Veterans. Mary Allyn joined the United Daughters of the Confederacy on November 13, 1900, and was active in its Pickett-Buchanan Chapter.

Allyn's health began to fail in his later years, and he died after a brief illness at the age of 63 on July 20, 1904. The funeral was held at his home at 128 Bute Street, and he was buried in Norfolk's Elmwood Cemetery.

JOHN COCKE ASHTON

John C. Ashton was a native of Portsmouth, Norfolk County, Virginia. His father, John Newton Ashton, was a descendant of the Ashton family who immigrated to Westmoreland County, Virginia about 1625, and he had moved to Portsmouth in 1839. It was here that he had married Elizabeth Cocke, whose ancestor, Richard Cocke, had immigrated from Worcestershire, England and settled at Malvern Hill in Henrico County, Virginia about 1626. Elizabeth's father, John Cocke (who had come to Portsmouth in 1829), and her husband, John N. Ashton, were both prominent, successful merchants in Portsmouth who occupied various positions in the local municipal government.

John Cocke Ashton was born October 29, 1844, and attended various public and private schools in Virginia. He was in school in Portsmouth when the city was evacuated by the Confederate forces in 1862. In the spring of 1864, he ran the blockade to Petersburg where on July 29, he volunteered for service in the Norfolk Light Artillery Blues. He arrived in the lines just in time to participate in the Battle of the Crater, then served in the remaining battles of this company. He was made a prisoner of war with his company at the fall of Petersburg on April 2, 1865, and was imprisoned at Point Lookout, Maryland until May 31, 1865.

He returned to Portsmouth, and in 1869, entered the mercantile business of this city, which he continued to control for many years. In 1880, he married Martha Everard Cole (1857–1947), the daughter of Dr. William Cole of Prince George County. John and Martha

John C. Ashton

Ashton had one daughter, Clara Maupin Ashton (1881–1933), who later married Henry MacKinzie. On June 2, 1890, Ashton became a member of the Stonewall Camp of Confederate Veterans and later held the position of treasurer of this group. In 1886, he was appointed the superintendent of Portsmouth City schools. Under his guidance, the number of city schools increased from 20 to 38. The Fifth Ward School, built in 1897 at the corner of Cook and North Streets (later known as the Cooke Street School, then the John Marshall School), was one of these. He also laid the cornerstone for Portsmouth High School at King and Washington Streets in January 1909, a short time before his retirement.

Ashton passed away on August 17, 1918, at the age of 73 at the Cole cottage in Virginia Beach. His funeral was held at the family home at 406 Middle Street in Portsmouth, and he was buried in Cedar Grove Cemetery of that city.

The butternut-colored shell jacket which Ashton had worn while serving with the Blues was passed to his daughter, and later Judge Henry MacKinzie donated it to the Naval Shipyard Museum of Portsmouth where it was put on display. Ashton's shell jacket is the only article of Confederate uniform of the Blues believed to have been saved.

RICHARD DAINGERFIELD BAGNALL

Richard Bagnall was born on March 11, 1839, to William Douglas Bagnall and Elizabeth Daingerfield Bagnall of Princess Anne County. He graduated from the University of Pennsylvania before Virginia seceded from the Union. He then enlisted as a private in the Norfolk Light Artillery Blues and served with the battery through the summer of 1861. On October 18, 1861, he was appointed an assistant surgeon in the Confederate army and transferred out of the artillery. One of his brothers, John Seldon Bagnall (1844–1922), fought with the VMI Cadets at the Battle of New Market.

Following the war, Dr. Bagnall practiced medicine in Norfolk and in Baltimore. He died at the age of 80 on November 1, 1918, in Hampton, where he had lived the last two years of his life. He was buried in his family's plot in Elmwood Cemetery in Norfolk.

RICHARD B. BANKS

Richard Banks was a 25-year-old notary public and a clerk with Dulton Wheeler on Widewater Street in Norfolk when he joined the Norfolk Light Artillery Blues as a sergeant at the outbreak of the War Between the States. He was quickly elected first lieutenant and was one of the first of the battery to go into action when he helped to destroy the lights and buoys marking the channel in the Elizabeth River to Norfolk and the Navy Yard. On February 19 of the following year, Banks married Miss Mary Virginia Lee, the 21-year-old daughter of Reverend LeRoy M. and Virginia Lee, and the sister of two of the Blues, LeRoy Lee, Jr. and F. Dean Lee. Banks left Norfolk for Petersburg with the Blues in May and except for a two-week hospital stay in late December of 1862, he served in all engagements of the company. During the Battle of the Wilderness in the spring of 1864, he was made adjutant of Richardson's Battalion. He was captured during the fall of Petersburg on April 2, 1865, and was taken to Old Capitol Prison in Washington, D.C., and then to Johnson's Island, Ohio. After his release on June 18, 1865, he returned to Norfolk, where he later became a member of the Pickett-Buchanan Camp of Confederate Veterans. He died of cancer in the City Almshouse on September 1, 1906, at the age of 71, and was buried in Elmwood Cemetery by the Reverend Tucker of St. Paul's Church.

C. D. BARRAUD

C. D. Barraud was a Confederate soldier who, according to the post Civil War minutes of the battery, served for a time with the Norfolk Light Artillery Blues.

H. BEALE

Listed in the service records as Howard or Haywood Beale, he enlisted as a private with the Norfolk Light Artillery Blues on April 13, 1862, at Sewell's Point. He served throughout the War Between the States except for several months in 1863 when he was confined to a Richmond hospital due to sickness. Captured with the Blues at Petersburg on April 2, 1865, he was taken to City Point (later Hopewell) and then to Point Lookout, Maryland. He was released upon taking the Oath of Allegiance or, as the Confederates called it, the "iron-clad" oath on June 24, 1865.

ALBERT S. BELL

Albert Bell enlisted as a private in the Norfolk Light Artillery Blues when Virginia seceded from the Union, and was present for duty with his company throughout the War Between the States. He was taken prisoner when Petersburg fell on April 2, 1865, and was put on a boat at City Point, Virginia for Point Lookout, Maryland. He took the Oath of Allegiance and was released on June 23, 1865.

NORMAN BELL

Norman Bell was one of five sons of Alexander and Margaret Bell who served in the Confederate army. Bell was born August 30, 1844. He attended Norfolk Academy before traveling to Albemarle County and enlisting in the Norfolk Light Artillery Blues at the age of 17 on May 1, 1864. Except for a short stay in a Richmond hospital during June, he served as a private with this company for about six months. On November 21, 1864, he was assigned to special duty as a clerk on the staff of General Robert E. Lee. In this position he occasionally served as a secretary for Lee, and he copied Lee's famous farewell address for distribution at Appomattox Court House. He was paroled as part of a detail under Captain G. W. Shell at Appomattox, then returned to Norfolk where he took the "Iron-clad Oath" on May 27, 1865, and returned to civilian life.

Bell then became successful in the cotton business and became superintendent of the Norfolk-Portsmouth Cotton Exchange in 1879. He was married to Ellen Herbert, the 27-year-old daughter of Edward and Margaret Herbert on November 22, 1881, by Reverend N. A. Okeson. Although their first son, Norman, Jr., died at the age of six, the couple eventually had a large family. Bell remained active in the city's business and social affairs until about a year before his death on October 20, 1916, at the age of 72. He passed away at his home at 210 W. Freemason Street after a brief illness. Major C. W. Grandy, brother of the late captain of the Blues, served as an honorary pallbearer. Bell was buried in Elmwood Cemetery in Norfolk.

Alex Bell, one of Norman and Ellen's four surviving children, later served as the Norfolk City treasurer. He was the special guest speaker on November 11, 1954, when Battery B of the 111th Field Artillery (the modern descendent of the Blues) was presented a Confederate Battle Flag in honor of the unit's Confederate service.

OTIS S. BENSON

O. S. Benson was born about 1840 to Edward P. and Mary N. Benson in Matthew's County, Virginia. His family moved to Norfolk where he found work as a clerk in the post office. On March 18, 1862, he enlisted as a private in the Norfolk Light Artillery Blues at Sewell's Point. He served as a private with the battery during the War Between the States and was slightly wounded on October 5, 1864, in the lines around Petersburg, Virginia when a spent bullet hit his arm. He was taken prisoner by the 20th New York Cavalry after the fall of Petersburg. After the war, he returned to Norfolk where he found a job as a steamship agent with the Old Dominion Steamship Company. On March 22, 1870, he married Miss Lizzie M. Lee, the daughter of Nath B. and Ellen Lee of Princess Anne County.

WILLIAM JAMES E. BISHOP

W. J. E. Bishop was born about 1841 to William and Mary Bishop of Princess Anne County, Virginia. As a young man, he worked in Norfolk as a journeyman coach trimmer for the carriage and harness company of A. Wrenn on Union Street. He joined the Norfolk Light Artillery Blues as a private on June 11, 1860, and was enlisted for Confederate service with this company on March 10, 1862. Except for a period in early 1864 when he was sick, he served continuously with the battery and was appointed an artificer on October 1, 1864.

He returned to Norfolk after the war and on April 17, 1867, was married by the Reverend LeRoy Lee, Sr. (the father of two other Blues) to Miss Lenora Diggs of Norfolk. He worked for the rest of his life as a coach trimmer, and was active in both the Royal Arcanum and the Odd Fellows societies. William Bishop died at the age of 60 of paralysis at his home at 110 S. Reservoir Avenue in the Brambleton section of Norfolk, leaving his wife Lenora and his son Charles. He was buried in Elmwood Cemetery and his pallbearers included members of the Blues, the Royal Arcanum, and the Odd Fellows.

WALTER W. BLOW

Walter Blow enlisted as a Confederate soldier on July 18, 1861, with the Norfolk Light Artillery Blues. In August of the following year, a doctor recommended he be transferred to duty as a hospital clerk due to his poor health, but instead, on October 14, 1862, he was made a clerk in the Inspector Generals Office of the Ordnance Department. He served in this department for the remainder of the war.

WILLIAM BOOTH(E)

William Booth(e) supported his family by working for the firm of Walters & Co. in Norfolk. On March 10, 1862, he enlisted in the Norfolk Light Artillery Blues. He was made a corporal with this unit and served throughout the War Between the States until April 2, 1865, when the lines west of Petersburg were overrun and most of the battery was captured. Booth(e) was killed in this battle at the age of 33, one week before the Army of Northern Virginia was compelled to surrender at Appomattox Court House.

CHARLES BORUM

Charles Borum was born in Matthew's County, Virginia on May 26, 1833, to Sterling and Hannah Borum. He moved to Norfolk at a young age and became a sailor, eventually commanding a number of commercial vessels. Charles married Cordelia March, the 26-year-old daughter of Seth and Virginia March in Norfolk on June 14, 1860. He enlisted in the Norfolk Light Artillery Blues as a private on May 1, 1862, and participated in several battles of the battery. On November 4, 1863, he transferred to the Confederate navy and was commissioned a master. He commanded several gunboats until the fall of Richmond in 1865. He evacuated the city and was paroled at Farmville, Virginia the day following General Lee's surrender.

After the war, he became a paint dealer in Norfolk and he joined the Pickett-Buchanan Camp of Confederate Veterans. Failing health eventually forced his retirement, and he died on October 16, 1899, three years after the death of his wife. He was buried in Elmwood Cemetery.

OTEY BRADFORD

O. Bradford enlisted as a private with the Norfolk Light Artillery Blues in Caroline County on May 30, 1863. He appeared in

Richmond before a Naval Exchange Board on July 31, and on September 21, 1863, was discharged from the Blues and appointed a lieutenant in the Confederate navy where he served for the rest of the war.

JOHN B. BRANHAM

John Branham was born about 1821 in Portsmouth, Virginia. Prior to the Civil War, he was a member of the Norfolk Light Artillery Blues and was elected second lieutenant. He served for several years as the Norfolk City assessor and lived at 7 North Catherine Street with the Graves family. When Virginia seceded and the war began, he served with the Blues for a short time before being detailed as a clerk in Richmond. He returned to Norfolk after the war, served as the city's commissioner of the revenue, and was a member of the Pickett-Buchanan Camp of Confederate Veterans. He died of spinal paralysis on May 4, 1903, at the age of 82 at his home at 427 Hamilton Avenue in the Ghent section of Norfolk. His funeral was conducted by the Reverend R. D. Smart of Epworth Episcopal Church and was attended by delegations from the Blues and the Pickett-Buchanan Camp. Alexander Goodrich served as one of his pallbearers. He was buried in Elmwood Cemetery in Norfolk.

BENJAMIN D. BRICKHOUSE

B. D. Brickhouse was born about 1842 to S. L. and Elizabeth Brickhouse of Northampton County, on the Eastern Shore of Virginia. He moved to Norfolk where he worked as a blacksmith before enlisting as a private in the Norfolk Light Artillery Blues in April of 1861. He and his older brother, Smith Brickhouse, both served with the Blues during the War Between the States. Brickhouse was admitted to the CSA Hospital in Charlottesville on Christmas Day of 1863, but stayed less than three weeks before he returned to his battery. He was appointed an artificer on October 1, 1864. After the war, he returned to Norfolk where he married Louisa A. Wellons, the 22-year-old daughter of Walter and Louisa Wellons on February 15, 1866. He worked in Norfolk as a blacksmith and a carriage maker for many years.

SMITH NOTTINGHAM BRICKHOUSE

Smith N. Brickhouse was born to Smith L. and Elizabeth Brickhouse in August 1837 in Northampton County, Virginia. He moved to Norfolk at a young age and worked as a shoe salesman and clerk for Herman & Co. He enlisted in the Norfolk Light Artillery Blues on April 13, 1862, as a private and served throughout the

Smith N. Brickhouse

War Between the States. He spent two short periods in hospitals but returned to the Blues and was promoted to corporal in the summer of 1864. He went into position with the company at the Rives Salient in June of 1864 and remained there until February 22, 1865, when he was detailed to the Quartermaster Department at Gaston for 60 days under Major C. W. Grandy. After the surrender at Appomattox Court House, he turned himself in to Federal pickets near Suffolk on April 27, 1865, and was paroled.

Following the war, he became one of the best known wholesale shoe dealers in Eastern Virginia as the junior member of the firm of Whitehead and Brickhouse. He was later with the Richmond firm of Elliot and Crump. He married Miss Cornelia M. Peterson, the 22-year-old daughter of Peter and Lucy Peterson of Petersburg, on December 28, 1871.

Brickhouse was a member of the Queen Street Methodist Episcopal Church, and frequently served as a delegate to annual Methodist conferences. In 1876, he became a member of the Board of Trustees of Norfolk Academy, and held this position for the rest of his life. He was also a member of the Pickett-Buchanan Camp of Confederate Veterans.

Brickhouse died at the age of 68 at Norfolk Protestant (later Norfolk General) Hospital on March 17, 1905, after an illness of several weeks. He was survived by his wife Cornelia, a son, and four daughters. He was buried in Elmwood Cemetery.

LYSANDER A. BROCK

L. A. Brock enlisted as a private in the Norfolk Light Artillery Blues in Richmond on July 24, 1864. Captured with this battery during the fall of Petersburg on April 2, 1865, he was transferred from City Point, Virginia to Point Lookout, Maryland where he was held as a prisoner. On June 12, 1865, he took the "ironclad" oath and was released.

E. W. BROOKS

E. W. Brooks enlisted in Petersburg on July 24, 1862 as a private in the Norfolk Light Artillery Blues. He served with the battery throughout the War Between the States until the fall of Petersburg, when he was captured. He was held in Libby Prison in Richmond.

ROBERT SOUTHER BROUGHTON

Robert Broughton was born in 1841, the oldest child of Thomas and Joan Broughton. He enlisted as a private in the Norfolk Light Artillery Blues on June 4, 1861, was promoted to 4th corporal on November 5, 1862, and served in all the engagements of the company during the War Between the States. He was wounded on April 2, 1865, during the collapse of the lines around Petersburg, and was sent to a hospital in Lynchburg to recuperate. He was paroled at the hospital about a week after Lee's surrender.

After the war, he worked as a salesman. He helped to reorganize the Norfolk Light Artillery Blues and was elected 4th sergeant in May of 1871. He was also a member of the Pickett-Buchanan Camp of Confederate Veterans and of the Second Presbyterian Church. On April 24, 1890, at the age of 49, he married Anna S. Peet, the widow of Lieutenant William Peet who had died in 1877. Three years after Anna's death, he married Miss Aline Herbert (1848–1919) on August 3, 1896. She was the daughter of C. M. and E. Herbert of Portsmouth. Both of Broughton's marriages were performed by William S. Lacy.

Robert Broughton was among the old members of the battery invited to the 78th anniversary banquet of the Blues in 1906, at which the battleflag of the battery was returned. In 1911, he served as a pallbearer at the funeral of Samuel Veale. He died of heart failure at the age of 76 at his home at 257 York Street in Norfolk on March 7, 1916, and was buried in the Ferguson family lot in Cedar Grove Cemetery in Norfolk.

CHARLES BROWN

According to the records of the Pickett-Buchanan Camp of Confederate Veterans, Charles Brown served as a private with the Norfolk Light Artillery Blues during the War Between the States.

E. P. BROWN

E. P. Brown (or Browne) enlisted late in the Civil War on October 25, 1864, in Petersburg with the Norfolk Light Artillery Blues. He served as a private for some six months, was captured by Union forces, and was paroled in Richmond on April 15, 1865.

HENRY CLAY BROWN

Henry Brown, the son of Captain James Brown of Portsmouth, joined the Norfolk Light Artillery Blues as a private in April 1861. He served with the company only a short time before he was discharged due to disability and assigned to duty in the laboratory at the Gosport Navy Yard. When the area was evacuated, he was transferred to the laboratory in Charlotte, North Carolina and served there as a private in Company G, Naval Brigade. He was detailed as a guard for the treasury train at Abbeville, South Carolina when the end of the war came.

After the war, he returned to Portsmouth where he married and worked as a clerk. He belonged to the Portsmouth Elks Lodge and joined the Stonewall Camp of Confederate Veterans on June 5, 1888. He died at his home at 1005 Dinwiddie Street on May 4, 1908, from a stroke, and was buried in Portsmouth's Cedar Grove Cemetery.

JAMES W. BROWN

James Brown was born in Portsmouth about 1839. He enlisted in the Company K, the "Old Dominion Guards" on April 20, 1861, and served with this company at Pinner's Point near Portsmouth during the first twelve months of the War Between the States. He was transferred to the Norfolk Light Artillery Blues on May 19, 1862, after the troops in the Norfolk area were moved to Petersburg, and was then assigned to Fort Clifton where he served during the Seven Days Battle. In the autumn of 1862, Brown was sent to Hospital Number 4 in Richmond due to rheumatism. Because of this disability, he was detailed on February 14, 1863, to serve as a clerk at this hospital. On December 16, 1864, he was transferred to the Medical Director's Office in Richmond where he served as a clerk for the rest of the war.

He returned to Portsmouth where he worked as a bookkeeper. He joined the Stonewall Camp of Confederate Veterans in November of 1887, and died nine years later on July 23, 1896.

JOHN B. BROWN

A native of Portsmouth, Virginia and a machinist by trade, 23-year-old John B. Brown enlisted for Confederate service as a private in the Norfolk Light Artillery Blues on April 18, 1861. He was promoted to 3rd sergeant in the autumn of 1862. On March 20, 1863, he was discharged from the Blues by Lieutenant William Peet to accept an appointment as a 3rd assistant engineer in the Confederate navy.

JOSEPH SAMUEL BROWNE

Joe Browne was born in Portsmouth, Virginia. He joined the Old Dominion Guards on April 20, 1861, as a private when Virginia seceded from the Union, and served with this company for just over a year. On May 19, 1862, he and Private James Brown transferred to the Norfolk Light Artillery Blues. He was slightly wounded and narrowly escaped death in the opening hours of the Battle of Chancellorsville on April 29, 1863. While he was standing by a limber chest, an enemy sharpshooter's bullet struck one of the limber's horses, went through the lid of the ammunition box, and struck him on the chest. Fortunately for him, the bullet had slowed, and Joe Browne was only bruised. He served with the company for the remainder of the war, and was captured and paroled on April 15, 1865, in Raleigh, North Carolina.

VICTOR H. BROWNE

Victor Browne was born September 8, 1840; the oldest son of Hamlin Browne. He worked as a clerk for George Reid in Norfolk, and joined the Norfolk Light Artillery Blues on March 9, 1860. He was enlisted as a private in this unit on April 18, 1861, served throughout the War Between the States, and was paroled when Lee surrendered at Appomattox Court House. After the war, he worked as a clerk and later as a salesman in Norfolk. He and his wife, Jane E. Browne (1845–1943) had two daughters, Jennie L. and Lucy B. He died July 21, 1880, at his residence in Brambleton at the age of 39. His funeral was held at St. Paul's Church, and he was buried in Elmwood Cemetery, Norfolk. Both of his daughters were later members of Pickett-Buchanan Chapter 21, United Daughters of the Confederacy.

CHARLES HENRY BUSKEY

Charles Buskey was born in 1838 in Princess Anne County. He worked in Norfolk and boarded at Mrs. Walker's along with John Walters until April 17, 1861, when he enlisted in the Norfolk Light Artillery Blues. He was made 2nd corporal and served in every engagement of his company until June of 1863 when he was detailed with the 3rd Corps Chief of Artillery under Colonel Walker. In October of 1864, he was detailed to act as bookkeeper for Colonel James L. Corley, the chief quartermaster of the Army of Northern Virginia. He was slightly wounded on two occasions, and remained at his post until paroled at Appomattox Court House.

After the war, he married Lucy Fatherly (1843–1919) and worked in Norfolk as a bookkeeper. When the Blues were reorganized in 1871, Buskey rejoined the unit as second corporal, and participated in the Blues' visit to Philadelphia in 1876 to celebrate the nation's centennial. He was also a member of the Pickett-Buchanan Camp of Confederate Veterans. He died at his home at 388 Bute Street on January 9, 1906, after an illness, and was buried in Elmwood Cemetery.

ROBERT M. BUTLER

Robert Butler was born in 1834 in Smithfield, Virginia to Reuben and Martha Butler. He worked as an agent for the Norfolk & Petersburg Railroad and was an active Mason. He moved to Norfolk and married C. Victoria Sheppard, the 27-year-old daughter of Smith and Sarah M. Sheppard, on November 24, 1858. Butler joined the Norfolk Light Artillery Blues on January 30, 1860. He was enlisted for Confederate service as a private on April 18, 1861, and was promoted to corporal in March of 1862. Except for brief periods of sickness in November of 1862 and January of 1863, he served continuously with the battery throughout the War Between the States. He was killed during the Battle of the Crater in the lines around Petersburg, Virginia on July 30, 1864. On March 31, 1866, his remains were returned to Norfolk with those of several other members of the Blues, and lay in state in the Court House until the following day when they were re-interred in an elaborate ceremony. Butler's body was buried in the Sheppard family plot in Norfolk's Cedar Grove Cemetery. Mrs. Butler later moved to Baltimore, where she died on February 8, 1887.

LEONARD O. CAPPS

Leonard Capps was born in 1843, the oldest of two sons of Ryland and Melissa Capps. He enlisted on June 30, 1861, and served continuously as a private in the Norfolk Light Artillery Blues during the War Between the States. After the war, he worked as a grocer at his shop on North Church Street in Norfolk. He died in 1873, and was buried in the family plot in Cedar Grove Cemetery.

WILLIAM S. CARROLL

A resident of Baltimore, Maryland, William Carroll enlisted as a private in the Norfolk Light Artillery Blues in Petersburg on May 13, 1862. He was present for service with the battery throughout the War Between the States, and was captured after the surrender at Appomattox Court House in Lynchburg on April 13, 1865. He took the Oath of Allegiance and was paroled on May 15, 1865, in Eastville, Virginia.

ANDREW E. CHAMBERLAINE

Andrew Chamberlaine was born in Norfolk Virginia in 1843, the oldest son of Captain Edward and Anna A. Chamberlaine. He enlisted in the Norfolk Light Artillery Blues at the age of 18 on March 10, 1862. He served with the company as a private throughout the War Between the States except for a short stay in Chimborazo Hospital in September of 1864. He was captured at Hatcher's Run during the breaking of the lines around Petersburg on April 2, 1865, and was sent to Point Lookout, Maryland where he was imprisoned until May 27 of that year.

Chamberlaine returned to Norfolk after his release and worked as a clerk and bookkeeper for several Norfolk cotton firms. He later joined the Pickett-Buchanan Camp of Confederate Veterans. He died on July 13, 1899, in his room at #10 Bank Street, and was buried in Elmwood Cemetery.

WILLIAM T. CLARKE

On April 18, 1861, William Clarke enlisted as a private in the Norfolk Light Artillery Blues. He was made 12th corporal in September of 1862, and by October 1 of the following year, he had advanced to the rank of sergeant He served continuously with the company for the remainder of the Civil War.

PHILIP ST. GEORGE COCKE

Philip Cocke was the second of four sons born to General Philip St. George Cocke (April 17, 1809 to December 26, 1861) and Sally Elizabeth Bowdoin Cocke of Surry County. He was born at "Belmead," the family estate in Powhatan County in 1844. His grandfather, General John H. Cocke (1780–1866), was one of the founders of the University of Virginia, and his father served as a brigadier general in the Confederate army, commanding the 1st Brigade at the First Battle of Manassas.

Philip Cocke entered the Virginia Military Institute on August 15, 1862, at the age of 18. He was a cadet-private in Company A when the students of VMI participated in the Battle of New Market on May 15, 1864. He left VMI on March 6, 1865, and traveled to Petersburg, where he enlisted in the Norfolk Light Artillery Blues, the company which his younger brother William Cocke had previously joined. He served with this company during the Siege of Petersburg and for the remainder of the war.

After the war, he became a farmer on a Mississippi cotton plantation until about 1875, when he returned to Powhatan County in Virginia. He sold his farm about 1895, and moved to "Lower Bremo," the estate of his late brother. He lived there until his own death on December 31, 1913.

WILLIAM RUFFIN COLEMAN COCKE

William R. C. Cocke was the third son of eleven children born to General Philip St. George Cocke (April 17, 1809 to December 26, 1861) and Sally Elizabeth Bowdoin Cocke of Surry County. He was born August 7, 1846, at "Belmead," the family estate in Powhatan County.

William Cocke enrolled in the Virginia Military Institute on September 3, 1863, a year after his brother Philip, and rose to the position of number one in his class of 187 students. He served as a cadet-private in Company B when the VMI cadets were called to fight in the Battle of New Market on May 15, 1864. He left VMI shortly afterward on June 27, 1864, to enlist in the Confederate army. On October 9 of that year he became a private with the Norfolk Light Artillery Blues. He was captured with his battery on the lines around Petersburg on April 2, 1865, and was sent to Point Lookout, Maryland, where he remained until his release on June 11 of that year.

Cocke returned to college after the war. He attended the University of Virginia for three years, and was admitted to the bar as an attorney in 1868. He then moved to Malvern Plantation near Columbus, Mississippi, and later practiced law in Montgomery, Alabama where he met and married Clara Vernon Pollard on April 26, 1871. About 1875, he and his wife moved to the Cocke family estate "Lower Bremo" in Fluvanna County, Virginia where they had seven children. Cocke died July 31, 1883, at the age of 36.

W. W. COLLINS

On October 17, 1863, W. W. Collins enlisted as a private with the Norfolk Light Artillery Blues in Richmond. He served with the company except for a time in the early spring of 1864 when he was detailed to guard the ordnance train. He was paroled at Appomattox Court House on April 9, 1865.

JOHN S. COOKE

John Cooke was a resident of Mecklinburg County, Virginia who joined the Norfolk Light Artillery Blues in Richmond on August 2, 1864, as a private. He served with the company until his capture near Petersburg on April 3, 1865. Sent to prison at Hart's Island, New York, he was released after taking the Oath of Allegiance on June 20, 1865.

MERRITT TODD COOKE

Merritt Cooke was born in Norfolk, Virginia on October 17, 1846, the oldest child of A. T. M. and Mary L. Cooke. He attended grammar school with Walter Doyle, Andrew Higgins, and Ignatius Higgins under Miss Serena Holden in 1852. In the summer of 1864, he and several other young men slipped out of occupied Norfolk and made their way to Richmond, where Cooke enlisted in the Confederate army on September 29. He requested to serve in the Norfolk Light Artillery Blues, and joined that company at the Rives Salient in the lines around Petersburg. He was wounded once, and was later detailed to a mortar battery under Lieutenants Johnson and Crenshaw. When Petersburg was evacuated on April 2, 1865, Cooke was ordered to Lynchburg, where he was paroled on April 13.

Following the War Between the States, he returned to Norfolk where he worked in real estate and as merchant. On May 8, 1879, he and Miss Mary F. Dickson were married by Reverend O. S. Barton. Mary was the daughter of Richard and Kate Dickson of Norfolk.

Cooke was elected city collector of taxes in 1872, served on city council, and was Norfolk's representative to the Virginia Legislature from 1891 to 1898 and again from 1903 to 1910. He also served as president of the board of pilot commissioners and was a member of the Pickett-Buchanan Camp of Confederate Veterans. He passed away on July 12, 1922, in the same house at the west end of Bute Street in Norfolk where he had been born. He was buried in Elmwood Cemetery.

HENRY CORNICK

Henry Cornick enlisted as a private in the Norfolk Light Artillery Blues on April 16, 1862, at Sewell's Point. He served with the company until April 1, 1863, when he transferred to the navy as a Master. His father, James Cornick, was a surgeon in the Confederate navy.

WILLIAM R. COX

On June 4, 1861, William Cox donned a Confederate uniform as a private in the Norfolk Light Artillery Blues. He served throughout the War Between the States with this company as a private. From October 24 through December 30, 1862, he remained in a Richmond hospital suffering from bronchitis. He was also sick for two weeks in early March of 1864, but was otherwise present for duty. Captured in Petersburg when that city fell on April 2, 1865, was taken to City Point, and placed on a boat for Point Lookout, Maryland. Cox was held there until June 12, 1865, when he took the "iron-clad" oath and was released.

WILLIAM S. CUTHERELL

When Virginia seceded from the Union, William Cutherell enlisted as a private in the Norfolk Light Artillery Blues. He spent a short time in a hospital in Lynchburg in the late autumn of 1862, but was otherwise present for duty with his company. On January 18, 1864, he wrote to the chief of ordnance, stating that he had been a gunsmith prior to the war, and requested a detail to the Ordnance Department. Instead, he was made assistant surgeon of Richardson's Artillery Battalion. Captured during the fall of Petersburg on April 3, 1865, he was taken to Old Capitol Prison in Washington, D.C. two days later. He remained here until May 11 when he was sent to prison at Johnson's Island, Ohio where he was eventually paroled.

JOHN HENRY DAY

John Day was born July 12, 1839, in Portsmouth, Virginia. He moved to Norfolk as a young man and enlisted in the Blues at the outbreak of the War Between the States. On May 1, 1863, he was on the crew of the company's rifled gun which was engaged during the battle of Chancellorsville. During the hour-long fight, the Blues' gun and a gun from Jordan's Battery fired against Weed's Battery of the U.S. Army. Day was one of several men wounded during this engagement. He was wounded a second time on July 30, 1864, during the Battle of the Crater. From October 4, 1864, to February 21, 1865, Day was confined to Chimborazo Hospital in Richmond suffering from tonsillitis.

Day returned to Norfolk after the war and worked as a commission merchant at Roanoke Dock. He married Martha Emma Day and the couple had one daughter. Day was a member of the Pickett-Buchanan Camp of Confederate veterans, and was one of the honored guests of the Blues at their 78th anniversary banquet when the unit's battleflag was returned by the state. He died on November 10, 1907, at the age of 68, and was buried in Elmwood Cemetery.

D. N. DEFORD

D. N. DeFord enlisted as a private in the Norfolk Light Artillery Blues at the age of 22 on April 18, 1861. He spent one week in Hospital Number 7 in Richmond in September of 1862, but otherwise served with this company throughout the War Between the States.

ALEX J. DENSON

Private Denson transferred from Company H, 6th Virginia Regiment, to the Norfolk Light Artillery Blues on March 17, 1863, at U.S.

Ford on the Rappahannock River. He served with the Blues until November 9, 1863, when he was admitted to Chimborazo Hospital with dysentery. Upon his release from the hospital in January of 1864, Denson was transferred to Company B, 19th Virginia Regiment.

H. S. DOUGHTIE

Private Doughtie transferred from Company E, 6th Virginia Regiment, to the Norfolk Light Artillery Blues on March 18, 1863, at U.S. Ford on the Rappahannock River. He spent several months of 1864 sick in hospitals in Charlottesville, Lynchburg, and Richmond, but eventually regained sufficient health to rejoin the battery in the lines around Petersburg. He was serving with the section of Napoleon guns on April 2, 1865, when the Confederate lines were overrun. Doughtie was wounded and taken prisoner during this battle. He was held at Libby Prison in Richmond and eventually paroled.

WALTER HERRON DOYLE

Walter Doyle, the second of nine children of Captain John E. and Mary Doyle, was born July 20, 1845, in Norfolk, Virginia. He was the oldest son, and was named for his father's employer. When Virginia seceded from the Union, his father, Captain John Doyle, took command of a cavalry troop in the 2nd Virginia Cavalry. Walter enlisted in the Norfolk Light Artillery Blues at the age of 16 on May 10, 1862, while the Confederate forces were being evacuated from Norfolk. Except for a short hospital stay due to sickness, he served as a private in all the engagements of the company, and was posted with the mortar detachment in the final days of the Siege of Petersburg. On the second of April 1865 he was being visited by his brother John E. Doyle, Jr., (who was on leave from the cavalry) when the Confederate lines were overwhelmed. Doyle, his brother, and several other men remained with the mortars until

Walter H. Doyle

dusk, when they made their way through the confusion to rejoin their forces. Doyle was present at the fight at Appomattox Station just before Lee surrendered the Army of Northern Virginia, and was paroled on April 9, 1865, at Appomattox Court House. He returned home to Norfolk just before the deaths of his three-year-old sister, Rose Grace, and his mother.

Doyle returned to civilian life as a clerk in the firm of Kader Biggs Company. In 1867, he became a clerk at the Citizen's Bank; in 1879 he succeeded W. W. Chamberlaine as bank cashier, and in 1900, he became president of the bank. Doyle also served as treasurer of the Norfolk Railway and Light Company, and as the president of the Norfolk and Berkley Bridge Company. He also found time to help reorganize his old battery and was elected 5th sergeant of the Blues in May of 1871. On December 9, 1880, at the age of 35, he married Virginia Barron Camp, the daughter of George W. and Elizabeth Camp of Norfolk. The couple eventually had four children: Bessie, Edward Fitzgerald, Walter Herron, Jr., and John E. Doyle. Walter was also active in the Pickett-Buchanan Camp of Confederate Veterans and was a member of Norfolk's prestigious "Virginia Club." His wife, who joined the United Daughters of the Confederacy in 1900, served as the president of its Pickett-Buchanan Chapter Nr. 21.

Doyle died on February 29, 1904, at his home at 238 Pembroke Avenue of heart trouble at age 58. His funeral was held at Sacred Heart Catholic Church, and he was buried in Elmwood Cemetery, Norfolk.

CHARLES HENRY DRUMMOND

Charles Drummond was born June 25, 1844, to William S. and Ann T. Drummond, and attended Miss Serena Holden's grammar school in 1854. He followed his older brother R. Joseph and enlisted as a private in the Norfolk Light Artillery Blues on August 1, 1862, in Petersburg. He served continuously with the battery throughout the Civil War. In February 1864, he was given leave to take his brother to CSA Hospital in Charlottesville. Captured at the end of the war, he was held at Point Lookout until his release on June 11, 1865.

After the war, he married Nora Bradford Holland (1849–1930), the daughter of Dr. Griffin W. and Margaret Holland on October 29, 1873, and they had one daughter, Margaret. He later became a member of the Pickett-Buchanan Camp of Confederate Veterans. Charles died June 7, 1881, and was buried in Elmwood Cemetery.

RICHARD JOSEPH DRUMMOND

R. Joseph Drummond was born in 1840, the second son of Captain William S. and Ann Drummond. He enlisted as a private in the Norfolk Light Artillery Blues on March 27, 1862, at Sewell's Point and served throughout the War Between the States along with his younger brother Charles. He was admitted to CSA Hospital in Charlottesville on February 16, 1864, suffering from rheumatism, and was released from Hospital Number 9 in Richmond in March, but was confined with the same ailment at Chimborazo from September 19 to December 27, 1864. Taken prisoner at the end of the war, he was paroled in Richmond on April 15, 1865, after taking the Oath of Allegiance.

After the war, he returned to Norfolk and worked for the Adams Express Company. He was later employed as an express messenger by the Seaboard and Roanoke Railroad, where his brother Captain W. R. Drummond was a conductor. After being ill about three weeks, he died on April 5, 1875, at his father's home at 84 York Street. He was buried in Cedar Grove Cemetery in Norfolk.

J. R. DUNN

Private J. R. Dunn served in the Norfolk Light Artillery Blues until dying from illness in a Petersburg hospital on September 4, 1862.

WILLIAM H. DUNN

Private William H. Dunn is listed on several rolls of the Norfolk Light Artillery Blues who served during the War Between the States.

JULIUS AUGUSTUS ELLIOTT

J. A. Elliott was born in 1841, in Northampton County, Virginia to J. T. and Margaret Elliott. He moved to Norfolk where he worked for Allyn, Rose & Co. as a clerk. Elliott was reported to have been the first to raise a Confederate flag in the city of Norfolk. The flag was flown from a house April 2, 1861, some two weeks before the state voted to secede from the Union. When secession came, he joined the Norfolk Light Artillery Blues, was enlisted on March 10, 1862, as a private, and served throughout the War Between the States. He was captured twice, the first time on July 14, 1863, at Falling Waters during the return from Gettysburg. He was taken to Old Capitol Prison in Washington, D.C., then transferred on August 9 to Point Lookout, Maryland. He was exchanged seven months later on March 3, 1864. Captured again at the fall of Petersburg, he was held a second time at Point Lookout where he was released on June 11, 1865.

Afterward, he became a hardware salesman, and for many years was employed in the store of Watters and Martin. On May 13, 1869, he married Annie Elizabeth Welton, the 25-year-old daughter of

Elizabeth Welton of Norfolk. He was a member of the Pickett-Buchanan Camp of Confederate Veterans, and attended the 78th anniversary banquet of the Blues in 1906 as a special guest. He died on December 13, 1912, of an apparent heart attack. He had arrived at Martin's Store in his usual good health, but was found dead at his desk by Mr. Martin. He left three sons, Walter W. and Gilmer T. Elliott (both attorneys), and Harry H. Elliott. The funeral was held at his home at Reservoir and Claiborne Avenues by Reverend Vernon I'Anson, D.D., and he was buried in Elmwood Cemetery.

JOHN W. ELLIOTT

Enlisting as a private with the Norfolk Light Artillery Blues on March 10, 1862, at Sewell's Point, John Elliott served throughout the American Civil War with this battery. He was promoted to 10th corporal on May 1, 1863, and achieved the rank of 6th corporal by the end of the conflict.

THOMAS E. ELLIOTT

Thomas Elliott was born on August 20, 1834, in Northampton County on the Eastern Shore to J. T. and Margaret Downs Elliott. He attended school in the county, then moved to Norfolk at the age of 14 where he worked briefly in lumber and commission businesses before being hired as a clerk for Allyn, Rose, & Capps. After three years, he became the head clerk and general manager of this hardware firm. In December of 1858, he married Mary Eliza Davis, the daughter of Miles Davis. When Virginia seceded from the Union on April 18, 1861, he immediately enlisted in the Norfolk Light Artillery Blues at Craney Island and served with his brother J. A. Elliott as a private throughout the War Between the States. He fired the last three rounds fired by the battery in the war and was taken prisoner on April 2, 1865, in the lines around Petersburg. He was released from prison at Point Lookout, Maryland on June 10, 1865, after taking the required "iron-clad" oath.

Elliott returned to Norfolk, and entered the hardware business in the firm of Taylor and Martin. He later became a partner in the firm of Taylor, Elliott, and Watters. He and Walter H. Taylor later founded the Norfolk Supply Company, which eventually became Taylor-Parker. He was a member of the Pickett-Buchanan Camp of Confederate Veterans and served on the Board of Directors of the Norfolk College for Young Ladies. He and his wife had six children: four girls and two boys.

On November 28, 1891, Elliott died at his home on Wood Street after a long illness. He was 57 years old at the time of his death. He was buried in the family plot in Elmwood Cemetery.

THOMAS H. ELLIOTT

Thomas Elliott was a clerk in Norfolk before April 18, 1861, when he enlisted in the Norfolk Light Artillery Blues as a private at the age of 27. He remained in General Hospital Number 7 in Richmond for most of the autumn of 1862 with an intermittent fever, and returned to the battery on December 21. During the retreat from Gettysburg, he was captured in Hagerstown, Maryland on July 5, 1863. He was sent to Fort Delaware four days later, and remained there for the rest of the war before finally being paroled on June 16, 1865.

RICHARD EVANS

Richard Evans was born June 20, 1847, in Norfolk, Virginia. He was the son of Captain Richard Evans and Jane M. Bissell Evans who lived at 9 Boush Street. Richard was a grammar school student of Miss Serena Holden in 1854. He ran the blockade to Petersburg in the spring of 1864 and on December 7 at the age of 17, was enlisted as a private in the Norfolk Light Artillery Blues. He served on a wood gathering detail for about a month, then was posted to the mortar battery during the Siege of Petersburg. When the city was evacuated on April 2, 1865, he left with an advance group of the army, and served in an artillery fight near Farmville under General Walker on April 9. He was paroled on April 12, 1865, and walked to Richmond where he took the official Oath of Allegiance on April 18.

With the war over, he returned to Norfolk, where he married Fannie D. Atkinson, the 21-year-old daughter of Joseph A. and Emily Atkinson of Smithfield, Virginia on February 19, 1874. Evans worked as a bookkeeper in the firm of Evans and Grandy, and was a member of the Pickett-Buchanan Camp of Confederate Veterans. He passed away at the age of 43 at his residence at 117 York Street on December 14, 1890, after a lingering illness. He was buried in Elmwood Cemetery.

D. FITZGERALD

D. Fitzgerald enlisted as a private in the Norfolk Light Artillery Blues on June 3, 1864, at Cold Harbor and served with the battery during the Siege of Petersburg in the final months of the War Between the States.

EDWIN FITZGERALD

Private Edwin Fitzgerald enlisted with the Norfolk Light Artillery Blues on May 9, 1862, as Norfolk was being evacuated by the Confederate forces. He served in most of the battles of the company, but was confined in General Hospital Number 7 in Richmond from September of 1862 until January 7, 1863, then he was transferred to Chimborazo Hospital, where he stayed until May 20, 1863. During the Siege of Petersburg, he was assigned to the mortar battery and served there until April 2, 1865, when the lines around the city were broken. He was paroled in Richmond on May 13, 1865.

W. FITZGERALD

W. Fitzgerald enlisted late in the War Between the States on October 25, 1864, and served as a private with the Norfolk Light Artillery Blues. He was posted with the mortar battery when the lines around Petersburg were overrun and was paroled with the Army of Northern Virginia at Appomattox Court House on April 9, 1865.

FRANK FLETCHER

On New Year's Day of 1846, Frank Fletcher was born at Jenkin's Bridge in Accomack County on the Eastern Shore of Virginia. He attended private elementary schools near his home, and was a student at Hampden-Sidney College when Virginia seceded in 1861.

Fletcher enlisted in the Norfolk Light Artillery Blues as a private on July 15, 1863, and served with the Blues through the War Between the States. He was captured at Petersburg on April 2, 1865, taken to City Point, then confined at Point Lookout, Maryland until taking the Oath of Allegiance on June 12, 1865. He made his way to Washington, D.C. after his release and was given transportation to Baltimore.

With the return of peace, Fletcher was accepted at the University of Virginia where he studied medicine. He graduated from the Jefferson Medical College of Pennsylvania and returned to his home on the Eastern Shore where he began his practice as a physician. Dr.

Dr. Frank Fletcher

Fletcher married Miss Emma

Hudgin of Matthews County, Virginia, and they had three sons, Ashton, Donald, and Dr. Richard Fletcher. In the 1870s, the citizens of Accomack County twice elected Dr. Fletcher as their representative in the Virginia State Senate. He also served as the commander of the county Confederate Veterans camp from the time of its organization until February 23, 1920, when he passed away at the age of 74.

JOSEPH W. FLOYD

On June 4, 1861, 19-year-old Joseph Floyd left his job as a clerk with W. T. Capps and Co. and enlisted as a private in the Norfolk Light Artillery Blues. He was present for duty at Sewell's Point, Petersburg, and Fredericksburg. On May 1, 1863, he was on the crew of the Blues' rifled gun which engaged Weed's Battery during the Battle of Chancellorsville, and was wounded in this fight when an enemy shell struck his right arm above the elbow. His arm was amputated at the shoulder and Floyd was sent to General Hospital Number 12 in Richmond to recuperate. A year later, he was assigned to the Commissary Department of Chimborazo Hospital, where he served as a clerk until being retired as an invalid on December 16, 1864.

JOSEPH M. FREEMAN, JR.

The son of a well known Norfolk jeweler, Joseph Freeman, Jr. enlisted as a private with the Norfolk Light Artillery Blues on May 13, 1862, in Petersburg. A year later on May 13, 1863, he transferred to the Confederate States Navy as an assistant engineer.

JOHN O. GAMAGE

John Gamage was born about 1838 to Elisha and Mary A. Gamage. He worked as a clerk for his father and joined the Norfolk Light Artillery Blues prior to the War Between the States. He served as the company collector from July 16, 1860, to April 1, 1861, then enlisted as a private in the company for Confederate service on April 18. On October 24, 1861, he married Bell Sarah Williams, the 24-year-old daughter of Reverend Peter and Nancy Clay Williams of Northampton County. He left Norfolk when the Blues were sent to Petersburg, spent three months from November 22, 1863, to February 6, 1864, in Chimborazo Hospital, Richmond with rheumatism, and was wounded while serving with the company at the Battle of the Crater. Gamage recovered and returned to his unit in the lines west of Petersburg, and was captured there with a portion of his battery on April 2, 1865. He was held at Point Lookout, Maryland until being paroled on May 28, 1865.

After the war, Gamage returned home to Norfolk where he and his wife raised their four daughters, Mary, Nancy, Ida, and Edna. On December 20, 1866, Gamage won a raffle sponsored by the ladies of St. Mary's Catholic Parish in Norfolk. As winner, he was given the honor of presenting a cane, locally made from a piece of oak salvaged from the wreck of the C.S.S. *Virginia (Merrimac)*, to Confederate President Jefferson Davis, who was then imprisoned at Fort Monroe. Gamage became a dealer in shell lime and other building materials in a business which was located at 101 and 103 Water Street, and later became a member of the Pickett-Buchanan Camp of Confederate veterans. He passed away on February 24, 1910, at the age of 72, dying at his home at 202 Bute Street from an apparent heart attack. He was buried in Elmwood Cemetery and his funeral was attended by many of the Blues including Captain M. C. Keeling. Following his death, his daughter Nancy and his heirs kept his building material business open until about 1931. In 1917, the Blues were called for service in the World War, and the citizens of Norfolk took up a collection to have a flag made for the battery. Nancy Gamage evidently made a memorial donation, for John Gamage was listed as one of the contributors to this flag.

GEORGE OSCAR GASKINS

George Gaskins was born on June 6, 1840. He was the second son of James Scott and Ann Woodhouse Gaskins who lived on Cumberland Street in Norfolk. Gaskins volunteered for service as a private in the Norfolk Light Artillery Blues at the outbreak of the war on April 17, 1861, when he was 20 years old and he served throughout the conflict with the battery. His older brother, Dr. James H. Gaskins, served the Confederacy as a doctor at the Poplar Lawn Hospital in Petersburg. Gaskins spent several months of his Confederate service in hospitals; he was sick in the winter and much of the late spring and summer of 1863, was in General Hospital Number 9 in March of 1864, and was in Chimborazo from September 19 to October 5, 1864. Five months later, Gaskins died of disease in a hospital at Petersburg, Virginia on March 11, 1865. His body was returned to Norfolk on December 16, 1865, and he was buried in the family lot in Elmwood Cemetery, not far from the plot of the Blues.

J. A. GATCH

Enlisting on April 13, 1862, as 10th corporal of the Norfolk Light Artillery Blues, J. A. Gatch served with the battery until April 4, 1863, when he was transferred to Company H, 6th Virginia Regiment and promoted to 1st lieutenant.

HORACE GHISELIN

Horace Ghiselin was born about 1841 to John and Catherine Ghiselin. He enlisted as a private in the Norfolk Light Artillery Blues on March 10, 1862, and served with his younger brother Richard. He served in most of the battles of the unit, but was confined to Chimborazo Hospital during the autumn and early winter of 1863, and again for a short period in December of 1864. He was also in a hospital in Richmond when that city was captured by Federal forces. Ghiselin was taken to Jackson Hospital in Richmond on April 9, and he was paroled there on April 20, 1865.

RICHARD GHISELIN

Richard Ghiselin, born on May 22, 1843, was the son of John D. and Mary T. Ghiselin. He enlisted in the Norfolk Light Artillery Blues on April 18, 1861, at the age of 17, and served with his brother as a private throughout the War Between the States. Like his brother, Horace, he spent a few months in the autumn of 1863 in Chimborazo Hospital in Richmond, but returned to the Blues more quickly and remained on duty. He was in the lines around Petersburg on April 2, 1865, when the battery's guns were overrun, and was taken prisoner, sent to City Point, and transferred to Point Lookout. Ghiselin took the Oath of Allegiance and was released on June 12, 1865. He returned to Norfolk where he died on March 10, 1909, at the age of 65, and was buried in the family plot in Cedar Grove Cemetery. Ghiselin was survived by his wife Lucy, who died January 5, 1920.

JAMES W. GILMER

James Gilmer was born October 20, 1830, and lived in Norfolk nearly all his life. He entered the hat business at a young age, and alternately worked for R. H. Stevens and Brother and for Stevens and Butt. He joined the Norfolk Light Artillery Blues when Virginia seceded from the Union on April 18, 1861, and was elected third lieutenant before the Blues left Norfolk in May of 1862. He was slightly wounded on the lines around Petersburg in 1864 when a shell fragment ricocheted from the ground and struck him in the forehead. Gilmer commanded the company's two Napoleons on the Boydton Plank Road, and was among the officers captured April 2, 1865, taken three days later to Old Capitol Prison in Washington, D.C., and sent on April 9 to Johnson's Island in Ohio. His mother, Elizabeth Landing, wrote a personal letter to General U. S. Grant on June 8 asking for his release. On June 18, Gilmer took the oath of Allegiance and was paroled.

After the war, Gilmer returned to Norfolk, and went back into the hat business with J. D. Reed. He later opened a hat and cap business of his own which he ran successfully for the rest of his life. He married the former Miss Lelia F. Moore, the daughter of Franklin G. Moore of Norfolk who had served the Confederacy as an ordnance officer.

Gilmer helped to reorganize the Norfolk Light Artillery Blues and was elected 1st lieutenant in May of 1871. On April 20, 1874, he was elected captain. He resigned his command on October 1 of the following year, but was re-elected on February 21, 1879. Gilmer served for the second time until March 1, 1889, when he again resigned and was succeeded by Captain M. C. Keeling. Besides being a member of the Blues, Gilmer served on the Norfolk City Council, the executive committee of the Blues Memorial and Benevolent Association, and was a member of the Pickett-Buchanan Camp of Confederate Veterans.

Gilmer died after a long illness at 12:30 on the morning of July 6, 1899 in his home at the corner of Olney and Colonial Avenue in Ghent. He was 69 years old. His funeral was held at the Cumberland Street Methodist Church the following day, and he was buried in Elmwood Cemetery.

ALEXANDER JOSEPH GOODRICH

Alexander Goodrich

Alex Goodrich, the son of Eason L. Goodrich, was born on March 13, 1839, in Isle of Wight County. As a young man, he worked in Norfolk as a clerk for S. Ullman & Co. When Virginia seceded, his father and his brother Bartholow both joined the Confederate Ordnance Department while he enlisted in the Norfolk Light Artillery Blues as a private. Goodrich served with the Blues throughout the War Between the States, except for three months in the winter of 1862–1863 while he was in a Lynchburg hospital with typhoid fever. Captured at Hatcher's Run on April 2,

1865, Goodrich was imprisoned at Point Lookout, Maryland until he took the Oath of Allegiance and was released on June 12. Following the war, he returned to Norfolk and became a clerk. He opened a grocery business with his brother Bartholow in 1873, and became an active member of the Pickett-Buchanan Camp of Confederate Veterans. He retired from the grocery after twenty years and became a director of the city gas company, then a member of the street sewerage and drainage board. He died on Saturday, December 6, 1913, at his home at 336 Fairfax Avenue in Norfolk after a long illness, and was buried in Elmwood Cemetery. Goodrich never married, but was survived by three sisters, Miss Alice Goodrich, Mrs. Annie Turner, and Mrs. R. Ligon.

GEORGE WASHINGTON GORDAN

George Gordan was born on May 3, 1842, the son of John D. Gordan, Sr. At the outbreak of the War Between the States, he enlisted in the Young Guards, under Captain W. A. S. Taylor, and on May 9, 1862, he transferred to the Norfolk Light Artillery Blues where he served with his brother Joseph as a private throughout the War Between the States. After the war, he returned to Norfolk and worked as a clerk in the firm of Shelton, Blamire & Co. He was among those who reorganized the Blues as a militia company in 1871. Beside the Blues, Gordan was a member of the Pocahontas Council Nr. 493, Royal Arcanum. He was married twice (both times by Reverend N. A. Okeson of St. Paul's Church); the first time on October 13, 1869, to Kate Hunter, the 20-year-old daughter of William H. and E. F. Hunter, and the second time on April 13, 1875, to Miss Ida Elizabeth Johnson from Nashville, Tennessee. George and Ida Gordan eventually had four children. He died of consumption on August 28, 1887, at the Gordan family residence at 74 Bermuda Street, and was buried in Elmwood Cemetery. Four of the Blues, William E. Taylor, Joseph T. Allyn, R. S. Broughton, and R. Frank Vaughn served as pallbearers.

JOSEPH P. GORDAN

Joseph Gordan was born in 1839, one of several children of John D. Gordan, Sr. He worked as a clerk in his father's firm until he enlisted in the Norfolk Light Artillery Blues on March 10, 1862. He served as a private in this company throughout the War Between the States along with his younger brother George. Captured on April 2, 1865, during the fall of Petersburg, he was taken to City Point, then transferred to Point Lookout, Maryland where he was held until June 9, 1865.

After the war, he returned to the family home at 74 Bermuda Street in Norfolk, and worked as a clerk in the family brokerage firm (later bank) of John D. Gordan & Co. At the death of his older brother John D. Gordan, Jr. at age 50 in 1879, he and his partner, William V. Taylor, assumed control of the bank, and continued to operate under the name John D. Gordan & Co. at their 155 Main Street location. Gordan remained at the family home with his brothers, sisters, and their families until April 16, 1889, when he died at the age of 50 from "cerebral rheumatism" after having suffered for several months. He was buried in the family plot in Cedar Grove Cemetery with his parents and his brother John, Jr.

MORTON GORDON

Morton Gordon was born on August 28, 1845, to Cornelius T. and Sarah Gordon of Norfolk. On March 18, 1864, at the age of 18, he enlisted as a private in the Norfolk Light Artillery Blues in Albemarle County. Aside from a short stay in Chimborazo Hospital in January 1865, he served with the company during the final year of the War Between the States. He returned to Norfolk after the war and found a job as a clerk. He married Caroline Bockover (1850–1931), the daughter of Benjamin T. and Sarah E. Bockover on December 18, 1872. The couple had one son whom they named Terry. About ten years later, Morton Gordon went into the grain business and became a hay weigher. He moved his family to a home on Mason's Creek in Norfolk County where he lived for the rest of his life. He died on March 23, 1910, at the age of 64 and was buried in the Gordon family plot in Norfolk's Elmwood Cemetery.

Captain Charles R. Grandy

CHARLES R. GRANDY

Charles R. Grandy was born August 18, 1834, the eldest son of Cyrus Wiley Grandy, Sr. and Anna D. Grandy. C. W. Grandy moved his family from Camden County, North Carolina to Norfolk in 1844. He joined in business with John H. Stout as commission merchants in Norfolk in 1845 as "Grandy & Stout" at Ferguson and Milhado's Wharf.

Charles R. Grandy entered the College of William and Mary in 1852, received a bachelor's degree in 1854 and a master's degree in 1855. He then worked as a "student of law" for Norfolk attorney Charles B. Duffield on Main Street and was a member of the United Fire Company of Norfolk for several years. He was described as robust, about five feet, nine inches tall, with light hair and blue eyes.

At the outbreak of the War Between the States, he enlisted in Company B of the 6th Virginia Volunteers and was elected lieutenant. On December 21, 1861, he was elected captain of Company H, 16th Virginia Regiment, the "Norfolk Light Artillery Blues" following the resignation of Captain Jacob Vickery. The Blues, or "Grandy's Battery" as they then became known, joined Lee's Army of Northern Virginia at Fredericksburg in November 1862 and took part in all the major engagements which followed. In addition to his field duties, Grandy was called to serve on courts-martial from the end of October 1862 through April of 1863, and for the first four months of 1864.

On March 31, 1865, Grandy assumed temporary command of his artillery battalion when his superior, Colonel Charles Richardson, was wounded. On April 2, his battery, consisting of four guns and

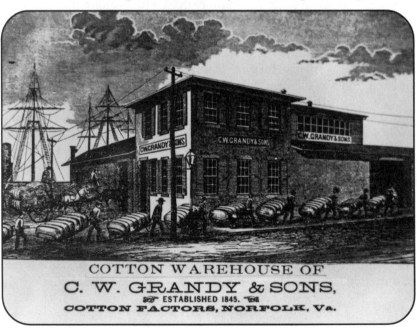

COTTON WAREHOUSE OF
C. W. GRANDY & SONS,
☞ ESTABLISHED 1845. ☜
COTTON FACTORS, NORFOLK, VA.

An advertisement for the firm of C. W. Grandy & Sons which appeared in the Norfolk City Directory.

Courtesy Norfolk Public Library

58 officers and men, was captured in front of Petersburg near the Boydton Plank Road. His enlisted men were sent to Point Lookout, Maryland, and Grandy and his officers were taken to Old Capitol Prison in Washington, D.C. on April 5 before being sent to Johnston's Island on Lake Erie four days later. His friends believed that Grandy contracted the pulmonary disease from which he later died while he was held in this prison. He took the Oath of Allegiance and was released on June 18, 1865.

Following his release, Grandy returned to Norfolk, where he became a partner with his father and his brother, C. W. Grandy, Jr. in the firm of C. W. Grandy and Sons at 6 Commercial Row. He died just two years later on April 1, 1868, at the age of 33. His funeral on April 3 was held at the family home at 90 West Bute Street, and was attended by members of the Blues, the Masons, and the United Fire Company among many others. He was buried in Elmwood Cemetery, Norfolk, Virginia.

CHARLES MALLORY GRAVES

Charles Graves was born in 1842 in Norfolk. Prior to the outbreak of war, Graves and his family lived with Lieutenant Branham of the Norfolk Light Artillery Blues. When Virginia seceded on April 18, 1861, he enlisted as a private in that company, and served with the Blues throughout the war. He spent almost two months in Richmond's General Hospital Number 9 in August and September of 1863 and was slightly wounded at the Battle of Spotsylvania Court House. Captured April 2, 1865, and sent to prison at Point Lookout, he was released on June 12, 1865. He returned to Norfolk and later served as the deputy commissioner of the revenue for the city for over twenty years. He joined the Pickett-Buchanan Camp of Confederate veterans, and was an honored guest of the Blues on February 22, 1906, when the Old Battery's battleflag was returned. After a long illness, he died on August 30, 1923, at the age of 81 at the home of his son-in-law, Dr. R. H. Walker, and was buried in Elmwood Cemetery. He was survived by his wife, Eugenia Hinton Graves, a daughter, Mrs. Sue B. Walker, three sons, J. H. Graves, E. L. Graves, and Charles M. Graves, Jr., and by ten grandchildren and one great-grandchild.

J. T. GWALTNEY

Private J. T. Gwaltney enlisted with the Norfolk Light Artillery Blues on April 18, 1861, at the age of 21 and served during the American Civil War.

RICHARD H. GWALTNEY

Richard Gwaltney was born about 1834 in Isle of Wight County, Virginia. He worked as a clerk for S. S. Dawes in Norfolk, then joined the Norfolk Light Artillery Blues on April 18, 1861. He served as a private throughout the War Between the States, and was in all the battles of the company, except for a two-week stay in April of 1864 in a Charlottesville hospital due to pneumonia. He was captured April 2, 1865, at the fall of Petersburg, taken to City Point, and then to Point Lookout where he was paroled on June 13, 1865. Gwaltney then moved to Norfolk where he lived at 100 Boush Street, worked as a clerk, served as 1st corporal of the reorganized Norfolk Light Artillery Blues, and became a charter member of the Pickett-Buchanan Camp of Confederate Veterans. In 1911, he served as a pallbearer at the funeral of Samuel Veale.

JAMES M. D. HAINES

James Haines of Portsmouth, Virginia enlisted as a private with the Norfolk Light Artillery Blues in Richmond on November 1, 1864. He spent five months on duty with the company until the lines around Petersburg were overrun, and he was taken prisoner. He was released from Point Lookout, Maryland on June 13, 1865, after taking the "ironclad" oath.

WILLIAM R. HALLETT

William Hallett joined the Norfolk Light Artillery Blues just before Virginia seceded from the Union, and was enlisted as a private on April 18, 1861. He served continuously with the battery throughout the War Between the States, was captured in Petersburg on April 2, 1865, and taken to Point Lookout, Maryland by way of City Point, Virginia. He took the Oath of Allegiance and was released on June 13, 1865.

RICHARD T. HALSTEAD

Richard Halstead was a native of Norfolk, Virginia who left that occupied city to join the Confederate forces defending Petersburg. He enlisted as a private in the Norfolk Light Artillery Blues on November 30, 1864, and served for the remainder of the Petersburg siege. He was paroled from Libby Prison in Richmond on April 20, 1865, and returned to Norfolk where he worked as a clerk. He later joined the Pickett-Buchanan Camp of Confederate Veterans and the Elks Lodge. He died on July 10, 1888, at the Confederate Soldier's Home in Richmond at the age of 40. His remains were returned to Norfolk on the steamer *John Romer*, and following a funeral at St. Luke's Church, he was buried in "Elks Rest" in Elmwood Cemetery.

JOHN F. HATTON

John Hatton lived in Norfolk with his brother James and sister Sarah. At the outbreak of the War Between the States he enlisted as a private in the Norfolk Light Artillery Blues at the age of 18. He was known as "a most agreeable associate, a perfect gentleman, and an excellent soldier." He became ill with chronic dysentery and was taken to Chimborazo Hospital on August 22, 1864. On September 8 he was transferred to a Petersburg hospital where his condition worsened. He was moved to his uncle's home in Prince Edward County where he died at the age of 21 on February 11, 1865, of cancer of the stomach.

ARMISTEAD J. HAUGHTON, JR.

On April 19, 1861, twenty-year-old Armistead Haughton enlisted as a private in the Norfolk Light Artillery Blues and except for seven days on sick call, he was with the company throughout the American Civil War. Haughton was captured on April 2, 1865, at the fall of Petersburg, was taken to City Point, and was transported to Point Lookout, Maryland. He took the Oath of Allegiance and was released on June 13, 1865.

ANDREW HIGGINS

Andrew Higgins served as a private with the Norfolk Light Artillery Blues from his enlistment on May 9, 1862, in Norfolk to his capture on April 2, 1865, in Petersburg. He arrived at Point Lookout, Maryland from City Point, and was held there until June 13, 1865, when he took the Oath of Allegiance and was released.

IGNATIUS HIGGINS

Ignatius Higgins was born in 1843. He was a student with Walter Doyle, Merritt Cooke, and his younger brother Andrew Higgins in Miss Serena Holden's 1852 grammar school class. He enlisted on April 14, 1861, and except for a two-week stay in a Petersburg hospital in the autumn of 1863, he served continuously as a private in the Norfolk Light Artillery Blues. He was wounded on June 7, 1864, in the fighting at Turkey Ridge during the Battle of Cold Harbor, when a stray bullet struck his left shoulder and punctured his lung. He was taken to Wayside hospital Number 9, then transferred to Chimborazo Hospital in Richmond where he contracted pneumonia in addition to his wounds. He died on July 21, 1864, at the age of 21. His body was returned to Norfolk on March 31, 1866, and was interred in St. Mary's Catholic Cemetery.

ALBERT HILL

Al Hill enlisted at Orange Court House on October 25, 1863, as a private in the Norfolk Light Artillery Blues. He served with the company until January of 1864 when he was made acting courier for Richardson's Battalion.

JOHN M. HODGES

John Hodges was born in Norfolk County, Virginia. He enlisted in the Norfolk Light Artillery Blues as a private on June 15, 1864, in Petersburg, Virginia at the age of 16. He served during the siege, then followed Lee's Army to Appomattox Court House, where he was paroled. He became a farmer after the war, and resided in Norfolk. Hodges was a member of the Pickett-Buchanan Camp of Confederate Veterans. He died on June 26, 1907.

SAMUEL HODGES

Samuel Hodges was born in Norfolk about 1842 to Samuel H. and Emily Hodges. At the beginning of the War Between the States, he was a drillmaster for North Carolina with the rank of first lieutenant. He resigned in 1862 to join the Norfolk Light Artillery Blues as a private. He served with the battery at Sewell's Point, and remained with the battery for the rest of the war. He was slightly wounded three times, and was taken prisoner on April 2, 1865. After the war, he was released from prison and returned to Norfolk where he worked as a wholesale hat and cap merchant.

Hodges helped to reorganize the Norfolk Light Artillery Blues and was elected 2nd sergeant in May of 1871. He rose to the rank of 1st lieutenant before being elected captain of the battery on October 1, 1875. Under his command, the Blues represented the Commonwealth of Virginia at the Philadelphia Independence Centennial. He resigned from the position the following October. Hodges became a charter member of the Pickett-Buchanan Camp of Confederate Veterans shortly before he passed away on December 4, 1883.

WILLIAM H. HOLMES

William Holmes was a native of Southampton County, Virginia who moved to Norfolk prior to the Civil War. He made his way to Petersburg in August of 1864 and enlisted in the Norfolk Light Artillery Blues as a private on October 2, 1864, at about the age of 16. He served in the lines around Petersburg until captured and taken to Point Lookout, Maryland, where he was held until June 13, 1865. After the war, he returned to Norfolk and worked as a commission merchant. He was elected 5th corporal of the newly reorganized

Norfolk Light Artillery Blues and was a member of the Pickett-Buchanan Camp of Confederate Veterans.

GEORGE C. HUDGINS

When Virginia seceded from the Union, George Hudgins enlisted in the Norfolk Light Artillery Blues as 2nd sergeant. He was present for duty throughout the War Between the States, and provided his own horse for service, for which he received an extra forty cents pay per day. Hudgins was captured at the end of the war and was paroled in Richmond on April 15, 1865.

RICHARD GREGORY HUME

Richard Hume was born in Portsmouth, one of four children of the Reverend Thomas and Mary Hume. Reverend Hume served as the director of the bank of Portsmouth. Richard Hume opened the Hume Book and Stationery Store at 224 High Street. He left the store in April 1861, and on June 2 he enlisted as a private in the Old Dominion Guards at Pinner's Point near Portsmouth. On May 19, 1862, he transferred to the Norfolk Light Artillery Blues and served with this company for the rest of the War Between the States. Following the war, he returned to his book shop, which became one of the largest in the area. He married Sarah Lucretia Nash, the daughter of John Nash (mayor of Portsmouth, 1862) and Ann L. Nash, and the couple had three sons: Thomas, Richard, Jr. and John Nash Hume. He became a partner with his brother J. H. Hume in the firm of Hume & Brother on High Street. He passed away at the family home on Middle Street after a short illness of typhoid pneumonia on October 9, 1878, at the age of 40. He was buried in the family plot in Cedar Grove Cemetery in Portsmouth.

JAMES FRANCIS HUNTER

J. "Frank" Hunter was born November 1, 1844, the fourth of seven children born to William H. and Eliza Francis Hunter. He enlisted in the Norfolk Light Artillery Blues on June 23, 1862, and served as a private during the War Between the States. He was in Hospital Number 7 in Richmond from September 21 to October 10, 1862, and was in Hospital Number 9 for two days in April and in August of 1864, but was otherwise present in all of the company's engagements. Hunter was paroled in Richmond on April 22, 1865. Following the war, he returned to Norfolk where he helped to reorganize his old battery, and was elected secretary in May of 1871. Frank Hunter married Nannie McClellan Tunstall, the daughter of Robert and Elizabeth Tunstall on November 2, 1876. He worked as a clerk for the Norfolk and Western Railroad, served as deputy city sergeant, and joined the Pickett-Buchanan Camp of Confederate Veterans. He died at his home at 460 Freemason Street of apoplexy at the age of 55 on Christmas Day, 1899 and was buried in the family plot in Elmwood Cemetery.

HENRY W. JAMES

Henry James was born in Princess Anne County in 1847, and enlisted in the Norfolk Light Artillery Blues in Petersburg on October 27, 1864, at the age of 17. He was detailed to the wagon yard during the siege of Petersburg, and was captured April 2, 1865. He was held as a prisoner at Point Lookout until paroled on June 14, 1865. After the war, he became an agent of the Norfolk and Western Railroad in Petersburg. He still considered Norfolk his home, however, and joined the Pickett-Buchanan Camp of Confederate Veterans in that city. He died in Orange County, Virginia on Sunday April 5, 1903. His funeral was held at the home of his nephew, Mr. J. W. Lee of Norfolk, and he was buried in Elmwood Cemetery.

AMES C. JOHNSON

A. C. Johnson served with the Norfolk Light Artillery Blues before transferring to the Confederate States Navy.

AUGUSTUS W. JOHNSON

Gus Johnson enlisted on September 15, 1863, at Orange Court House and served with the Norfolk Light Artillery Blues as a private during the War Between the States. In the closing days of the war, he was assigned to the Napoleon section in the lines west of Petersburg. During the Union attack on April 2, 1865, he was wounded, but like John Walters, he evaded capture and made his way to the rear of the Confederate lines. He was taken to a Richmond hospital to be treated, and was captured in the hospital when Richmond fell. Johnson was held in Libby Prison until April 23, 1865, when he was released and given transportation to Newport News, Virginia.

JOHN W. JOHNSON

John Johnson of Northampton County, Virginia enlisted as a private in the Norfolk Light Artillery Blues on June 4, 1861. He was present in all battles of the battery, and spent only a few days in Richmond's Hospital Number 9 in February of 1864. He was captured on April 3, 1865, after most of the company had been taken prisoner, and was paroled at Newport News after taking the Oath of Allegiance on June 30, 1865.

GEORGE JONES

On March 10, 1862, twenty-one-year-old George Jones enlisted as a private in the Norfolk Light Artillery Blues. Except for a short stay in Hospital Number 9 in Richmond in January of 1865, he served continuously through the War Between the States. He was paroled in Lynchburg on April 14, 1865.

R. HENRY JONES

Henry Jones was born in Norfolk on August 11, 1844, to Jesse and Jane Jones. When Norfolk was being evacuated by Confederate troops on May 9, 1862, he left school and enlisted as a private in the Norfolk Light Artillery Blues. Except for December of 1862 which he spent in Hospitals 7 and 12 in Richmond, and a two-day stay in Hospital Number 9 in February of 1865, he served continuously with the company in all its engagements until paroled at Appomattox Court House in April of 1865.

After the war, he worked as a merchant in Norfolk, and was a member of the Pickett-Buchanan Camp of Confederate Veterans. He died on June 26, 1908, and was buried in Elmwood Cemetery.

CUSTIS T. JOYNES

Custis Joynes was born in Onancock, Virginia in 1844. He joined Company A, 3rd Virginia Regiment, as a private on April 19, 1861, at Portsmouth, Virginia, and was enlisted for Confederate service on October 16, 1861, in Richmond. Joynes served with the infantry at Williamsburg and Sharpsburg, and was discharged in September of 1862. He then transferred to the Norfolk Light Artillery Blues as a private. He first saw action with the battery at the Battle of Fredericksburg in December of 1862. He was detailed to collect forage and pack hay in Buckingham County in the winter of 1864. Joynes was wounded June 20, 1864, in the right knee during the fighting around Petersburg, and spent two months in Chimborazo hospital recuperating. He rejoined the battery in Petersburg and was captured with a portion of the battery on April 2, 1865, when the lines were overrun. The prisoners were marched to City Point where they boarded boats which took them to Point Lookout, Maryland. Joynes was released from prison after taking the Oath of Allegiance on June 14, 1865. He returned to Norfolk and was employed as a policeman by the city. The readers of the Norfolk Landmark for January 30, 1894, may have been relieved to find that "Police Officer C. T. Joynes, after being confined to his residence about three weeks from la grippe, was again on duty last night." Custis Joynes was a member of the

Pickett-Buchanan Camp of Confederate Veterans for many years. He died in November of 1905 and was buried in Cedar Grove Cemetery in Norfolk.

SOLON H. JOYNES

Private S. H. Joynes, a resident of Norfolk, enlisted in the Norfolk Light Artillery Blues on April 18, 1861, and served with the company for the duration of the War Between the States. He was paroled at Point Lookout, Maryland on June 14, 1865, after taking the Oath of Allegiance.

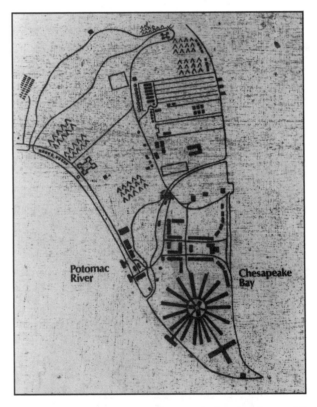

A diagram of the Federal facilities at Point Lookout, Maryland in 1865. The spoke-shaped lines are hospital buildings for Union soldiers. As many as 20,000 Confederate prisoners were held in Camp Hoffman, the center compound marked by three rows of Vs, representing the tents in which the Rebels were housed.

Drawing by Maryland Department of Forests and Parks

WILLIAM COLONNA JOYNES

William Joynes was born in Hampton, Virginia on July 8, 1845. He joined the Confederate army in Richmond on September 10, 1862, at the age of 16, and was severely wounded in the side by a shell fragment at the Battle of Seven Pines. When he recovered, he transferred to the Norfolk Light Artillery Blues. On April 2, 1865, the battery was overrun in the lines around Petersburg and Private Joynes, who was serving as number four man on one of the Blues' guns, was captured and ordered to fire on the retreating Confederates. He responded by throwing his pouch of primers in the water which prevented his gun from being fired. He was held prisoner at Point Lookout, Maryland until June 14, 1865, when he took the Oath of Allegiance and was released.

Shortly after the war, he married Miss Sallie Curry. He died at his home in McKinney, Texas on May 18, 1913, after a long illness, and was survived by his wife of 45 years.

JOHN E. KEELING

John E. Keeling was born in Norfolk, Virginia about 1833 to John W. and Mary D. Keeling. He and his brother Melville joined the Norfolk Light Artillery Blues as privates at the outbreak of the War Between the States on April 18, 1861. Keeling served in most of the battles in which the battery was engaged except for Chancellorsville and the Wilderness. He was promoted to corporal in the autumn of 1862, was appointed an artificer in October of 1864, and served as commissary sergeant. He was paroled in Richmond on April 15, 1865. After the war, he worked as a master builder (contractor) in Norfolk and married Mary Ann Gamage, the 23-year-old sister of Private John Gamage, on November 13, 1867. He later became a member of the Pickett-Buchanan Camp of Confederate Veterans.

JOHN L. KEELING

John L. Keeling enlisted on April 18, 1861, as a private in the Norfolk Light Artillery Blues at the age of 29 and, except for a stay in Chimborazo Hospital from August 10 to September 13, 1863, he served with the company throughout the War Between the States.

MELVILLE COX KEELING

M. C. Keeling was born in Williamsburg, Virginia on October 7, 1838 to John W. and Mary D. Keeling. His ancestors had originally come to Williamsburg from England and were members of the Episcopal Church. He was named after the Reverend Melville Beveredge Cox, a well known missionary who left Norfolk for Liberia in 1833.

M. C. Keeling's father moved the family to Norfolk while he was still an infant. At the age of 20, he joined the Norfolk Light Artillery Blues as a private, and paraded with the company for the first time on February 22, 1858.

Keeling and his older brother John enlisted for duty on April 18, 1861, when the Blues were called into active service. He remained with the company throughout the War Between the States, and was made 8th corporal in the spring of 1863. He was wounded in the left ankle by shrapnel at Chancellorsville on May 1, 1863, during an artillery duel with a Union battery. After spending two

M. C. Keeling was elected captain of the Norfolk Light Artillery Blues on March 1, 1889, and served in this position for seventeen years.

months in Banner Hospital in Richmond, he was captured by Stoneman's Raiders while returning to his company, but was exchanged a short time later. He was wounded a second time during the Battle of the Crater and was sent to the camp hospital for six weeks. Captured again at Hatcher's Run on April 2, 1865, he was taken to Point Lookout, Maryland. He remained there until June 5, 1865, when he was released.

After returning home, Keeling married Sally Walker of Norfolk on August 12, 1866. They had two children: Emily Armistead Keeling (who later married C. W. Robertson) and Harry Walker Keeling (who later married Lucy Scott). He supported his family by working in the Norfolk City Market.

Keeling was one of those who reorganized the Norfolk Light Artillery Blues in 1871. He became first sergeant on May 12, 1880, and traveled with the company on all of their trips, including those to Boston and Philadelphia. During the trip to New Orleans for Mardi Gras in 1895, he was made "Duke of Norfolk" by the king of the carnival.

He was elected captain of the company on March 1, 1889, having served continuously with the Blues over 30 years in every rank. He celebrated his 40th year with the company and 9 years of command in 1898. He eventually attained the rank of major in the Virginia State Militia. Beside his military service, Keeling served as president of the Berkley Town Council and was elected Berkley's mayor in 1899. He served as superintendent of the Chestnut Street Episcopal Church Sunday School for many years, was an active Mason, and was a member of the Pickett-Buchanan Camp of Confederate veterans. His last position was justice-of-the-peace. Keeling died on January 9, 1923, at the age of 85, and was buried in Magnolia Cemetery in Berkley.

WILLIAM TURPIN KILBY

William Kilby was originally a native of Suffolk. He enlisted in the Old Dominion Guards on April 20, 1861, and was later transferred to the Norfolk Light Artillery Blues by Special Order 108 of Major General Huger on May 19, 1862. He spent most of the autumn and winter of 1862 and the spring of 1863 in Richmond hospitals with chronic dysentery. Due to this condition, he was declared unfit for field service and was detailed as a clerk in the medical director's office in Richmond on June 28, 1863. Near the end of the war, he was posted on temporary duty with the provost marshal's office of the Confederate army. He was captured in Richmond when that city fell, and was paroled there on April 18, 1865

After the war, he returned to Norfolk where he married Lucrece Selah Jordan, the daughter of Madison and Eliza Jordan. Kilby opened a clothing business and later joined his family's grocery and liquor business in Maupin's Hall in Portsmouth, and lived at 810 Court Street. Following his retirement, he lived for about fifteen years in Brooklyn, New York. He returned to Portsmouth suffering from consumption, and died at a relative's home on October 1, 1895. He was buried in the family plot in Portsmouth's Cedar Grove Cemetery.

WARRINGTON CRANE KING

Warrington King was born in Washington, D.C. In March of 1862 at the age of 15, he enlisted in the Confederate navy in Norfolk, Virginia. He served on board the gunboat C.S.S. *Jamestown* as the captain's clerk, then transferred to the artillery in Richmond on May 23 of the same year. He then became a private in the Norfolk Light Artillery Blues and fought in all the battles of the company. Captured at Petersburg in April of 1865, he was sent to Point Lookout, and remained in prison until May of 1865. He returned to Washington and became a commercial agent.

He was a member of the Pickett-Buchanan Camp of Confederate Veterans.

WILLIAM A. LAND

William Land was born in Princess Anne County on February 12, 1849. He enlisted as a private in the Norfolk Light Artillery Blues on October 26, 1864, during the War Between the States. After the war, he married Leoline C. Land (1849–1883) of Princess Anne County. He lived in Norfolk where he was self-employed, then later worked as a clerk for Mr. W. A. Shipp. On Friday, May 19, 1899, while in the store of Malbon and Turner at Church and Bute Streets, he died suddenly of heart failure. He was buried in Elmwood Cemetery.

W. C. LAND

W. C. Land was employed as a clerk by J. D. Gammon in Norfolk and joined the Norfolk Light Artillery Blues as a private on February 27, 1860. He enlisted for Confederate service with the battery on March 10, 1862, at Sewell's Point. Land was the first member of the battery to be killed in combat. He died during an artillery duel between one of the Norfolk Light Artillery Blues' rifled guns and a four-gun Union battery during the Battle of Chancellorsville on May 1, 1863. His remains were returned to Norfolk on March 31, 1866, and were buried in the Blues' plot in Elmwood Cemetery on April 2, 1866.

JOHN W. LECOMPTE

John LeCompte was born in 1839 to Gaston and Mary LeCompte of Norfolk. He enlisted as a private in the Norfolk Light Artillery Blues on April 23, 1861, and served with the unit throughout the Civil War. He returned to Norfolk after the war and married Maggie L. Saunders, the 23-year-old daughter of John and Mary Saunders of Norfolk on April 18, 1866. LeCompte worked as a clerk before opening a boot and shoe store on Market Square and later opened a feed store on Water Street. He enlisted as a member of the Norfolk Light Artillery Blues when the battery was reorganized in 1871, but declined to be uniformed and was dropped from the rolls. LeCompte died suddenly at the age of 56 from an apoplectic coma which occurred at his home at 102 Boush Street in Norfolk, on October 29, 1896. His funeral was held at St. Luke's Church and he was buried in Elmwood Cemetery. Several of his pallbearers, including J. H. Watters and R. Henry Jones, were also former members of the Blues.

FRANK DEAN LEE

Dean Lee, the 17-year-old son of Reverend LeRoy Lee of Norfolk, enlisted as a private with the Norfolk Light Artillery Blues on June 22, 1861, at Sewell's Point. His messmate, Joseph Allyn, described him as a soldier who "really enjoyed a battle and urged for a fight." He was wounded twice during his service in the War Between the States. The first time was on June 20, 1864, when he was struck in the head by a bullet. He spent about two months in the hospital, then returned to his company in the lines around Petersburg. Lee was wounded again that year on October 31 and was disabled for further service by his second wound.

LEROY M. LEE, JR.

LeRoy Lee was named for his father who was the pastor of the Granby Street Methodist Episcopal Church in Norfolk and the presiding elder of his district. On January 12, 1864, Lee joined his older brother as a private with the Norfolk Light Artillery Blues. He met the company in Albemarle County where he was enlisted by Captain Grandy, and served for the remainder of the War Between the States. He was captured at Harper's Farm on April 6, 1865, and taken to Point Lookout, where he was held until June 8, 1865.

HENRY C. LOVITT

Henry Lovitt was born in 1843 to W. H. C. and Jane Lovitt. He worked in his father's millinery goods business on Main Street in Norfolk, enlisted as a private in the Norfolk Light Artillery Blues on April 8, 1862, at Sewell's Point, and served the Confederacy throughout the Civil War with his brother Robert. He was seriously wounded at Petersburg on November 5, 1864, when a bullet entered his right hip and exited just above the knee. He recovered from this wound and returned to service. After the Army of Northern Virginia surrendered at Appomattox Court House, he joined Johnston's Army until that unit surrendered in North Carolina. Following the war, he operated a hat shop in Norfolk at 188 Church Street for several years. He moved his family to Dinwiddie County, Virginia where his daughter Jane was born on January 3, 1881. His wife, Ella H. Lovitt, passed away in 1900, and Lovitt himself died on May 15, 1918, at the age of 75. His body was returned to Norfolk, and was buried in Elmwood Cemetery during a grave side service conducted by Reverend J. L. Bray of the Cumberland Street Methodist Episcopal Church. He was survived by a sister, Mrs. James Browne of Norfolk, his daughter, Jane Lovitt, and two sons, John H. and Henry C. Lovitt of Dinwiddie County.

ROBERT C. LOVITT

Robert Lovitt was born in 1838 to W. H. C. and Jane Lovitt. He worked with his father and brother in the family hat and cap business on Main Street in Norfolk as a clerk. He joined the Norfolk Light Artillery Blues on April 11, 1861, and served with his brother Henry as a private with the company during the War Between the

States. Captured at Amelia Court House on April 6, 1865, he was held at Point Lookout, Maryland until June 11 of that year. He returned to Norfolk, where he died in 1876 at the age of 38 and was buried in Elmwood Cemetery. He was survived by his wife, Mary Dianna Lovitt (who later died at their home at 417 Olney Road in Norfolk on April 23, 1924), a daughter, Mrs. John Shepherd Land, and his brother Henry.

OSCAR L. MALBORN

On October 26, 1864, Oscar Malborn, a resident of Princess Anne County, Virginia, enlisted for Confederate service in Richmond as a private with the Norfolk Light Artillery Blues. He was captured in Petersburg on April 4, 1865, and was released from Point Lookout, Maryland on June 12 of that year.

FRANK J. MASI

Frank Masi was a cadet in the Confederate artillery corps before enlisting as a private in the Norfolk Light Artillery Blues on January 26, 1864, at their winter camp in Albemarle County, Virginia. He spent much of his service in Chimborazo Hospital due to illness. Captured on April 1, 1865, he was paroled in Richmond on April 15, 1865, and took the oath of allegiance two days later.

GEORGE WASHINGTON O. MAUPIN, JR.

George Maupin, Jr. was born September 13, 1845, to U.S. Army surgeon Dr. G. W. O. Maupin, Sr. and Ann Augusta Maupin of Portsmouth. His grandfather was Gabriel Maupin, a Huguenot immigrant who had settled in Williamsburg. During the War Between the States, Maupin slipped out of occupied Portsmouth as soon as he was 18 and made his way to Petersburg, where he enlisted as a private in the Norfolk Light Artillery Blues on June 14, 1864. He served with the battery until Lee's surrender at Appomattox Court House, and was paroled on May 17, 1865. He later attended the University of Virginia, became a doctor, then returned to Portsmouth where he set up his practice and married Mary Wilson Maupin. He joined the Stonewall Camp of Confederate Veterans on March 19, 1861, and served as the Camp Surgeon. He was also active in the Portsmouth Elks Lodge, the Portsmouth Council Royal Arcanum, and Trinity Episcopal Church. At the time of his death on September 17, 1912, at the age of 67, Dr. Maupin was the oldest physician in the city. He died suddenly of a cerebral hemorrhage at his home at 100 Middle Street and was buried in the family plot in Cedar Grove Cemetery in Portsmouth.

ALEXANDER DAVID MCCARRICK

David McCarrick was the son of Captain Patrick McCarrick of Ballina County, Ireland and Margaret Collins McCarrick of Richmond. He attended Miss Serena Holden's grammar school in 1851. During the War Between the States, he left Union-occupied Norfolk and joined the Norfolk Light Artillery Blues as a private at the age of 17. He died about two months later on August 26, 1864, in Petersburg from a disease contracted while in the army. After the war, his remains were brought to Norfolk, and his funeral was held at St. Mary's Catholic Church on December 17, 1865. He was buried in the family plot in St. Mary's Cemetery next to his brother, Patrick H. McCarrick of the C.S. Navy, who died October 27, 1865.

JOSEPH B. MCGUIRE

Joseph McGuire enlisted as a private in the Norfolk Light Artillery Blues in Richmond on November 1, 1864. He served with the battery in Petersburg and was captured on April 2, 1865, when the lines around the city were broken. He was taken to Point Lookout and held until June 5, 1865.

C. K. MCKOWN

C. K. McKown (or McKeown) enlisted in the Norfolk Light Artillery Blues as a private on March 10, 1862, at Sewell's Point at the age of 19. He was slightly wounded in the back during the Battle of Chancellorsville on May 1, 1863, while serving on the rifled gun that fought against Weed's Federal Battery. He was captured on April 2, 1865, when the lines around Petersburg were taken, and was sent to Point Lookout.

WILLIAM D. MONTAGUE

William Montague was born on November 5, 1828. He joined the Norfolk Light Artillery Blues and served as a corporal in the company during the War Between the States. He was wounded slightly during the battle of Chancellorsville on May 1, 1863. Just over a year later, he was wounded again while in charge of an eight-inch mortar in the siege lines around Petersburg. A shell fragment struck him in the side and broke one of his ribs.

After the war he returned to Norfolk and worked as a salesman. About 1872, he opened a successful grocery business at 259 Church Street. He also served on the Norfolk Board of Health, and was a member of the Orient Lodge, Number 734 of the Knights of Honor. On October 5, 1881, he died of double pneumonia at his home at 52 Falkland Street at the age of 52. His funeral was held at the Freemason Street Baptist Church and he was buried in Elmwood Cemetery. James Gilmer and R. Frank Vaughn of the Norfolk Light Artillery Blues were two of his pallbearers.

HENRY V. MOORE

Henry Moore was born April 10, 1835, in Norfolk, Virginia. He married Julia Smith Fatherly (1845–1931) on November 14, 1860, then enlisted in the Norfolk Light Artillery Blues on April 18, 1861, at the age of 26. He served as a sergeant, was elected 4th lieutenant in the summer of 1862, and served with this company in all its engagements during the War Between the States except for a short time in October of 1864 when he was in Chimborazo Hospital in Richmond. He commanded a mortar battery in the rear of Rives Salient in the final days of the Siege of Petersburg. He was paroled on April 9, 1865, when Lee surrendered his army.

He returned to Berkley where his son, W. L. Moore, was born in 1866. Henry worked as a lumber inspector after the war, and his son eventually joined him in this business. He served on the executive committee of the Blues Memorial and Benevolent Association, and in December of 1883, he became a charter member of the Pickett-Buchanan Camp of Confederate Veterans. He died on March 3, 1886, and was buried in Cedar Grove Cemetery, Norfolk.

JOHN W. MOORE

John Moore was born in Norfolk County, Virginia in 1832 and grew up in Portsmouth. He later moved to Norfolk, where he lived at the National Hotel and worked in the dry goods store of Foster & Moore. He enlisted as a private in the Norfolk Light Artillery Blues at the outbreak of the War Between the States, and served until May of 1862, when he was transferred to the Quartermaster's Department. In 1864, he was appointed captain and assigned to the staff of Major George W. Grice in Columbia, South Carolina where he collected supplies for the Army of Northern Virginia. He was paroled at Greensboro, North Carolina in April of 1865.

After the war, he returned to Norfolk, where he held the positions of deputy collector of city taxes, assistant postmaster, and cashier of the post office. He later became cashier and bookkeeper for the *Norfolk Virginian* newspaper. He was a member of the Pickett-Buchanan Camp of Confederate Veterans. He died on Wednesday, January 21, 1891, in New York City where he had gone to be treated for cancer of the throat. He was survived by his wife, three sons, and a daughter.

JOSEPH PORTER MOORE, JR.

Joseph Moore, Jr. was born March 17, 1836, to Joseph and Caroline Moore. He enlisted in the Old Dominion Guards as a private on April 20, 1861, and later transferred to the Norfolk Light Artillery Blues where he served until the end of the war. He was wounded during the Battle of the Crater and was captured at the fall of Petersburg on April 2, 1865. After his release from prison at Point Lookout on June 9, 1865, he returned to Portsmouth. He married Mary Elizabeth Moore (1844–1913) and the couple had several children. He operated a hardware business in Portsmouth and was a member of the Knights of Pythias. He died July 11, 1882, at the age of 46 at his home on the corner of Court and Glasgow Streets of "congestion of the brain." His funeral was held the next day at Monumental M. E. Church, and he was buried in Cedar Grove Cemetery in Portsmouth.

DAVID P. MORRIS

David Morris was born on May 5, 1846, in Princess Anne County, Virginia, the third son of Davidton and Sarah Morris. During the War Between the States, he traveled to Petersburg and joined Lee's besieged army on November 9, 1864. He enlisted in the Norfolk Light Artillery Blues as a private, and was detailed to the caisson camp at Amelia Court House where his older brother John was serving. He was later detailed to bring firewood to the men in the front lines. When the army evacuated Petersburg, he was separated from his command, and joined General Shelly at Danville. He served with Shelly until the unit surrendered to General Wright at Burksville Junction on May 15, 1865.

Following the war, he moved to Norfolk where he worked as a bookkeeper and lived with his brother's family at 186 Church Street. He was a member of the Pickett-Buchanan Camp of Confederate Veterans. He died on November 19, 1890, at the age of 44 and was buried in Elmwood Cemetery.

JOHN JESSE MORRIS

John Morris was born on November 23, 1840, in Princess Anne County, Virginia, the third of four sons to Davidton and Sarah Morris. He enlisted in Company F at Craney Island as a private in 1861, but was discharged from the infantry on account of poor health. He joined the Norfolk Light Artillery Blues the following year as the battery left Sewell's Point, and remained in this company as a private until after it reached Orange Court House following the Battle of Gettysburg, when he was made battalion ordnance sergeant under Major Garnett. During the winter of 1864–65, he was made acting lieutenant and placed in charge of the battalion caisson camp at Amelia Court House. He remained there until the evacuation of Lee's Army. He was paroled at Appomattox Court House.

After the war, he returned to Norfolk where he supported his wife and children as a teacher, and later as a druggist at 186 Church Street. He was a member of the Pickett-Buchanan Camp of Confederate Veterans. He died on April 24, 1889, in Westmoreland, North Carolina where he had moved in an attempt to improve his health. He was buried in Elmwood Cemetery in Norfolk.

BURWELL NEWTON MORSE

B. N. Morse was a citizen of Norfolk who enlisted as a private in the Norfolk Light Artillery Blues on June 4, 1861. He served throughout the American Civil War as a private except for a short period in May of 1864 when he was in Chimborazo Hospital in Richmond. He returned to the battery and was captured at Petersburg on April 2, 1865, when the lines around the city were broken. Morse was released from Point Lookout, Maryland on June 12, 1865. He returned to civilian life in Norfolk after the war and operated a grocery store with D. C. Whitehurst on Water Street and later at 170 Cumberland Street. On February 8, 1866, he was accidentally wounded when a pistol being examined by policeman Larkin Davis unexpectedly fired. The bullet hit Morse in the right leg, but fortunately, the wound was not serious. Morse married Miss Virginia P. Cowell (1842–1928), the daughter of Joseph and Amanda Humphries Cowell of Currituck County, North Carolina, and the couple had one son, Joseph T. Morse. On April 11, 1900, Morse died at the age of 71 of paralysis at his home on Fenchurch Street, and he was buried two days later in the family plot in Elmwood Cemetery.

JOHN H. NASH

John Nash was a student prior to enlisting in the Norfolk Light Artillery Blues where he served as ordnance sergeant. He applied for a clerkship or desk job due to his poor health on July 13, 1862, and the following October, he was admitted to General Hospital Nr. 7 in Richmond at the age of 20, suffering from an abscess. He later served as a courier for General Pendleton from March 1864 to February 1865.

WADSWORTH NASH

"Wads" Nash transferred from Young's Harbor Guards to the Norfolk Light Artillery Blues on April 22, 1861, and served with the Blues as a private during the War Between the States. Captured on

April 2, 1865, during the fall of Petersburg, he was taken to Point Lookout and held there until released on May 21, 1865.

C. A. NEWTON

C. A. Newton was born about 1841 and worked as a clerk in Alexandria, Virginia before the Civil War. He enlisted in the Norfolk Light Artillery Blues in Petersburg on June 13, 1862, and served as a private. On August 13, 1864, while in the lines around Petersburg, he was struck on the lower left leg by a piece of shell during a Federal bombardment. His left leg was amputated and he was transferred to Chimborazo Hospital the next day. He was released from service in Richmond in January of 1865 as disabled.

POWHATAN E. NIMMO

P. E. Nimmo was the son of John and Margaret Nimmo of Norfolk. Although Nimmo joined the Norfolk Light Artillery Blues at the age of 23 on March 23, 1861, he was not enlisted for Confederate service until June 10, 1861. He married Miss Margaret K. Butt, the 21-year-old daughter of Arthur and Margaret Butt of Pasquatank County, North Carolina, on February 5, 1862, in the Granby Street Church in Norfolk while the Blues were stationed at Sewell's Point. In November of 1862 he was reported sick and was sent first to a Richmond hospital and later transferred to Huguenot Springs Hospital. He returned to service with the Blues in June of 1863 and remained with the company for the remainder of the War Between the States.

WILLIAM T. NIMMO

William Nimmo was a lieutenant in the Norfolk Light Artillery Blues before the outbreak of the American Civil War. He became the first of the company to die in Confederate service when he became ill and passed away at Sewell's Point on September 25, 1861. His remains were returned to Norfolk for burial.

JOSEPH CHAPMAN NORSWORTHY

J. C. Norsworthy was born in the town of Smithfield in Isle of Wight County on October 22, 1831. He joined the Norfolk Light Artillery Blues at Sewell's Point on July 30, 1861. Later that year, he was transferred to the Confederate Signal Corps, then became a scout. In January 30, 1864, he was in action against the Federal gunboats "Flora Temple" and "Smith Briggs" in Smithfield. Captured on June 6, 1864, he was taken to Point Lookout, Maryland. He later told his family that he and a friend, Sidney Lanier, were released from prison on February 6, 1865, because he had bribed an officer with $15.00 in gold. He returned to Richmond and resumed his scouting duties the day after he arrived. When Lee's Army surrendered, he made his way to Suffolk, surrendered, and was paroled in Norfolk. He remained in Norfolk and found work as a salesman of "staple and fancy dry goods." Norsworthy married Mariana Wakefield Vesey (1840–1921) and had a son, J. C., Jr. He later joined the Pickett-Buchanan Camp of Confederate Veterans. He lived until June 6, 1920, and his remains were buried in the family plot in Elmwood Cemetery in Norfolk.

C. R. NORVELL

On April 4, 1864, C. R. Norvell enlisted as a private in the Norfolk Light Artillery Blues just before the company left their winter camp in Albemarle County, Virginia.

JAMES D. PEET

Enlisting on April 18, 1861, James Peet served as a private with the Norfolk Light Artillery Blues until July of 1863, when he was appointed quartermaster sergeant and detailed to the Confederate Ordnance Department where he served for the remainder of the war.

WILLIAM T. PEET

William Peet was born in Norfolk to William and Frances Peet on the 4th of July, 1833, the same day the Norfolk Light Artillery Blues fired the first shot from their first cannon. He lived at the National Hotel and worked as a clerk in the firm of J. I. Bloodgood until he joined the Blues at the outbreak of war on April 18,1861, and was elected orderly sergeant. He was promoted to second lieutenant in June 1861 when the company was mustered into the Virginia Army, and was later made first lieutenant. He served as the Blues' second-in-command for the remainder of the war, and frequently commanded the battery, as Captain Grandy was often called away to serve on courts-martial. Peet was wounded in the leg at the Battle of Chancellorsville on May 1, 1863, when a shell burst near the gun and disabled most of the crew. Despite his wound, he with Grandy and two others continued to serve the piece until the Federal troops retired. Early on the morning of April 2, 1865, in the lines around Petersburg, he was severely wounded in the leg while directing the fire of the Blues' two rifled guns. Later this day, this section of the battery was captured. Although the rest of the captured officers were taken to Johnson's Island, Peet was placed aboard the hospital ship *Connecticut* at City Point (later Hopewell), Virginia and taken to Lincoln Hospital in Washington, D.C. He was released from this hospital on June 19, 1865, and after taking the "ironclad" oath, was permitted to return to Norfolk.

Peet entered the dry goods business in Norfolk with William J. Capps in the firm of Capps and Peet, and later became a successful wholesale merchant in the firm of Peet and Atkinson. During this time he was also president of the Blues Memorial and Benevolent Association, which kept the group together until it was allowed to reform as a militia company in 1871. On October 24, 1867, Peet married Anna S. Ferguson, the 24-year-old daughter of Elizabeth Ferguson and Captain Finlay F. Ferguson, who had commanded the Norfolk Junior Volunteers at the beginning of the war.

Peet retired from active business shortly before his death at age 44 on May 18, 1877. His funeral was attended by the Blues and the Masons, Atlantic Lodge No. 2, A.F. and A. M. and he was buried in the Ferguson family plot in Cedar Grove Cemetery.

JOHN CALVERT PETTY

John Petty was born in Princess Anne County in January of 1846, the son of John P. and W. Hanna Petty. He enlisted in the Norfolk Light Artillery Blues on September 29, 1864, in Richmond and served as a private with this unit for the remainder of the War Between the States. Near the close of the war, he was promoted to quartermaster sergeant. He was serving in the mortar battery near the Rives Salient when the lines around Petersburg were overrun on April 2, 1865. He followed Lee's army to Appomattox Court House, was paroled, and allowed to keep his own horse.

Following the war, Petty was elected clerk of the court in Norfolk. He enlisted in the U.S. Navy, and served as the paymaster clerk on board the U.S.S. *Essex* and the U.S.S. *Pensacola*. He then served for 18 years as the superintendent of sulfur mines in Louisa County, Virginia. He became ill in November of 1902 and eventually left Norfolk's DePaul Hospital to travel to a spa at Clifton Springs, New York, where he died on October 1, 1903, at the age of 57. His body was returned to Norfolk on the NYP&N Railroad, and his funeral was held at the home of his brother-in-law, W. C. Dickson, at 182 Freemason Street. Petty was survived by his mother and three sisters. He was buried in Elmwood Cemetery in a service conducted by the Reverend Carl E. Grammer of Christ Church. Three of his pallbearers were Merritt Cook, Colonel Walter H. Taylor, and Captain William E. Taylor.

ROBERT T. (Y.) PORTER

Robert Porter joined the Norfolk Light Artillery Blues in Richmond and served as a private with the company during the last four months of the War Between the States.

JOHN T. RAINIER

John Rainier was from Portsmouth, Virginia and served with the Norfolk Light Artillery Blues as a corporal after enlisting on April 18, 1861, in Norfolk. He was slightly wounded in the head on June 24, 1864, in the lines around Petersburg.

Following the war, he helped to reorganize the Norfolk Light Artillery Blues and was elected 3rd sergeant when the company was reinstated in May of 1871.

JOHN SPENCE REID

John Reid joined the Norfolk Light Artillery Blues in Norfolk on April 19, 1861, as a private. He was sick on several occasions during his Confederate service, and was wounded on November 27, 1864, in the lines around Petersburg when he was struck in the upper leg. He spent December of 1864 recuperating in Chimborazo Hospital in Richmond.

JOSEPH B. REYNOLDS

Reynolds served as a private in the Norfolk Light Artillery Blues during the War Between the States. On May 4, 1905, the Virginian *Pilot* reported that J. B. Reynolds, an old Confederate soldier, had committed suicide at the age of 68 by drinking a tincture of opium. He was found unconscious next to the Norfolk Southern Railroad tracks, and was taken to the Queen Street Police Station where he died. He was buried in an unmarked grave in Elmwood Cemetery. He left a wife and son, who at the time lived on Reservoir Street in the Brambleton area of Norfolk.

ROBERT EMMETT REYNOLDS

Robert Reynolds was born to Joseph P. Reynolds (originally of County Meath, Ireland, 1808–1853) and Jemima R. Reynolds (1801–1871) on October 10, 1842, in Portsmouth, Virginia. He enlisted on May 1, 1862, at Sewell's Point and served as a private in the Norfolk Light Artillery Blues during the War Between the States. He was captured while returning to Virginia after the Battle of Gettysburg on July 14, 1863, and died almost a year later at the age of 21 in a Union prison. Some sources indicate he was held at Point Lookout or at Fort Delaware; however, the official records state he died at Finn's Point, near Salem, New Jersey on June 12, 1864. His body was given to his mother and was later returned to Portsmouth where it was interred in the family plot in Cedar Grove Cemetery.

JOHN B. ROBERTS

John Roberts was born in Gloucester County, Virginia. He worked in Norfolk as a carpenter until April 18, 1861, when he enlisted as a private in the Norfolk Light Artillery Blues. He served in all the battles in which the company was engaged, and was shot in the left heel at Petersburg on June 24, 1864. His wound was treated at Chimborazo Hospital in Richmond and he returned to the company. He was paroled at Appomattox Court House.

Following the war, he joined the Pickett-Buchanan Camp of Confederate Veterans.

CRAWFORD S. ROGERS

Crawford Rogers enlisted as a private with the Norfolk Light Artillery Blues on March 10, 1862, at Sewell's Point. He was confined to Chimborazo Hospital in Richmond from September of 1863 to February of 1865 due to illness.

JOHN C. ROGERS

On June 20, 1862, John Rogers enlisted as a private with the Norfolk Light Artillery Blues. He served throughout the War Between the States and was captured at Petersburg on April 2, 1865. He was released from prison at Point Lookout on May 31, 1865.

THEODORE F. ROGERS

T. F. Rogers was a native of Norfolk born July 4, 1844, to John Randolph and Mary Ann Rogers. He was still a student at Norfolk Military Academy at the outbreak of the War Between the States on April 19, 1861, and left school at the age of fifteen to enlist in Young's Harbor Guards. He transferred to the Norfolk Light Artillery Blues on May 8, 1862, before the evacuation of Norfolk, and served with the company as a private in all of its engagements. He was severely wounded in the leg on May 12, 1864, at Spotsylvania Court House and was paroled in Richmond on May 10, 1865.

He returned to Norfolk after the war and found employment in a small lumber firm. Within a year, he had become a partner in this company. In 1884, he sold his partnership and entered the real estate business. He served as the president of the Boys' Home, the vice-president of the Chamber of Commerce, and for many years, as the High Constable of Norfolk. On May 30, 1867, he married Adelaide (Addie) March (1851–1924). They resided at 34 Bute Street and had a son and three daughters. As secretary pro tem, he helped to reorganize the Norfolk Light Artillery Blues in 1871. He attended the Freemason Street Baptist Church, was a member of the Pickett-Buchanan Camp of Confederate Veterans, the Knights Templar, and was a thirty-second degree Mason. On February 9, 1898, he was compelled after years of suffering from his war wound to have his leg amputated above the knee. The operation was successful, and he enjoyed many years of health before dying at the age of 66 in 1910. He was buried in the family plot in Elmwood Cemetery.

W. H. R. ROGERS

W. Rogers lived in Norfolk and worked as a clerk in the store of Nussbaum & Brother before enlisting as a private in the Norfolk Light Artillery Blues on April 18, 1861, at the outbreak of the Civil War. He died of illness in a Richmond hospital on September 24, 1862, at the age of 27.

SMITH S. SAUNDERS

Smith Saunders, the third of seven children born to John C. and Mary C. Saunders, was a native of Norfolk who attended grammar school under Miss Serena Holden in 1856 and 1857. During the War Between the States, he "ran the blockade" out of Norfolk, and enlisted as a private in the Norfolk Light Artillery Blues on October 6, 1863, at Orange Court House while still a teenager. He was wounded on June 24, 1864, in the lines around Petersburg when a shell struck the muzzle of the Napoleon gun he was serving and exploded, burning his face badly.

He returned to Norfolk after the war, remained a bachelor, and worked as a clerk in the shoe business, mostly at the wholesale boot and shoe company of Bottimore, Marrow, and Co. He continued to be active with the Norfolk Light Artillery Blues, was elected 6th corporal in May of 1871, and eventually reached the rank of sergeant; however, due to his failing health, he voluntarily resigned this position and returned to his former rank of private. He died of consumption (cancer) at the age of 35 on October 31, 1881. His funeral was held at his home at 112 Bank Street and was conducted by the Reverend O. S. Barton. Smith Saunders was laid to rest in Cedar Grove Cemetery in Norfolk by his comrades in the Blues.

N. C. H. SEBRELL

On May 2, 1862, N. C. H. Sebrell enlisted as a private with the Norfolk Light Artillery Blues in Petersburg.

THOMAS F. (G.) SEGAR

Tom Segar enlisted in Grandy's Battery later in the war on February 13, 1864, in Albemarle County, Virginia. He remained with the company through the fall of Petersburg and took the "ironclad" oath in Richmond on April 18, 1865.

BAINS A. SIMMONS

Private Bains Simmons served with the Norfolk Light Artillery Blues until his capture at the end of the war. He took the "ironclad" oath and was paroled in Richmond on April 22, 1865.

J. SIMMONS

J. Simmons served as a private with the Norfolk Light Artillery Blues during the War Between the States.

C. D. SMILEY

C. D. Smiley enlisted in the Norfolk Light Artillery Blues on May 9, 1862, as the Blues were evacuating Norfolk. He was always present for duty, and was burned on the face on June 24, 1864, when a Federal shell struck the gun on which he was serving in the lines around Petersburg. He returned to the Blues and joined the mortar battery in the rear of the Petersburg lines where he served until April 2, 1865, when the city was abandoned. He was paroled at Appomattox Court House with Lee's Army of Northern Virginia.

CHARLES A. SMITH, JR.

Charles Smith was born in 1846 to Charles A. and Sarah A. Smith, and at the age of 18, enlisted as a private in the Norfolk Light Artillery Blues on September 29, 1864, in Richmond. He was captured on April 4, 1865, and held at Point Lookout until his release on June 15. Smith died in Williamsburg, Virginia on June 5, 1884, and was buried in Elmwood Cemetery in Norfolk.

ELBRIDGE C. SMITH

On April 19, 1861, E. C. Smith enlisted as a private in the Norfolk Light Artillery Blues in Norfolk. He served with the battery during the War Between the States except for the period of May of 1863 to April of 1864 when he served as a teamster for the ordnance train. He was captured at the end of the war and held at Point Lookout until his release on June 19, 1865.

JOHN E. SMITH

John E. Smith, shown on some lists as James E. Smith, enlisted in Petersburg near the close of the war on October 18, 1864, and served the remainder of the war as a private in the Norfolk Light Artillery Blues.

JOHN W. SMITH

John Smith served as a private with the Norfolk Light Artillery Blues from his enlistment on April 18, 1861, to April of 1865 when he was captured by Federal troops and sent to Point Lookout by way of City Point (later Hopewell), Virginia. He was released on May 29, 1865.

WILLIAM SMYTHE

On June 26, 1862, William Smythe enlisted as a private in the Norfolk Light Artillery Blues in Petersburg.

J. S. STERRETT

Private J. S. Sterrett was one of six men from Maryland to join the Norfolk Light Artillery Blues. He became sick in the summer of 1862 and was taken to a Petersburg hospital where he died on June 14, 1862, at the age of 20. His remains were returned to Norfolk and interred in the Blues' plot in Elmwood Cemetery on April 2, 1866.

EDWIN STEEVER

Ed Steever was born about 1831 to George and Elizabeth Steever in Baltimore, Maryland. He was a commission merchant in the firm of Stuart and Steever at Maxwell's Wharf in Norfolk before enlisting as a private in the Norfolk Light Artillery Blues on April 13, 1862, at Sewell's Point. He spent September of 1862 in Hospital Nr. 7 in Richmond suffering from typhoid fever, but was otherwise present for duty throughout the War Between the States. Captured in April of 1865, he was taken to Point Lookout and held until June 11, 1865.

Edwin Steever moved to Dubuque, Iowa where he worked as a clerk after the war, but returned to Norfolk, Virginia to marry Miss Mary L. Nash, the daughter of Thomas and Lydia Nash. They were married on October 21, 1867, by Reverend Nicholas A. Okeson.

WILLIAM A. SWANK

W. A. Swank was born about 1830. An attorney in Norfolk, he enlisted in the Norfolk Light Artillery Blues as a private on September 26, 1862, in Richmond. He served with the company until taken prisoner in 1865, when he was taken to City Point, Virginia and then to Point Lookout, Maryland. He was released on June 19, 1865, and returned to Norfolk where he resumed his practice of attorney. He served on the committee formed to return the bodies of those who had died during the war, and served as secretary of the Norfolk Monumental Association organized to build a Confederate monument in Norfolk. He died on December 21, 1909, of cancer and was buried in Elmwood Cemetery.

J. THEODORE TAYLOR

Private J. Theodore Taylor served throughout the War Between the States with the Norfolk Light Artillery Blues. On July 30, 1864, during the Battle of the Crater, a shell from an enemy gun started a fire on the roof of a nearby powder magazine. While others around him ran, Private Taylor grabbed two buckets of water and single-handedly put out the fire. His quick thinking prevented the magazine from exploding. Just a few months later, on November 11, 1864, Private Taylor was killed at the age of nineteen by an enemy sharpshooter while on duty in the lines around Petersburg. He was eulogized as a "first class soldier, kind and obliging in all his actions among his associates, a very moral young man," and was buried the next day in the churchyard of Grace Church in Petersburg. His body was taken up after the war and was returned to Norfolk by steamboat from Richmond on March 22, 1866. He was laid to rest in Cedar Grove Cemetery in Norfolk in a ceremony attended by several of his old comrades of the Blues.

WILLIAM EYRE TAYLOR, JR.

William E. Taylor, Jr. was born in the borough of Norfolk in 1841 to Captain William E. and Margaret A. Taylor. His father had served as Captain of the Norfolk Light Artillery Blues from 1835 to 1838. His grandfather, Judge Robert B. Taylor (1774–1834), served as a general commanding the troops in the Norfolk area during the War of 1812. The younger William was well educated. He attended Miss Serena Holden's School in 1850 and later Norfolk Academy, and was admitted to Virginia Military Institute. He later attended the University of Virginia and earned a law degree, and studied for a time in Germany.

When Virginia seceded from the Union, his father was made a major in the Virginia Militia, and commanded the forces at Sewell's Point which battled the U.S.S. *Monticello* on May 19, 1861. On March 10, 1862, Taylor joined the Norfolk Light Artillery Blues and was elected sergeant at the age of 21. Taylor served with the Blues in all their battles until March of 1864, when both his arms were injured in an railroad accident on the Virginia Central Railroad. Although confined to the Confederate General Hospital in Charlottesville and removed from active duty, he remained in the Confederate army until Lee's surrender.

Taylor returned to Norfolk after the war and lived with his sister Sallie Eyre Taylor and his parents at the family home at 64 (later 164) Bute Street. General Robert E. Lee was entertained here during his last visit to Norfolk in 1870. The deaths of his father in 1870 and his mother in 1888 left him with a great deal of land in Norfolk and Norfolk County. One of his farms on the Elizabeth River in the Atlantic City section was sold to General Virginius Groner in 1888. When the Norfolk Light Artillery Blues were reorganized in 1871, the former sergeant was elected captain of the battery, and like his father before him, he served at this rank for three years. Taylor was also a member of the Pickett-Buchanan Camp of Confederate Veterans. Following his sister Sallie's death in 1900 he lived alone, as he had never married. He died on November 26, 1918, following a lingering illness. His funeral was held at the house two days later and was attended by the Pickett-Buchanan Camp. John J. Burroughs, the camp commander, and M. T. Cooke were among his honorary pallbearers. Taylor was interred in Cedar Grove Cemetery in a private ceremony.

WILLIAM J. TAYLOR

William J. Taylor was born July 27, 1843. He enlisted in the Norfolk Light Artillery Blues on January 21, 1861, as a private and served with the company throughout the War Between the States, taking part in all of its engagements. Private Taylor was captured on April 2, 1865, when the Confederate lines at Petersburg were overrun. He was attempting to sponge his gun when the enemy took the sponge from his hands and wounded him severely in the right foot. He was taken to Lincoln Hospital in Washington, D.C. where his foot was amputated and even though he was given an artificial foot, he still walked with a crutch for the rest of his life. He was released on May 29, 1865.

After the war, he returned to Norfolk for a short time before moving to Baltimore where he worked as a printer. In 1873 and 1874 he was the head of the Baseball department of the *Baltimorean* newspaper. He died on March 29, 1875, of consumption in Philadelphia where he had moved just a few months before, leaving a wife and two young sons. His funeral at Christ Church in Norfolk on April 5, 1875, was attended by the Blues, a detachment of the City Guard, and the Norfolk Typographical Union Nr. 86. His pallbearers included J. F. Hunter, R. J. Broughton, J. A. Elliott, and B. D. Brickhouse. He was buried in Elmwood Cemetery with an Episcopal burial service, after which the City Guard fired a salute.

BENJAMIN D. THOMAS

Benjamin Thomas enlisted as a corporal in the Norfolk Light Artillery Blues on April 18, 1861. He was promoted to quartermaster sergeant on July 1, 1863, and served throughout the War Between the States. He returned to Norfolk after the war and lived on Bermuda Street, where he died on May 14, 1870.

JESSE D. THOMAS

On April 18, 1861, twenty-four-year-old Jesse Thomas enlisted as a private in the Norfolk Light Artillery Blues. He was detached from the company in September of the following year, and was appointed to the rank of lieutenant in the Confederate army on October 31, 1864.

EBENEZER THOMPSON, JR.

Ebenezer Thompson was originally from Portsmouth, Virginia. He made his way to Petersburg, where he enlisted as a private with the Norfolk Light Artillery Blues on October 27, 1864. He served with the company for six months before taking the oath of allegiance in Richmond on April 26, 1865.

CRAWFORD H. TOY

Crawford Toy was the son of Jane Morton Toy and Dr. Thomas Toy, a well known druggist of Norfolk, and a founding member of the Freemason Street Baptist Church. He attended Norfolk Academy before enrolling in the University of Virginia, where he helped to establish the first college YMCA. After graduating in 1856, Crawford taught at the Albermarle Female Institute of Charlottesville until 1859, when he enrolled in the Southern Baptist Theological Seminary in Greenville, South Carolina. He served as a professor of Greek at Richmond University for a short time in 1861, then in May of that year, returned to Norfolk where he later began to preach at the Cumberland Street Church. In March of 1862, his father, Thomas Toy, closed his drug store and moved to Baltimore, and on April 13, 1862, Crawford Toy enlisted as a private in the Norfolk Light Artillery Blues, serving with the Confederate battery until January 1863, when he became the chaplain of the 53rd Virginia Regiment. He was captured later that year by Union troops and held as a prisoner of war.

After the war, he studied in Berlin, Germany and taught at several colleges before accepting the position of professor of semantic languages at Harvard University in 1879. Dr. Toy returned to Norfolk occasionally, visiting family (who had returned after the war) and friends.

EDWARD S. VAUGHAN

Edward Vaughn enlisted as a private in the Norfolk Light Artillery Blues on January 6, 1864, in Albemarle County, Virginia, and served with the company for the remainder of the War Between the States.

R. FRANK VAUGHAN

Frank Vaughan was born on the 1st of December, 1834, in Gloucester County. He was one of nine sons born to William P. Vaughan (January 1806 to January 1870), who was a prosperous farmer. As a young man, he worked as a bookkeeper for Walke & Co. He enlisted in the Norfolk Light Artillery Blues on April 18, 1861, as a private and later served as the first sergeant. He took part in every engagement of the battery during the War Between the States and was captured on April 2, 1865, during the fall of Petersburg. He was released from Point Lookout, Maryland on June 21, 1865.

Following the war, he married Miss Mary E. Hallett and opened an insurance business in Norfolk. One of his sons, F. Wade Vaughan who was born in 1870, later joined him in this business.

Frank Vaughan was president of the Blues Memorial and Benevolent Association, a member of the Pickett-Buchanan Camp of Confederate Veterans, the Masonic Lodge, and the Redmens Association, and was an elder of the First Presbyterian Church of Norfolk. He served with the Blues again as first sergeant following the reorganization of the company in 1871, and was elected captain on October 6, 1876, at the age of 41. He commanded the Blues for over two years before resigning on February 21, 1879. His son Wade served as ordnance sergeant on the staff of the 4th Virginia Regiment.

On May 9, 1895, Vaughan became ill while riding home on the streetcar from his insurance office, and died suddenly after arriving at his home at 119 York Street. Vaughan was 60 years old, and was survived by his wife and five children. He was buried in Elmwood Cemetery in Norfolk.

SAMUEL VEALE

Samuel Veale was born August 6, 1840. He worked as a clerk for Seth March before enlisting as a private in the Norfolk Light Artillery Blues on March 26, 1861. He served with the unit as a private throughout the War Between the States, was captured when the lines around Petersburg were broken on April 2, 1865, and was released from Point Lookout on June 5, 1865.

After the war, he helped to organize the Blues Memorial and Benevolent Association, and served as the secretary of this organization.

He later moved to Baltimore, where he died on January 9, 1911, of Brights Disease. His wife Kate (1860–1935) brought his remains to Norfolk two days later, and he was buried in Elmwood Cemetery in the family plot. The funeral was conducted by Reverend D. W. Howard of St. Luke's Episcopal Church and the Masons. Several of the old Blues, including Richard Gwaltney and Robert Broughton served as pallbearers.

JACOB VICKERY, JR.

Jacob Vickery, Jr. was born November 6, 1816; the first of four children of Jacob and Ann W. Vickery. Both his father and his uncle Samuel Vickery were successful ship owners. Jacob Vickery, Sr. also served as inspector of the customs in Norfolk until his sudden death from illness at the age of 70 in 1853.

Jacob Vickery, Jr. joined the Norfolk Light Artillery Blues on February 26, 1835, at the age of 19 and was elected 5th corporal. He was promoted to 4th corporal on February 19, 1839. He established "Vickery and Company, Booksellers" in 1843 and became a successful merchant. He served as captain of the Blues in the 1840s, and was re-elected to this position on November 28, 1859. He was still in command of the company at the outbreak of war in April of 1861 when the Blues were called to service by the governor.

On December 1, 1861, Captain Vickery resigned his command, citing his failing health. The Blues held a special meeting at their post at Sewell's Point to pass resolutions expressing their esteem for their captain and their regret at his resignation. Vickery returned to Norfolk and his family book and stationery store at Nr. 7 Bank Street. The store was completely destroyed in the Atlantic Hotel fire on January 8, 1867, but was eventually rebuilt and reopened.

In 1873, Vickery served as the chairman for a Committee of Arrangements, and introduced the guest speaker, when the reorganized Norfolk Light Artillery Blues were presented with a new flag by the city on Independence Day of that year.

In the 1880s, Vickery moved to Baltimore where he died of heart disease on November 3, 1887, just three days before his 71st birthday. He left a wife, an adopted daughter, and several grandchildren. His body was returned to Norfolk aboard the Bay-Line steamer *Georgia* on November 5, and was escorted to the family burial plot in Cedar Grove Cemetery by the Blues under the command of Captain James W. Gilmer.

ISAAC T. WALKE

On May 6, 1861, Isaac Walke enlisted as a private in the Norfolk Light Artillery Blues at Craney Island. During September and

October of 1862, he was sick in a Richmond hospital. Walke returned to duty, was assigned to Ordnance on May 31, 1863, and became ordnance officer of the 1st Corps Artillery on June 9.

R. P. WALKER

R. P. Walker enlisted in the Norfolk Light Artillery Blues as a private on June 10, 1862, in Petersburg. He was discharged on account of disability, and appointed to General Walker's staff on August 6, 1863, presumably satisfied with the amount of battle he had seen.

JOHN H. WALTERS

John Walters was born near Amsterdam, Holland to William and Hester Walters on January 21, 1835. He came to America as a boy and lived in Albany, New York where he worked for a short time in the offices of the New York State Senate. He later moved to Norfolk, where he entered into a partnership with Fredrick W. Clark in the blank book and bookbinding business "Clark & Walters" in 1859. He lived in a boardinghouse at Cumberland and Talbot Streets run by Mrs. Walker with Charles Buskey and several others. Walters enlisted as a private in the Norfolk Light Artillery Blues on June 4, 1861, shortly after Virginia seceded from the Union. He served continuously with the company throughout all its engagements during the War Between the States, was wounded April 2, 1865, at Petersburg, and was paroled at Appomattox Court House. He kept a diary of his experiences with Grandy's Battery from May 1862 to the close of the war.

John Walters in his Masonic regalia.
Courtesy of the Norfolk Masonic Temple

Following the war, Walters returned to Norfolk where he worked briefly at the office of the *Norfolk Journal* before opening a bookbinding shop at 54 Roanoke Square, just south of Water Street. He married Miss Virginia Phillips of Norfolk on February 3, 1870. Their first child, Mary Lee, was born later that year and was followed by William Duncan Walters in

1872 and Lottie Roper Walters in 1875. About 1882, Walters took on the position of clerk of the city market in addition to his book-binding shop.

Walters was also extremely active in several Masonic organizations in the city. He joined Atlantic Lodge No. 2 A.F. and A. M. on August 1, 1868, and three days later was initiated in the first degree. By the end of that month, he had risen to the degree of Master Mason. In December of that year, Walters served as acting treasurer of the lodge. He was elected Worshipful Master of the Atlantic Lodge on June 9, 1873, and served in that position for two years. He served for 13 years as the secretary of this lodge. In 1869, Walters became secretary of the Royal Arch Chapter No. 1, a position he would hold for almost fifty years. In July of that year, he was accepted as a member of the Grice Commandery No. 16, Knights Templar. He held the offices of Treasurer, Recorder, Standard Bearer, Captain General, and Generalissimo of the Grice Commandery before being elected Eminent Commander on April 10, 1882. He held this office for two years. He later served as Prelate, and then as Recorder for another eight years. Walters also belonged to the four Scottish Rite bodies of Norfolk; the McDaniel Lodge of Perfection, the Frederick Webber Chapter of Rose Croix No. 4, the Auld Consistory No. 3, and the John Moore Council of Kadash. He served as secretary for all of these bodies, and remained secretary of the McDaniel Lodge for twenty-five years. As a 32nd Degree Mason, he was elected to honorary memberships in both the Grice Commandery and in Atlantic Lodge No. 2.

In addition to his Masonic affiliations, Walters was a member of the Pickett-Buchanan Camp of Confederate Veterans where he served as color sergeant, and he also served as the Treasurer of the Blues Memorial and Benevolent Association. He was one of several surviving members of Grandy's Battery who were guests of the Blues at their 78th anniversary banquet in 1906, when the Civil War flag of the company was returned to the unit.

"Uncle John," as he was fondly known, joined McKendree Methodist Episcopal Church on Clay Avenue in Brambleton on May 3, 1885. He was an active member of the congregation for the rest of his life and was a member of the men's bible class.

At about the age of 50, Walters retired from his bookbinding business, moved his family from Wood Street to a new home at 147 North Reservoir Avenue at the corner of West Highland Avenue (later Olney Road), and worked for a while as a watchman, a clerk, and a boilermaker. Walters' wife, Virginia, passed away May 30, 1892, at the age of 46, and after her death, he became the proprietor of a grocery store on West Brambleton Avenue, which he operated from about 1894 to 1907.

Walters died after a brief illness on January 11, 1918, at the age of 82 at his residence at 807 Marshall Avenue (where he and his two daughters had moved in 1916). He was buried the following day next to his wife in Elmwood Cemetery with both Masonic and Knights Templar honors. Walters was further honored for his many years of service to the Masonic bodies when the "John Walters Chapter No. 68" was organized in July of 1922 and was chartered on October 25, 1922, under the United Royal Arch Chapter. Within a year, the John Walters Chapter had 268 charter members.

On August 22, 1956, Mary and Lottie Walters had the remains of their mother, father, and brother William (who had died soon after his father on May 12, 1918) re-interred in a new family plot in

John Walters surrounded by other members of McKendree Methodist Church about 1914. The church stood on the corners of Clay and Clairborne Avenues in the Brambleton section of Norfolk. John's home was just a few blocks away. Detail from a panoramic photo by Harry C. Mann.

Courtesy of Norfolk Public Library

Norfolk's Forest Lawn Cemetery. The two sisters, who like their brother had never married, had continued to live in Norfolk where Mary worked as a clerk for the Virginian Railway. In their later years, they moved from their home at 2705 Kimball Terrace to the Mary F. Ballentine Home on Granby Street. Lottie Walters died there on October 2, 1959. Her sister, John Walter's oldest child, lived only four months longer, dying February 6, 1960, at the age of 89.

JOHN T. WARD

John Ward was a resident of Norfolk who joined the Norfolk Light Artillery Blues in Petersburg on August 12, 1864. He was captured by Federal troops, and released from Point Lookout on June 22, 1865.

A. M. WATTERS

A. M. Watters enlisted as a private in the Norfolk Light Artillery Blues on August 7, 1862, in Petersburg. He was killed instantly at the age of 20 on June 24, 1864, during a heavy bombardment at the Rives (or Reeves) Salient, a portion of the Confederate lines around Petersburg. He was struck in the left shoulder by a shell which came out under his right arm. His remains were returned to Norfolk on March 31, 1866, and interred in the Blues' plot in Elmwood Cemetery two days later.

JAMES HATTON WATTERS

James Watters was born in Norfolk, Virginia on July 13, 1840, to James and Georgiana Martin Watters. He worked as a clerk from the age of 14 until he enlisted in the Norfolk Light Artillery Blues on April 18, 1861, as a private at the beginning of the War Between the States. He served on the crew of an 8-inch Columbiad at Sewell's Point which was dismounted by a shot from the *Monitor* on May 8, 1862. Except for a short stay in General Hospital No. 12 in Richmond recovering from wounds to his hands and wrists received on May 1, 1863, at the Battle of Chancellorsville and sickness in October of 1864, he served continuously with his company. He attained the rank of sergeant on the same day he was wounded, and was paroled in Richmond on April 14, 1865.

Following the war, he returned to Norfolk where he joined Walter H. Taylor and Thomas Elliott in the hardware firm of Taylor, Elliott, and Watters. He later became a partner with William A. Martin in the hardware store Watters and Martin on Commercial Place. He married twice, the first time to Margaret Garrett in 1882. They had three children: Garrett, James, Jr., and Margaret. After his wife's death in 1887, he married Martha Watts. Watters served two terms on the Norfolk City Council and in 1906 served as police commissioner. He served as vice-president of the Blues Memorial and Benevolent Association, was elected 3rd lieutenant when the Blues were reinstated in May of 1871, and was a member of the Pickett-Buchanan Camp of Confederate Veterans. He passed away at "Markham Cottage" in Princess Anne County on July 9, 1919, at the age of 78, and was buried in Cedar Grove Cemetery in Norfolk.

WILLIAM T. WEBB

William Webb enlisted on April 18, 1861, as a private and served with the Norfolk Light Artillery Blues at Sewell's Point and Petersburg, was sick in a hospital during September and October of 1862, and was discharged from the company on January 3, 1863.

JOSEPH S. WEST

Joseph West was born in Currituck County, North Carolina about 1843. He was living in Portsmouth, Virginia when he enlisted in the Norfolk Light Artillery Blues on April 18, 1861. He served as a private with the company until being transferred to the Confederate navy as an engineer on September 24, 1862.

WILLIAM M. WEST

William West enlisted as a sergeant in the Norfolk Light Artillery Blues on April 18, 1861, but was reduced to private, in which rank he served during the War Between the States. He died in Norfolk and was buried in Elmwood Cemetery on August 31, 1887.

CHARLES EDGAR WHITE

Charles E. White was born on May 13, 1846, the son of James G. and Mrs. Pricilla Potts White. He enlisted in the Norfolk Light Artillery Blues as a private on September 27, 1864, in Richmond and served the remainder of the War Between the States. He was captured on April 2, 1865, sent to City Point, Virginia, and from there to Point Lookout, Maryland where he was held until May 29, 1865.

He returned to Norfolk and married Olivia Frances White. The couple had two sons, Charles E. White, Jr. and W. W. White, and two daughters, Ida O. Wright and Mrs. H. Zimmerly. Charles White died at his home in the Botetourt Apartments at 500 Botetourt Street on December 2, 1935, at the age of 89. His funeral at Elmwood Cemetery was the last for a member of Grandy's Confederate battery.

NATHANIEL ELISHA WHITE

Nathaniel White was born in Portsmouth on May 28, 1827, and enlisted during the War Between the States as a private in the Norfolk Light Artillery Blues on November 4, 1864, in Richmond. He was captured and was held at a prisoner camp in Winchester, Virginia until April 19, 1865. After the war, he opened a dry goods business in Portsmouth at 318 High Street, and lived at 43 Court Street. He died at the home of his son-in-law, Horace Hardy, in Norfolk's Ghent section on October 31, 1892, at the age of 65, and was buried in Cedar Grove Cemetery, Portsmouth.

LUKE HILL WHITEHURST

Luke Whitehurst was born on Knotts Island in Currituck County, North Carolina on December 14, 1830. He came to Norfolk as a young man and worked as a salesman and a clerk in the dry goods store of J. D. Gammon. He enlisted on June 4, 1861, as a private in the Norfolk Light Artillery Blues and served with the company throughout the War Between the States. He was captured during the fall of Petersburg on April 2, 1865, and taken to Point Lookout, Maryland. After his release on June 12, 1865, he returned to Norfolk and was employed in the dry goods store of J. D. Gammon at 336 Main Street. When Mr. Gammon passed away, Luke bought the store and ran it successfully for nearly forty years. He married Annie M. Granbery (1842–1927), the sister of Bishop John C. Granbery of the Methodist Church, and they had two daughters. Luke was an active member of the Cumberland Street Methodist Church, acted as a church delegate at several district and annual conferences, and was a member of the church official board. He was finally forced to retire from his dry goods business due to failing health, and passed away about a year later from pleurisy on February 13, 1911, at his home at 244 Bank Street at the age of 80. His funeral service was conducted by the Reverend R. Finley Gayle of the Cumberland Street Church. He was buried in Elmwood Cemetery, just across from the grave of Captain Grandy. John Walters served as one of his pallbearers.

STEVEN T. WHITEHURST

Steven T. Whitehurst was born in Norfolk County on February 3, 1846. In April of 1863, at the age of 17, he traveled to United States Ford on the Rappahannock River where on April 19 he enlisted as a private in the Norfolk Light Artillery Blues. He served throughout the remainder of the War Between the States, except for a two-week stay in a hospital. After the war he moved to Princess Anne County where he worked as a farmer. He was a member of the

Pickett-Buchanan Camp of Confederate Veterans. He died on January 19, 1905, at the age of 58, and was buried in the churchyard of Emmanuel Episcopal Church in Kempsville.

JOHN R. WHITING

John R. Whiting enlisted as a private in the Norfolk Light Artillery Blues under Captain Grandy in Richmond on January 26, 1863.

JOHN S. WHITING

John S. Whiting served as a private in the Norfolk Light Artillery Blues until October 10, 1861, when he was detailed to service as a hospital steward.

THOMAS B. WHITING

Thomas Whiting enlisted as a private in the Norfolk Light Artillery Blues on March 10, 1862, at the age of 22. Except for two brief stays in hospitals during October of 1862 and again in February of 1865, he was continuously present for duty with the battery during the War Between the States.

C. WHITMORE

Private C. Whitmore served in the War Between the States with the Norfolk Light Artillery Blues.

CHARLES L. WILKINS

Charles Wilkins was born about 1836. He worked in Norfolk as a bookkeeper for Rowland and Reynolds and lived on Cumberland Street prior to the American Civil War. He joined the Norfolk Light Artillery Blues on February 25, 1861, and served with the company as a private during the war. He was hospitalized due to illness at General Hospital No. 7 in Richmond during October and November of 1862, and was in Chimborazo Hospital during August of 1864. A month prior to his second illness, Wilkins became acting battalion quartermaster sergeant, and was forage master for Richardson's battalion from November of 1864 to the end of the war.

He died in Norfolk on January 27, 1883, at the age of 47, and was buried in Elmwood Cemetery.

GEORGE W. WILKINS

George Wilkins became a private in the Norfolk Light Artillery Blues upon his enlistment on February 21, 1862, in Norfolk. He served with the company throughout the War Between the States and was paroled in Richmond, Virginia on April 18, 1865, after taking the "ironclad" oath.

JOHN F. WILKINS

John Wilkins joined the Norfolk Light Artillery Blues on February 25, 1861, before the outbreak of the American Civil War. He was enlisted as a private for Confederate service on June 4 of that year, and served continuously with his company.

THOMAS J. WILKINS

On February 21, 1861, Thomas Wilkins joined the Norfolk Light Artillery Blues at the age of 23. He served as a private when the company was called to service with the Confederacy, and was promoted to corporal on May 1, 1863, during the Battle of Chancellorsville. He spent July and August of that year in Chimborazo Hospital before rejoining his battery. Captured during the fall of Petersburg on April 2, 1865, he was confined at Point Lookout, Maryland until his release on June 17, 1865.

WALTER A. WILKINS

On March 10, 1862, 19-year-old Walter Wilkins enlisted as a private with the Norfolk Light Artillery Blues at Sewell's Point. After the battery was first posted in Petersburg, Private Wilkins was taken to the Ladies Hospital at the corner of Bollingbroke and Third Streets, suffering from typhoid fever. He died there on August 7, 1862. His body was returned to Norfolk after the war and interred in the Blues' plot in Elmwood Cemetery on April 2, 1866.

JAMES WILKINSON

James Wilkinson was born in Norfolk, Virginia and enlisted in the Norfolk Light Artillery Blues on April 18, 1861, at the age of 32. He served in the company as a private throughout the War Between the States and took part in all its engagements. He was captured on April 2, 1865, when the lines around Petersburg were broken, was confined at Point Lookout, and paroled on May 31, 1865. He returned to Norfolk where he worked as a lumber inspector and became a member of the Pickett-Buchanan Camp of Confederate Veterans. He died September 28, 1902, and was buried in the Blues plot in Elmwood Cemetery.

CLARENCE HENNING WILLIAMSON

Clarence Williamson was born March 13, 1846, to Lieutenant Thomas and Caroline Williamson in Portsmouth, Virginia. He enlisted in the Norfolk Light Artillery Blues on November 1, 1864, in Richmond and served as a private for the remainder of the War

Between the States. His brother Charles H. Williamson served as a surgeon in the Confederate Army. Clarence Williamson died March 12, 1911, and was buried in the family plot in Cedar Grove Cemetery in Portsmouth.

D. C. B. WILSON

Cary Wilson caught up with the Norfolk Light Artillery Blues on June 13, 1864, at Cold Harbor, Virginia and was enlisted by Captain Grandy as a private. He spent September through November of that year in Chimborazo Hospital, then returned to his company in Petersburg, where on November 27, he was severely wounded in the upper left leg by a sharpshooter's bullet. He took the "ironclad" oath in Richmond on May 17, 1865, and was paroled.

RICHARD C. M. WINGFIELD

Born in Portsmouth on June 3, 1837, Richard Wingfield was the son of John H. Wingfield, D.D. He enlisted in the Norfolk Light Artillery Blues as a private on April 20, 1861, at Pinner's Point after transferring from the Old Dominion Guards. He was with the Blues throughout the War Between the States, except for a period in 1862 and 1863 when he was sent to Chimborazo Hospital for rheumatism, and was detailed as a commissary sergeant. He was paroled with Lee's Army at Appomattox Court House in April 1865.

Wingfield married Elizabeth Susan Hudgins (1844–1926), the daughter of Robert K. and Sarah J. Hudgins. He worked as an insurance agent in Norfolk after the war, and rejoined the Blues as a corporal when the unit was reorganized in 1871. He was present when the Blues represented Virginia at the Centennial Celebration in Philadelphia in 1876. He was also a member of the Pickett-Buchanan Camp of Confederate Veterans and the Pocahontas Council, Royal Arcanum. He died October 15, 1890, at the age of 53. His funeral was held at Trinity Episcopal Church in Portsmouth, and was attended by the Blues, the Old Dominion Guard and Rifles, the Pickett-Buchanan Camp, and the Royal Arcanum. Robert Broughton and James Gilmer served as pallbearers. He was buried in Cedar Grove Cemetery, Portsmouth, and the Blues fired a three-volley salute from one of their guns over his grave.

JOHN WOODHOUSE

John Woodhouse arrived at the Confederate Conscript Camp in Petersburg on April 15, 1864, and was assigned to duty as a private in the Norfolk Light Artillery Blues on April 18. He joined the company in Albemarle County and served for the remainder of the War Between the States. He was captured at Petersburg the following April.

PHILIP D. WOODHOUSE

Philip Woodhouse lived in Norfolk and worked as a clerk in the drug store of George Dey and Company. He first joined the Norfolk Light Artillery Blues on January 23, 1860, at the age of 22. He served with the company as a private until September 15, 1862, when by special order, he was detailed as a hospital steward. He returned to duty with the Blues on December 23, 1864, and remained with the company for the rest of the war.

W. W. WOODWARD

W. Woodward enlisted as a private with the Norfolk Light Artillery Blues on October 26, 1864, in Petersburg.

JAMES R. WORRELL

On May 22, 1861, James Worrell enlisted for Confederate service in Richmond. From September of 1862 through February of 1863, he was confined to a Richmond hospital due to illness. On his release, he joined the Norfolk Light Artillery Blues and was wounded while in service with the battery during the Battle of Chancellorsville on May 1, 1863.

EDWIN L. WRIGHT

Edwin Wright joined the Blues on March 8, 1860, as a private and was enlisted for Confederate service on April 18, 1861, at the age of 21. During July and August of 1863, he was absent due to illness, but he otherwise served continuously with the battery and was promoted to the rank of corporal. He was captured, held for a time at Point Lookout, and was released on June 22, 1865.

JAMES R. WRIGHT

James Wright joined the Norfolk Light Artillery Blues on January 21, 1861, and enlisted as a private for Confederate service with the company on April 18, 1861, at the age of 20. He was promoted to 5th sergeant in September of 1862, and to 4th sergeant in May of 1863. He was captured and held prisoner at Point Lookout until June 22, 1865.

MINTON A. WRIGHT

Minton Wright was the second of eight children and the oldest son born to Penelope and Dr. David Minton Wright. He lived most of his youth in Edenton, North Carolina. In 1854, his father moved the family to Norfolk, Virginia, where he set up his home and practice at 20 West Main Street, near the U.S. Customs House. Dr. Wright earned the respect of the citizens of his new home when Yellow Fever swept Norfolk the following year and he remained to treat its many victims.

Minton Wright became a civil engineer, and on September 17, 1862, he enlisted in the Norfolk Light Artillery Blues as a private in Richmond. He transferred to the 57th North Carolina Infantry Regiment on April 7, 1863, and was appointed a second lieutenant. He was declared missing in action after the Battle of Gettysburg and presumed killed, although his body was never found. A few months later on October 23, 1863, his father was executed by hanging for shooting and killing a Federal lieutenant on the streets of Norfolk on July 11, 1863.

WILLIAM S. WRIGHT

William Wright enlisted as a private in the Norfolk Light Artillery Blues on October 17, 1862, in Richmond. He was present for service with the battery except during September and October of 1863 when he was sick. He took the "ironclad" oath in Richmond on April 16, 1865, thus ending his Confederate service.

ALEXANDER C. ZILLS

On May 9, 1862, just prior to the evacuation of Norfolk, Alexander Zills joined the Norfolk Light Artillery Blues. He was sick during November and December of that year, but otherwise served continuously as a private during the War Between the States.

JULIUS A. ZILLS

Julius Zills enlisted as a private in the Norfolk Light Artillery Blues on April 18, 1861, when Virginia seceded from the Union. He served as a private with the company until his parole in Richmond on April 13, 1865, almost exactly four years.

JOHN M. ZILLS

John Zills enlisted on April 18, 1861, and served the Norfolk Light Artillery Blues as a corporal during the War Between the States. He was captured when the lines around Petersburg were broken on April 2, 1865.

Bibliography

Sources

In addition to John Walters' diary, the information for this book was gathered from the microfilm files of Norfolk newspapers printed between 1829 and 1992 of the Kirn Memorial (Norfolk Public) Library, the collection of Norfolk City Directories in the Sargeant Memorial Room of the Kirn Memorial Library, and the following sources:

Published Works:

Burton, Harrison W. (Harry Scratch). *The History of Norfolk Virginia.* Norfolk: Norfolk Virginian Job And Print, 1877.

Historical Sketch of the Volunteers of Norfolk And Portsmouth, Virginia. Norfolk: 1898.

Porter, John W. H. *A Record of Events in Norfolk County, Virginia from April 19, 1861 to May 10, 1862, With a History of the Soldiers and Sailors of Norfolk County, Norfolk City, and Portsmouth Who Served in the Confederate Army or Navy.* Portsmouth: W. A. Fiske, 1892.

Sifakis, Stewart. *Who Was Who in the Civil War.* New York: Facts On File, 1988.

Stewart, William H. and Benjamin H. Trask, ed. *A Pair Of Blankets, War-Time History In Letters To The Young People Of The South.* Wilmington: Broadfoot Publishing Co., 1990.

War of the Rebellion, Official Records of the Union and Confederate Armies, 128 Volumes. Washington, D.C.: Government Printing Office, 1880.

Wise, Jennings C. *The Long Arm of Lee or The History Of The Artillery Of The Army Of Northern Virginia,* 2 Volumes. Lynchburg: J. P. Bell Co., 1915.

Unpublished Sources:

The Chrysler Museum. Todd, Westwood A. "Reminiscences of the War Between The States," as quoted in a letter from C. W. Grandy to Colonel William Sands, January 28, 1935. Chrysler Museum Archives, Norfolk Virginia.

————. Secretary's Minute Book, 1829–1841, Norfolk Light Artillery Blues, the Chrysler Museum Archives Norfolk, Virginia.

————. Secretary's Minute Book, 1860–1875, Norfolk Light Artillery Blues, the Chrysler Museum Archives, Norfolk, Virginia.

Macon, Thomas. "Reminiscences of the First Company of Richmond Howitzers." Richmond: Whittet and Shepperson.

National Archives, Washington, D.C., Compiled Service Records of Confederate Soldiers Who Served in Organizations From The State Of Virginia.

Norfolk Public Library, Norfolk, Virginia. United Confederate Veterans membership applications for the Pickett-Buchanan Camp in Norfolk (five volumes).

————. Records of Interment, Elmwood, Cedar Grove, Forest Lawn, and Magnolia Cemeteries, Norfolk, Virginia.

Office of the Clerk of Court. Marriage Records. Norfolk, Virginia.

United States Census, 1860.

University of Virginia, Alderman Library. Allyn, Joseph. Manuscript of a speech given to the Norfolk Light Artillery Blues. Charlottesville, Virginia.

Index

2nd Virginia Cavalry, 259
3rd Alabama Regiment, 22
3rd Virginia Regiment, 278
4th Virginia Regiment, 5, 301
5th Florida Regiment, 145
6th Virginia Regiment, 11, 14, 120, 258, 259, 266, 271
12th Virginia Regiment, 218
13th Virginia Cavalry, 42
16th Mississippi, 49
16th Virginia, 11, 271
18th Georgia, 35
19th Mississippi Regiment, 60
19th Virginia Regiment, 259
20th New York Cavalry, 247
29th "Blue and Gray" Division, 236, 237
41st Virginia, 120
46th Virginia (Richmond Blues), 185
53rd Virginia Regiment, 300
57th North Carolina Regiment, 313
61st Virginia, 36
64th Georgia Regiment, 134
99th New York Vol., 10
111th Field Artillery, VNG, 236-238, 247

A
Abbeville, South Carolina, 252
Alabama, CSS, 133
Albany, New York, 1, 154, 303
Alexandria, Virginia, 290

Allyn, Pvt. Joseph T. (NLAB), 15, 16, 239, 242, 243, 269, 283
Amelia Court House, Virginia, 177, 219, 220, 285, 288, 289
Amsterdam, Holland, 1, 29, 154, 155, 303
Anderson, Gen. Richard H. (CSA), 62, 64, 98, 134, 173
Division, 46, 67, 73, 97, 98, 101, 109, 115, 116, 121
Anderson's Station, Virginia, 120
Andrews, Gov. John (Massachussets), 140
Appomattox Court House, Virginia, 218, 219, 221, 230, 243, 246, 248, 250, 253, 254, 256, 260, 264, 275, 278, 284, 285, 289, 294, 296, 303, 311
Appomattox River, 210, 220, 227
Aquia, Virginia, 111
Aquitania (troop ship), 236
Archer, Gen. F. H. (CSA), 126
Archer, Gen. James J. (CSA), 77, 93
Tennessee Brigade, 93
Army of Northern Virginia, 17, 46, 219, 224, 248, 253, 260, 264, 271, 284, 287, 296
Army of Tennessee, 109, 181
Ashby, Gen. Turner (CSA), 87
Ashland, Virginia, 121
Ashton, Pvt. John C. (NLAB), 239, 243, *244*
Atlanta, Georgia, 135, 150, 151, 160, 194
Atlantic Lodge, Nr. 2, A. F.& M., 234, 292, 304
Averell, Gen. William (USA), 118, 131

316

B

Bagnall, Pvt. Richard D. (NLAB), 239, 245
Baltimore and Ohio RR, 176
Baltimore, Maryland, 6, 132, 245, 254, 264, 297, 299, 300, 301, 302
Banks' Ford, Virginia, 53, 54, 55
Banks, Pvt. Richard (NLAB), 6, 239, 245
Barksdale, Gen. William (CSA), 77
Barraud, Pvt. C. D. (NLAB), 239, 246
Bartlett, Gen. (USA), 138
Barton, Gen. Francis S. (CSA), 96
Battery (Fort) Gregg, Petersburg, Virginia, 211, 212
Battery 45, Petersburg, Virginia, 205, 206, 210, 211, 212, 217
Beale, Pvt. H. (NLAB), 239, 246
Beauregard, Gen. Pierre G. (CSA), 113, 125, 160
Beaver Dam, Virginia, 37
Bee, Gen. Barnard E. (CSA), 96
"Beefsteak Raid", 156
Bell, Pvt. Albert S. (NLAB), 239, 246
Bell, Pvt. Norman (NLAB), 239, 246
Benjamin, Judah P., 197
Benson, Pvt. O. S. (NLAB), 161, 239, 247
Berkley, Virginia, 282, 287
Bermuda Hundred, Virginia, 25, 125
Berryville, Virginia, 69
Beverly Ford, Virginia, 42
Bishop, Pvt. William J. E. (NLAB), 239, 247
Blackwater River, 19
Blackwater Swamp, 156
Blow, Pvt. Walter W. (NLAB), 239, 248
Blue Ridge Mountains, 39, 69, 88, 93, 95, 188
Blues Memorial and Benevolent Association, 231-233, 243, 268, 287, 292, 301, 304, 307
Boisseau Farm, Petersburg, Virginia, 210, 212, 218
Boonsboro, Maryland, 80
Booth(e), Corp. William (NLAB), 219, 239, 248
Borum, Pvt. Charles (NLAB), 83, 239, 248
Boston, Massachussets, 281
Boush's Bluff, Virginia, 6, 8
Bradford, Pvt. Otey (NLAB), 83, 239, 248, 249
Bragg, Gen. Braxton (CSA), 91
Brandy Station, Virginia, 35, 41, 45, 51, 99
Branham, Pvt. John B. (NLAB), 239, 249
Breckenridge, Maj. Gen. John C. (CSA), 118, 120, 131, 157, 189

Brickhouse, Pvt. Benjamin D. (NLAB), 239, 249, 299
Brickhouse, Pvt. Smith N. (NLAB), 239, 249, 250
Bristoe, Virginia, 96, 98
Broad River, 98
Brock, Pvt. Lysander A. (NLAB), 239, 250
Brooklyn, New York, 282
Brooks, Lama, 32, 36
Brooks, Pvt. E. W. (NLAB), 239, 251
Brown, Col. John Thompson (CSA), 112
Broughton, Corp. Robt. (NLAB), 216, 239, 251, 269, 299, 302, 311
Brown, John, 4, 72, 140
Brown, Pvt. Charles (NLAB), 239, 251
Brown, Pvt. E. P. (NLAB), 239, 251
Brown, Pvt. Henry C. (NLAB), 239, 252
Brown, Pvt. James W. (NLAB), 239, 252, 253
Brown, Pvt. John B. (NLAB), 83, 239, 252
Browne, Pvt. Joseph S. (NLAB), 239, 253
Browne, Pvt. Victor H. (NLAB), 239, 253
Buchanan, Cdr. (Adm.) Franklin (CSN), 15, 142
Burgess Mill, Virginia, 214, 215
Burkville Junction, Virginia, 225, 228, 288
Buskey, Corp. Charles H. (NLAB), 239, 253, 254, 303
Butler, Corp. Robert (NLAB), 138, 231, 239, 254
Butler, Gen. Benjamin (USA), 10, 13, 84, 125

C

Caledonia, Pennsylvania, 74
Camp Hoffman, Maryland, 279
Camp Lee, Virginia, 236
Capps, Pvt. Leonard O. (NLAB), 239, 254
Carolina War Maneuvers, 236
Carroll, Pvt. William S. (NLAB), 239, 254, 255
Cashtown, Pennsylvania, 74
Cedar Grove Cemetery, Norfolk, Virginia, 231, 251, 254, 261, 267, 270, 279, 287, 292, 295, 298, 299, 302, 307
Cedar Grove Cemetery, Portsmouth, Virginia, 244, 252, 276, 282, 285, 288, 293, 308, 311
Cedar Run, Virginia, 40
Chaffin's Bluff, Virginia, 159
Chamberlaine, Pvt. Andrew E. (NLAB), 239, 255
Chambersburg, Pennsylvania, 141, 160
Chambliss, Col. John R. (CSA), 36, 42

Chancellorsville, Virginia, 62, 63, 64, 68, 101, 112, 113, 157, 253, 258, 265, 280, 281, 283, 286, 291, 306, 310, 312
Charleston, South Carolina, 141
Charles Town, (West) Virginia, 31, 70-72
Charlotte, North Carolina, 252
Charlottesville, Virginia, 32, 110, 118, 249, 259, 260, 261, 273, 298, 300
Chesterfield Station, Virginia, 51, 64
Chester Gap, Virginia, 69
Chicago, Illinois, 149
Chickahominy River, 122
Chilesburg, Virginia, 65
Chimborazo Hospital, 103, 255, 258, 259, 261, 264, 265, 266, 267, 270, 274, 278, 280, 285, 287, 289, 290, 293, 294, 309, 310, 311
Cincinnati, Ohio, 195
City Point (Hopewell), Virginia, 246, 250, 257, 264, 267, 269, 273, 274, 278, 291, 297, 307
Clark, Frederick W., 2, 3, 16, 53, 58, 303
Clark Mountain, Virginia, 93, *95*
Clark, Pvt. William T. (NLAB), 239, 255
Clifton Springs, New York, 292
Clingman's Brigade, 114
Clover Hill (Appomattox), Virginia, 221, 222
Cobb, Gen. Thomas R. (CSA), 48
Cobham Station, Virginia, 106
Cocke, Pvt. Phillip (NLAB), 239, 255, 256
Cocke, Pvt. William R. C. (NLAB), 239, 256
Coggin's Point, Virginia, 30, 156
Cold Harbor, Virginia, 263, 274, 311
Collins, Pvt. W. W. (NLAB), 239, 256
Colquit, Capt. (CSA), 8, 9
Colston, Gen. R. E. (CSA), 126
Columbus (Georgia) Light Guard, 8
Columbia, South Carolina, 287
Confederate Soldiers Home, Richmond, Virginia, 273
Congress, USS, 15
Cooke, Gen. John R. (CSA), 97, 98, Brigade, 114
Cooke, Pvt. John S. (NLAB), 239, 256
Cooke, Pvt. Merritt T. (NLAB), 218, 239, 257, 274, 292, 299
Corley, Col. James L. (CSA), 253
Cornick, Pvt. Henry (NLAB), 83, 239, 257
Cox, Pvt. William R. (NLAB), 239, 257
Craney Island, Virginia, 2, 6, 17, 262, 288, 302
Crater (the Battle of), 139, 140, 168, 244, 254, 258, 265, 281, 288, 298
Crenshaw Battery, 115, 145, 211, 214

Criglersville, Virginia, 89
Culpepper Court House, Virginia, 40, 68, 94, 96, 99
Cumberland Court House, Virginia, 220
Cumberland, USS, 15
Custer, Gen. George A. (USA), 223
Cutherell, Pvt. William S. (NLAB), 240, 258
Cutt's Battalion (CSA), 143, 152

D

Dacotah, USS, 15
Dales, Brig. Gen. (CSA), 117
Danville (Richmond &) Railroad, 194
Danville, Virginia, 158, 219, 288
Davis, President Jefferson, 16, 83, 172, 187, 196, 197, 235, 266
Davis' Brigade, 114, 121, 155
Day, Pvt. John H. (NLAB), 64, 240, 258
Deep Bottom, Virginia, 136
DeFord, Pvt. D. N. (NLAB), 240, 258
Denson, Pvt. Alex J. (NLAB), 240, 258
Deshler, Col. James (CSA), 27
Dimmock Line, 126
Dinwiddie Court House, Virginia, 178, 211, 213
Dismal Swamp Canal, 14
Donaldsonville (Louisiana) Artillery, 46, 66, 67, 111, 150, 201, 214
Doughtie, Pvt. H. S. (NLAB), 216, 240, 259
Doyle, Pvt. Walter H. (NLAB), 218, 240, 257, *259, 260, 274*
Drewry's Bluff, Virginia, 25, 26, 27, 31, 125, 142
Drummond, Pvt. Charles H. (NLAB), 240, 260
Drummond, Pvt. Richard J. (NLAB), 240, 260, 261
Dubuque, Iowa, 297
Dunn's Hill, Virginia, 19, 20, 125
Dunn, Pvt. J. R. (NLAB), 240, 261
Dunn, Pvt. William H. (NLAB), 240, 261
Dutch Gap, Virginia, 157

E

Eagle, Capt. Henry (USN), 9
Early, Gen. Jubal A. (CSA), 131, 141, 147, 150, 156-158, 160, 165
Corps, 175
Division, 86
Eastville, Virginia, 255
Edenton, North Carolina, 312
Edinburg, Virginia, 86, 87
Ege, Eddy M., 33, 34, 103, 135, 146, 149, 150, 151, 152, 153, 155, 156, 162, 165, 166, 172, 206, 209, 210

Ege, J. L., 32, 36, 103, 105, 136, 191, 195, 199, 228
Ege, John B. and Mrs., 21, 23, 28, 34, 103-105, 125, 128, 130, 134-136, 141, 142, 143, 147, 153, 162, 164, 165, 166, 174, 176, 178, 180, 181, 190, 199, 200, 201, 204, 205, 207, 208, 209, 217, 228, 229
Elizabeth City, North Carolina, 14
Elizabeth River, 6, 8, 14, 15, 245, 299
Elliott, Brig. Gen. Steven Jr. (CSA), 138
Elliott, Pvt. John W. (NLAB), 240, 262
Elliott, Pvt. Julius A. (NLAB), 5, 83, 240, 261, 262, 299
Elliott, Pvt. Thomas E. (NLAB), 240, 263, 306
Elliott, Pvt. Thomas H. (NLAB), 83, 240, 262
Elliott Salient, 139
Elmwood Cemetery, Norfolk, Virginia, 85, 231, 232, 234, 237, 243, 245, 247-250, 253-255, 257, 258, 260, 262, 263, 266, 268-270, 272, 273, 277, 278, 283-285, 287-289, 291-293, 295-297, 299, 301, 302, 305-310
Essex, USS, 292
Ettricks, Virginia, 217
Evans, Pvt. Richard (NLAB), 240, 263
Ewell, Lt. Gen. Richard (CSA), 68, 74, 76, 92, 96, 97, 99, 113, 114, 118, 119
Corps, 90, 101, 112, 131
Express (steamboat), 13

F

Fairfax Gap, Pennsylvania, 79, 81
Fairfield, Pennsylvania, 78
Falling Waters, (West) Virginia, 261
Falmouth, Virginia, 47
Fanny (gunboat), 13
Farmville, Virginia, 220, 226, 227, 248, 263
Fayetteville, Pennsylvania, 73
Featherston, Gen. Winfield S. (CSA), 53
Fenn, Will, 207-209, 217, 229
Fields, Gen. Charles W. (CSA), 134
Division, 134, 135
Finegan, Gen. Joseph (CSA), 121, 170
Florida Brigade, 145, 152
Finn's Point, New Jersey, 293
Fisher's Hill, Virginia, 157, 158
Fitchburg, Massachusetts, 10
Fitzgerald, Pvt. D. (NLAB), 218, 240, 263
Fitzgerald, Pvt. Edwin (NLAB), 218, 240, 263, 264
Fitzgerald, Pvt. W. (NLAB), 218, 240, 264
Five Forks, Virginia, 211
Fletcher, Pvt. Frank (NLAB), 240, 264, 265

Flint Hill, Virginia, 69
Floyd, Pvt. Joseph W. (NLAB), 62, 64, 240, 265
Floyd's Brigade, 242
Forest Lawn Cemetery, Norfolk, Virginia, 234, 237, 306
Forrest, Gen. Nathan B. (CSA), 139, 160
Forts
    Clifton, Virginia, 252
    Darling, Virginia, 26
    Delaware, Delaware, 263, 293
    Fisher, North Carolina, 181, 182, 189
    Gains, Alabama, 142
    Gilmer, Virginia, 159
    Harrison, Virginia, 159
    Monroe, Virginia, 6, 8, 9, 10, 13-16, 31, 48, 125, 235, 266
    Morgan, Alabama, 142
    Norfolk, Virginia, 6, 84
    Oglethorpe, Georgia, 236
    Pillow, Tennessee, 138-140
    Sumter, South Carolina, 5, 30, 138
    Wagner, South Carolina, 140
    Wool, Virginia, 13
Frankstown, Pennsylvania, 73
Fredericksburg, Virginia, 36, 42, 43, 47, 52, 55, 59, 63, 65, 67, 113, 141, 228, 265, 271, 278
Frederick's Hall, Virginia, 38
Freeman, Pvt. Joseph M. Jr. (NLAB), 36, 37, 83, 240, 265
French, Brig. Gen. Samuel G. (CSA), 30
Frogtown, Pennsylvania, 79
Front Royal, Virginia, 69, 85

G

Gaines Mill, Virginia, 122, 125
Gamage, Pvt. John O. (NLAB), 16, 151, 186, 240, 265, 266, 280
Garnett, Lt. Col. John J. (CSA), 63, 66, 67, 76, 82, 106-109, 111, 289
Artillery Battalion, 69, 106-109
Gary's Brigade (CSA), 220
Gaskins, Pvt. George O. (NLAB), 206, 231, 240, 266
Gatch, Pvt. J. A. (NLAB), 240, 266
Germanna Ford, Virginia, 94, 113
Gettysburg, Pennsylvania, 76, 78, 83-85, 90, 91, 161, 261, 263, 288, 293, 313
Ghiselin, Pvt. Horace (NLAB), 240, 267
Ghiselin, Pvt. Richard (NLAB), 240, 267
Gilmer, Lt. (Capt.) James W. (NLAB), 218, 234, 240, 267, 268, 287, 302, 311
Gilmer, Mr. John A., 197

Gilmore, Mr. J. Y. and Mrs. Maggie, 148, 153, 159, 166, 172, 178, 180, 186, 190, 191

Goodrich, Pvt. Alex J. (NLAB), 240, 249, *268*

Gordan, Pvt. George W. (NLAB), 240, 269

Gordan, Pvt. Joseph P. (NLAB), 240, 269, 270

Gordon, Lt. Gen. John B. (CSA), 117
    Corps, 224

Gordon, Pvt. Morton (NLAB), 240, 270

Gordonsville, Virginia, 38, 39, 42, 51, 85, 87, 89, 91, 102, 103, 110, 112, 114, 157

Gosport Navy Yard, Virginia, 4, 6, 15, 17, 252

Gracie, Gen. Archibald Jr. (CSA), 177
    Alabama Brigade, 141, 168

Grandy, Capt. Charles R. (NLAB), 14, 24, 37, 63, 64, 67, 76, 106, 177, 189, 216, 218, 219, 228, 231-233, 240, *270-272*, 284, 291, 308, 309, 311

Grandy, Maj. C. W. (CSA), 247, 250

Grant, Gen. Ulysses S. (USA), 113, 114, 116-120, 122, 124, 130-132, 136, 139, 142, 144, 149, 158, 159, 162-164, 173, 178, 185, 201, 203, 210, 213, 215, 216, 223, 267

Graves, Pvt. Charles M. (NLAB), 240, 272

Greensboro, North Carolina, 287

Greenville, South Carolina, 300

Greenwich, Virginia, 97

Gregg, Gen. Maxcy (CSA), 48

Grice Commandery, Knights Templar, 304

Grice, Maj. George W. (CSA), 287

Groner, Gen. Virginius (CSA), 299

Gwaltney, Pvt. J. T. (NLAB), 240, 272

Gwaltney, Pvt. Richard H. (NLAB), 240, 273, 302

H

Hagerstown, Maryland, 72, 80, 263

Haines, Pvt. James M. D. (NLAB), 240, 273

Hallett, Pvt. William R. (NLAB), 240, 273

Halstead, Pvt. Richard T. (NLAB), 240, 273

Hampton, Gen. Wade (CSA), 113, 156, 157, 168, 179

Hampton Roads, 8, 10, 13, 14, 235

Hampton, Virginia, 245, 280

Hancock's Corps, 115

Hanover Junction, Virginia, 37, 64, 119

Hardee, Gen. William J. (CSA), 135

Harper's Ferry, Virginia, 4, 131, 140

Harrison's Landing, Virginia, 29

Harris' Brigade, 114, 116, 120, 145, 152, 168, 171

Hart's Island, New York, 256

Hatcher's Run, Virginia, 211, 255, 268, 281

Hatton, Pvt. John F. (NLAB), 201, 240, 274

Haughton, Pvt. Armistead J. (NLAB), 240, 274

Hays, Gen. Alexander (USA), 114

Hays' Brigade (Gen. Harry T.) (CSA), 99

Hazel River, 96, 99

Heth, Maj. Gen. Henry (CSA), 77, 134, 168
    Division, 69, 70, 81, 97, 101, 115, 148

Hicksford, Virginia, 109

Higgins, Pvt. Andrew (NLAB), 240, 257, 274

Higgins, Pvt. Ignatius (NLAB), 123, 124, 135, 231, 240, 257, 274

Hill, Gen. Ambrose P. (CSA), 61, 92, 97, 134
    Corps, 69, 80, 90, 101

Hill, Gen. Daniel H. (CSA), 30

Hill, Pvt. Albert (NLAB), 240, 275

Hoag's Brigade, 99

Hodges, Pvt. John M. (NLAB), 240, 275

Hodges, Pvt. (Capt.) Samuel (NLAB), 234, 240, 275

Hoge, Rev. Dr. Moses, 196, 198

Hoke, Gen. Robert F. (CSA), 114
    Division, 122, 175

Holcomb Legion, 168

Holden, Miss Serena, 242, 257, 260, 263, 274, 286, 295, 298

Hollywood Cemetery, Richmond, Virginia, 235

Holmes, Maj. Gen. Theophilus (CSA), 27

Holmes, Pvt. William H. (NLAB), 240, 275, 276

Hood, Gen. John B. (CSA), 77, 135
    Texas Brigade, 129, 134

Hooker, Gen. Joseph (USA), 56, 61, 113

Hudgins, Sgt. George C. (NLAB), 240, 276

Huger, Gen. Benjamin (CSA), 11, 14, 282

Huger, Capt. (Col.) Frank (CSA), 11, 221
    Battery (Norfolk Light Artillery), 11, 14, 46, 66, 67, 111, 150, 214, 215, 237

Hume, Pvt. Richard G. (NLAB), 240, 276

Hunter, Maj. Gen. David (USA), 131

Hunter, Senator Robert M. T., 194, 196

Hunter, Pvt. James F. (NLAB), 240, 276, 277, 299

I

Imboden, Brig. Gen. John D. (CSA), 118, 131

"Ironclad Oath" of Allegiance, 230, 246, 250, 255-257, 261-264, 267, 269, 272-274, 277-280, 285, 292, 295, 296, 300, 309, 311, 313

J

Jackson, Lt. Gen. T. J. "Stonewall" (CSA), 31, 47, 61, 63, 65, 66, 128, 157, 196, 197
  Corps, 59
James, Gen. Wm. E. (CSA), 118, 132
James, Pvt. Henry W. (NLAB), 240, 277
James River, 17, 26, 29, 30, 120, 124, 136, 161, 229
Jamestown, CSS, 282
Jamestown Exposition, 235
Jenkins, Gen. Micah (CSA), 113
Johnson, Capt. Marmaduke (CSA), 92
Johnson, Gen. Joseph E. (CSA), 113, 131, 181, 194, 213
  Army, 284
Johnson, Gen. Bushrod (CSA), 168, 171, 173
  Division, 101, 116, 174, 183
Johnson's Island, Ohio, 232, 245, 258, 267, 272, 291
Johnson, Pvt. Ames C. (NLAB), 83, 240, 277
Johnson, Pvt. Augustus W. (NLAB), 216, 240, 277
Johnson, Pvt. John W. (NLAB), 240, 277
John Walters Chapter Nr. 68, 234, 305
Jones, Brig. Gen. John M. (CSA), 112
Jones Crossroads, Maryland, 72
Jones, (Gen. D. R.) Division, 109
Jones, Pvt. George (NLAB), 240, 278
Jones, Pvt. R. Henry (NLAB), 240, 278, 283
Jordan's Battery, 62, 64, 258
Joynes, Pvt. Custis T. (NLAB), 127, 240, 278, 279
Joynes, Pvt. Solon H. (NLAB), 240, 279
Joynes, Pvt. William C. (NLAB), 240, 280

K

Kahukee (tugboat), 8
Keeling, Pvt. John L. (NLAB), 240, 280, 281
Keeling, Pvt. (Capt.) M. C. (NLAB), 63, 234, 240, 266, 268, 280-282
Keeling, S(QM) John E. (NLAB), 240, 280
Kershaw, Gen. Joseph B. (CSA), 136, 157
  Division, 122, 175
Kilby, Pvt. William T. (NLAB), 240, 282
King, Capt. Miles (NLAB), 3
King, Pvt. Warrington C. (NLAB), 240, 282
Kirkland, Gen. William W. (CSA), 97, 98
  Brigade, 114
Knights of Honor, 286
Knights of Pythias, 288
Knights Templar, 294, 304, 305
Knotts Island, North Carolina, 308

L

Lamar, Col. John H. (CSA), 145
Lamb, Capt. William W. (CSA), 8
Lamb, W. W., 16
LaMountain, John, 13
Lander's Brigade, 92
Lane's Brigade, 101, 218, 242
Land, Pvt. William A. (NLAB), 240, 282, 283
Land, Pvt. W. C. (NLAB), 62, 64, 231, 240, 283
Landry, Capt. R. Prosper (CSA), 111
LeCompte, Pvt. John W. (NLAB), 240, 283
Lee, Gen. Robert E. (CSA), 16, 29, 30, 36, 44, 45, 49, 61, 63, 64, 74, 77, 79, 91, 100, 106, 109, 111, 113, 118, 121, 125, 130, 131, 134, 149, 150, 153, 159, 163, 164, 173, 175, 177, 178, 181, 182, 188, 192, 196, 197, 203, 211, 213, 220, 221, 223-225, 242, 246, 248, 251, 253, 260, 271, 275, 285, 287-289, 291, 298, 311
Lee, Maj. Gen. William. H. (CSA), 225
Lee, Pvt. F. Dean (NLAB), 67, 127, 170, 171, 240, 245, 283, 284
Lee, Pvt. Leroy M. Jr. (NLAB), 240, 245, 284
Lee, Rev. Leroy, 67, 245, 247, 283
Leitersburg, Maryland, 73, 80
Letcher, Gov. John (Virginia), 5, 6
Lewis, Capt. John W. (CSA), 67, 76
  Battery (Pittsylvania Artillery), 44, 46, 47, 54, 66, 67, 76
Lexington, Virginia, 118, 120, 131
Libby Prison, Richmond, Virginia, 251, 259, 273, 277
Liberty Mills, Virginia, 110
Lightfoot, Lt. Col. Charles E. (CSA), 32, 36
Lincoln, President Abraham, 5, 16, 17, 35, 56, 57, 84, 135, 155, 158, 169, 172-174, 187, 196
Lincolnton, North Carolina, 221
Lindsay's Turnout, Virginia, 102, 106
Longstreet, Gen. James (CSA), 73, 91, 114, 219, 220
  Corps, 40, 44, 46, 73, 76, 90, 122
Louisa Court House, Virginia, 38
Lovitt, Pvt. Henry C. (NLAB), 171, 240, 284, 285
Lovitt, Pvt. Robert C. (NLAB), 240, 284, 285
Luray Valley, Virginia, 157, 158
Lynchburg, Virginia, 67, 118, 131, 148, 153, 157, 221, 222, 251, 254, 257-259, 268, 278

M

MacClellan, Gen. George B. (USA), 25, 29, 30, 31, 149, 155, 158, 169, 172, 173
Macon, Georgia, 147
Macon, T. J. (CSA), 55
Madison Court House, Virginia, 89
Magnolia Cemetery, Berkley, Virginia, 282
Mahone, Gen. William (CSA), 19, 59, 127, 128, 134, 137-139, 144, 145, 168, 170, 221, 229
   Brigade, 57, 60, 61, 64, 81, 97, 114, 116, 127, 137, 151,168, 174
   Division, 173
Malborn, Pvt. Oscar J. (NLAB), 240, 285
Malvern Hill, Virginia, 29, 124, 243
Manassas, Virginia, 11, 12, 96, 174, 255
Martinsburg, (West) Virginia, 82, 131
Masi, Pvt. Frank J. (NLAB), 240, 285
Massanutten Mountain, 87
Massaponax Church, Virginia, 52
Mattaponi River, 51
Maupin, Pvt. George W. O. Jr. (NLAB), 240, 285
Maurin, Capt. Victor (CSA), 67, 76
McCarrick, Pvt. Alex D. (NLAB), 148, 231, 240, 286
McGowan's Brigade, 101, 210, 211
McGrath's Ford, Virginia, 44
McGuire, Joseph B. (NLAB), 240, 286
McIntosh's Battalion, 97, 98
McKeown, Pvt. C. K. (NLAB), 63, 64, 240, 286
McKinney, Texas, 280
McLaws, Maj. Gen. Lafayette, (CSA), 61
McPherson, Maj. Gen. James (USA), 135
Meade, Gen. George G. (USA), 90-92, 100, 101, 120
Mechanicsville, Virginia, 110, 121
Merrimac (CSS Virginia), 15-17, 19, 266
Mexican Punitive Expedition, 236
Middleton, Virginia, 85, 86
Milroy, Gen. Robert H. (USA), 68, 71, 89, 90
Minnesota, USS, 15, 17
Mitchell Station, Virginia, 94
Mobile, Alabama, 142
Monitor, USS, 15, 16, 18, 19, 27, 235, 306
Montague, Cpl. William. D. (NLAB), 108, 177, 240, 286, 287
Montgomery, Alabama, 256
Monticello, USS, 8, 9, 298
Moore, Capt. Joseph D. (CSA), 67, 76
   Battery, 111, 115

Moore, Lt. Henry V. (NLAB), 177, 218, 240, 287
Moore, Pvt. John W. (NLAB), 240, 287
Moore, Pvt. Joseph P. Jr. (NLAB), 240, 288
Morgan, Brig. Gen. John H. (CSA), 118
Morris, Pvt. David P. (NLAB), 240, 288
Morris, Pvt. John J. (NLAB), 240, 288, 289
Morse, Pvt. Burwell N. (NLAB), 241, 289
Mosby, Col. John S. (CSA), 132
Mosley's Artillery Battalion, 180
Mount Jackson, Virginia, 86
Mullins, Lt. Col. Thornton, 237
Mystic, USS, 15

N

Nash, Lt. Thomas, Jr. (CSA), 8
Nash, Pvt. John H. (NLAB), 241, 289
Nash, Pvt. Wadsworth (NLAB), 241, 289, 290
Nashville, Tennessee, 269
New Baltimore, Virginia, 96
New Market, Virginia, 65, 86, 87, 88, 255, 256
New Orleans, Louisiana, 235, 281
Newport News, Virginia, 10, 277
New Store, Virginia, 221
Newton, Pvt. C. A. (NLAB), 143, 241, 290
Newtown, Virginia, 83, 85, 86
New York, New York, 5, 109, 287
Nimmo, Lt. William (NLAB), 14, 46, 241, 290
Nimmo, Pvt. Powhatan E. (NLAB), 241, 290
Norfolk Academy, 246, 250, 298, 300
Norfolk and Petersburg RR, 19, 229, 254
Norfolk and Western RR, 235, 277
"Norfolk Beacon", 2
Norfolk City Guard, 299
Norfolk Harbor Guards, 6, 8
"Norfolk Journal", 230, 303
Norfolk Juniors, 6, 8, 9, 292
"Norfolk Landmark", 278
Norfolk Light Artillery (Huger Battery), 11, 14, 46, 66, 67, 111, 150, 214, 215, 237
Norfolk Naval Base, 235
Norfolk Southern RR, 293
Norfolk, Virginia, 1-3, 5, 6, 8, 9, 11, 13, 14, 16-20, 22, 23, 28-30, 33, 40, 41, 45, 53, 58, 59, 66, 71, 84, 91, 92, 125, 134, 148, 151, 167, 177, 218, 228-238, 242, 243, 245, 247-249, 253-255, 257-263, 265-300, 302, 303, 306-309, 311-313
   Churches
      Chestnut Street Church, 282
      Christ Church, 292, 299

Cumberland Street Church, 268, 284, 300, 308
Epworth Episcopal Church, 249
First Presbyterian Church, 301
Freemason Street Baptist Church, 287, 294, 300
Granby Street M. E. Church, 284, 290
McKendree M. E. Church, 234, 304, 305
Queen Street M. E. Church, 250
Sacred Heart R. C. Church, 260
Saint Luke's Episcopal Church, 273, 283, 302
Saint Mary's R. C. Church, 231, 266, 286
Saint Paul's Episcopal Church, 243, 245, 253, 269
Second Presbyterian Church, 251
"Norfolk Virginian", 287
Norsworthy, Pvt. Joseph C. (NLAB), 241, 290, 291
Northampton (ship), 13
North Anna River, 119, 120
Norvell, Pvt. C. R. (NLAB), 241, 291
NYP&N (New York, Phila. & Norfolk) RR, 292
Ny River, 51, 115

O

Oak Grove, Virginia, 20, 28, 31
Ocean View, Norfolk Co. Virginia, 8, 16
Odd Fellows Society, 247, 248
Okeson, Rev. Nicholas A., 243, 246, 269, 297
Old Capitol Prison, D.C., 245, 258, 261, 267, 272
Old Dominion Guards, 252, 253, 276, 282, 288, 311
Old Dominion Steamship Company, 247
Old Point Comfort, Virginia, 8, 19
Omaha Beach, 237
Onancock, Virginia, 278
Orange & Alexandria RR, 35, 39, 94, 97, 98, 113
Orange Court House, Virginia, 40, *41*, 91, 100, 102, 157, 275, 277, 288, 295

P

Parker's Store, Virginia, 113
Pawnee, USS, 6
Peet, Lt. William T. (NLAB), 37, 63, 64, 218, 219, 241, 251, 252, 291, 292
Peet, Pvt. James D. (NLAB), 241, 291
Pegram, Lt. Col. William (CSA), 145
Pegram's Battalion, 119, 215
Pegram's Battery, 76, 138

Pemberton, Lt. Gen. John C. (CSA), 130
Pender, Maj. Gen. William D. (CSA), 77
Division, 70, 81
Pendleton, Gen. William N. (CSA), 30, 66, 109, 111, 289
Penick, Capt. Nathan (CSA), 111
Pensacola, USS, 292
Perrin, Brig. Gen. Abner M. (CSA), 117
Perry's Brigade, 56, 60, 61, 121, 156
Pershing, Gen. John J., 236
"Petersburg Express", 148, 210
Petersburg "Rifles", 12th Virginia, 218
"Petersburg Sun", 22
Petersburg, Virginia, 16, 17, 19, 21-25, 27, 29, 31-34, 43, 46, 58, 59, 71, 103, 104, 113, 124-126, 133, 136, 139, 141, 147, 156, 158, 164, 177, 189, 193, 199, 203, 205, 209, 217-220, 228, 229, 231, 233, 242-248, 250-252, 254-266, 269, 272-275, 277, 278, 280, 282, 284-301, 303, 306-308, 310, 311, 313
Churches
Grace (High Street) Church, 22, 153,160, 166, 173, 180, 186, 204-206, 229, 298
Market Street M. E. Church, 19, 208, 210
Saint Paul's Church, 204, 206
Pettigrew's (Brig. Gen. J. J.) Brigade, 68
Petty, Pvt. John C. (NLAB), 218, 241, 292
Philadelphia Centennial, 235, 275, 311
Philadelphia, Pennsylvania, 254, 281, 299
Phillips, Major Louisa (CSA), 195
Pickett-Buchanan Camp, Conf. Veterans, 233, 243, 245, 248-251, 254, 255, 257, 258, 260, 262, 263, 266, 268, 269, 272, 273, 275-280, 282, 287-289, 291, 294, 299, 301, 304, 307, 309, 310, 311
Pickett-Buchanan Chapter, UDC, 232, 243, 253, 260
Pickett, Maj. Gen. George (CSA), 77, 113, 235
Division, 79, 215
Pittsburgh, Pennsylvania, 141
Pittsylvania Battery, 46, 67, 111
Po River, 51, 116
Poague's (Lt. Col. William T.) Battallion, 97, 114, 119, 145
Point Lookout, Maryland, 244, 246, 250, 255-257, 260-262, 264, 265, 267, 269, 272-275, 277-282, 284-286, 288-290, 293, 294, 296, 297, 301, 306-308, 310, 312
Porter, Pvt. Robert T. (NLAB), 241, 292

Portsmouth Artillery, 2
Portsmouth, Virginia, 6, 13, 16, 17, 84, 177, 243, 244, 249, 251-253, 258, 273, 276, 278, 282, 285, 287, 288, 293, 300, 307, 308, 310, 311
  Churches
    Monumental M. E. Church, 288
    Trinity Episcopal Church, 285, 311
Posey's Brigade (Gen. Carnot) (CSA), 57, 97, 114
Potomac River, 72, 80, *81*, 131
Price, Gen. Sterling (CSA), 118

Q

"Quaker" gun, 93
Queen Mary (troop ship), 236
Quincy, Pennsylvania, 73

R

Raccoon Ford, Virginia, 42
Rainier, Pvt. John T. (NLAB), 128, 241, 293
Raleigh, North Carolina, 253
Ransom, Gen. Robert, Jr. (CSA), 32, 132
  Brigade, 114
Rapidan Ford, Virginia, 92, 100
Rapidan River, 40, 42, *92*, 93, 94, 95, 99, 100, 102, 106, 110
Rapidan Station, Virginia, 91, 92
Rappahannock River, Virginia, 36, 47, 55, 96, 98, 259, 308
Redman's Association, 301
Reid, Pvt. John S. (NLAB), 176, 241, 293
Reynolds, Pvt. Joseph B. (NLAB), 241, 293
Reynolds, Pvt. Robert E. (NLAB), 83, 241, 293
Richardson, Maj. Charles (Col.) (CSA), 82, 111, 215, 228, 271
  Battalion, 113, 237, 245, 258, 275, 309
Richmond and Fredericksburg RR, 51
Richmond Blues (46th Va.), 185
Richmond Grays, 41
Richmond Howitzers, 55
Richmond, Virginia, 6, 16, 22, 26, 29-32, 36, 43, 45, 48, 50, 51, 56, 58, 61, 66, 79, 83, 102, 103, 105, 106, 113, 120, 123, 125, 130, 135, 136, 141-143, 145, 153, 157, 158, 164, 169, 172, 174-176, 178, 184, 187, 189, 190, 191, 199, 202, 203, 210, 217, 219, 228, 229, 233, 246, 248, 249-252, 256-259, 261, 263-266, 272, 273, 276-282, 285-287, 289- 298, 300, 303, 306-313
  Churches
    African Church of Richmond, 195
    Saint John's Church, 191

Rip Raps (Fort Wool, Virginia), 10, 13
Rippon, (West) Virginia, 70
Rives, Timothy, 125, 187
Rives Salient, 126, 218, 250, 257, 287, 292, 306
Roanoke Island, North Carolina, 14
Roanoke, USS, 15
Roberts, Pvt. John B. (NLAB), 128, 241, 294
Robinson River, 89, 100, 102
Robinson's Ford, Virginia, 93
Rodes, Maj. Gen. Robt. (CSA), 61, 157
Rogers, Pvt. Crawford S. (NLAB), 241, 294
Rogers, Pvt. John C. (NLAB), 241, 294
Rogers, Pvt. Theodore F. (NLAB), 241, 294, 295
Rogers, Pvt. W. H. R. (NLAB), 46, 241, 295
Rosecrans, Maj. Gen. William (USA), 91
Rosser's Brigade (Gen. Thomas), 112
Royal Arcanum Society, 247, 248, 269, 285, 311
Royal Arch Chapter Nr. 1, 304
Ruffin, Edmund, 30

S

Saint Mary's Cemetery, Norfolk, Virginia, 148, 231, 274, 286
Sanders, Brig. Gen. John C. (CSA), 117, 138, 145
  Alabama Brigade, 117, 137, 145
San Jacinto, USS, 15
Saunders, Pvt. Smith S. (NLAB), 128, 241, 295
Sawyer Gun, 10, 11, 16, 19
Sawyer, Sylvanius, 10
Scales' Brigade, 101, 183
Seaboard and Roanoke RR, 261
Seales' Brigade, 173
Sebrell, Pvt. N. C. H. (NLAB), 241, 295
Seddon, John A., 189
Segar, Pvt. Thomas G. (NLAB), 241, 295
Seminole, USS, 15
Semmes' Brigade, 64
Semmes, Capt. Raphael (CSN), 133
Seven Pines, Virginia, 35, 280
Sewell's Point, Virginia, 8-11, 15-18, 46, 235, 242, 246, 247, 257, 261, 262, 265, 275, 283, 284, 286, 288, 290, 293, 294, 297, 298, 302, 306, 307, 310
Sharpsburg, Maryland, 72, 278
Sherwood (ship), 13
Shenandoah River, 69, 86
Shenandoah Valley, Virginia, 118
Shepherdstown, (West) Virginia, 71
Sheridan, Gen. Phillip T. (USA), 157, 158, 160, 165

Sherman, Gen. William T. (USA), 131, 160, 175, 178, 213
Sigel, Maj. Gen. Franz (USA), 118, 131
Simmons, Pvt. Bains S. (NLAB), 241, 296
Simmons, Pvt. J. (NLAB), 241, 296
Simms' Brigade, 62
Smiley, Pvt. C. D. (NLAB), 128, 218, 241, 296
Smithfield, Virginia, 254, 263, 290
Smith, Gen. Gustavus (CSA), 36
Smith, Gen. M. L. (CSA), 134
Smith, Gen. Edmund K. (CSA), 118
Smith, Gov. William "Extra Billy", 80
Smith, Pvt. Charles A. (NLAB), 241, 296
Smith, Pvt. Elbridge C. (NLAB), 241, 296
Smith, Pvt. John E. (NLAB), 241, 296
Smith, Pvt. John W. (NLAB), 241, 297
Smythe, Pvt. William (NLAB), 241, 297
Southampton, Virginia, 140
South Mountain, Pennsylvania, 78
Southside RR, 124, 144, 201, 221
Spotsylvania Court House, Virginia, 63, 114, 115, 116, 117, 272, 294
Stafford, Brig. Gen. Leroy A. (CSA), 112
Staunton, Virginia, 87, 118, 131, 157
Steever, Pvt. Edwin (NLAB), 241, 297
Sterrett, Pvt. J. S. (NLAB), 23, 46, 231, 241, 297
Stevens Alexander H., 194
Steuart, Brig. Gen. George H. (CSA), 116
Stoneman's Raiders, 281
Stonewall Camp, Confederate Veterans, 244, 252, 285
Stoney Creek Station, Virginia, 179
Strasburg, Virginia, 86, 157
Stuart, Gen. J. E. B. (CSA), 90, 117
Suffolk, Virginia, 16, 30, 34, 91, 250, 282, 291
Susquehanna, USS, 15
Swank, Pvt. William A. (NLAB), 241, 297
Swift Creek, Virginia, 23
Sykes' (US) Division, 64, 65

T

Tanner's Creek, 6, 17, 18
Taylor, Col. Walter H. (CSA), 292, 306
Taylor, Gen. Robert B., 298
Taylor, Maj. William E. (CSA), 8, 9
Taylor, Pvt. J. Theodore (NLAB), 139, 173, 241, 298
Taylor, Pvt. William J. (NLAB), 219, 241, 299
Taylor, Sgt. (Capt.) William E. (NLAB), 108, 110, 233, 234, 241, 269, 292, 298, 299

Thomas Freeborn, USS, 8
Thomas, Sgt. Benjamin D. (NLAB), 241, 299, 300
Thomas, Pvt. Jesse D. (NLAB), 241, 300
Thompson, Pvt. Ebenezer, Jr. (NLAB), 241, 300
Tilghmantown, Maryland, 72
Todd, Westwood A. (CSA), 218
Toy, Pvt. Crawford H. (NLAB), 241, 300
Tredegar Iron Works, 48
Tucker, J. Randolph, 198
Turkey Ridge, Virginia, 274
Turner's Rebellion, 140
Twin Sisters Mountain, Virginia, *95*

U

United Daughters of the Confederacy, 126, 232, 243, 253, 260
United Fire Company, Norfolk, 232, 271, 272
United Royal Arch Chapter, 234
United States Ford, Virginia, 53, 57, 64, 259, 308

V

Vaughn, Pvt. Edward S. (NLAB), 241, 301
Vaughn, Sgt. (Capt.) R. Frank (NLAB), 234, 241, 269, 287, 301
Veale, Pvt. Samuel (NLAB), 241, 251, 273, 301, 302
Verdiersville, Virginia, 100, 102
Vickery, Capt. Jacob, Jr. (NLAB), 2, 11, 14, 233, 241, 271, 302
Vicksburg, Mississippi, 53, 83, 130
Viele, Gen. Egbert (USA), 84
Villa, Pancho, 236
Virginia Beach, Virginia, 244
Virginia Central RR, 37-39, 102, 106, 110, 117, 118, 120, 131, 298
Virginia Club, 260
Virginia, CSS (*Merrimac*), 15-17, 19, 266
Virginia Military Institute (Cadets), 245, 255, 256, 298
Virginia National Guard, 232, 236-238
"Virginian Pilot", 293
Virginian Railway, 306

W

Wadsworth, Gen. James S. (USA), 114
Walke, Pvt. Isaac T. (NLAB), 241, 302, 303
Walker, Brig. Gen. James A. (CSA), 115, 224, 263
Walker, Col. Reuben Lindsay (CSA), 189, 253
Brigade, 92, 94

Walker, Pvt. R. P. (NLAB), 63, 241, 303
Walters, Lottie L., 233, 234, 304, 305, 306
Walters, Mary Lee, 233, 234, 303, 305, 306
Walters, Pvt. John H. (NLAB), 241, 253, 277, *303-305*, 308
Walters, Virginia Phillips, 233, 234, 303, 304
Walters, William D., 233, 234, 303, 305
Ward, Pvt. John T. (NLAB), 241, 306
Warren, Gen. Gouverneur K. (USA), 210, 211
Warrenton Springs Ford, Virginia, 96
Warrenton, Virginia, 96
Washington Artillery, 32, 46, 109, 143
Washington, D.C., 120, 132, 245, 258, 261, 264, 267, 272, 282, 291, 299
Washington, George, 11, 45, 70, 233
Watson, Lt. Malbone F. (USA), 64
Watters, Pvt. A. M. (NLAB), 128, 129, 231, 241, 306
Watters, Pvt. James H. (NLAB), 15, 62, 64, 241, 283, 306, 307
Waynesboro, Pennsylvania, 73, 80
Webb, Pvt. William T. (NLAB), 241, 307
Weed, Capt. Steven H. (USA), 64
Weed's Regulars (Battery) (USA), 64, 65, 258, 265, 286
Weldon RR, 124, 144, 147, 159, 169, 179
Westmoreland, North Carolina, 289
West, Pvt. Joseph S. (NLAB), 83, 241, 307
West, Pvt. William M. (NLAB), 241, 307
White Post, Virginia, 69, *70*
White, Pvt. Charles E. (NLAB), 234, 241, 307
White, Pvt. Nathaniel E. (NLAB), 241, 308
Whitehurst, Pvt. Luke H. (NLAB), 241, 308
Whitehurst, Pvt. Steven T. (NLAB), 241, 308, 309
Whiting, Pvt. John R. (NLAB), 241, 309
Whiting, Pvt. John S. (NLAB), 241, 309
Whiting, Pvt. Thomas B. (NLAB), 241, 309
Whitmore, Pvt. C. (NLAB), 241, 309
Wigfall, Senator Louis T., 194
Wilcox's Brigade, 92, 168
    Division, 99, 101, 119, 148, 173
Wilderness, 113, 114, 245, 280
Wilkins, Pvt. Charles L. (NLAB), 241, 309
Wilkins, Pvt. George W. (NLAB), 241, 309
Wilkins, Pvt. John F. (NLAB), 201, 204, 207-209, 241, 310
Wilkins, Pvt. Thomas J. (NLAB), 64, 241, 310
Wilkins, Pvt. Walter A. (NLAB), 31, 46, 231, 241, 310

Wilkinson, Pvt. James (NLAB), 231, 241, 310
Williamsburg, Virginia, 278, 280, 285, 296
Williamson, Pvt. Clarence H. (NLAB), 241, 310, 311
Williamsport, Maryland, 80, 81
Wilmington, North Carolina, 143, 181, 182, 189
Wilson, Pvt. D. Cary B. (NLAB), 176, 241, 311
Winchester, Virginia, 69, 82, 84, 86, 156, 157, 308
Wingfield, Pvt. R. C. M. (NLAB), 241, 311
Wise, Gen. Henry A. (CSA), 14, 193
    Wise's Brigade, 161, 184
Woodis Rifles, 8, 9
Woodhouse, Pvt. John (NLAB), 241, 311
Woodhouse, Pvt. Philip (NLAB), 241, 312
Woodstock, Virginia, 86
Woodward, Pvt. W. W. (NLAB), 241, 312
Wool, Gen. John E. (USA), 16
Worrell, Pvt. James R. (NLAB), 241, 312
Wright's Georgia Brigade, 60, 114, 116, 117, 121, 134, 137, 138, 145
Wright, Dr. David, 85, 312, 313
Wright, Sgt. James R. (NLAB), 201, 208, 209, 241, 312
Wright, Pvt. Edwin L. (NLAB), 241, 312
Wright, Pvt. Minton A. (NLAB), 85, 241, 312, 313
Wright, Pvt. William S. (NLAB), 241, 313

Y

Yorktown Centennial, 235
Young, Capt. John J. (CSA), 8
    Harbor Guards, 269, 289, 294
Young's Brigade, 175

Z

Zills, Pvt. Alexander (NLAB), 241, 313
Zills, Pvt. Julius A. (NLAB), 241, 313
Zills, Pvt. John M. (NLAB), 241, 313
Zuni, Virginia, 19